KALEIDOPHONIC MODERNITY

Kaleidophonic Modernity

TRANSATLANTIC SOUND, TECHNOLOGY, AND LITERATURE

Brett Brehm

FORDHAM UNIVERSITY PRESS   NEW YORK 2023

Fordham University Press gratefully acknowledges financial assistance and support provided for the publication of this book by the College of William & Mary

Copyright © 2023 Fordham University Press

All rights reserved. No part of this publication may be reproduced, stored in a retrieval system, or transmitted in any form or by any means—electronic, mechanical, photocopy, recording, or any other—except for brief quotations in printed reviews, without the prior permission of the publisher.

Fordham University Press has no responsibility for the persistence or accuracy of URLs for external or third-party Internet websites referred to in this publication and does not guarantee that any content on such websites is, or will remain, accurate or appropriate.

Fordham University Press also publishes its books in a variety of electronic formats. Some content that appears in print may not be available in electronic books.

Visit us online at www.fordhampress.com.

Library of Congress Cataloging-in-Publication Data available online at https://catalog.loc.gov.

Printed in the United States of America
25 24 23   5 4 3 2 1

First edition

Contents

Introduction: Acoustic Spectra 1

1 Paleophonics: Charles Cros's Audiovisual Worlds 27

2 Poe's *Tintamarre*: Transatlantic Acoustic Horizons 74

3 Tattered Sound:
Baudelaire's Paris, Noise, and the Protophonographic 102

4 The Amazing Chorus:
Whitman and the Sound of New York City 136

5 Nina's Song: Music, Sound, and Performance
in the Salon of Nina de Villard 155

Conclusion: Pyrophonica and the Rhythms of Inspiration 193

ACKNOWLEDGMENTS 205

NOTES 209

BIBLIOGRAPHY 253

INDEX 269

KALEIDOPHONIC MODERNITY

Introduction
Acoustic Spectra

Researchers practicing the strange new art of "archaeophony" (the archaeology of sound, as some define it) made a startling discovery in 2008. They were able to listen back to a previously unheard moment in time. With a special optical method, they recovered a sound recording that predated Thomas Edison's phonograph by nearly two decades. Until this discovery, history had generally regarded Edison's phonograph as the first device capable of mechanical sound recording and reproducibility. The earlier recording, however, was made in 1860 by French inventor Édouard-Léon Scott de Martinville with a device he called the phonautograph.[1] At the official presentation of his mechanical device to an audience of scientists and inventors at the Society for the Encouragement of National Industry in Paris in 1857, Scott employed the curious and partly ambiguous phrase "spectre sonore," which one might translate as an acoustic spectrum.[2]

Speaking to an idea of dialogue between media and their emergence, Scott posed this revealing question about the possibility of mechanically recording the human voice: "The particular movement that produces the sensation of sound, could it also create, like a ray of light [*un faisceau lumineux*], in every point of space that surrounds us, a spectrum gifted with a certain persistence for which a sensitive surface [*un écran sensible*] could be chemically marked [*impressioné*]?"[3] Scott then asserted: "No, the sonic spectrum [*le spectre sonore*] (please forgive me this inexact expression) is not permanent like the spectrum of light [*le spectre lumineux*]." Despite being qualified as "this inexact expression," the "*spectre*" here belongs, it would seem, to the scientific discourse on acoustics and means "spectrum" in the sense of a range. To help with potential ambiguity, English has both "specter" and "spectrum." In French, "spectre" can mean both.

Scott himself encouraged a spectral ambiguity when he proceeded to refer to the "chimeral" nature of his scientific investigations: "Ah, if only I could place on this air around me harboring all the elements of a sound, a quill [*une plume*], a needle [*un style*], this quill, this needle would form a trace on an appropriate fluid layer [. . .]. But to position a quill on this fugitive, impalpable, invisible fluid, it's a chimera, it's impossible!"[4] And then, of course, he would explain that, thanks to his invention, it was in fact possible. Scott, however, did not intend for those traces to reproduce audio. Strange as it may seem to us today, he meant only to visualize sound, not to use those chimeral traces for what we now tend to call playback.[5]

What the archaeophonists in 2008 managed to do was to educe audio from Scott's recordings. Since they were broadcast widely and with some fanfare in the media in March of that year, you may have even heard a few of them, on the radio perhaps, as I did (available now at the website firstsounds.org). In one of them, Scott, it is believed, sings a verse of "Au Clair de la Lune." The 2010 versions, which you may not have heard, sound significantly clearer because of some refinements in the reconstitution process, though their sound quality is still far from contemporary standards of high-fidelity audio recording. With their crackling, distant sound, the recordings are perhaps even spectral—or ghostly, a word my students have sometimes used to describe their impressions of the sound quality of Apollinaire's 1913 audio recording of his poem "Le Pont Mirabeau."

A year before the unveiling of Scott's invention, the photographer Félix Nadar (1820–1910) had, in 1856, speculated that one day a device might be able to produce what he called an "acoustic daguerreotype," something like a photograph of sound. Scott also drew a similar analogy with the daguerreotype when explaining the workings of his invention. He compared the surface on which the human voice would be written in his device to a "plaque daguerrienne" and a photographic negative. Just as Tiphaigne de la Roche, author of the novel *Giphantie* (1760), has been hailed as a key prophet of the protophotographic imagination, Nadar and Scott serve similar roles in the prehistory of phonography.[6]

The scholarly fields of media studies and media archaeology have taken due note of these developments, more so of Scott's invention than of Nadar's evocative idea. But how did these particular scientific imaginaries enter into dialogue with literature and aesthetic modernity of the period? In this book, I endeavor to answer that question.

In these pages, I uncover a hidden acoustic substrate in aesthetic modernity. I reveal audiovisual dynamics at play in the imaginations of scientists, writers, and artists in the nineteenth century while demonstrating how ideas about new media were imagined in relation to each other and other preexisting media. Scholarly attention to audio technologies, particularly in this historical period, has tended to congregate around the telephone and the phonograph (for which Scott's phonautograph was an important precursor). Arguments about the phonograph typically divide into two camps. Some scholars claim that in the decades before its technical realization, the idea of mechanical sound reproducibility was decidedly in the air. Others claim that when the phonograph was invented in 1877, no one knew what exactly to do with it or what its potential was. I argue firmly against the latter position while maintaining that if such ideas about sound recording *were* in fact in the air, such ideas need scholarly and critical grounding in relevant texts, discourses, and contexts. Once we have a method for looking at and listening to the nineteenth century in this way, a new field of audiovisual figures, including the protophonographic and protocinematic imagination, becomes available for our critical regard. Here, in this book, I offer this grounding. I locate ideas about audiovisual pasts, presents, and futures in specific poems, paintings, narratives, and historical documents both familiar and unfamiliar to scholarship and popular culture.

Ultimately, I reveal how the architecture of modern audiovisual relations emerged in nineteenth-century France and the United States, specifically in Paris and New York City, where the conditions of their need and possibility were elaborated. With this framework, I demonstrate how to discover important acoustic undercurrents in the lives and works of both canonical figures of urban modernity, here, namely, Edgar Allan Poe, Charles Baudelaire, and Walt Whitman, and more obscure figures, such as French poet and inventor Charles Cros (1842–1888) and his lover and muse, the celebrated musician and salonnière Nina de Villard (1843–1884). Poe listened to the sounds of the past for a "more absolute truth," while Baudelaire found "rags of music" in the streets of Paris, and Whitman heard "living and buried speech" in the streets of New York.

When considered together, these figures become singularly resonant with (though not determined by!) technological developments in audiovisual media and the soundscapes of modern life. From a comparative perspective of French and American authors and artists, this book is about the prehistory of modern audiovisual media and the aesthetics of sound recording and reproducibility.

This intersection of science, technology, and the arts finds a most compelling focus, I argue, in the enigmatic figure of Charles Cros, who is the subject of Chapter 1. Cros's scientific endeavors ranged from color photography to telecommunications to climatology to mechanical sound recording and reproduction. In his poetry, the Surrealists would find a close ancestor and early inspiration. André Breton, for one, in an homage to Cros, likened him to Marcel Duchamp, saying each was guided by "sources as luminous as the future."

Cros's singularly prescient writings, both literary and scientific, prove startling and relevant to our contemporary predicaments with technological media, from privacy to portability to big data. In 1878, for instance, he imagined something like digital photography. In the following year, echoing Cyrano de Bergerac and prefiguring Edward Bellamy, he penned a story about how technological networks of the future would lead to upheavals in the publishing world.

Here is how Lisa Gitelman refers to Cros in the first chapter of her illuminating and influential *Scripts, Grooves, and Writing Machines* (1999), a cultural history of the phonograph, Edison, and phonography in the "Edison age": "With his invention, Edison made history in the banal sense of priority: he had done something that only he and maybe a secretive Frenchman named Cros could yet do."[7] This is the sole reference to Cros in that book, as is the case with Edmund Morris's recent biography *Edison* (2019), in which Cros appears briefly only once. In the influential but polarizing *Gramophone, Typewriter, Film* (1999), media theorist Friedrich A. Kittler praises the elegance of Cros's scientific script but criticizes Cros's imagination and ultimately deems him a poor prophet of the future of audio technologies. No doubt Cros lived and died poor, but he was far more prophetic than Kittler would have us believe.

What if, then, we look more closely at this "secretive Frenchman"? Part of what I propose more broadly with this initial turn to Cros is the necessity of a comparative approach between French and American histories and prehistories of these audiovisual inventions, histories still somewhat splintered in the scholarly literature. One could look at Cros and Edison more closely together, which I do here primarily from a cultural perspective. But I have chosen to consider as much and more closely other American voices, namely Edgar Allan Poe and Walt Whitman, to uncover the poetic, literary, and cultural dimensions of the technological audiovisual imaginations of the age.

In his collaborations with Manet, Cros contributed to publishing innovations of his own time with a short volume that some scholars have called the "first modern illustrated book" and, some years later, with the first mass-reproduced photographic copy of an artwork in color.[8] His works thus provide a unique perspective, from someone who was both poet and scientist, someone tuned both to technological media and to its content, on the origins of our present-day obsessions with and anxieties about audiovisual media. Despite his prescience and the respect accorded his ideas and writings by contemporaries who included members of the French Académie des Sciences and poets such as Paul Verlaine, Cros has since been consigned as an oddity, more thoroughly cursed than other *poètes maudits* of his generation, to the margins of literary studies and histories of science. Here I demonstrate the truly pioneering side of his works in the context of relations between the arts and the mechanical reproducibility of sound, movement, and color. In tandem with his scientific works, Cros's literary production offers new means of evaluating the emergence of modern audiovisual media. I argue that these literary texts also anticipate the types of issues that animate our contemporary debates about privacy and technological surveillance.

Nina de Villard, Cros's lover and muse, has similarly languished in near obscurity despite having presided over the most daring intellectual salon in France of the Second Empire and early Third Republic. For nearly twenty years she welcomed artistic and literary luminaries such as Cézanne, Manet, Mallarmé, Maupassant, Turgenev, Verlaine, Renoir, and Degas. A salonnière, poet, journalist, celebrated musician, and composer, Villard cultivated a social space for the rise of novel performance practices, ones involving music and poetry in particular. Her salon was a veritable crucible of the artistic avant-garde and a precursor to the famous Chat Noir cabaret. The Goncourt brothers described her salon as a place for "manifold debaucheries of thought, [. . .] the most daring paradoxes and the most subversive aesthetics [. . .]. A sort of intellectual haschisch-tinged drunkenness, [. . .] an orgiastic exertion of conversation."[9] I highlight her salon's importance to revolutionary aesthetics while illustrating how it shaped scientific discourses alongside such movements as Zutism, Impressionism, and Symbolism. By examining and revising the caricatural image of Villard drawn by a group of fin de siècle novelists, I relate an untold story in which she figures as a key voice in the rise of modern performance culture and its nascent forms of technological reproducibility in audiovisual media.

Part of the reason behind the scholarly neglect of Charles Cros and Nina de Villard, I suspect, is the need for an interdisciplinary approach to elucidate their full historical and cultural significance. The pair straddles rigidly defined fields in their own time and in ours.[10] Cros's scientific writings, for example, may initially appear formidable in a way akin to the forbidding cosmological theories articulated in Poe's *Eureka* (1848). It is, for instance, both striking and revelatory of Cros's particular poetic and scientific sensibility to see a chemical formula in the pursuit of synthesizing diamonds, rubies, sapphires, and other gemstones "$2\,(C^2\,Az\,H) + 6\,(HCl) = C_4Cl_4 + 2(Az\,H_4Cl)$" in Cros's "L'Alchimie moderne" published alongside Mallarmé's "Le Démon de l'analogie," and an etching by Manet (of Villard, in fact) in Cros's short-lived periodical *Revue du monde nouveau* in 1874. Nouveau indeed.

Because Villard left relatively few published texts, her most important contributions to her artistic and intellectual world are of a less immediately tangible nature. Here, I examine some of those writings that she did see published in various periodicals, and these texts offer a means of reexamining her voice in her own words.

Given our media-saturated present, I argue that now is the moment of Cros and Villard's knowability. At the very least, it presents a distinct opportunity to get to know them better. And as we come to know them, they help sharpen and reorient our perspectives on the more familiar Edgar Allan Poe, Charles Baudelaire, and Walt Whitman, together with the spectacularly lit and deafeningly loud cityscapes of Paris and New York in the nineteenth century.

Photographing Sound

Before we turn to their worlds, let us return to Scott's phonautograph invention, specifically to his elusive *"spectre sonore."* Scott's idea, ghostly or not, and Nadar's "acoustic daguerreotype" can together serve as unexpected but revealing points of departure for a reading of an unassuming short story about photography, "La Légende du daguerréotype," written in 1863 by Jules Champfleury, art critic, author of the 1857 manifesto "Le Réalisme," friend of Baudelaire, and sometimes a thorn in the side of Nadar. The voice that remains at this story's end speaks to the broader layers of meaning in the works that I excavate throughout this book.

Often cited in the early history of relations between literature and photography, Champfleury's story, as I want to argue here, can also be read in the context of a prehistory of phonography.[11] The story ends with a ghost who haunts with his voice alone, a singularly acoustic specter, a "spectre sonore" perhaps. Reading the story in this context allows us to see literature not only responding to and representing existing technology, not only anticipating what might emerge down the line, but also elaborating the terms, understanding, and uses of those future technologies, while laying the groundwork for their emergence and reception. This approach helps us resist the tendency to view historical periods as dominated by the most successful media (the digital age, the Internet age, or the Edison age for example) and instead allows us to probe the sources of our obsessions with and anxieties about those media even before their appearance on the scene.[12]

In "La Légende du daguerréotype," a hint of things going awry appears early in the story when the daguerreotypist says to his unsuspecting victim: "We are going to make for you, monsieur, an admirable portrait. No one will recognize you." The narrator heightens the sense of impending disaster with the question: "Wasn't it dangerous to be exposed in front of a mysterious machine that coldly, with its immense somber eye, contemplated the seated man?"

Indeed, the man sitting for his portrait, the ill-fated M. Balandard, who has traveled to Paris from the provinces and wants a souvenir, a daguerreotype portrait of himself, to bring home to his wife, finds himself the victim of the comically inept photographer Carcassonne, a former barber's assistant with ambitions of becoming Paris's first celebrated daguerreotypist.

Carcassonne's first attempts to produce an image result only in "three times the same irritating black square [. . .] on the glass." Successive attempts yield images of Balandard's individual facial features: first his nose, then his ears, then his toupee, his right eye and then the left, each feature alone against a black background. And each time, Carcassonne protests that Balandard has moved, that his movement is the cause of each failed portrait, that he is in fact "perpetual movement" itself. Repeatedly the photographer tells the poor man to stay still. And eventually, Carcassonne does succeed in producing a portrait, but at that point he no longer has a sitter to hand it to (see Figures 1a, 1b). "Fifty successive attempts had annihilated little by little the body of the model. Of M. Balandard, only a voice remained! [*De M. Balandard, il ne restait qu'une voix!*]" Only, *only* a voice, I would emphasize.

Carcassonne subsequently abandons the dangerous profession of daguerreotypist and resumes his work as a barber, but the narrator of the tale reports: "But incessantly, like an eternal punishment, the shadow of M. Balandard would follow him everywhere and incessantly beg him to render him back into his former self."

As critics have noted, Champfleury's story illustrates an anxiety—one shared by the likes of Balzac, Gautier, and Nerval among others—that the

Figures 1a and 1b. Original illustrations by Gérard Morin in Jules Champfleury's "La Légende du daguerréotype." 1863.

daguerreotype process might interact with the human as a kind of gradual corrosion, that this new process of representation could strip away layers of the body or soul. The story intimates these concerns when the narrator reports that M. Balandard, after feeling all manner of strange sensations across his body, "felt like a shell of his former self [*ressentait comme une diminution de lui-même*]."[13] In his memoir *When I Was a Photographer* (*Quand j'étais photographe*) (1900), Nadar explains Balzac's theory of "specters" and photography, which animated the novelist's fear of being in front of a camera. According to Balzac, as Nadar relates, each body is "composed of a series of specters [*séries de spectres*], in infinitely superimposed layers," and "every Daguerreian operation would catch, detach, and retain [. . .] one of the layers of the photographed body [. . .]." Nadar concludes his summary of Balzac's theory: "With every repeated operation, there was an evident loss of one of its specters [*perte évidente d'un de ses spectres*], [. . .] a part of its constitutive essence."[14]

Champfleury's tale, in the way the portrait process endangers the life of the sitter, might call to mind Poe's "The Oval Portrait," in which the painting of a portrait results in the death of the sitter. Unlike Poe's decidedly more gothic tale, however, Champfleury's is highly comic, charming even; most crucially, it does not end with the death of the sitter, but with the absence of the sitter's body. At the core of the story's essential irony, a technology intended to preserve the visual image of the human subject is able to do so, but at the expense of rendering the sitter invisible. Of the sitter, the daguerreotype process leaves only a haunting voice behind. M. Balandard remains in a way forever audible, a visual specter on the daguerrotype plate, but a "*spectre sonore*" in the air. Sound resides even in the name of the barber daguerreotpyist Carca*sson*ne.

Like the "living foot" in Frenhofer's painting in Balzac's philosophical tale "The Unknown Masterpiece," Balandard's disembodied voice, in a way, remains living, having similarly, as with Frenhofer's "Belle Noiseuse," escaped a slow and progressive destruction—fifty attempts to produce a daguerreotype portrait. In Balzac's story, Frenhofer's realization of his masterpiece's ruined state leads to the artist's demise. For Champfleury, the artist's end is far less dramatic. Carcassonne simply abandons the profession of daguerreotypist and returns to cutting hair and shaving beards, albeit in the company of a voice that won't leave him alone. The death of the artist is denied while, for the sitter, for poor M. Balandard, symbolic death and an uncertain ethereal life are ultimately evoked more through the disembodied voice than the photographic portrait.

The story's tone leads us to conceive of Balandard's eternal voice as ultimately more symbolic of bodily destruction than of immunity to dangerous chemicals, absence more so than presence. Simultaneously, and perhaps just as much, the narrative voice inspires wonder about the possibility of a human voice speaking in the absence of a human body and in the presence, instead, of a mechanical device.

A similar effect appears in Nathaniel Hawthorne's novel *The House of the Seven Gables* (1851), in which a daguerreotypist also figures in the character of Holgrave. At the very conclusion of the novel, Maule's well produces "a succession of kaleidoscopic pictures" as a strain of music is heard from the harpsichord of the deceased Alice Pyncheon (a Romantic trope, this sound buried in a musical instrument, as in the tales of E. T. A. Hoffmann). In the conjunction of the kaleidoscope and the evocation of ghostly sound that persists, there is an element of what we might call the kaleido*phonic*. And I want to suggest that with this conjunction, as with "La Légende du daguerréotype," there is greater intermedial overlap—synesthetic, yes, to an extent, but not always—than we might presume in literature of this period more broadly; indeed, literature served as a kind of laboratory for configuring these kaleidophonic relations. The prophetic powers of literature not only shape what we might call the precinematic, not only anticipate what future technologies might be like, but also lay a groundwork for the future reception, understanding, and uses of such devices. And there is a specificity to this groundwork that remains to be probed and explored in nineteenth-century literature.

Literature and the arts of this era spoke in secret ways to the auditory, to the acoustic future, to their audiovisual present, to literary metaphors, such as acoustic daguerreotypes or the eternal voice of a M. Balandard. Those figures were, in turn, preparing for historical ruptures in media and representation. Nineteenth-century texts about photography (but certainly not limited to texts about photography) might be hiding, somewhere somehow, secret acoustic dimensions. The search for those sonorous elements might both involve questions of lack (as Walt Whitman exclaimed of the photographs he saw in Plumbe's Gallery on Broadway in July 1846: "Ah! what tales might those pictures tell if their mute lips had the power of speech [. . .] an immense Phantom concourse—speechless and motionless, but yet *realities* [. . .] a new world [. . .] though mute as the grave") *and* questions of becoming.[15] M. Balandard's disembodied voice sprung *both* from period fears that photography could strip away spectral layers of a person's body and from unconscious literary participation in a discourse that shaped how and what a photography of sound could mean. In this way, "La Légende du daguerréotype" instantiates such prophetic powers of literature and speaks to an aesthetic unconscious that harbored the promise of new audiovisual possibilities.

Sound Awakenings in the City

In a fragment from the *Arcades Project*, Walter Benjamin proposes: "The nineteenth century—to borrow the Surrealists' terms—is the set of noises that invades our dream and which we interpret upon awakening."[16] Though Benjamin specifically invokes the Surrealists, he may have Proust in mind as well, particularly in relation to the experience of awakening. In an extended meditation on sound and deafness in *The Guermantes Way*, Proust writes about awakening: "Today, on the surface of silence spread over our sleep, a shock louder than the rest manages to make itself heard, gentle as a sigh, unrelated to any other sound, mysterious; and the demand for an explanation which it exhales is sufficient to awaken us."[17] Scholarship on the nineteenth century is itself awakening more and more to the study of sound and noises in an expanded acoustic field and how that study might help probe and uncover what some have called the auditory culture or soundscape of modernity.[18]

Stress falls more on the metaphorical than the literal sense of the "noises" in Benjamin's and the Surrealists' phrases. Still, the effort to interpret involves some manner of grasping those noises, rendering them solid and preserving what would otherwise melt into air. This acoustical preservationist impulse was an issue not only for science in the nineteenth century but also for literature and aesthetics as well. At the same time the nineteenth century witnessed an increasing valorization of the "new" and of forward progress, aesthetic and scientific currents led to the preservation of sounds of the past, marking an unsettling temporal ambivalence in the acoustic field.

Scholars committed to framing and establishing the field of sound studies have frequently invoked the study of visual culture as a point of departure for their explorations.[19] Though formulated in different ways in recent years by a growing cadre of sound studies scholars, the core question of this "auditory turn" bears repeating: So much attention has focused on the question of vision and a perceived hegemony of the visual field of modernity (termed an "ocularcentrism" by some), what about the acoustic? Might attention to the acoustic imagination open up a new register of questions in the humanities?

My study follows in this lineage in the way I seek to reveal a fertile, turbulent acoustic field at a historical moment more often examined through the lens of a visual field in massive flux. Specifically, I argue that inquiry into acoustic phenomena in nineteenth-century literature yields questions and concepts that complement and deepen those inspired by study of the visual field: a panacoustic for the panoptic, a noisy *tintamarre* for the dazzling spectacle, a "luminous noise" for the "disenchanted night."[20] My attention to the auditory imagination in literature likewise complements historical and sociological approaches to the question of soundscapes and auditory culture as historical and theoretical categories, as in the scholarship of Jonathan Sterne, Alain Corbin, Lisa Gitelman, and Jean-François Augoyard, among others.[21]

While scholars in visual culture studies commonly locate a "modernization of vision" in nineteenth-century practices and phenomena (the invention of photography, urbanization, and popular optical devices, to name a few), scholarship continues to negotiate the implications of that era's modernization of listening and sound.[22] In what follows, I argue that auditory phenomena reverberating in the modern city, as represented in the works examined here, struck modern listeners in a way that opened up a space within which new acoustic technologies could be imagined and where the diverse uses of those technologies could be shaped and critiqued.

In these pages, I make a case for the quality of sounds and listening practices in the nineteenth-century city, where writers discovered modes of attention to urban acoustics and the means of imagining novel audiovisual devices and their cultural impact. Such states of acoustical attention, together with their literary representations, changed with concepts of the modern listening subject. One could argue, however, that cities had long been known for their chaotic noise, great diversity of sounds, and aesthetic responses to the urban soundscape.[23] William Hogarth's engraving from 1741, "The Enraged Musician" (see Figure 2), is a case in point. The picture vividly illustrates how urban acoustics could be a source of conflict for a certain social and artistic elite. Hogarth's musician figures in a lineage of artists and musicians bothered by the disturbance of urban noise, from Schopenhauer, who complained about how the noise of Frankfurt disrupted his contemplation, to Hoffmann, who once likened himself to the "enraged musician" of Hogarth's print, to Poe, who published newspaper articles about how the noise of Brooklyn could drive one mad, to Proust in his famous cork-lined room in Paris.[24]

Still, the nineteenth century witnessed the development of new attitudes regarding diverse urban acoustical phenomena, especially the sounds of crowds, technology, and industry. Amidst this cacophony, and as urbanites took to circulating beyond the confines of their neighborhoods in spaces becoming ever more multilingual and punctuated by a kind of urban machinery, the task of hearing one's self and hearing others came under increasing stress. At the same time, such stress, acoustical shock, and disorientation encouraged ways of navigating what might seem, for some, like chaos, and for others, like a field of vast aesthetic possibility, the two not always necessarily opposed. How could

Figure 2. William Hogarth, "The Enraged Musician," 1741. Etching and engraving on paper. © Tate, London / Art Resource, NY.

one listen to the city? And how was the activity of listening itself, in everyday life and in the more specialized spheres of art and science, changing in the space of the city?

Passages from two nineteenth-century writers, one famous and the other obscure, help illustrate this emergent wonder about urban sound in the nineteenth century. First, consider this passage from the beginning of Charles Dickens's novel, *The Old Curiosity Shop* (1840), in which the narrator, in recounting the experience of his nocturnal wanderings, asks the reader to imagine listening to the acoustic chaos of London:

> That constant pacing to and fro, that never-ending restlessness, that incessant tread of feet wearing the rough stones smooth and glossy—is it not a wonder how the dwellers in narrow ways can bear to hear it! Think of a sick man in such a place as Saint Martin's Court, listening to the footsteps, and in the midst of pain and weariness obliged, despite himself (as though it were a task he must perform) to detect the child's step from the man's, the slipshod beggar from the booted exquisite, the

lounging from the busy, the dull heel of the sauntering outcast from the quick tread of an expectant pleasure-seeker—think of the hum and noise being always present to his senses, and of the stream of life that will not stop, pouring on, on, on, through all his restless dreams, as if he were condemned to lie dead but conscious, in a noisy churchyard, and had no hope of rest for centuries to come.

Dickens offers conceptual means of parsing this "hum and noise . . . always present to his senses" by juxtaposing young and old, poor and wealthy, idle and industrious as audible dualities. On the subject of urban *flânerie* and Dickens, Walter Benjamin has observed: "When Dickens went traveling, he repeatedly complained about the lack of street noises, which were indispensable to him for his work."[25] In this way, urban noise served for Dickens as a kind of background source of nourishment for creation, while in the passage from the novel, the noise comes to the foreground by presenting the sick man with "a task he must perform." Each case speaks to a kind of evolving urban auditory attention and consciousness of the surrounding hum.

Little-known French composer and urban ethnographer Jean-Georges Kastner authored *Les Voix de Paris* (1857), a study of street cries in Paris and other world cities. Like Dickens, Kastner voluntarily immersed himself in the urban "hum and noise," in which he sought to reconcile the musical and social worlds so starkly opposed in Hogarth's print. Kastner went beyond studying and collecting individual street cries and melodies to make the remarkable claim that "the very noise of a city forms part of its distinctive character [*le bruit même d'une ville fait partie de son originalité*]."[26]

Indeed, Kastner posed questions similar to those asked in recent years as part of what some have called an "auditory turn" in the humanities.[27] Interested in the broad acoustic spectrum of the city, which he calls its "chaos sonore," Kastner helps us to consider the auditory culture of a past age and the distinctive ways of listening to the city. He was interested in attunement to the cries of individual street vendors and, crucially, to the denser aural fabric of the city, in which cries overlap with the architectural and social forces that shape the listener and the listening.[28]

By cataloging and transcribing the metropolitan street cries and melodies of his era, Kastner sought to write a musical score documenting content that was typically shared through oral tradition.[29] His transcription of street cries into musical notation marked a significant turn in the range of attempts to capture and preserve the sound and music of these cries in writing. This ethnographic effort would take another dramatic turn when urban ethnographers would record such street cries with phonographs as early as 1892.[30]

Though Kastner was neither the first nor the only collector of Parisian street cries (Victor Fournel and Joseph Mainzer were other important *confrères* in this activity), his comparative analysis of Paris's *chaos sonore* with the acoustic ambiances of other world cities distinguishes his efforts.³¹ Comparative study and global reach provided a model for a later generation of ethnographers that included Hubert Pernot, whose sound recordings from a field expedition to the Greek isles in 1898 were rediscovered only recently, in 2011; Léon Azoulay, who inaugurated an immense collection of phonographic recordings at the Colonial Exhibition by hailing a "new era of sounds and noise" circa 1900; and Victor Segalen, who provided an ethnographic study of Polynesian music and sound in his 1907 essay "Dead Voices: Maori Music," in which he made the striking assertion: "the particular aspect of sound in Polynesia both stuns and disconcerts us [*La qualité du son, en Polynésie, nous étonne et nous déconcerte*]."³²

Reflecting on the field of sound studies, Peter Szendy has warned that, in the shift of scholarly and theoretical attention to the acoustic, dialogue between the visual and the acoustic risks being lost.³³ In this book, I stake a claim on the importance of particular acoustic epistemologies, or "acoustemologies," as elaborated, for example, in anthropologist Steven Feld's scholarship or Valeria Luiselli's 2019 novel *Lost Children Archive*. At the same time, with Szendy's warning in mind, I am interested in how the acoustic helps to reframe the visual in novel ways. Hence, I aim to illuminate and amplify the singularity of modern audiovisual relations and their literary representations.

The kaleidophone provides an especially vivid example of nineteenth-century audiovisual interaction and a bridge between aesthetic and scientific fields. As an instrument and material artifact giving onto broader aesthetic and theoretical imaginations, the kaleidophone did not rattle the human sensory world nearly as dramatically as the kaleidoscope, its inspiration and more famous counterpart. Like Scott's phonautograph, the kaleidophone served as a tool for visualizing sound. I adopt the device here for its suggestive name and interweaving of the audio with the visual in an age sometimes known for stark sensory separations.³⁴ The kaleidophonic, as a concept I elaborate in these pages, speaks more broadly to evolving listening practices and transformations of sound in the nineteenth century while pointing to audiovisual collisions between images and sounds in discourses on acoustics and new media, such as the idea of an "acoustic daguerreotype" or a "musical daguerreotype."³⁵

English inventor Charles Wheatstone developed the kaleidophone in 1827. Calling it both a new "philosophical toy" and a "phonic kaleidoscope," he declared his creation a device for "creating beautiful forms."³⁶ In this pursuit, he acknowledged inspiration from Sir David Brewster's kaleidoscope. The beautiful forms in Wheatstone's device were visual figures and patterns made by different sounds as produced by objects such as a violin bow or hammer. Set in motion by these objects, thin vibrating metal rods with light focused on small silvered beads at their ends would trace patterns (in some cases projected onto a screen), where the effect of the afterimage on the human eye—similar to its exploitation in precinematic devices such as the phenakistiscope, zoetrope, and praxinoscope—enabled less the appearance of movement, as in those devices, than of figures in a "continuous line of light" corresponding to sounds musical or otherwise, sometimes with colors added to enhance the aesthetic effect.[37] Essentially, for a general idea of the kaleidophone's workings, picture these forms (see Figure 3) as continuous streams of light—more about afterglow than afterimage in this way—accompanied by the sounds of vibrating metal rods. In the configuration of luminous streams powered by the vibrations of different sounds, the kaleidophone's "beautiful forms" have their own acoustic undersides. In short, there's a buzz beneath the device's visual spectacle.

Though the kaleidophone never attained the degree of popularity and renown that Brewster's kaleidoscope enjoyed, Wheatstone's audiovisual imagination informed the principles and invention of the microphone and the stereoscope (an optical device to create the illusion of depth), the latter a device that Jonathan Crary has called "the most significant form of visual imagery in the nineteenth century, with the exception of photographs."[38]

Tracing the kaleidophone's ancestry back into the eighteenth century reveals an obscure progenitor in the historical play of visualized sound and optical music. The idea of an ocular harpsichord [*clavecin oculaire*], as dreamed by Jesuit Father Louis Bertrand Castel (1688–1757), received an entry in Diderot's *Encyclopédie* (Figure 4).[39] In an article from 1725, Castel stated that he wished to use color to "paint sounds" and all kinds of music.[40] He dreamed of helping the deaf enjoy music and the blind enjoy color. In the twentieth century, the kaleidophonic lineage and aesthetic would live on, drawing on the development of color organs, perhaps most vividly in Thomas Wilfred's Clavilux and Lumia works of the 1930s, some of which look like the aurora borealis in a cabinet or dreamier, psychedelic versions of the screen savers we used to see so frequently on computer screens in the 1990s (see Figures 5 and 6). Less immediately apparent are the shared audiovisual concerns and designs between Wilfred's color record from *Unit #50* and Marcel Duchamp's rotoreliefs, which I consider in Chapter 1.

Bracketing the visual, if only momentarily, to listen deeply to an acoustic field can disclose particularities of that field distinct from visual experience. This goal of uncovering singularities of the acoustic is, in part, what theorists

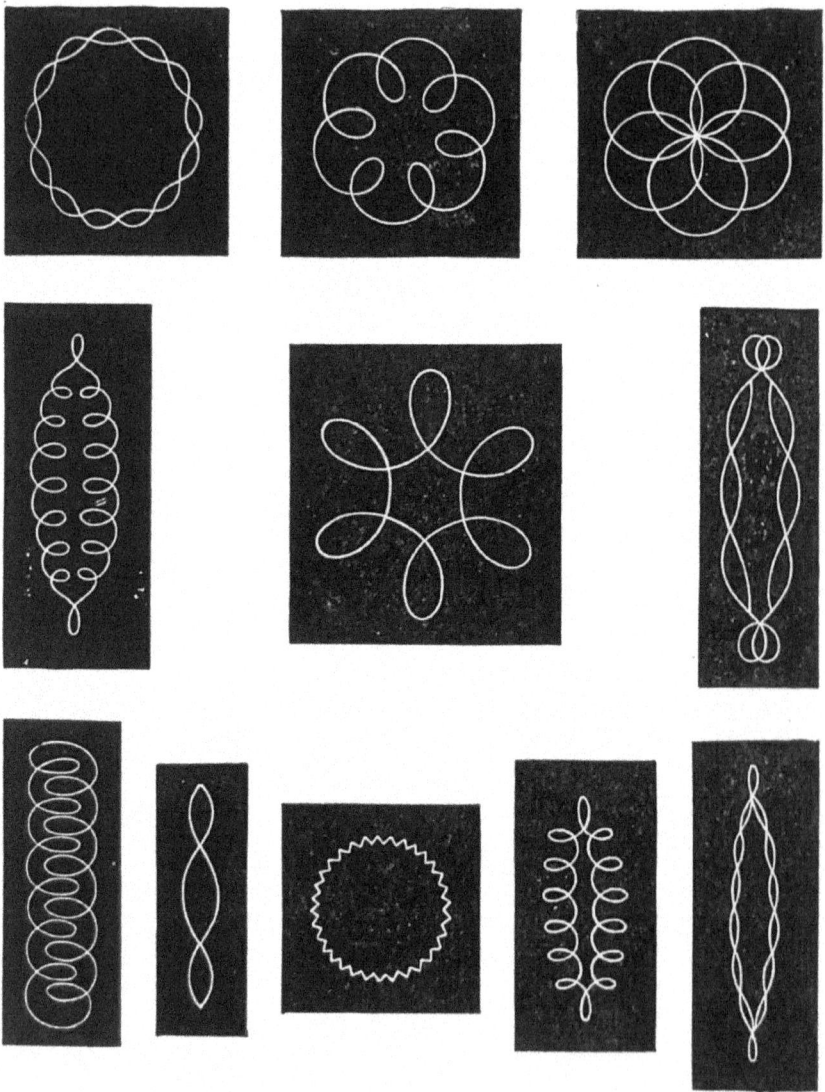

Figure 3. Charles Wheatstone, Kaleidophone figures. From H. Holbrook Curtis, *Voice Building and Tone Placing* (New York: D. Appleton and Company, 1914), 221.

Figure 4. Jesuit Father Louis-Bertrand Castel with his ocular harpsichord. Part of the text reads: "Le Père Castel—rapport des sons et des couleurs [relation between sounds and colors]." From Charles-Germain de Saint-Aubin, *Livre de caricatures tant bonnes que mauvaises*, circa 1750. Courtesy The Rothschild Foundation Waddesdon.

Figure 5. Thomas Wilfred. *Unit #50, Elliptical Prelude and Chalice*, From the *First Table Model Clavilux (Luminar)* series, 1928. Courtesy Yale University Art Gallery / Gift of Thomas C. Wilfred.

Figure 6. Thomas Wilfred, hand-painted disc for use with *Unit #50*. Courtesy Yale University Art Gallery / Gift of Thomas C. Wilfred.

such as Jean-Luc Nancy, Roberto Casati, and Jérôme Dokic have taken as their point of departure for immersion in listening and probing of the sonorous, a search for philosophical knowledge, as Nancy explores, in terms of such auditory qualities as "accent, tone, timbre, resonance, and sound."[41] Such theoretical sensory separation could be read as a distant echo of Proust's theory, which follows his reflections on sound and deafness in *The Guermantes Way*, that the loss of a sense might add "as much beauty to the world as its acquisition." The kaleidophonic, as I uncover in these pages, speaks to the discovery of a strange beauty between sensory acquisition and sensory loss, in the multisensory play of literary and artistic expression with new media technologies in the nineteenth century.

Ancestors

It is striking that scholars, when discussing the phonograph, a technology invented in 1877, have often invoked a passage from as far back as François Rabelais's *Le Quart Livre* (c. 1552) as a startling anticipation of the device, as perhaps the first elaboration of the concept of sound storage.[42] It should be noted, however, that a closer look at early twentieth-century chronicles of the phonograph and its legends yields ancestors dating even further back in time than Rabelais's text and from more diverse regions of the globe, namely, a Chinese legend from some three thousand years ago about a spoken message contained in a case brought to the emperor, or the story of a seventeenth-century explorer discovering an island where the natives used sponges to soak up spoken words to be transmitted over great distances to their recipients who would, in turn, squeeze the sponges to hear the words reproduced.[43] As that account goes, musical concerts were recorded and reproduced with this method "in the most refined and delicate of their sponges [*dans les plus fines de leurs éponges*]." However apocryphal these legends might be, the key is perhaps in the authors' ultimate claim. André Coeuroy and Geneviève Clarence, with their collection of phonographic legends and ancestors, submit: "poetry has always paved the way for science to follow [*toujours la poésie a devancé la science*]."[44]

If we turn to Rabelais's famously prophetic passage, we find Pantagruel and his companions, during their journey, encounter what Rabelais describes as "frozen speech [*paroles gelées*]," words and diverse sounds that have been frozen in time and that mysteriously appear to the travelers in a form resembling "sugared almonds of diverse colors [*des dragées perlées de diverses couleurs*]." In their frozen state, these spoken words are visible to the eye:

> After they had been warmed up a little in our hands, they melted like snow, and we actually heard them [*nous les entendions réellement*] but did not understand them, for they were in some barbarous tongue [*un langage barbare*], save for a rather tubby one which, [. . .] made a sound such as chestnuts make when they are tossed un-nicked on to the fire and go pop. It gave us quite a start [*nous fit tous tressaillir de peur*].

Fear turns to "some excellent sport [*un bon passe-temps*]," as the travelers warm, melt, and subsequently listen "réellement" to more of these sounds and words from a mysterious source and unknown moment in time. This "realness" of hearing suggests an auditory register over and above the echoes normally heard and produced in nature; these reproduced sounds are echoes of another sort, of another register or spectrum of hearing.

Jean-François Augoyard argues that this passage in Rabelais represents an astonishing "prophecy about the invention of phonography [*prophétie sur l'invention de la phonographie*]." He maintains that scholars, however, have been less attentive to the ways the passage can be read as a fable of a different resonance, the question of how sound might be gathered and retained in space, in the materials and environments built by human hands.[45] In the way Pantagruel and his companions warm the frozen words and sounds in their hands, Augoyard suggests that something similar can be done with the city, an activity that would make the sounds that have filled its spaces resound for historians' ears, albeit in indirect ways. Augoyard argues that architectural historians today can examine the built environment for vestiges of its "audible past," to quote Jonathan Sterne and his eponymous study, another kind of archaeology of sound.[46]

In turn, I argue that nineteenth-century literary representations of the city, together with metaphors formed in the confluence of literary and scientific discourse on new acoustic technologies, helped to elaborate an aesthetics of acoustic reproducibility in the decades before the invention of the phonograph. Literary representations of urban life in the nineteenth century made sound newly available for both new literary possibilities and technological processes. Literature in the nineteenth century primed the aural fabric of the city for the reception of recorded sound, the city variously conceived as an absorptive space that not only deadens sound or roars with a deafening noise, but also creates the conditions and the impulse for sound recording in an environment that would echo in a distinctly different way. Consequently, the grooves and cylinders of acoustic technologies and phonographs might be conceived as continuous with the fabric of urban space, less in the way of visual resemblance than in the way the city was imagined as an acoustic environment that could absorb sound so that it would be preserved and eventually recovered.

Balzac, for instance, in a passage on the Parisian flâneur in his *Physiologie du Mariage* (1829), cites the "paroles gelées" passage from Rabelais: "Who is the foot soldier of Paris in whose ear has not fallen, like projectiles on the day of a battle, thousands of words spoken by passers-by, and who has not seized one of these countless conversations, frozen in the air [*paroles, gelées en l'air*], of which Rabelais speaks?" Scholars have highlighted the activity of "seizing" words that Balzac describes here as evidence that the flâneur could at times be an active multisensory seeker, possessing a "gastronomy of the eye," as Balzac goes on to write, and of the ear for diverse sounds, voices, words, and conversations in the city.[47] As the notion of an acoustic or aural flânerie begins to take hold in scholarship, I want to stress that the prehistory of phonography, as it took shape in literature, needs to be considered as part of this activity.[48] The nineteenth-century city, specifically literary representations of it, acted as the crucible for the meeting of discourses on mechanical sound recording and the developing flâneurial taste for words and sounds seized out of the urban air. Scientific and aesthetic possibilities arose out of these urban confluences and encounters.

In this respect, I respond to technological determinist thought by demonstrating how literature can shape scientific thought and technological progress, with an emphasis on how reciprocal exchange occurs between artistic and scientific discourses. While I do not deny that great aesthetic transformations followed technological inventions in the nineteenth and early twentieth century, my area of inquiry is different. I look more to the literary elaboration of what Jacques Rancière calls an "aesthetic regime" as a sphere for the negotiation of aesthetics that would interact most intensely with the invention of certain technologies. I depart from the perspective that questions how preexisting modern technologies inflect subsequent artistic movements and possibilities, that is to say, the question of artistic rejection or embrace of technological modernity as a preexisting field, the sometimes one-way street of inventions transforming representation. Did a particular writer embrace the typewriter, for instance? Or, how might a painter's antipathy to or delight in cinema, Matisse's, for example, be manifest in their works? These *are* fundamentally important and compelling questions, but they are not the types of questions I pose here. Instead, I investigate reciprocal negotiation across aesthetic spheres, imagined devices, real inventions, and the discourses that live on in states of dynamic possibility. Such is my aim in uncovering a prehistory of modernist aesthetics of noise and sound. My study focuses less on the stage of a particular device's emergence for a public and more on figures left waiting in the wings and ones that hardly set foot on stage, together with all the backstage machinations largely invisible to that public.

In this way, I build upon claims by scholars of literature and the history of science who emphasize the confluences between nineteenth-century technologies and aesthetics. Jacques Perriault, for example, has claimed that the phonograph took shape in the confluence of "the world of engineers and the universe of poets."[49] Likewise, Laura Otis has, for example, examined not only George Eliot's knowledge of scientific developments and how that knowledge informs *Middlemarch*, but also how the novel and Eliot's literary networks offered something to science. Hence, Otis stresses that this exchange was not simply a "unilateral flow." For Otis, it was neither a question of the influence of science on the novel nor how Eliot borrowed a metaphor from scientific research and discourse. Rather, this exchange was a fruitful interplay between the two.[50]

Jacques Rancière, in elaborating his theory of aesthetic modernity and an "aesthetic regime," emphasizes the complex relationships between nineteenth-century scientific and literary programs in the way that literature, as he argues, offered an understanding of ordinary life and "sensory micro-events" for subsequent historical, artistic, and scientific analysis.[51] I, in turn, examine how a literary prehistory of phonographic technology involved a priming of the auditory field, one that made sound newly available to scientific and artistic investigation.

Apollinaire's self-proclaimed status as a "poète phonographiste," the futurists' adoption of noise into their aesthetic programs, and Erik Satie's innovations in "furniture music" and film scoring, to name a few early twentieth-century examples, while shaped by phonographic technology, I maintain, have origins and continuity with literary aesthetics of sound in the era before the invention of the phonograph.

Chapter 1 considers how Cros's works look back to figures like Castel and how they speak to our "information age." While demonstrating how the scientific and the literary are mutually inflected in Cros's imagination, the chapter examines his stories about subjects ranging from technological surveillance in a dystopian Paris of the future to telecommunications to disability studies (Cros taught at a school for the deaf) to the origins of cinema. Ultimately, I argue that Cros's visions for and about the future of society, by turns satiric, skeptical, and filled with wonder, harbor both optimism and pessimism about the progress of human knowledge through scientific research and the place of art in the capitalist marketplace. Cros represents technology in his poetry and prose fantasies as a potentially dangerous tool in acoustic surveillance and as a means to arrest time. In this way, he reimagines the ephemeral and eternal sides of art elaborated in Baudelaire's modernity.

The primary field of exploration in Chapter 2 involves a broad protophonographic imaginary in Edgar Allan Poe's writings and the particular trajectory of this thought in transatlantic audiovisual culture. Poe's writings about science, urban life, and modern technological innovations offer points of intersection with Cros and Baudelaire especially. Acoustic figures in Poe's literary works form part of Poe's search for a "more absolute truth" discoverable by listening to the past, as in his mystifying text *Eureka* (1848), written after he had left Manhattan to live in the then pastoral setting of a cottage in Fordham. For Poe, a decisive link exists between the fascination inspired by the sound of new technologies and new urban phenomena. By examining the conflicts arising from acoustic perception in the multilingual spaces of the modernizing city,

I argue that Poe's representations of mysterious unnerving sounds belong to a nascent protophonographic logic even as they evoke madness in the form of auditory hallucination.

While the transnational Poe-Baudelaire connection is well established, a fecund and largely unexplored dialogue exists between Poe and the other authors here, especially Cros in the scientific context and Villard in the literary context. By probing these connections, I reveal a trajectory and legacy of Poe that is different from the well-recognized literary reception of Poe in France by Baudelaire, Mallarmé, and Valéry.[52]

Chapter 3 helps to reorient recent scholarly inquiry about Baudelaire and the noise of Paris, as in the scholarship of Aimée Boutin and Ross Chambers among others, by setting noise in dialogue with the technological. I also reevaluate Baudelaire's ambivalence about photography by introducing an acoustic element to the photographic.

Sounds of the past mingle with sounds of the modern city in Baudelaire's life, writings, and in his friendship and sometimes rivalry with the photographer Félix Nadar, who spoke of an "acoustic daguerreotype," a means of "seeing noise," decades before the invention of mechanical sound recording. I approach Baudelaire and nineteenth-century Paris from the nexus of optical devices, protophonography, and Nadar as incarnation of modern "progress," a term that generated so much conflicted revulsion and contempt *chez* Baudelaire. The contingency of modern interpersonal relations, I argue, often viewed through something like the glimpse of the "passante" highlighted by Walter Benjamin, can also be heard, as in the way Baudelaire describes a "rag of music," by chance in the city street. This rag of music forms part of a deeper undercurrent of the city's acoustic residue in Baudelaire's poetry and of latent aesthetic value in the dreams of new audiovisual media forms.

Chapter 4 examines the desire to imprint Walt Whitman's poetic speaking voice "on record," an impulse that speaks to an emerging aesthetic of poetic performance for the machine, which is part of a broader imaginary about the place of performance in modern society and the societal desire to preserve such performance. I ultimately demonstrate how Whitman's desire to capture all sounds, with a democratic ear, compares with emergent audiovisual media of the era. Whitman discovers "living and buried speech" resonant in the streets of New York City, as in his "omnibus jaunts" along Broadway. Urban street noise functions as an immersive source for Whitman's singing.

Finally, Chapter 5 illuminates Nina de Villard's role in shaping avant-garde thought in Paris and concepts of performance at the dawn of mechanically recorded sound. Revising the traditional view of Villard as a modern muse, I suggest an alternative perspective: Villard as the architect of a social space with particular acoustic features central to the prehistory and early history of modern audiovisual culture. In Villard's bohemian salon, I locate a point of origin for the popular musical "hits" of the twentieth century. Her salon also helped to cultivate a performance culture and aesthetic that entertained and portended different directions in modern music, both for the Wagnerians (Villard was an early supporter) and for more eccentric modes of performance (less German, more French) of the sort, a figure like Erik Satie, in his singularly "montmartrois" and then Dadaist way, would come to exemplify as a "phonometrographer" (Satie's word), someone who measures the weight of sounds.

In their explorations of the sounds of the past, historians have sought to reconstruct what might be called a *period ear*, inspired in part by the influential notion of a "period eye" in art history from Michael Baxandall.[53] What did a specific time and place sound like, and how was meaning constructed in sound at that historical moment? Though I occasionally draw from this kind of scholarship, my aims are somewhat different. To return to the quotations about awakening from Benjamin and Proust cited earlier, the task for the scholar writing about nineteenth-century sound before the invention of the phonograph may resemble the experience they describe, of awakening to a sound heard on the other side of a dream. My goal is not so much to identify that sound's source or even its precise meaning. Rather, I examine how, for the authors I discuss, their own literary awakenings in sound led, and can still lead, to other awakenings in sound.

1
Paleophonics
Charles Cros's Audiovisual Worlds

What constitutes invention? What makes an inventor an inventor? Before Alfred, Lord Tennyson would record himself reciting poetry on Thomas Edison's newly improved phonograph in the late 1880s, before Guillaume Apollinaire would declare himself "un poète phonographiste," and before Victor Segalen would write poetry inflected by a phonographic logic, an enigmatic French poet, who was also an accomplished inventor and contributor to the French Académie des Sciences, formulated the core principles of mechanical sound reproducibility.[1] Charles Cros (1842–1888) called his would-be device a "paléophone" (literally, the voice of the past) and filed a blueprint of its design in a sealed envelope at the French Académie des Sciences in April 1877, roughly eight-and-a-half months before Edison would register a US patent for his "phonograph" in December of the same year. In the summer of 1877, Cros, destitute and struggling to secure funds and support from his patron, the Duke of Chaulnes, lacked the resources necessary to realize his vision and build this invention.[2]

Edison built the first working audio recording machine, but the status of inventor and invention remains hazier. Though the historical record commonly grants Cros partial credit for the invention of mechanical sound recording and reproduction, Edison has continued to occupy the spotlight. In his novel *L'Ève future* (1886), Cros's friend Villiers de l'Isle-Adam attributed to his fictionalized version of Edison certain ideas about the phonograph that had originated with Cros, while Emile Berliner borrowed directly from Cros's writings on mechanical sound reproducibility to develop a means of mass reproduction of sound on disc in the late 1880s and early 1890s, a device that Berliner would call the gramophone.[3]

Stories detailing the origins of phonography in Cros's life remain fragmented, at best, in the scholarly literature. This chapter constructs a more complete and synthetic account of these origins and will help to deepen understanding of the historical currents that shaped the development of phonography, its technology, and the literary innovations that accompanied and followed upon it, specifically prose poetry and imagery that would inspire Surrealist and modernist writers. André Breton, for instance, pays homage to Cros in *Anthologie de l'Humour Noir*: "The fingers of Charles Cros, like those of Marcel Duchamp, are guided by butterflies the very color of life, which feed on the essence of flowers but which are attracted by no other light sources than those of the future. These fingers are those of a perpetual inventor."[4] Breton's characterization of Cros as a specifically *"perpetual"* inventor speaks both to the astounding diversity of Cros's visions and inventions, in areas ranging from climatology to interplanetary communication and languages, and to his vexed relationship with time.

In his poem, "Inscription," for example, Cros conceives of sound reproducibility as a means to arrest time and grapple with the speed of modernity. His transatlantic race with Edison to invent and patent audio technology emblematized speed in one such respect. Indeed Cros's ambivalence regarding the fabrication, ownership, and commercialization of his scientific visions speaks to a tension, perhaps even a divide, in his life and writings: On the one side is Cros as the poet, theorist, dreamer, and on the other side is Cros the inventor, who alternately disdained and actively sought participation in an economy of technological progress through patent ownership and commercial exploitation. Edison's enterprise, most would say, was primarily profit driven. With Cros, the origins and motivations in sound recording are obscure, as elsewhere in his life and works. But in that obscurity, in the theory and dream of the unconstructed paleophone, as I argue here, we can discover a hidden side of the literary imagination as it touches on the early understanding and possibilities of audio and visual media technologies. Those possibilities involved the reproducibility of sound, color, and movement especially, together with broader relations and conflicts between science and the arts in the nineteenth century.

Though scholars cite Cros for his efforts to develop sound reproduction technology and color photography, less has emerged about the relationships between his scientific explorations, his literary texts, and broader aesthetic developments in the nineteenth century. Scholars have tended to marginalize the contribution of Cros's literary texts and his other scientific investigations to the invention and early history of audio and visual technologies of the era.[5] Though Villiers's *L'Ève future* is among the first and earliest of literary texts invoked in studies of literature and the phonograph—a group that includes Jules Verne's *Le Château des Carpathes* (1892), Albert Robida and Octave Uzanne's "La fin des livres" ("The End of Books") (1894), and Edward Bellamy's "With the Eyes Shut"(1889)—Cros's short story "Le Journal de l'avenir" ("The Newspaper of the Future") (1880), which predates them all, also offered a deeply unsettling and prescient vision of the direction that audiovisual technologies might take. This was a direction tending toward mass media, surveillance, and their relationships in the wake of the newly invented telephone and phonograph. In this way, Cros probed society's overabundant faith in technological progress.

Cros's cynicism and sarcasm in that particular story resemble Baudelaire's sentiments about progress, such as, for example, his scorn for something like photography's infringement on the realm of fine art. Ironically, shortly after Cros penned that story, he would employ his latest trichrome color photographic method on a painting by the artist we have come to identify with Baudelaire's "Painter of Modern Life," Édouard Manet. Cros's collaboration with Manet represents a happy union of technology and art, while the story voices deep concern about such a union.

Throughout Cros's life and writings, it is striking to observe such transformations and divergences of thought on issues related to technology, art, and societal progress. As a poet, Cros demonstrated an abiding affinity for Baudelaire with, for instance, motifs of flowers and ennui in his first published volume of poetry, *Le Coffret de santal* (1873). At the same time, Cros's views on science and the means of mechanical reproducibility can both coincide with and diverge from those of Baudelaire. The dark humor in "Le Journal de l'avenir" echoes the cynicism and contempt that Baudelaire expressed in texts such as "Le Public Moderne et la Photographie," while an ebullient letter from Cros to Manet about their experiment with color photography, which would lead to the very first mass photographic copy of an artwork in color, evidences opposing ideas.[6]

Friedrich A. Kittler, for his part, has stressed what he believes are the limits of Cros's poetic imagination in the face of the phonograph, a device so new in its power and significance that Cros, so Kittler has argued, failed to comprehend its possibilities.[7] However, a closer examination of Cros's poetic and literary imagination yields new insights into the state of technology in the 1870s and 1880s, and into the transatlantic scientific and literary dialogue between France and the United States. Cros's literary texts furthermore reveal how innovations in poetry developed in tandem with new acoustic and graphic technologies, and how ideas about sound reproducibility connected with photography and Impressionism.

His literary production adopted several different forms: poems in both verse and prose (some of which were set to music by Cros's contemporaries and by composers of a slightly later generation, Claude Debussy and *vers libre* pioneer Marie Krysinska among them), short stories (sometimes conceived as "fantasies in prose"), and monologues (which he and others typically performed at the Chat Noir and other Parisian cabarets).

By investigating Cros's "paleophonic" origins, we might continue to examine the idea of modernity as a radical break with the past, specifically the break that pertains to the relationship between literature and phonography.[8] Edison's phonograph and Cros's paleophone from 1877–1878 mark one moment in a long history of the profound transformation of listening and sound in the nineteenth century. Dramatic changes in literary and artistic expression indeed arose out of the aesthetic field opened up by the expansion of phonographic technology, with the gramophone especially. However, there is a veritable literary imagination about modern ways of listening, modern sound, and its mechanical reproducibility that has been overlooked.[9] Cros's life and works stand squarely within this lineage, at a veritable center of scientific discourse and innovation.

Outside of Menlo Park, literature provided another laboratory for exploring "paleophony," the reproducibility of sounds, and the voices of the past. In the person and work of Cros, some scholars have offhandedly pinpointed a phonographic zeitgeist and a veritable contest over the phonographic imagination.[10] But questions remain: How specifically did Cros's work participate in other discourses of the era, and how did it speak for an audiovisual technological zeitgeist?

We know Rimbaud as a singular *"voyant"* ("seer"), but his one-time host (Cros was there with Verlaine to welcome the young phenom to Paris and to house him for several weeks) and forgotten rival (Rimbaud allegedly poured sulfuric acid into Cros's drink one day at a cafe!) can also lay claim to another conception of that label that is distinctly his own and that, at the same time, evokes broader changes in the nineteenth-century mediascape.

Paleophonic Origins

One of Cros's unpublished papers succinctly states the goal of his scientific research into sound and how his research innovated upon previous technologies. Cros gave himself this task: "Étudier l'enregistrement et la reproduction des phénomènes sonores" ("Study the recording and reproduction of sonorous phenomena").[11] The key term is "reproduction" because, as discussed in this book's Introduction, Scott's phonautograph in 1857 could record sound but could not reproduce it as such, a feat that illustrates both the diversity and the limits of the period's imagination about the uses and possibilities of these new mechanical audio and graphic devices.[12]

There is a telling irony in the title of an essay that Cros wrote as part of his examinations to become a teacher at a school for deaf children in Paris, a position he held as a young man for roughly three years, from 1860 to 1862. Asked in the first part of the examination to discourse on the subject "of language, its essence, its forms and the modifications to which it is susceptible," Cros mistakenly heard "its essence [son essence]" as "its birth [sa naissance]," near-homophonic phrases in French.[13] The misheard phrase could be read as a sign of Cros's poetic and performative imagination concerning the sound of words and as a portent of his participation in the literary and scientific currents that would give birth to a new means of hearing. Cros's writings at the Institute reveal that, as part of his pedagogical theory for teaching deaf students at the school, he began to formulate a way of studying "all the known sounds that make up the languages of the globe."[14] Grounded in the study of language, this investigation into "all the known sounds" would suggest possibilities for sonic inscription that include and exceed language, speech, music, or poetry, hence a broader acoustic field to be known and examined.

On the question of deafness and sound reproducibility, Kittler asserts that Edison's first recorded words hardly resembled the kind of sound recordings that Cros imagined and described in his poem "Inscription." Edison's words were so unlike the "beloved voices" or "musical reveries" of Cros's poem partly because Edison, believed to have been half-deaf, effectively screamed into his machine. On this point, Kittler concludes: "A physical impairment was at the beginning of mechanical sound recording—just as the first typewriters had been made by the blind for the blind, and Charles Cros had taught at a school for the deaf and mute."[15] This observation, however, leaves open the question of *how*, beyond the biographical coincidence between Cros and Edison, deafness factored into the origins of mechanical sound recording. As we saw in the Introduction, the importance of deafness as a key element in the history of mechanical audio devices stretched back into at least the eighteenth century with Castel's dreams of painting music in colors for the deaf.

Cros worked with students at the Institut des Sourds-Muets in Paris at a time when the school was grappling with a pedagogical debate about deafness and language.[16] A central question in this debate was whether these students should learn to speak and read lips or whether they should learn sign language. Cros took an active part in this debate at the school, where he taught students who were deaf from birth and those who became deaf later in life.[17] Cros's close friend, writer and humorist Alphonse Allais, believed that the idea for a phonographic machine emerged, in part, from Cros's immersion in this debate on the teaching of speech to the deaf and his subsequent desire to build a machine that would serve as an oral prosthesis for the deaf: "Cros hoped that his students would carry the instrument in a kind of shoulder strap with a provision of phrases for the day."[18] This particular vision is consistent with several currents in Cros's thought, one of which concerned portability and the possibility of a portable device for audio playback (portability being a historically important practical step in making mechanical recording and reproduction technologies more accessible to a wider public).

More importantly, developing such an instrument could form a potential bridge between separate worlds and cultures, facilitating communication across many divides. Cros would explore this idea in work with telegraphs and theorize it further with designs for optical arrangements in the service of interplanetary communication.[19] A third element, and one that is easy to overlook in this brief description, is the assumption of daily utility in a machine that provides phrases "for the day." This everyday quality is easily overlooked in the era before widespread mechanical sound recording and reproduction. Today we hear prerecorded speech daily, in welcome and unwelcome circumstances, without a thought. Cros imagined something similar before it ever existed, the specifically quotidian element of mechanically recorded and reproduced speech. The very possibility for mechanically reproduced sound to become a part of everyday life is a key and unexpected element to emerge from Cros's engagement with deafness and its ramifications for how we consume sound in our present.

For Baudelaire, as we will see, deafness and deafening contributed to the experience of modern urban life, as in the opening line of his famous "À une passante" poem, "La rue assourdissante autour de moi hurlait" ("The Deafening Street around Me Was Howling"), and in his essay "Notes nouvelles sur Edgar Poe," which I will discuss in more detail in Chapter 3. The everyday has its place in Baudelaire's text as well, in that the deafening street becomes—or had, in Baudelaire's time, already become—a normal occurrence and the setting for the urban drama that ensues in Baudelaire's poem. Viewed in the now-familiar Benjaminian frame, the noise of this deafening street presents itself as something to be "parried," a "shock" to and within Baudelaire's system. When compared with Cros's theoretical instrument, however, and with the accent placed on the everyday rather than the shocking, the deafening disorder of Baudelaire's city street still appears as a force to avoid (by retreat, Proust-like, into a sound-proof interior) or to overcome (with more howling, as we will see in Whitman, or with something like, roughly a half century later, composer Charles Ives's polytonality), but also as an origin for new communications media in the conjunction of deafness and the everyday. In the experience of deafness, deafening, and the everyday, and in a certain sense of the everyday, Cros and Baudelaire ever so glancingly cross paths. Indeed, Baudelaire planned but never could write a prose poem with the title "La sourde-muette" ("The deaf woman").

Jacques Perriault has revealed that Cros, while teaching at the school for the deaf, consulted one of the foundational publications in the debate on sign language, De Gérando's *De l'Education des sourds-muets de naissance* (*On the Education of the Deaf from Birth*) (1827), in which several of De Gérando's points are striking in the way they describe the idea of a speaking machine: "It would not be an issue of making the deaf person into a speaking automaton [*un automate parlant*]." On the question of the mechanization of speech, De Gérando suggests: "The study of the mechanism of speech, obtained by anatomy, with the help of wax models, engravings, speaking machines, will be very useful to the teacher of the deaf to guide them in their progress."[20] From these elements, Perriault concludes that Cros was struck by the idea of a mechanical prosthesis for speech.[21]

It is also likely that Cros, after leaving the school to pursue medical studies for a while, came into contact with another auditory prosthesis: the stethoscope. His brother Antoine, a doctor, was famous for practicing a form of mediate percussion auscultation, "l'organographie plessimètre," which provided a means of imaging the body's internal organs *in vivo*.[22] Through his two brothers, with whom he was close and shared ideas in Nina de Villard's salon, Charles became familiar with the medical practice of auscultation, which involved mechanical prostheses for hearing and visualizing the body's interior together with the idea of a prosthesis for speech. These elements all figured as sources for his desire to study the recording and the reproduction of sound.

Cros's connection to deafness was thus both mechanical and intensely human, from his personal connection to the students he taught to their particular sensory world and the languages that both he and they could use to communicate to the mechanics of real and dreamed-of instruments (a lineage we could draw, albeit schematically, from paleophone to phonograph to gramophone), the kind of devices that would eventually become part of everyday life.

Player piano recording technology was another source for Cros's early interest in the mechanical reproducibility of sound that would later take on innovative literary dimensions in his prose poetry.[23] Charles's brother Antoine, with whom Charles collaborated on musical compositions as a child, related that Charles often delighted in improvisations on the piano.[24] From these "musical reveries," the two brothers recognized the need for a device that could record the piano improvisations directly from Charles's playing, which would obviate the need for musical notation. Hence they envisioned a device that could mechanically allow the piano to repeat what had been played on it, a certain stenography of music.[25] These efforts to mechanize help to contextualize Cros's prose poem "Le Vaisseau-Piano," one of his three "fantaisies en prose" that he based on aquatints by his brother Henry, an artist who worked in a variety of media.

Cros's poem presents a sequence of arresting images: "esclaves de diverses races imaginaires" ("slaves of various imaginary races") row a boat over the "océan de la fantaisie" ("the ocean of fantasy"), the vessel presided over by "la Reine des fictions" ("the Queen of fictions"), who sits at a piano on an elevated platform.[26] A contradiction exists between the rowers' enslavement and the boat's constant forward momentum, which evokes liberation from the confines of the real world. Cros uses language to temper this contradiction, describing the slaves as "courageous" and celebrating their power and the diversity of their imaginary races, their bodies in colors "rares ou impossible chez les races réelles" ("rare or impossible with real races"). The speaker elaborates: "Il y en a de verts, de bleus, de rouge-carmin, d'orangés, de jaunes, de vermillons, comme sur les peintures égyptiennes" ("There are greens, blues, carmine-reds, oranges, yellows, vermillions, as in Egyptian paintings").[27] With the poem's concluding repeated refrain, "en avant!" ("forward!"), Cros responds to the call of Baudelaire's prose poem, "Anywhere Out of the World," to depart into other worlds. Each prose poem shares a desire to take flight. While Baudelaire expresses that desire through the inadequacy of distant—but still worldly—places to satisfy the yearnings of his soul, Cros leaps straight into the realm of explicit fantasy.

The strange conjunction of images in the poem constitutes part of that leap, one being the piano in the middle of the ship:

> In the middle of this ship is an elevated platform and on the platform a very long grand piano.
>
> A woman, the Queen of fictions, is seated before the keyboard. Beneath her fingers of rose, the instrument renders silky and powerful sounds that neutralize the whispering of the waves and the hearty sighs of the rowers [*Sous ses doigts roses, l'instrument rend des sons veloutés et puissants qui couvrent le chuchotement des vagues et les soupirs de force des rameurs*].
>
> The ocean of fantasy is tamed, no wave would be so audacious as to spoil the surface of the piano, masterpiece of cabinetmaking in shimmering rosewood, or to soak the felt of the hammers or to rust the steel of its strings.[28]

The poem celebrates a kind of mechanical transcendence in the piano's inner mechanics, in their resistance to rust and moisture, mechanics Cros knew well. In their plans for musical stenography, the Cros brothers would describe, in the blueprint for the device, how a band of paper "resulting from the action of the writing apparatus, receives imprints in various colors as representations of the sounds produced."[29] Though the brothers ultimately abandoned the technical plans for patenting a new mechanical device, Charles did not altogether forget these "imprints in various colors" as a "representation of sounds produced," a correspondence between color and sound that harked back potentially to Castel (see Figure 4). Their imprint resurfaces in his poetry, in the "colors, rare or impossible in real races" of the rowers in "Le Vaisseau-Piano." In this way, a certain idea of race, of escaping from race as it was *seen* in "real" waking life, was also present, together with deafness, at one point of origin in the protophonographic imagination. Several of his contemporaries saw Cros as an other in racial terms. One contemporary described him as "presque nègre" ("almost black") in appearance and physiognomy.[30] Sometimes exoticizing ("Je rêve de passer ma vie en quelque coin [. . .] En Orient, [. . .]"), he was at the same time himself exoticized and seen as a racialized outsider by some in his social circle.[31]

The literary evocation of fantastical felt and hammers in Cros's "Le Vaisseau-Piano" would also point toward new outsider literary domains and the potential influence of Cros's prose poetry and imagery therein on Rimbaud. In particular, "Le Vaisseau-Piano" might be read as an influence on Rimbaud's "Le Bateau Ivre" and the prose poetry of his *Illuminations*.[32] Beyond the similar nautical imagery of the poems, it is more the juxtaposition of poetic images and the revolt against traditional literary forms and values of the time—Cros's dream of "the art of tomorrow"—that would briefly unite the two poets, in life and in poetry. (Rimbaud, to recall, stayed with Cros for roughly two weeks during his first trip to Paris to see Verlaine, during which time the three poets read and discussed each other's works.)[33]

In another prose poem, "L'Heure Froide," a transitional work between the prose poetry of Baudelaire's *Spleen de Paris* and Rimbaud's *Illuminations*, Cros describes a drunkenness of youth and of Paris suggestive of that particular kind of revolt, which might be found in the city's enchantments. The speaker relates how, again recalling Baudelaire, "just speaking the very words 'evening twilight [*crépuscules du soir*], splendors of setting suns' allows me to evoke both solemn memories of a past life and the enchantments of drunken youth [*les ravissements de jeunesse enivrée*]." Rendered in the poem as a source of both enchantment and terror, Paris offers the speaker another source of intoxication, specifically in the acoustical field. As the night grows deeper, the speaker muses on the sounds of the city, in particular how "women selling pleasures of the flesh whisper their offers, modest because of the late hour" and how "others miss the liveliness, now interrupted, and get drunk on melodies and cries in the air."[34] The poem's metaphorical intoxication from *plein air* songs and cries signifies one way of capturing and inscribing sound and incidental urban song in poetry.

Cros's "Soir," a poem of five quatrains in verse, likewise includes nocturnal urban imagery similar to that encountered in "L'Heure Froide": gas lamps, shadowy passing figures in the street, and echoing voices. The speaker obliquely references Nina de Villard and her salon through invocation of his "bien-aimée" ("beloved") and "les tapis de son boudoir" ("the carpet of her boudoir"). Sounds of the city transport him back into the past and stir up his memories. Interior and exterior spaces blur in like fashion to the present and the past as the speaker hears the voice of his lover brought back to him once again, echoed in the city that turns into clouds or the carpet of her boudoir beneath his feet:

Le gaz s'allume aux étalages . . .	Gas takes light in the window displays . . .
Moi, je crois, au lieu du trottoir,	Me, I think, instead of the sidewalk,
Fouler sous mes pieds les nuages	I tread beneath my feet on cloudy haze
Ou les tapis de son boudoir.	Or the carpet of her boudoir.
Car elle suit mes courses folles,	She follows me with every crazy choice,
Et le vent vient me caresser	And the wind caresses my face
Avec le son de ses paroles	With the sound of her voice
Et le parfum de son baiser.[35]	And the fragrance of her embrace.

The wind, blowing through a city illuminated with modern gas lamps and transformed by the poet's "courses folles," allows the sound of his lover's voice to echo. The city thus begins to resemble the "coffret" ("case") of the poetry collection's title, an ambivalent stimulus to and container of memory, and in this way recalls the dedication to Villard at the beginning of *Le Coffret de santal*. Just as the wind blows through the city with the sounds of her voice and the fragrance of her kiss to caress the fugitive poet, preserving them in his memory in "Soir," her summertime perfume lingers in the sandalwood case of poetry he dedicates to her:

| Ton capiteux parfum d'été | Your sensuous summertime perfume |
| Seul, parmi d'autres, est resté. | Alone, out of all others, can I exhume. |

And in "Inscription," Cros's ode to his inventions and, even more so, to the "visions" that guided their conceptualization, one could imagine Villard's voice as one of the "voix aimées" ("beloved voices") that are, for him, "un bien, qu'on garde à jamais" ("a keepsake, which one holds onto forever").[36] In this way, Cros reveals his desire to still the passage of time and to preserve sound that is metamorphosed by both poetry and mechanical invention. His vision is of a harmonic union between art and science inscribed in memory through poetry and scientific visions, the product of love both tumultuous and newly timeless in sound. In doing so, Cros anticipates something like the fascination with preserving La Stilla's voice in Jules Verne's *Le Château des Carpathes* (1892).[37] Part of Cros's debt to Baudelaire, on the other hand, together with Cros's dilemma in the face of the ephemeral and eternal crosscurrents of modernity, reveals itself through his other desire, namely his impulse to part with these containers, to disdain new technologies or material trinkets in favor of seemingly more ephemeral charms, flowers of the moment:

Quel encombrement dans ce coffre!	What a weight in this coffer!
Je vends tout. Accepte mon offre,	I'll sell it all. Accept my offer,
Lecteur. Peut-être quelque émoi,	Dear reader. Perhaps some glee,
Pleurs ou rire, à ces vieilles choses	Tears or laughter, from this old stuff
Te prendra. Tu paieras, et moi	Will seize you. You'll pay, and me
J'achèterai de fraîches roses.[38]	I'll buy some sweet roses.

If Cros's prose poetry draws on Baudelaire's *Spleen de Paris* and at the same time anticipates Rimbaud's prose poetry aesthetic in *Illuminations*, Cros's literary forms speak to a union between literary and scientific ideas about developing acoustic technologies, however ambivalent Cros feels toward their development and uses. His ideas about sound intersected with the period's new ways of seeing, in particular an impulse to refine and expand the possibilities afforded by photography. Dialogue between the visual and acoustic fields unfolds in Cros's poetry as in his scientific research.

When recounting the history of phonographic technology, scholars commonly stress the ways in which telegraphic innovations and the invention of the telephone helped make the technical realization of the phonograph possible.

There was also, as I want to stress, a distinctive visual source for Cros's conception of acoustic technology.[39] Cros's investigations into the nature of vision, for one, in his *Principes de mécanique cérébrale*, a treatise that joins the science of optics with a theory of visual perception, led him, as he explains, to explore similar issues with hearing. It was in the course of these investigations into aural perception and possibilities of mechanically mediated listening, he reveals, that he lit upon the idea for his paleophone.[40]

For nearly twenty years, from the late 1860s into the late 1880s, Cros also committed himself to efforts to develop a means of color photography. This research inspired him to reflect deeply on mechanical reproducibility across different media with different effects. His 1867 text entitled "Procedure for Recording and Reproduction: Of Colors, Forms, and Movements" is among his most important. Cros begins the work with a description of the phenakistiscope, developed in the early 1830s by Belgian scientist Joseph Plateau. It is an optical toy that provides the illusion of continuous motion through a series of drawings and a screen that produces an after-image on the retina (see Figures 7, 8).[41] In an attempt to develop this technology, Cros proposed substituting photographs for the drawings, which would enable a better illusion of continuous movement, one drawn from "the very trace of reality itself."

Figure 7. Émile Tilly & C. Gilbert. The phenakistiscope. *La Nature* 448 (Dec. 31, 1881), 72.

Figure 8. The phenakistiscope in the Living Pictures Optical Illusion Set. Circa 1840–1860.

For one to visualize Cros's innovations, a good visual reference would be Eadweard Muybridge's or Étienne-Jules Marey's chronophotography, to which Walter Benjamin refers in his theory of the "optical unconscious." Cros's 1867 text demonstrates a unity in his thought about the mechanics of representational devices. Like the superior illusion of movement drawn from "the very trace of reality itself" in his theoretical photographic phenakistiscope, the color field that Cros attempted to reproduce in his quest to develop a color photographic process similarly enhanced the preexisting technology. Cros, in effect, attempted to gift that technology with something beyond its then proper technical and epistemological domain or limits, in the way Baudelaire imagined a "kaleidoscope gifted with consciousness" or Félix Nadar imagined an "acoustic daguerreotype."

Nadar, in fact, took several photographic portraits of Cros, which are some of the most vivid images of the poet we have (see Figure 9). Though better remembered for his work with sound, Cros's profound engagement with mechanical reproducibility developed primarily across years of work on color photography. This raises the urgent question of whether, in the years leading

Figure 9. Photograph of poet and inventor Charles Cros by Félix Nadar, 1878. Courtesy Bibliothèque Nationale de France.

up to the invention of the phonograph, Cros was ever aware of Nadar's prophetic concept of the "acoustic daguerreotype." Little is known about Cros's relationship with Nadar or its precise chronology, leading Perriault to report that the surviving written correspondence between the two provides no answer to that question.[42] It is, however, reasonable to imagine that, depending on the chronology of their relationship, Cros and Nadar likely discussed Cros's attempts to develop mechanical sound reproducibility.[43] Such connections between the two would suggest that photography, though not an essential part of the technical mechanics leading to the phonograph, still played an ongoing role in conceptualizing such a device and possibility, both explicitly and in broader, even unconscious ways.

Cros's efforts to develop color photography also animated his dialogue with Manet, with whom Cros would maintain a close friendship for approximately ten years. These endeavors included Cros's experiments with a photographic reproduction of at least one of Manet's paintings in color, Manet's celebrated allegory of spring in *Printemps-Jeanne*, which the painter exhibited along with his *Bar aux Folies-Bergère* at the Salon of 1882. Thanks to advances in chromolithography, Cros's trichrome photograph of Manet's painting appeared on the cover of Ernest Hoschedé's *Impressions de mon Voyage au Salon de 1882* (see Figure 10). It was possibly the first photographically mass reproduced copy of an artwork in color.[44] In such a way, Cros worked at the convergence of different artistic practices—painting, printmaking, photography, and poetry—joined by mechanical techniques to reproduce visual artworks together with a distinct kinship between poetic and painterly visions. Cros's experiments with the Manet painting evidence his contribution to a new means of recording and mechanically reproducing the fleeting impressions of modern life and also reveals a vision—which Villard shared—of the "art of tomorrow." Like Mallarmé, Cros appreciated Manet's talent at a time when the painter's critical recognition in the art world was far from given. Ever the polymath and, in the words of Breton, ever the "perpetual inventor," Cros sought to bring out the nuances of tone in poetic language, photographically reproduced color, and phonographically reproduced sound. Though ruptured by divides between vision and actualization in each of these domains, these various aspirations still reveal a polymathic unity to Cros's thought, a unity that connected silent media such as painting or photography with the sound of emergent phonography.

Although Breton's comparison between Cros and Duchamp derived more from their perpetually inventive natures than from their formal affinities, there is one affinity in particular between the two that crystallizes the dialogue between different media highlighted here, from phenakistiscope to chronophotography to cinema to mechanically recorded and reproduced sound, a certain intermedial field. The "rotoreliefs" that Duchamp devised in the 1920s harkened back to nineteenth-century toys like the phenakistiscope, but their movement and illusion of depth borrowed the motion of a then more recent device: the gramophone. The circular movement of the gramophone effectively animates the illustrations on the discs and produces the illusion of three-dimensional depth (see Figures 11 and 12). Cros had imagined the possibility and practicality of sound recordings on disc rather than on the cylinders used by early phonographs. Duchamp's rotoreliefs would feature in several films, including *Anémic Cinéma* (1926), which the artist produced with Man Ray.

Figure 10. The front cover of Ernest Hoschedé's *Impressions de mon Voyage au Salon de 1882*, with chromolithographic print of Cros's photographic reproduction of Manet's painting. Printed and published by Tolmer et cie, 1882. Courtesy National Gallery of Art Library, David K. E. Bruce Fund, Washington DC.

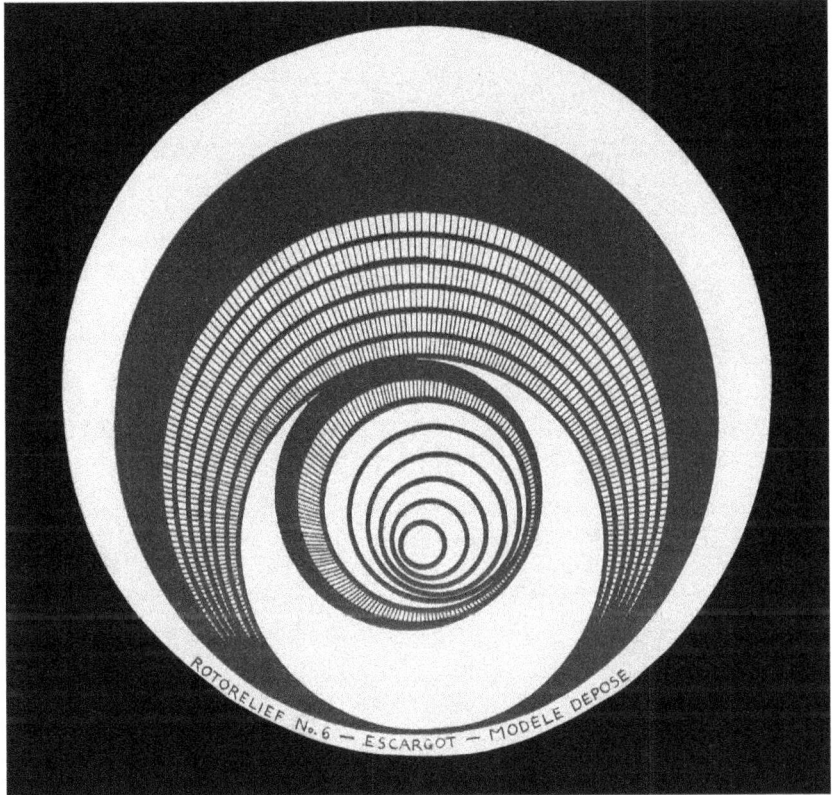

Figure 11. Marcel Duchamp, *Rotorelief no. 6—Escargot*, 1935. © Association Marcel Duchamp / ADAGP, Paris / Artist Right's Society (ARS), New York 2021.

Regardless of whether Duchamp had Cros in mind when creating the rotorelief discs, we can say that the discs play *with* and *across* different media. They play *on* film with a circular form recalling the phenakistiscope, the apparatus with which Cros effectively anticipated cinematic movement. They play as discs *on* the gramophone, which animates their movement and depth. They play on the gramophone without sound, however, and in so doing, they play, perhaps most importantly, *with* the expectations of what particular media should produce (be it sound, color, movement, or depth). The gramophone was a device for listening to sound, yet Duchamp characteristically treated it as a "found object" for something else, for viewing movement and three dimensions instead.[45] At the same time, the rotoreliefs demonstrate a historical lineage by looking back to the phenakistiscope and looking forward (perhaps also silently listening forward) to the first "talkie" films. With his rotoreliefs,

Figure 12. André Raffray, *Duchamp at Concours Lépine Inventor's Fair*, 1935 (detail). From Jennifer Gough-Cooper and Jacques Caumont, *La Vie illustrée de Marcel Duchamp, avec 12 dessins d'André Raffray* (Paris: Centre National d'Art et de Culture Georges Pompidou, 1977).

hence, Duchamp effectively played with and broke down the discrete sensory domains of particular media technologies, while also, consciously or not, evoking the very intersensory play that was at work in Cros's imagination for what these devices, in their prenatal and infant stages, could do outside of their intended sensory or representational frame, be it visual or acoustic, static or mobile, flat or three-dimensional.

Interplanetary Romance, Sounds on the Surface of the Sun

Though Cros called his would-be invention for sound reproduction the "paléophone" in 1877, he used the term "phonograph" to refer to an idea for sound reproducibility that he developed in a short story published in 1872, five years before Edison's realization of the technology. In "Un drame interastral," a science fiction love story set in the year 2872, the narrator tells of how Glaux, the son of a famous astronomer on Earth, falls in love with a woman on Venus via advanced audiovisual telecommunications between the two planets: a love story over Skype or Zoom from the nineteenth century.[46] Glaux initially shows little interest in astronomy, and instead prefers to paint and write poetry. When his father's eyesight begins to deteriorate, Glaux takes up the work of exchanging photographs between Earth and Venus in the service of mutual scientific study of equatorial flora. In the course of this exchange he glimpses a woman, a "Vénusienne," and soon falls in love.

Through their correspondence, a strange idea emerges. Perhaps they might attach sound to the images transmitted between planets. Speaking about the effects of this particular interplanetary dialogue, the narrator generalizes: "It was not in fact until these events that it was possible to transmit and receive acoustic phenomena. But the practical use of this ability has been rejected [*On a nié l'utilité de cela*]."[47] Here, "*on*" refers to political and scientific societies described in the story that impose repressive laws upon astronomers and the public alike, laws that the poet and lovestruck visionary dreamer Glaux flouts as he exchanges sound and song with Venus. The narrator elaborates on the political restrictions on thought and communication: "They say that we hardly understand a thing about Venusian music and that, as for spoken languages, we can only make them audible with the help of the mechanical speaking device [*l'articulateur mécanique*]."[48] Here, Cros may have drawn on his experiences at the Institut des Sourds-Muets to conceive the idea of an "articulateur mécanique" and the sign language that the story's star-crossed lovers initially use, the "signs exchanged . . . of the interastral language [*signes échangés . . . du langage interastral*]."

Glaux's artistic and scientific aspirations merge as the couple communicate via extraordinary representational means:

Ils crurent vaincre la distance qui les séparait en échangeant les traces les plus complètes de leurs personnes. Ils s'envoyèrent leurs photographies, par séries suffisantes à la reproduction du relief et des mouvements.

Glaux, aux heures où l'observation était close, s'enfermait dans une salle et reproduisait dans des fumées ou des poussières l'image mouvante de sa bien-aimée, image impalpable faite de lumière seule. Il en réalisa aussi la forme immobile en substances plastiques.[49]

(They believed themselves able to overcome the distance that separated them by exchanging the most complete traces of themselves. They sent each other their photographs, in series that allowed for the reproduction of depth and movement.

Glaux, during the hours when observation was unavailable, would hide himself away in a room and reproduce the moving image of his beloved in smoke or in dust, an impalpable image made of light alone. From these activities he also created her immobile form in plastic materials.)

In these passages, and in his description of the photographic series in particular, Cros uses tender and intimate terms to narrativize the idea he described in his 1867 scientific treatise on the recording and reproduction of movement through the convergence of photography and the phenakistiscope. The phenakistiscope, to recall, played on the effect of visual afterimages on the human eye to produce the illusion of movement.

Similar to the way that the phenakistiscope conjured afterimages on the eye, the story's lovers transmit traces of themselves to one another. Here, "traces" signifies both their physiognomical features and that which appears through repetition—that is, through procedures yielding new forms of representation with the reproducibility of movement (to help visualize this sequence in the text, one might think of the first image of Princess Leia in *Star Wars: Episode IV–A New Hope* [1977]), a recorded hologram akin, I would argue, to Cros's vision of an "impalpable image made of light alone," or to La Stilla in Jules Verne's *Le Château des Carpathes* (see Figure 13).

Cros's narrative then takes a surprising turn to the acoustic:

It was at that point that they endeavored to send each other the sound of their voice, their speech, and their songs. All these things were recorded by curved lines and reproduced in the electric apparatus of

Figure 13. Léon Bennett. Original illustration in Jules Verne's *Le Château des Carpathes*. 1892.

tuning forks [*l'appareil électrique à diapasons*]. I can say nothing about the particular speech and song (?) that came from so far away.[50]

Deserving special attention here is the element of reproduction, in contradistinction to Scott's idea of his phonautograph's principal function, to record. The narrator cannot discuss recorded speech or song in detail because, he notes, records of these communications are stored in the "central archives," and access is highly restricted: "All of Glaux's papers, photographs, photosculptures, and phonograms [*phonographies*] are stored in the central archives. It is necessary, as I have already noted, to be of the eleventh degree in order to consult them."[51] Though the narrator cannot reveal the content of these transmissions, he does describe how these new representational practices fostered new means of private correspondence that could leave "traces" for preservation in an archive. In that era, the words *"photosculptures"* and *"phonographies"* were arresting neologisms in their own right. In the plural, the terms suggest the remains left by an otherwise seemingly ephemeral and intangible exchange and simultaneously imply the existence of multiple discrete records documenting photographic three-dimensionality and sound. Sound recordings and enhanced photographic representations enable private amorous communication between Glaux and his beloved, albeit on a system intended to support rational scientific discourse. In this way, Cros evokes an ambivalent position between positivist scientism and poetic dreaming.

In "Le Journal de l'avenir" (1880), Cros would imagine acoustic technologies—specifically the telephone and phonograph—as devices for the mass communication of news and mass reproducibility, but in "Un drame interastral" the technologies emerge from and serve intimate private interpersonal telecommunication. They emerge, too, from the need to "annihilate distances," a phrase that has become something of a cliché in nineteenth-century studies with the development of railroads, for instance. In Cros's imagined world, however, the annihilation of distances involves drawing the interpersonal into greater proximity through vivid means of representation and mediation, and through proliferating layers of communication.

The story's conclusion, in which political forces seize Glaux's correspondence, speaks to nineteenth-century anxiety about evolving state surveillance and threats to privacy under audiovisual communications monitoring. As the narrator repeats, Glaux's amorous communication with his beloved violates the protocols dictated by the astronomical society; the lovers were, after all, appropriating public resources for their own interpersonal communications. The Paris Commune and its aftermath might have informed the political subtext of this anxiety and inspired the reported changes in imagined political regimes at the story's beginning and end.[52] Authorities used photographs of Communards to track down those who escaped the first violent repressions. Soon thereafter, police forces enlisted photography as a key resource in tracking criminals. This use of photographic technology parallels the story's description of a future in which the state archives and guards records of illicit correspondence conducted over advanced telecommunication technologies.[53]

In the story's conclusion, the brief paragraph describing the archiving process stands as an early example of an author articulating the idea that a state agency or large organization would preserve records of personal correspondence produced through the use of *audiovisual* telecommunication technologies. Because such technology had not yet been developed at the time Cros was writing, there is every chance that he was the first author to address this subject. The electric telegraph, whose messages were susceptible to interception and monitoring, had been invented decades earlier. But the telephone, in its newborn working form, would not be invented for another four years, in 1876, by Alexander Graham Bell. And the video chat, as this story also seems to presage, would not emerge in the form of a practical working device until many years afterward.

Cros's story invites us to consider what function and value reside in the "photosculptures" and "phonographies" on which records of the interplanetary correspondence are preserved. The narrator is silent on the topic, stating only that the records were saved and that future access to them would be restricted. Ironic and deadpan, his statement allows the reader to imagine that future technological media platforms for telecommunication could produce valuable, perhaps scandalous artifacts of the content flowing on those networks. As Cros imagines, oversight and preservation of these records cannot escape political and administrative centralization.

Shades of the Photophonic

Ultimately, "Un drame interastral" imagines sound reproducibility in the crucible of existing optical representational technologies that included photography and an early idea of silent film ("photographs in series allowing for the reproduction of depth and movement"). No less important to the story is the concept of love, which inspires the narrative of sound transmission and reproducibility in the protagonists' desire to overcome physical distance by exchanging "les traces les plus complètes de leurs personnes" ("the most complete traces of themselves"). Studies of early sound technologies frequently identify death as a crucial issue in the conception and early understanding of these technologies. Here, however, it is love that resolutely animates and frames imagined audio telecommunications and sound recording. Though the transmission of sound and speech across great distances would appear to herald the invention of the telephone, that Cros includes the element of reproduction is a defining feature of what would become the phonograph.

In its notion, however vague, of transmitting sound by optics, the story contains the germ of a lesser-known audiovisual technology that Bell invented in 1880, the "photophone" (see Figures 14a and 14b). Not only does this invention illustrate the breadth of Cros's imagination regarding mechanized sound and communication, but it also highlights close connections between ideas about the visual and the acoustic at this historical moment in both the literary and scientific domains. In more general terms, seemingly discrete audio or visual imaginaries and media in the nineteenth century harbor hidden audiovisual (and, in some cases, multisensory) dimensions that are theoretical and material. A certain prehistory of the phonograph, I maintain, is, for example, latent in the early history of photography, particularly in literary and art critical discourse on photography such as Champfleury's "Legend of the Daguerreotypist" (1863) and in the works of Baudelaire and Nadar, as we will see in Chapter 3. Alphonse Allais, Cros's friend and confrère in the comic arts, wrote of Cros's idea for a device similar to the "photophone": "In his *Cerebral Mechanics*, Charles Cros described a theoretical apparatus that truly made the Académie des Sciences laugh: light that could speak! [*la lumière qui parle!*]"[54] Two years later, Allais notes, someone else—Bell—patented such a device for "the production and reproduction of sound through light" and called it the photophone.[55] Here Allais throws into relief a deep irony that attended his friend's writings and life: Cros was both serious and comic, innovative in his humor and humorous in his innovations, and at times—depending on his audience—too much so. Though it would be decades before other inventors applied the photophone's technology for practical purposes, Bell would describe the device as "the first wireless telephone ever invented," and its technological principles would influence the development of cinema and sound films in particular.[56] Thanks to his early photophone experiments, Bell, in an 1880 letter to his father, exclaimed: "I have been able to hear a shadow."[57]

As seen in "Un drame interastral," Cros's communication technology designs were intended for interplanetary communication, another venture that he explored in both literary texts and scientific circles. It is striking, then, that shortly after the invention of the photophone in 1880, Bell followed a path similar to that of Cros's fictional character Glaux in the literary fantasy of Glaux's efforts to overcome interplanetary distances through audiovisual technologies. With its imagined sounds optically transmitted between Earth and Venus, Cros's "Un drame interastral" anticipated, by eight years, a photophone

PALEOPHONICS: CHARLES CROS'S AUDIOVISUAL WORLDS

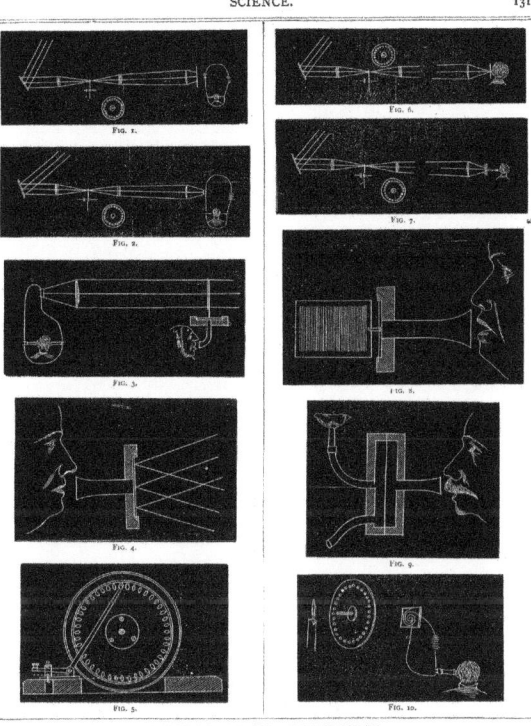

Figure 14a. Illustrations of the photophonic procedure. From Alexander Graham Bell, "The Photophone," *Science* 1, no. 11 (Sept. 11, 1880), 131.

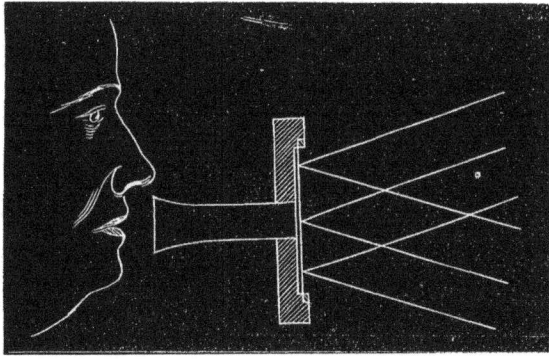

Figure 14b. (Detail)

experiment that Bell conducted with French astronomer Jules Janssen. At the time, Janssen was famous for his photographs of the sun, and Cros was likely to have known him through their mutual association with the Académie des Sciences in Paris and from Janssen's photographs of Venus.

In October 1880, Bell traveled to Janssen's observatory in the town of Meudon, outside Paris, intending to use the photophone in a study of "the noises taking place on the surface of the sun."[58] The meeting of Janssen's images and Bell's photophonic apparatus resulted in "the idea of reproducing on earth the sounds caused by great phenomena on the surface of the sun."[59] Though the experiment did not yield satisfying results at the time, the attempt to "recueillir les échos du soleil" ("harvest the sun's echoes"), a very Surrealist thing to do, as André Breton would later describe it (160), prompted further theorization. The experiment attests to the range and depth of Cros's involvement with contemporaneous scientific theories and practices that exploited distinctly audiovisual configurations. The reproduction of sound was both imagined and realized through multiple modes of inscription on different surfaces—inscribed not only on foil or wax, as in early models of the phonograph, but in light as well. Light could now be manipulated as a mechanical conduit and container of information.

The oneiric imagery of Cros's "Un drame interastral," with its reproduced "moving image of his beloved, impalpable image made of light alone," would appeal to the Surrealists, to Breton, and to Aragon especially, while the story's fantasy of interplanetary communication through optical acoustics anticipated astronomical theories like Bell's and Janssen's experiment with the sounds of the sun. That experiment, together with the literary text and notion of the "acoustic daguerreotype" that Félix Nadar and others variously imagined in the decades before the invention of the phonograph, illustrates the breadth of what one might call the photophonic theory of the age. This theory involved not only anticipation of a new invention, as an analogy of doing for sound what the daguerreotype did for light, but a conception of a photograph being itself visually inscribed with sound, to be made audible by certain mechanical means, as Cros theorized and as Bell and Janssen attempted to realize.[60] One might then, as Nadar proposed, be able to "see noise."[61]

What are the broader implications of a photophonic theory of the age? For one, can we imagine something like photophonic Impressionism? Might the photophonic enable, among other things, a rethinking of Impressionism's traditional associations with natural light and the era's artificial lighting, which included gas, arc, and electric illumination?[62] Photophonic Impressionism, then, if we can imagine it, would not be so much about images of people conversing over photophones (had they been built and mass marketed in that period) or about the buzz of gaslight ever so subtly evoked in brushstrokes or synesthetic prose (think of Pissarro's nocturnal boulevards or the "luminous noise" of gaslight in Mallarmé's "An Interrupted Spectacle"). Instead, it would be about sound and information converging in light over new communications networks, or at least in the dream of those networks.[63] Directed light between mechanical transmitters and receivers could be a novel communication medium.

Indeed, part of Bell's design and dream for photophonic communications touched on the form and aesthetic of modern urban space. Not wanting to encumber that space with masses of visible telephone wires, he envisioned a more elegant solution in a medium that would have hidden, or, more precisely, would have used a largely hidden medium (sightlines) to facilitate audio communication.[64]

Inscriptions

For Cros, inscription remained fluid even amid forces that aspired to more inscriptive permanence. What may have seemed newly permanent remained still labile, semi-fluid. "Inscription," the first poem in Cros's posthumous collection *Le Collier de Griffes* (1908), reads largely as a paean to Cros's various scientific aspirations and inventions, including interplanetary communication, color photography, sound reproducibility, gemstone synthesis, and studies of light in particular.[65]

Though some mocked certain of these visions, the Académie des Sciences and other venues for scientific research took them seriously and were a willing audience for Cros's scientific ventures.[66] The poet's homage in these verses to his own scorned visionary nature is framed, in part, by a bitterness at being excluded and denied recognition by a world insensible to his aspirations, both literary and scientific, the kind of world that Maupassant, imitating the form and spirit of Cros's famous "Le Hareng Saur" poem, described in a letter to Flaubert: "*je vois des choses farces, farces, farces et d'autres qui sont tristes, tristes, tristes, en somme tout le monde est bête, bête, bête, ici comme ailleurs*" ("I see things that are mad, mad, mad and others that are sad, sad, sad, in sum everyone is stupid, stupid, stupid, here as much as anywhere else").[67]

Inscription is more than a theme that binds these various visions in the poem. The dream of advanced technological inscription subtends and inflects the lyric voice of the poem, making and remaking that voice into something at once threatened with obsolescence but also endowed with a seemingly newfound permanence as a trace within a new acoustic machine.[68] The amorous embrace at the end of Cros's poem ("mes lèvres, . . . savaient les suprêmes baisers") invites comparison with Maurice Renard's "Death and the Shell" and with Kittler's interpretation of that literary text, which he situates within a "long series of literary phantasms that rewrite eroticism itself under the conditions of gramophony and telephony." My own point is that before Cros wrote "Inscription," eroticism in his oeuvre shaped the originary conditions for gramophony and telephony. In Cros's poetry and short fiction, romantic love first helped to articulate a desire for phonography and photophony, among other technological devices.

As a phenomenon, "inscription" adopts multiple forms across the poem. In the first stanza, the lyrical self speaks of how his life is reflected in his verse:

Aussi, malgré le mal, ma vie	Also, despite its pain, my life
De tant de diamants ravie	With so many diamonds rife
Se mire au ruisseau de mes vers.[69]	Scintillates in poetic runs.

If the lines of poetry hold the power to "reflect" and sing of the lyric self, other means of self-representation will require different instruments. Thus in the line that concludes the third stanza, in which the poet says he knows how to show the new world ("et montrer le monde nouveau"), such a demonstration is as much about a "new world" with new technology as it is about such new technological means of "showing" ("montrer") that new world.

The fourth stanza of the poem, read as a whole, appears to address Cros's investigations into color photography:

J'ai voulu que les tons, la grâce,	I wished that shades, grace,
Tout ce que reflète une glace,	Everything a mirror reflects to a face,
L'ivresse d'un bal d'opéra,	The drunkenness of an operatic spree,
Les soirs de rubis, l'ombre verte	Evenings of rubies, green shadow,
Se fixent sur la plaque inerte.	Would on the inert plate be hallowed.
Je l'ai voulu, cela sera.	I wished and dreamed, it will be.

At a time when much of the discourse on the phonograph centered on the preservation of the human voice, visual and auditory fields converge in the poem's reference to "un bal d'opéra," allowing one to interpret the line as an expression of the dream of recorded and reproducible music.[70] The element of color in the nights of rubies and green shadow could be read as a means of elevating photography to a new level of representation. Color draws the *"soirs de rubis"* in closer proximity to the diamonds of the poet's life, suggesting a lyricism of color photography, or photography coming closer to that lyricism in color.

The plate's inert quality, primed to receive the poet's inscription, also relates to the fugitive nature of modern life, as in the subsequent—and penultimate—

stanza in which the poet concludes: "Le temps veut fuir, je le soumets." The stanza describes the inscriptive ability of the paleophone, which enables a recording of the past, arresting the flight of time. Cros maintains the audiovisual interplay, analogizing the preservation of the sound of the past with the visual field, while obliquely referencing the domain of portraiture:

Comme les traits dans les camées	Like features in cameo portraits
J'ai voulu que les voix aimeés	I wished that beloved voices
Soient un bien, qu'on garde à jamais	Would become a keepsake, kept forever,
Et puissent répéter le rêve	That they would repeat the musical
Musical de l'heure trop brève;	Dream of the too brief hour;
Le temps veut fuir, je le soumets.	Time wants to flee, I arrest it.

To the extent that a life can be reflected or inscribed, such life resides in the use of an object like a cameo, in the way visual features or the tones of a "beloved voice" resolve into an object, "un bien." How that object is held, and for how long, "qu'on garde à jamais," depends on the inscriptive technology. The subject's ability to hold on to the object as a memory also connotes the object's ability to hold or save (*garde*) the subject. The subject both holds and is held by inscription.

The image of the cameo, evocative of carving and of layers and grooves, helps to set the auditory technology of the inscription itself in relief. "Traits," while denoting the features of a person's face, can also signify "traces," a word that Cros often uses to refer to the inscriptions in his scientific writings on phonography; they are the imprint that sound makes in a mechanical device. Cros's analogy suggests how the voice might be touched, in the way fingers might run over the features of the cameo, calling up the memory of a loved one. The inscription, in this way, might be touched in addition to being read, seen, and heard.

The poem's contest with fugitive time continues to develop when the beloved voices enter into a musical register. Repetition nuances the act of saving ("un bien, qu'on garde à jamais"). And from that repetition emerges a kind of music, the preservation of a musical dream ("Le rêve/Musical de l'heure trop brève").[71] As in the suggestive ambiguity of acoustic and colorful tones earlier in the poem, the phrase expresses a mode of inscription, signifying both a "musical dream" and the possibility of dreaming of music *musically*.[72] In this way, the phonograph not only preserves voices like material mementos but also shades those voices with the tone of fleeting time and imbues them with musicality in an ephemeral key.

Cros's "beloved" voices additionally testify to the power of love to inspire the need and desire for sound reproducibility, as we saw in "Un drame interastral." In contrast with Poe, with whom Cros would share literary interests in science-fiction fantasies of the protophonographic imagination, Cros's narratives of audiovisual recording are less obsessed with death and more awash in anguished love and ambivalent beauty.[73] Though death frequently haunts images of love in Cros's poetry, he writes the dream of sound reproducibility more often through a drama of love than a drama of mortality and morbidity.[74]

Framed by amorous embrace, "Inscription" concludes with a return to the life of the poet and the poetic self. In the poem's final stanza, sound and sight might, in self-aggrandizing self-deprecating jest, find their pinnacle in touch, in a kiss from past to future. Inscription returns to the human body.

Patent Timing

To the extent that the poem connotes both physical and textual possession, Cros's "Inscription" reveals a broader historical context for Cros's literary meditation on his scientific works. Two elements heighten the acutely fugitive perception of time in the poem: newfound mechanical techniques to arrest time, and the way those techniques were themselves legally possessed—that is to say, the way those techniques were "inscribed'" in a particular textual form, in patent form to be precise.[75] For Cros, one side of this conflict arose from the gap between his visions on the one hand and their strictly timed inscription as patented inventions in a material and textual form on the other. Bell's initial patents on telephone technology preceded his material realization of the device.[76] Thus, we can read the line "Le temps veut fuir. Je le soumets" in the poem both as a perception of what the phonograph could do to time and as an implicit acknowledgment of fugitive time in the competition to patent this and other technologies. If the phonograph could effectively freeze the flight of time and consequently mitigate the fear of arriving too late to an event, inventors still struggled to be the first to go "on record," both with a working device and with foundational principles and improvements to the technology. Claims of being the first in the scientific world were a constant concern and point of conflict.[77]

As an inventor, Cros fell victim to the rush of time in the race to patent first. Repetition, as an acoustic specter of sorts, haunted him as a mechanical acoustic question in his scientific and literary works and as a social phenomenon when he repeatedly lost legal claims to priority. In negotiating Cros's dual legacies—he was a visionary dreamer content to theorize the principles of scientific innovation and let others realize them, and he was an accomplished inventor who could himself realize those visions—it is important to account for the social and economic context in which these innovations were documented and patented. For example, because the early work of the Cros brothers on musical stenography coincided with the contemporaneous work of other inventors, Pierre Richard has concluded that the Cros brothers abandoned their efforts in the face of others laying claim to being the first to patent such principles.

More dramatic in this respect, in the near simultaneity of scientific discovery and presentation, was one of Cros's early attempts to demonstrate and promote his color photography technique. On the day Cros was scheduled to present his method to the Société Française de Photographie, another inventor, Louis Ducos du Hauron, was also presenting a similar color photography process.[78] Cros and du Hauron, each unknown to each other before they met that day, came to share credit for the similarly innovative principles of their work. These principles effectively laid the groundwork for subsequent successful procedures for color photography, a moment some have celebrated as the true invention of the medium.

Cros was to have a similar experience with his work on the phonograph. Vested economic interests drove the circulation of information about patents, and about the race to patent, an economy of yet unrealized visions, from which Cros wished to escape if he could not in some way negotiate, entangled as he was in that economy. In this way, too, the inventor-poet experienced modernity as a headlong flight of time, one he wished to arrest. He would vent his frustrations about this race in an embittered 1876 letter as he sought funding for his scientific work: "Justice will perhaps eventually be served: but in waiting, there is in these things an example of the scientific tyranny of capital [*la tyrannie scientifique du capital*]. Such tyranny is notably evident in this kind of saying: 'theories are but things in the air and have no value; show us results [*des faits*].' And the money then in order to conduct these demonstrations? And the money in order to produce these results? In such a way so many things are impossible in France."[79]

While developing disc-based mass sound reproduction technology in the 1890s, Emile Berliner would not only draw on Cros's principles of the paleophone but also investigate the legal status of Cros's claim on the technology.[80] Because it had been envisioned but never realized in material form, Cros's paleophone presented no obstacle to Berliner's incorporation of its principles in the mechanics of his own sound reproduction process. Still, Berliner's concern to investigate on legal grounds, together with his explicit acknowledgment of a scientific debt to Cros, reveals how abstract visions, once "inscribed" and inserted into scientific circles and legal text, were subject to evolving market forces and the increasing speed of modern technological innovation. These visions and this speed were effectively working against the flight of time even as they helped to accelerate that flight. Often unable to afford the cost of securing a patent, Cros, for his part, instead filed his work under a form that was less expensive but legally ambiguous and precarious at the Académie des Sciences.[81]

It was not only in patenting scientific work but also in performance and literary innovations that Cros would suffer from claims to ownership. The comic monologues that he would write and popularize as a form of performance in Parisian cabarets in the 1880s would help to launch the career of, among others, the actor Ernest Coquelin Cadet, who in performing Cros's material enjoyed great financial success, while Cros continued to languish in poverty.[82] I make this less as a biographical point and more as a means of highlighting the multiple historical valences of "inscription." Despite the appearance of a "plaque inerte" in the poem, "inscription" can be read as a still labile field shifting between visions of scientific advances, as a textuality subject to literary-critical and rapidly evolving legal, economic forces. Inscription also encompassed texts written for performance as live ephemeral spectacle, the sounds of which were soon to be mass reproduced in the form of discs commodified for the gramophone—a device that Cros's paleophone had inspired.

The Pinwheel Phonograph

In 1878, the year following Edison's realization of the phonograph, Cros would continue to write about the technology and propose different possibilities and diverse means of improving and refining the device. These documents demonstrate his efforts to imagine the future of the device. A closer look at one of these texts, in particular, helps to reveal the diversity and depth of the literary imagination concerning the early understanding of mechanical sound reproducibility. Within these documents, one proposal stands out for its link to a celebrated literary source.

The relevant text contains Cros's design for "small phonographs purely for playback, at a reduced price."[83] At the time, between 1877 and 1887, phonographs were used to both record and reproduce sound. Cros, however, imagined a smaller, more portable phonograph whose only function was to play back prerecorded material: "One draws the thread or the metallic ribbon that has the imprint of a word, a short phrase spoken or sung, or of any ordinary sounds or noises [. . .]. All that is required is to pull on the thread to hear the sounds inscribed on the thread played back by the phonograph receptor."[84] Note, once again, elements of the ordinary and everyday. Cros describes his miniature device as "almost a toy" and imagines that its form could resemble a pinwheel.[85] Essentially, his proposal was a primitive, portable sound reproduction device akin to the Walkman or iPod in size and portability. Expanding on its possibilities, he notes: "It would even be possible to sell separately various threads containing various phonographic recordings [*phonogrammes variés*] according to the buyer's tastes."[86] The idea for metallic threads containing varied "*phonogrammes,*" or voices of the past, might have originated in Cros's poem "L'Archet," in which the strands of the dead beloved's hair are used to make the bow for a violin.[87] In each case the thread, whether played over a "*violon de Crémone*" or a "*petit phonographe pûrement répétiteur,*" resonates with the sounds and songs of the past.[88]

If the resemblance between Cros's "petit phonographe" idea and contemporary portable music players should seem too anachronistic, there exists another potential source of inspiration for Cros's idea. The source in question is a literary text that scholars have discussed in connection with Cros, but never in direct connection with either his literary texts or his particular document describing the pinwheel phonograph.[89]

In an essay titled "Conserver les sons," Pierre Liénard cites a celebrated passage from Cyrano de Bergerac's *Voyage dans la Lune* (1657), one of the first literary works of the genre that we would now label "science fiction." Liénard claims: "It is the science-fiction of Cyrano de Bergerac (1619–1655) that discovers, in the Empire of the moon, the portable magnétophone, and even the portable music player or *Walkman*."[90] Specifically, Cyrano describes an encounter on the moon with a strange and marvelous invention, a little box

> in an unknown metal substance, almost akin to our clocks full of altogether mystifying little springs and imperceptible machines. It is a book [. . .] where, in order to learn, the eyes are useless; all you need is your ears. When someone wants to read, [. . .] he turns the needle to the chapter he wants to listen to, and at the very same time arises, like from the mouth of a man or a musical instrument, all the distinct and different sounds that serve amongst the great Lunaires in the expression of language.

Liénard stresses that the device in Cyrano's text is conceived as eminently portable. Cyrano's narrator continues: "In one's room, out for a stroll, in the city, on a trip they can have in their pocket or attached to their belt a good thirty of these books for which all they have to do is connect a spring in order to hear a single chapter or several. [. . .] You have eternally around you all the greats, living or dead, who entertain you with a lively voice. This gift occupied me for well over an hour; and then, with them attached in the form of ear pendants, I went out for a stroll." From this, Liénard makes the startling assertion that, hundreds of years *avant la lettre*, Cyrano offered "the exact description, and the very terms, of the *Walkman*."

The parallels are indeed uncanny, though in Cyrano's text the reproduction versus the mechanical imitation of spoken language or instrumental music remains indefinite, as this phrase evidences: ". . . *like* from the mouth of a man or a musical instrument" (my emphasis). Also striking is the degree to which Liénard's reference to the Walkman (*baladeur*) dates his piece today, though he wrote it in 1987—not so long ago, especially compared to the centuries that had passed since Cyrano's text. In the twenty-first century, we might read the Cyrano passage more as presaging the audiobook. The idea of a pocket-sized portable device from the seventeenth century to play these audiobooks remains startling, though in the present day few people would carry a device like this that serves only a single function. Did some point in the past thirty years, perhaps in the years spanning the late-1980s to early 2000s, contain the moment when Cyrano's audiobook passage reached it most prophetic stage?

Another question remains, then, for the nineteenth century: How might Cros have felt the influence of Cyrano de Bergerac's text and this particular idea? Regardless of whether or not Cros was familiar with the text or had it in mind when conceiving the "petit phonographe répétiteur," there exist important conceptual parallels between the two texts, particularly the elements of portability and sound reproducibility.[91] Cyrano and Cros each imagined the possibility of listening to and playing prerecorded sound virtually anywhere, an idea akin, in some ways, to the device Cros imagined for his deaf students. With their shared tangible objecthood, Cros's conception of the petit phonographe répétiteur resembles Cyrano's talking book. Cros likened the petit phonographe to a pinwheel, a child's toy, while Cyrano stressed his imagined device's portable size, which would fit in one's pocket for a promenade "en ville." Inherent in the idea of the portable device is the possibility of creating a mobile acoustic space framed by mechanically reproduced sounds. For Cros, this acoustic space would draw on and alter the experience of urbanization in the latter part of the nineteenth century. Mass mechanically reproduced sound on disc in the early 1900s would satisfy the demand for recorded music born at the close of the nineteenth century, in part, out of the profusion of Parisian music halls, places that would, in turn, become music publishing houses for disseminating recordings on disc.[92] At the same time, portable devices that use mechanically recorded and reproducible sound to delimit an acoustic space both respond to and parry the increasingly ubiquitous mechanically produced noises in urban spaces. Cyrano's narrator, after all, goes walking with the device "attached in the form of ear pendants."

This theoretical device might also offer another historical context for Mallarmé's mysterious *"aboli bibelot d'inanité sonore* [abolished trinket of sonorous inanity]" in his famous sonnet in -x. Imagine the inanity produced by a toy in the hands of a child with the power to repeat mechanically over and over *"les traces d'un mot, d'une courte phrase parlée ou chantée, de sons ou de bruits quelconques."* The "ptyx" of Mallarmé's poem, when read as a container of the sound of the ocean (in the original Greek, one definition for "ptyx" is "seashell"), thus confronted the idea of a different kind of container: a container of mechanically recorded and reproduced sound.[93]

The Contest and Convergence of Technologies

Just as Cros's scientific writings can often provide the context and inspiration for certain scientific allusions in his literary works, the literary works, as we have seen in "Interastral," have their own way of unifying science and art, shaping the possibilities of scientific blueprints. In the intersection of blueprints and the literary imagination, Friedrich Kittler highlights an apparent difference between Cros's poem "Inscription" and Cros's 1877 formal scientific treatise on sound reproducibility, "Procedure for the recording and reproduction of phenomena perceived by hearing."[94] Kittler relates that Cros "with great technological elegance . . . formulated all the principles of the phonograph" in the text, and notes that Cros's grand vision for the invention involved the reproduction of both "sounds and noises."[95]

The poem however seems to omit this "noise" in favor of the more refined sounds of human speech ("les voix aimées") and music ("le rêve musicale de l'heure trop brève"). Kittler claims: "Certainly, phonographs can store articulate voices and musical intervals, but they are capable of more and different things. Cros the poet forgets the noises mentioned in his precise prose text. An invention that subverts both literature and music (because it reproduces the unimaginable real they are both based on) must have struck even its inventor as something unheard of."[96] In addition to a pun on the literal and figurative dimensions of the "unheard," Kittler's argument calls attention to the way that the phonograph and poetry confront each other on the field of "competing technologies." Writing, as technology, confronts phonographic inscription that, as Kittler claims, is unlike "ears that have been trained to immediately filter voices, words, and sounds out of noise."[97] The phonograph, he maintains, instead ". . . registers acoustic events as such." How and in what particular ways literary texts might also "register" the acoustics of modernity is another important question, and one, I want to stress, that Cros did not neglect, noise and all.

Kittler distinguishes Cros the poet from Cros the scientist when he claims that the poet forgets the noises mentioned in the "scientific" text. André Breton, in contrast, appreciated the *convergence* of poetry, literature, and science in the writer's works: "Charles Cros saw words themselves as 'processes,' which he held just as dear as the processes whose discovery and application mark the stages of scientific progress. The unity of his twin vocations—poet and scientist—comes from the fact that, for him, the goal was always to wrest from nature [*arracher à la nature*] a part of her secrets."[98] While Breton emphasizes the "unity" of Cros's inquiry into the secrets of nature through poetic words and technical processes alike, Kittler's assertion of a divide between Cros's poetry and his formal scientific writing supposes something like acoustic totality—sounds *and* noises, in contradistinction to the voices and music of poetry celebrated in the poem "Inscription" that have already passed through the filter of human perception and aesthetic judgment. Kittler's impression of the poem's contracted acoustic field opens onto his broader argument that writing and poetry fall into crisis as forms of technology in competition with the phonograph. Once the phonograph was invented, Kittler claims, writing (and poetry especially, with its rhymes and meters functioning as mnemonic devices) no longer held a "monopoly" on sound storage and memory.[99] Cros's writings, however, demonstrate lively experimentation with the interactions of literature and new media technologies, experimentation that could shift the balance of such purported monopoly. Cros's irreverent and satirical texts aimed, in part, to upset technological and political orders.

Another prose text by Cros, unmentioned by Kittler, engages the contest of technologies in a sociopolitical power struggle, a contest in which literary production confronts the expansion of mechanical industry. "Le Journal de l'avenir," a dystopian fantasy in prose in the vein of Villiers de l'Isle-Adam's *L'Ève future* or Jules Verne's *Paris au XXe Siècle*, imagines another fate for the phonograph or consequence of its invention: "No one knows how to read or write anymore—that's what we call progress—thanks to the aforementioned phonograph."[100] This is how Cros imagines a future for publishing, literature, and media in the story, in which the phonograph of the future is used to deliver an audio version of the *Chat Noir* newspaper to its subscribers, an idea that has been compared to radio, but which might now seem more akin to podcasts. Here, again, the influence of Cyrano's lunar audiobooks might be intuited in Cros's imagination.

Cros biographers Louis Forestier and Gérard Bobillier each describe "Le Journal de l'avenir" as an anticipation of Charlie Chaplin's *Modern Times*.[101] The story is also startlingly prophetic in its conjunction of elements about state surveillance and mass mechanical gathering of information through telephones.

In the story, millions of people are subscribers to the "*journal parlé* (audio newscast)," a form of mass media that literally and figuratively seizes the minds of the public. Bobillier characterizes "Le Journal de l'avenir" as "the text of a man whom bitterness pushed to an overwhelming lucidity."[102] Such bitterness is manifest most explicitly in the narrative's comic and derisive references to fictional American inventors. "Tadblagson," whose name in French is loosely heard as "tas de blagues son," or "full of jokes" Edison, has transformed "the social order by rendering talent proportional to fortune," while "Humbugson" (a kind of composite of Scrooge and Edison) has, in one of the story's more oneiric absurdist passages, invented a powder to kill hummingbirds, "une poudre colibricide."[103] The story's lucidity and prescience, however, as I want to stress, are not the products of Cros's personal despair and bitterness alone, but also of a long period of deep reflection on the mechanics of acoustic technologies and of their potential effects on society, their social possibilities, both utopian and dystopian. Cros's dream of marrying science and art morphs into a darkly comic nightmare in a story that on the surface *is* very funny but no less serious in its warnings about the centralization of power through technological devices.

Certain alternate—if not opposing—conceptions of phonography in the nineteenth century, for one, involved a democratizing element, as Jacques Perriault has argued: "Phonography was also in that era phonetic writing. It was defended by workers' organizations as a possibility for democratizing culture."[104] This possibility for democratizing culture through phonetic writing was more the social current out of which Cros's vision for phonography was born, together with Cros's dream of communication with other worlds, such as with the deaf or with other planets, a more utopian vision, or one at least committed to empowering those at the risk of remaining voiceless.[105] His dream was to make the technology accessible to all. In "Le Journal de l'avenir," he vents his pessimism for the fate of such technology once appropriated by high capitalism and a kind of multilayered state surveillance.

The story begins with its unnamed narrator (whom we might presume is Cros) entering the offices of the *Chat Noir*, where he is seized by "an unknown vertigo." He then finds himself magically transported from the *Chat Noir* offices in the year 1886 to the same offices in the year 1986.[106] Alphonse Allais, one of Cros's close friends, along with Rodolphe Salis, founder of the *Chat Noir*, explain to the narrator the various changes that have transpired in the past hundred years. Salis and Allais describe something like a lobotomized society in which human brains are made out of platinum (the most expensive being made out of the molds of famous individuals such as Victor Hugo and Sarah Bernhardt, duly stored and cataloged at the Hôtel de Ville), are bought and sold as commodities on the open market, and are, if by chance they are naturally talented, subject to seizure by the state. Allais explains:

> Now the axiom is: no money, no talent. There are some rare exceptions of penniless people who are born with intelligence and wit; but our tribunals render prompt justice in those cases by expropriating those people of their brain, of which each model becomes the property of the state.[107]

The *Chat Noir* has invested heavily in reproductions of the most talented of those brains, which the journal puts to use for writing poetry, among other things. Allais continues to explain:

> The *Chat Noir* of 1986, which desires to interest its readers at any cost, has made the greatest of investments to enrich its collection of brains. Hence, the ten writers in the back, two of them writing in verse, have a value of more than five million sitting on their heads. That one there, on the left, has a Victor Hugo brain; have a look. Ten past five o'clock [...] and he's already written two hundred lines of poetry, twenty per minute.[108]

Part of the story's irony and dark humor, in addition to this barb at Hugo's prolific output and historical dominance as a poet in France, arises out of the implied connection between the state's literal seizure of human brains and the journal's huge investment in reproductions of those brains to seize the public imagination and recapture as many subscribers to the journal as possible. Literature is caught in a feedback loop of commercialized industrialized mechanical production and reproduction. Poet Ernest Raynaud, one of Cros's contemporaries, in an essay reflecting on literary bohemia in the Second Empire, explained Cros's resolute opposition to such industrialization of literature: "The 'zutisme' of Charles Cros is a magnificent lesson in disinterestedness, a barrier against commercial ideas, opposed to industrialized and commercialized literature."[109]

A surveillance apparatus also structures the way in which the story's *Chat Noir* writers, each supplied with a reproducible brain machine, use telephones. Again, Allais provides exposition: "Here we have the writers of the *news*, telephones reveal to them what is happening everywhere [*les téléphones leur révèlent ce qui se passe partout*], and they write it down with the talent they draw from these singular hats."[110] Note the shift in Cros's thought about possible uses of the telephone: in "Un drame interastral," telephones were devices for private telecommunication between individuals, but here the author depicts them as a tool for monitoring the public and listening in on events "everywhere." In this future, telephones serve as devices for the mass mechanical collection of information. And though the reader might intuit that human agents use telephones to speak to the writers at the *Chat Noir*, the text, in its suggestive withholding of details, in its abbreviated description (in contrast to some of Cros's scientific papers that *do* spell out mechanical procedures in detail), emphasizes that the instruments themselves, perhaps even absent a mediating human presence, reveal the various events of the day to the writers at the *Chat Noir*. It is already almost only the telephones that speak, not the human subject, not the human voice. This kind of listening comes across as a marvelous possibility, tainted however by the specter of control by the state. Cros illustrates the risk of such technological capabilities to fall prey to particular political or economic interests.

While Villiers de l'Isle-Adam's *L'Ève future* and Jules Verne's *Le Château des Carpathes* represent sound in the telephone and phonograph as a fetishization of the disembodied voice, Cros's imagination for what the technologies could do looks in a different direction, more toward the ability of the telephone and phonograph to register and record the full spectrum of acoustic events, "ce qui se passe partout." Here in the ubiquity of mechanical listening prostheses is where we might find the "noise" that Cros the poet, according to Kittler, apparently left out of his poem "Inscription." The *Chat Noir* apparatus of telephones, platinum brains, and phonographs is capable of recording and reproducing the very noise of society, all the daily "actualité." Unlike Verne's narrative of acoustic spying by telephone in *Le Château des Carpathes*, which happens between a rural village and a remote, isolated chateau, Cros locates the center of the telephonic listening apparatus in a city, with an ambiguous though broad reach, "partout" ("everywhere"). This mode of overhearing in the story signals a radical departure from a conception of lyric poetry as poetry in which the reader listens in on the poet, since the telephones effectively help the poets of the 1986 *Chat Noir* to listen in on all of society.

As the telephone's hearing ability is diffused—indeed dislocated—in the extreme across a vast telephonic listening network, information is still routed back to a central office. Here, as in "Interastral," telecommunications media with the potential to decentralize are still in effect controlled by a powerful center. The difference between the two texts, and particularly between their respective conclusions, reveals the scope of Cros's imagination for what content, from interpersonal correspondence to recorded news reports, might travel over such networks. In "Interastral," sound recordings are stored in a central archive, whereas in "Le Journal" sound recordings are disseminated by a central source, the largely state-controlled *Chat Noir*, to the public. Between archival storage and mass dissemination, different modern modes of listening could then take shape and proliferate. In these narratives, listening remains both centralized and politicized.

The "Panacoustic"

The listening apparatus in "Le Journal de l'avenir," its imagined use of telephones in conjunction with mechanically manufactured brains, exploits what Peter Szendy has theorized as a "panacoustic" apparatus.[111] Indeed, Cros may have been responding to Thomas Edison's 1878 essay in *The North American Review*, in which the American inventor reflected on the phonograph and its potential uses that included "the captivation of sounds, with or without the knowledge or consent of the source of their origin."[112] When working in this way, without the knowledge or consent of those being surveyed, the phonograph effectively acts as a secret listener and recorder. As early as 1881, New York City prisons used an improved version of the microphone (first invented in 1827 by English inventor Charles Wheatstone, who also invented the kaleidophone), hidden inside prison walls and in conjunction with a telephone, to surveil conversations between prisoners who were left alone without any visible monitor.[113]

In "Le Journal de l'avenir" the point of listening does have a kind of center, albeit an unstable one, in the panacoustic apparatus at the *Chat Noir* of phonographs and telephones, which both collect and disseminate information. This listening apparatus reinforces the condition of a heightened audibility of time and events. In contrast with the phonograph/paléophone of "Inscription," which can preserve elements of the past, the phonograph in the short story is a key instrument for the diffusion of news, and it opens up a new audibility of the present—or the presentness of the future as imagined in the past. The phonograph heralds a new technologically mediated relation to presentness, and to a moment ever more shaped by speed and saturated with news and information. The story's Allais explains:

> I won't even speak about the underground space for printing, where in fact we don't print at all; because now we have people with exquisite voices who dictate the copy to phonographs whose reproduced imprints in the form of millions of copies will offer the newspaper *in spoken form* [*le journal* parlé] to subscribers. (emphasis in original)[114]

Cros imagines the demise of print media in the face of phonographic inscription and mass communication to millions of subscribers.[115] It is after this revelation that Allais relates that people no longer know how to read or write. But it is more the emphasis on the reproduced voice, "le journal *parlé*," the "spoken" newspaper, that links the subscribers to the writers in the panacoustic condition, when the subscribers hear news in a format that seems like radio or podcasting.[116] The subscribers hear all that has been surveyed by the newspaper writers, filtered, however, through expropriated, manufactured, and reappropriated brain machines.

Reporting of *all* the news heard through these telephones seems almost total and automatic. The reporters write on paper that is mechanically driven "in continuous bands that a machine unrolls in front of them," a detail that implies a sort of industrialized endlessness and speed to their output and to their listening abilities.

"Progress," as imagined in this particular tale, heralds a grim future. At this point in his life, and especially with this text, Cros could be read as antipositivist, though not exactly as a decadent writer (witness, for example, the ire Cros inspires in Huysmans's Des Esseintes in the novel À *Rebours*). The irony of Allais's pronouncements in the story on technological progress contrast with Cros's more optimistic feelings about scientific invention in the papers he delivered throughout his life at the Académie des Sciences. Nonetheless, the story's humorous tone and some of its details belie the horror felt by its author about some forms of progress. And this is part of the very subtlety and challenge of this text and of classifying Cros's work and life more broadly. One point in the circuit of representation that remains partly immune to state control and technological mediation is the stage of transfer to the phonograph by "people gifted with an exquisite voice [*des personnes d'une voix exquise*]." Both Cros's "Inscription" and "Le Journal de l'avenir" stress the beauty of the recorded voice in the phonographic apparatus.[117] Against the bleak future envisioned here, the "exquisite" sonority of the human voice is one surviving remnant of the human in a society ruled by state surveillance and capitalist exploitation and appropriation of brains and talent. Sonority, in the form of exquisite, beautiful human voices, as textualized and imagined in Cros's literary *oeuvre*, might then be heard as a point of resistance within a new regime of technological sound.

Despite the foreboding light cast over the dissemination of news and literature in "Le Journal," such transmission does not come across as an entirely bad thing. The antipathy and fear about it pertain less to the technical possibilities of such an apparatus than to the political and economic structures that could taint the promise and use of these new media technologies. The important conceptual shift that occurs between "Interastral" and "Le Journal" hinges on the way telecommunications are imagined as a mass medium. In "Le Journal," telecommunications—specifically, the telephone—do not exist to facilitate knowledge-sharing and interpersonal communication between individuals and cultures as they do in "Interastral." Instead, the apparatus facilitates mass mechanical data collection, news gathering, and dissemination. Indeed, dehumanized and depersonalized telephones in "Le Journal" function more like the microphones used at the time in New York City prisons to spy on the incarcerated, as mentioned previously, than like the interpersonal telecommunication apparatus of "Interastral."

In both texts, Cros's satirical wonder, wit, and prescience target reigning political and economic powers. Opposition to would-be state and high capitalist control of technological inventions mingles with a sense of wonder about communicational possibilities that could bridge great spatial, cultural, and linguistic divides. However, each text tempers its awe and optimism with the warning that political and administrative centralizing forces could employ mass media to consolidate power and at the same time constrain the liberating, decentralizing potential of new audiovisual media. Cros suggests that society will need to confront not only political and economic control over nascent audiovisual telecommunications networks but also centralized control of the data that travel on those networks, both as information is disseminated and as it is gathered.

I conclude this chapter with a word on a text by one of Cros's immediate successors in this line of thought and fiction. Albert Robida (1848–1926) was a prolific popular illustrator and a novelist who has been compared to Jules Verne. Robida's novel *The Twentieth Century* (1882) reads like an extension of "Le Journal de l'avenir" in both its humor (early in the novel, for example, home food delivery services of the future result in a dining room flooded with soup from pneumatic tubes) and in its turns toward forecasting the possibilities of audiovisual technologies.

Ten years after Cros's "Insterastral" and its dream of interplanetary video chatting, Robida imagines a "telephonoscope" device, "the wonder that allows one to see and hear at the same time an interlocutor one thousand leagues away" (43).[118] Among its various uses, the narrator explains, the telephonoscope offers a way of keeping in touch with loved ones at a distance (see Figure 15). The idea is continuous with Cros's thought, in the way audiovisual technologies, both for telecommunication and for conservation of sound and image, frame and are framed by love. Like Cros's "Inscription" poem, Robida's description of a retrospective theater and of its "clichés phonographiques" ("phonographic snapshots") (67) anticipates the impulse behind Ferdinand Brunot's Archives de la Parole, where Apollinaire, among others, would record his voice in 1913.

The telephonoscope device could also be used for home entertainment, including the broadcasting of theater performances especially: "With the telephonoscope—the word says it all—one could both see and hear [. . .] actors

LA SUPPRESSION DE L'ABSENCE.

Figure 15. The telephonoscope for "La Suppression de l'absence [Overcoming absence]." Original illustration by Albert Robida in Le vingtième siècle, 1882.

appear with the sharpness of direct vision on the large crystal screen. Thus, one virtually attends the performance, sights and sounds alike. The illusion is complete, absolute, as if one were sitting in the front row" (52–53). In that context, as the narrator explains, the device could transmit *all* the sounds of the theater—from main act to incidental noise—into the home. The total "illusion" that the device renders, in both sight and sound, has a certain reciprocal effect in the near-ubiquity of the devices and their adoption in manifold situations and places in everyday life, especially as they enter the bedroom, where the dangers of surveillance and overstimulation are both manifest.

Wonders can thus readily transform into nuisance and danger. Early in the novel, for instance, a telephone transmits a theater review in the middle of the night and awakens the protagonist Hélène, who is bathed in the glow of electric blue light, despite a special filter that transmits "only very serious news" (31). Already the telephone, as in Cros's "Journal," appears as a device both for interpersonal communication *and* for the broadcasting and consumption of news. The initially unceasing flow of news delivered by telephone, before Hélène discovers how to turn it off, keeps her awake. Beyond the both comically dreamy

Figure 16. The telephonoscope for "Le Journal téléphonoscopique [News on the telephonoscope]." Original illustration by Albert Robida in *Le vingtième siècle*, 1882.

and nightmarish turns of this episode, Robida's vision of how news would be consumed resembles the way telephones relate to journalism and the news in Cros's "Journal." Human voices recede in order to give way to a particular telephonic voice and presence. As in Cros's text, it is the telephone, the device itself (not a recognizable personality over it) that speaks and that will not stop speaking. Both authors suggest a rapid stream of information in the presence of that voice, a stream both wondrous and overwhelming, like the soup that inundates the household or even something like the startling aspect ratio of a domestic telephonoscope screen in one of Robida's illustrations for the novel (182) (see Figure 16).

Furthermore, on the possibility of surveillance, Robida makes explicit what was more implicit in Cros's "Journal." Mr. Ponto, the novel's patriarch, explains how "the telephonoscope is also excellent for surveillance" (65), both intentional, in the way family members spy on each other to verify their physical whereabouts, and inadvertent, because "people wanted telephonoscopes everywhere, even in their bedrooms" (65), and because those same people often forgot to turn off their machines or to turn on their safety modes (64).

Such a concerted stream of information, of sights and sounds, also inflects no less than the distribution of music in *The Twentieth Century*. Proust, despite his aversion to noise, was an avid subscriber to the théâtrophone (see Figure 17), and Robida's novel imagines something like that (66), but also a system that sounds in some ways more like an ancestor of our present-day music streaming services, in some ways like radio, yes, but also not exactly, because the system is not exactly wireless.[119] In an authorial aside, Robida details the distribution of prerecorded operatic orchestra music to subscribing theaters, so that the music played for audiences is not live but, "thanks to a special phonographic system," stored in tubes (55). Later, the narrator describes music subscription services for the home, for the domestic sphere, with the result that Europe becomes one nation with a single idiom (100–1).

Finally, a more monumental vision of the interaction between telephone, telephonoscope, and journalism arrives later in the novel with the description of huge telephonoscope screens that crown Paris rooftops and broadcast the images and sounds of war, all visible and audible to observers in the streets below: a Times Square–like vision, we might say, in nineteenth-century Paris. This urban scene contrasts with Bell's roughly contemporaneous designs for the photophone and his intention to avoid overwhelming the city—visually, at any rate—with the telecommunications medium. Robida imagines the opposite with sound and image that become spectacularly huge, the audiovisual system in the telephonoscopic screens likened to "twin moons" (177) that loom over urban space. In contrast, Bell's photophonic apparatus would have largely hidden the medium of telecommunication. Hence, between Robida and Bell, something of an audiovisual dialectic emerges as it relates to the form of the modern city, spectacularly visible and audible (Robida's vision) versus everywhere present but largely invisible and inaudible (Bell's vision), except for those positioned at the ends of photophone receivers.

Ultimately, Robida's text develops ideas at the heart of Cros's "Journal" for longer-form narratives, ones with rich visual illustration, in the manner of a Daumier for a technology-saturated generation.[120] It would be hard to imagine that Robida, with his penchant for humorous writing and witty illustrations, had not read or otherwise been familiar with the *Chat Noir* periodical in which Cros's tales were published. Robida once produced a shadow-theater performance at the Chat Noir cabaret. Without positing a direct case of influence, it is still possible to see Cros's ideas in texts like "Le Journal" take flight and impart broader impact through Robida's novels, which—unlike the majority of Cros's works—sold widely and found a broad readership into the early twentieth century before they were mostly forgotten.

Figure 17. Jules Chéret. *Théâtrophone*. Lithographic poster, circa 1890. © RMN-Grand Palais Art Resource, NY.

Like the popular success of Coquelin's dramatic performances launched by Cros's monologues, Robida's popular success, I would emphasize, grew out of a literary genre that Cros helped to initiate.[121] Where Robida's texts (like those by Bellamy and Villiers) offer more technical detail about the devices and more narrative heft than Cros's at this historical juncture, Cros, who had the practical scientific knowledge to fill out such detail in his literary texts, instead offers prose that is ultimately more poetic, more allusive in its biting satire and ambivalent attitudes about the future of society, texts that might ultimately prove more timeless in the elision of those details even as the prophetic sides might only emerge as prophetic in particular times, whenever a certain generation spies the germs of its becoming in these futures of the past.

2
Poe's *Tintamarre*
Transatlantic Acoustic Horizons

Like Baudelaire, Poe has been hailed as an acute observer of urban life, one whose vision was shaped, in part, by dramatic advances in nineteenth-century optical technologies, most notably the daguerreotype. Like Cros, Poe drew inspiration from the photographic field and the sciences more broadly. As a journalist, Poe wrote something of an encomium to the daguerreotype soon after news of its invention reached American shores. Poe called the daguerreotype "the most important, and perhaps the most extraordinary triumph of modern science," and in the years before his death, he would pose for several photographic portraits.[1] Like Cros, Poe imagined what uses the technology might serve (lunar mapping, astronomy, and other practical uses) while also discovering a beauty in its images. Poe's enthusiasm for and interest in optical technologies was, however, not limited to photography. When Poe was living in Fordham near the end of his life, he composed a lengthy prose poem titled *Eureka* (1848), an equal parts astonishing and baffling exploration of cosmology and astronomy. In it, he responds to the recent invention of the world's then largest telescope, Lord Rosse's "Leviathan," which was completed in Ireland in 1845.

Soon after its completion, Rosse's telescope, as an authority whose power had to be constantly negotiated in public representations and more specialized scientific forums, demanded something of a new vocabulary to accommodate its new art of seeing.[2] As such, the telescope was crucially involved in mid-nineteenth-century competitions to produce scientific representations, most importantly debates about nebula, nebulosity, and the resolvability of nebula into discrete stars once seen by a powerful enough telescope.

Poe's enigmatic description of this device develops out of a meditation on concepts of the infinite in the universe and the perception of visible voids in space, made newly visible by Rosse's telescope. Ironically, Baudelaire, in the *Salon de 1859*, mocks the Parisian public's enthusiasm for Wheatstone's stereoscope by describing the public as avidly gazing into the stereoscope's twin peepholes *as if* they gave onto a vision of the infinite, as if the viewing holes were "the skylights [*lucarnes*] of the infinite."[3] But Poe, in *Eureka*, displays a profound, genuine fascination with the ability to ponder the infinite versus the ostensibly visible limits of luminosity and darkness/non-luminosity in the cosmos granted by the new optical technology, which functioned through the use of huge mechanically produced mirrors.

It is striking, then, that Poe employs an acoustical metaphor to describe the staggering visual images provided by the new telescope: "There are nebulae, however, which, through the magical tube of Lord Rosse, are this instant whispering in our ears the secrets of a million of ages by-gone."[4] Granted, Poe's interest here is primarily with time (his emphasis on "this moment" might also relate to evolving discourses and concepts of instantaneity in photography at that moment), specifically the age of the light emitted by stars and the time it took to reach observers on earth. He likens light from the stars to "phantoms of processes completed long in the past" and continues to elaborate on the nebulae's light as the trace of these "by-gone" ages: "In a word, the events which we behold now—at this moment—in those worlds—are the identical events which interested their inhabitants *ten hundred thousand centuries* ago."[5] But it is altogether curious that the telescope, with its powerful and widely celebrated optics, should be "whispering" to the ear instead of speaking, at least in Poe's poetic language, to the eye.

Poe's whispering telescope could be described in this instance as synesthetic, to the extent Poe plays on a subtle confusion of the eye and the ear in this cosmological epistemology. As an auditory prosthesis of sorts, the telescope offered a broader view of the heavens, of great distances and time, in sound. Recall, as we saw in the previous chapter, Alexander Graham Bell's experiment with French astronomer Jules Janssen to listen to "sounds on the surface of the sun" with photophonic technology, an experiment recognized by André Breton for its kinship with Cros's theories about light that could speak. Poe speaks to something like that effort here. And as with the kaleidophone, the afterglow of luminous phenomena has an acoustic dimension, or at least the possibility of one.

The synesthesia can be read as an example of one of the more poetic passages in a text elaborating scientific theories (often in a seemingly more factual, rational mode and tone), an example of how Poe wished for *Eureka* to be judged in the end "as a poem only," as he professes in his brief preface to the text.[6] Still, the rhetoric animating that wish suggests that *Eureka* would also elicit comparison with other modes of writing, with discourses other than purely literary or scientific. *Eureka* thus falls ultimately somewhere in between. Poe's acoustical metaphor here encapsulates a recurrent motif in Poe's fiction, the hearing of extraordinary sounds. At the same time, the whispering telescope speaks to a nascent audiovisual aesthetic of sound preservation, the means, technological and literary, of listening to the past and to the otherworldly. The synesthesia is motivated by Poe's broader interest in the idea of listening to extraordinary sounds at the margins of life and death, between past and present, sounds that register unnerving temporal fluctuations and new possibilities for representation in his tales and poetry. Here it could be said that he entertains the idea of auscultating the cosmos, hearkening to the universe with our ears, to fainter sounds and lights, things to which he was perhaps more sensitive at the time after having left the bustle of Manhattan for the relative tranquility of Fordham village.

I highlight this passage from *Eureka* to demonstrate how Poe's language about visual technologies might also harbor an acoustic undercurrent, one of Poe's many "undercurrents of meaning," in this case through the synesthetic relationship of ear and eye.[7] What Poe finds, then, in the nebulae's secrets whispered through the telescope is the idea of both a luminous and an "audible past," to quote again Jonathan Sterne's felicitous phrase, or more precisely, a past that is audible in light, whispers of the visible "phantoms of processes completed long in the past." Poe's metaphor participates in and, in a way, anticipates Nadar's conception of an "acoustic daguerreotype"(first articulated in 1856 and again in 1864), and the discourse around the need for such an invention, the conditions of its possibility, mentioned in this book's Introduction and which I explore in more detail in Chapter 3 with Baudelaire.

For now, I mean to emphasize that Poe's contemplation of optical technologies involves both a connection and a split between sight and sound. Poe tests the limits of ocular proof and, in the face of those limits, the possibility of sound to offer an alternative path to knowledge. In Poe's 1840 article celebrating the invention of the daguerreotype, he likens it to a mirror for the startling fidelity of its visual reproduction. The mirror analogy could be understood as a kind of remediation, the understanding of a new technology by means of an older existing technology, though one that was, at that time, newly industrialized, as with the mirrors of Rosse's telescope.[8] Poe then contrasts the daguerreotype with painting with the help of the microscope, arguing: "If we examine a work of ordinary art, by means of a powerful microscope, all traces of resemblance to nature will disappear—but the closest scrutiny of the photogenic drawing discloses only a more absolute truth, a more perfect identity of aspect with the thing represented."[9] At the birth of this new visual technology, Poe thinks about supplementing it with the microscope, with an existing optical technology, to reveal not so much what Benjamin theorizes as an "optical unconscious" of photography (though it could be read with that theory in mind) but what Poe calls "a more absolute truth" and "a more perfect identity." Poe's suggestion to apply a microscope to the daguerreotype, however, might also betray something to the contrary, instead of a belief in the "more absolute . . . more perfect," an unconscious distrust and ambivalence about the new technology, hence a skepticism of its "ocular proof." In *Eureka* as well, Poe voices some skepticism about ocular evidence: "Thus it was supposed that we 'had ocular evidence'—an evidence, by the way, which has always been found very questionable—of the truth of the hypothesis."[10]

One could argue that the idea of applying a microscope to the daguerreotype involves an inherent suspicion of its presumed representation of this "more absolute truth," even as Poe celebrates that visualization. This ambivalence, I want to suggest, in turn animates the auditory turn in his description of the telescope, evidencing Poe's wonder about what the acoustic field contains and what it might disclose amidst so much excitement about the visual. In the way Poe imagines how a microscope applied to the daguerreotype offers the possibility of a more truthful vision, sound associated with the light of distant ages through the telescope implies the question of how we might listen to the past and the otherworldly for another kind of truth. The idea of a "more perfect identity" granted through powers of vision itself becomes nebulous and split between sight and sound, reflecting a dissociation of knowledge and self-identity in Poe's other writings, especially in his tales "The Lighthouse," "The Black Cat," and "The Fall of the House of Usher," to which we will turn in a moment.

Sounds of technology and the modern city intersect in Poe's writings. These intersections yield a distinctive acoustical aesthetic with implications for subsequent auditory imaginaries and audiovisual technologies in the nineteenth century.

In a reading of Poe's short story "The Facts in the Case of M. Valdemar," Roland Barthes generalizes about narrative: "A narrative is not a tabular space, a flat structure; it is a volume, a stereophony . . . there is a field of listening in a written narrative."[11] Barthes's reflections on the "volume," "stereophony," and "field of listening" in a narrative are not necessarily specific to Poe or Poe's story alone. Barthes means these terms to be understood more broadly as metaphors for the polysemy of narrative and narrative form.

In this chapter, however, I aim to demonstrate that there are indeed specific "fields of listening" and "stereophonies" in Poe's texts, these fields of listening being evocative of the particular acoustical phenomena of technological and urban modernity. Literally speaking, "stereophony" can denote, as Jonathan Sterne has examined with the development of the stethoscope in the nineteenth century, a "three-dimensional sense of the auditory field."[12] Here, I would like to use the term to designate an idea of acoustic space in dialogue with the visual illusions of stereoscopy. Though the explicit notion of stereophony historically did not emerge until after the development of stereoscopic devices (when inventors began experimenting with differential stethoscopes, binaural headsets, and then "stereophonic" telephones in the late 1870s and 1880s), I would argue that the germs of such stereophonic thought can be found in Poe's writings.

In Poe's narratives specifically, the "field of listening" often figures as a source of mystery and conflict that leads to critical reflection on sound and voice. My readings of Poe's works in this chapter thus are guided by this central question: How does Poe articulate an idea of a radical transformation of listening practices and of sound in his era, as when the narrator in "Valdemar," attempting to describe what he hears, declares that "no similar sounds had ever jarred upon the ear of humanity"?[13] While harking back to Romantic theories of the sublime in his representations of sound, Poe also furnishes an idea of radically new acoustics, of both what and how humanity had never heard before.[14]

Critics and scholars have approached the question of sound in Poe's writings from many angles. Early on, Baudelaire would famously celebrate, among other qualities of Poe's œuvre, his poem "The Raven" as invigorated by "the most sonorous of all rhymes [*une rime la plus sonore de toutes*] (nevermore, *jamais plus*)."[15] T. S. Eliot, in contrast, while examining the influence of Poe on French poetics, criticized what he saw as a frequent disconnect between sound and sense in some of Poe's poetry. And among recent scholarly works in sound studies, Poe has most often been cited for his arresting descriptions of auditory hallucination, especially in "The Tell-Tale Heart."[16]

Though certainly an apt phrase, auditory hallucination, for "The Tell-Tale Heart" and other stories by Poe with similar conflicts, does not capture the full stereophony of these passages in Poe's narratives. The multiple representations of apparent auditory hallucinations in Poe's tales can be approached from an angle other than the psychology or madness of the story's characters. Specifically, the concept of the acousmatic is one idea of listening that can help to frame the field of listening in Poe's stories as they explore the nuances of sensory perception between auditory hallucinations and truly hearing, hearing "*réellement*" as Rabelais described it.

Acousmatic sound has been broadly understood and defined as sound heard in the absence of its visible source.[17] Scholars have, for instance, described the telephone, phonograph, and radio as acousmatic technologies because they mediate sound by making it present or audible in the absence of a visible (real and original) source.[18] Brian Kane has recently emphasized the importance of approaching the question of acousmatic sound through the history, theory, and practice of acousmatic listening, with a corresponding focus on the listening subject's epistemological conflicts. Kane maintains that the history of acousmatic sound and listening predates the invention of mechanical sound reproducibility. With this attention to listening, certain understandings of the acousmatic have historically divided around the question of whether acousmatic sounds, in the absence of a readily identifiable source, were real or hallucinated. The understanding of the hallucinatory side of the listening experience prevailed in the nineteenth century in such areas as psychology and literature where, as Kane has examined, the element of auditory hallucination was strongly emphasized. Nineteenth-century scientific discourse on the *acousmatic*, however, encouraged an understanding of sound as an extraordinary product of nature, something strange and wonderful, but still real, not imagined by a hallucinating subject.

Acousmatic, as Kane explains, can refer to a listening practice based on the Pythagorean Veil, an activity developed out of the idea that Pythagoras encouraged his followers to listen to his lectures while he was hidden behind a veil. Though derived from this Greek term and history, the term "acousmate" has a different history and set of eighteenth- and nineteenth-century meanings in French. "Acousmate" was coined in 1730 by the Curé d'Ansacq when the inhabitants of this small French town were startled by a mysterious sound whose source they could not determine. The Curé wrote about this extraordinary event: "Doesn't the event in question authorize me to [. . .] appeal in the same way to what the ancients called Phenomena, the extraordinary objects that appeared in the air; can't I [. . .] designate the surprising and prodigious sound by the word *Akousmène*, or to speak more properly Greek in French, *Akousmate*?"[19] Kane highlights an important divergence in subsequent understandings of the word in the years following its coining by the Curé, with Abbé Prevost's definition from 1755 remaining close to the Curé's original intention: "*Acousmate*, s.m. A term newly formed from the Greek to describe a phenomenon that makes heard a great noise in the air, comparable, one says, to that of several human voices and diverse instruments."[20] The *Académie Française*, in the same period, defined the *acousmate* differently, as the "noise of human voices or instruments that one *imagines* hearing in the air" (my emphasis).[21]

With Poe, acousmatic listening in his tales is closely tied to anxiety about the phenomenology of urban space and technological acoustics. Not only does the acousmatic dimension of his texts involve sounds in the absence of a visible source, but there is an acute anxiety about such sounds in conflicts of hallucination, mediation, and representation. Poe's narratives of acousmatic listening elaborate a protophonographic aesthetic of "the strange and exceptional."[22]

For Poe, this kind of sound, isolated from other sense impressions, often generates mystery in the sense of prolonged or ultimate invisibility or unknowability of the sound's source. For example, in "The Murders in the Rue Morgue," witnesses to the murder, who hear but don't see it, struggle to identify a mysterious voice.[23] Accompanying that mystery is an ardent desire for knowledge, involving both fright and wonder central to Poe's aesthetic of the "strange and exceptional." Attention to the question of real or hallucinated sound helps us to reveal the specificity of the "fields of listening" in Poe's narratives and their relationships with urban and technological modernity. The acousmaticity of urban life involves the very spatial and architectural features of the built environment that make for heightened and frequent anxiety and annoyance about hearing sounds absent their visible source, such as hearing neighbors when living in apartment buildings or adjacent homes. Such sounds are training grounds, in the Benjaminian sense, for the encounter and reception of acousmatic technologies later in the century.[24]

Poe's narratives and their *dénouements* often hinge on acousmatic sound, whose strangeness and discordance create mystery, terror, and fascination. Poe's aesthetic exploits a practice of acousmatic listening that allegorizes conditions of modern urban life—such as hearing sounds between seemingly solid but newly permeable surfaces—and lays the groundwork for the aesthetics of mass audiovisual media technologies. The situation of acousmatic listening in his tales figures as the occasion for the effusion and collapse of language and acoustical metaphors. In Poe's texts, urban and technological modernity find a point of contact in the strangeness of modern sounds, a strangeness that tests the limits of rational behavior and explanation.

Like the noises heard by Benjamin and Proust's dreamers, acousmatic sound begs for interpretation. Poe depicts that begging in ways that both unnerve (as in "The Fall of the House of Usher") and inspire calculated rational thinking (as with Dupin) in his characters. More specifically, as a question of poetics, as a motif in his tales, acousmatic sound helps bring closure to his stories while bringing about a character's undoing, as with the minister in "The Purloined Letter," for example, who is distracted by noises and shouts in the street. As a "field of listening," then, the acousmatic serves as the terrain for conflicts about self-identity (the self-possession of a rational mind versus the physical and verbal effusions of madness), the urban, and the technological in Poe. Beyond the biographical fact that Poe lived and spent a great deal of time in cities where technology was in the process of transforming everyday life and where the practices of everyday urban life were in the process of transforming technologies, attention to sound enables us to examine the convergence of urban and technological imaginaries in Poe's fiction as they elaborate ideas of modern self-identity in an auditory frame, in the play of sounds newly caught between interior and exterior.

In the way Poe evokes horror and wonder about acoustics that unsettles the categories of human and nonhuman, human and machine, he anticipates a certain phonographic aesthetics that critics have typically identified primarily with late nineteenth- and early twentieth-century writers. For example, to the extent that we follow Ivan Kreilkamp in reading Joseph Conrad's *Heart of Darkness* (1898), with its insistence on disembodied voice, as "owing a precise debt to the new paradigm of sound, voice, and memory introduced by the phonograph," I want to suggest that Conrad's novel, at the same time, invokes and owes a debt to an earlier acoustical aesthetic, one we can find in Poe.[25] And this kinship between authors can be examined not only by their mutual turns to morbidity and horror, but by a phonographic textuality centered on the representation of disturbing acoustics. The phonographic aesthetics of late nineteenth- and early twentieth-century texts such as *Heart of Darkness* owe not only to the historical "introduction" of the phonograph, to the device itself, into public consciousness, but also to a protophonographic aesthetics of sonic astonishment elaborated by Poe within a broader literary auditory imagination of the nineteenth century.

Sound Technologies: Auscultation, Telegraphy, Living Wires

On the subjects of Poe and visual culture, *flânerie*, and the dynamics of vision in urban modernity, critics often begin and end with the narrator's point of view at the opening of "The Man of the Crowd" in the London coffee house. There, the narrator commands something of a panoramic perspective, one that, in giving onto the spectacular side of urban life with its big boulevards and their crowds, connects with a certain conception of visual modernity.

Though not inhabiting an urban locale, the narrator in Poe's unfinished story "The Lighthouse" (1849) might also be described as gifted with a panoramic point of view of the ocean outside. The cylindrical form of the lighthouse interior, I want to emphasize, resembles the form of dioramas and panoramas in the nineteenth century, structures that both represented and conditioned new forms of seeing in modernity.[26] The interior space of the lighthouse in Poe's story, however, becomes an uncanny place of looking *and* listening, in which the narrator is seized by anxiety over the acoustics of the lighthouse and their effect on words, or on one word in particular, "alone." Of his ambivalent desire for solitude, the narrator reveals:

> Besides, I wish to be *alone*. . . . . It is strange that I never observed, until this moment, how dreary a sound that word has—"alone"! I could half fancy there was some peculiarity in the echo of these cylindrical walls—but oh, no!—this is all nonsense. I do believe I am going to get nervous about my insulation. *That* will never do.[27]

It is curious that sound in the interior of the lighthouse should provoke the narrator's anxiety about insulation, should shake his "passion for solitude," when on the outside, while examining the sea, he reports: "nothing to be seen, with the telescope even, but ocean and sky, with the occasional gull."[28] Audible aloneness unnerves him, while visible, ocular solitude provides comfort. The interior space of the lighthouse, its particular "insulation," concentrates sound in a way that unsettles the narrator. There is, perhaps, something kaleidophonic about the lighthouse interior in the way the word "alone," spoken aloud, echoes within the cylindrical walls, akin to the way images are reflected inside the cylinder of the kaleidoscope. Unsure of his senses, the narrator reports that he "could half fancy there was some peculiarity in the echo," but then, in what seems like both a written and spoken effort to hold that "fancy" in check, he retorts: "—but oh, no!—this is all nonsense."

The ellipsis after the phrase "Besides, I wish to be alone" could be taken as, itself, marking a space of listening in the text, of the narrator listening to the word it would seem he has just written and then spoken aloud. (It is also possible to read the passage as if the narrator is saying some of these words aloud as he writes.) The "dreary sound" that he "observes" would seem to inhabit and resound (or perhaps pre-sound) in that ellipsis. Hence the ellipsis could also signify the echo or the anticipation of the echo and its "peculiarity." The second use of the word "alone" would appear to signify, in addition to the narrator's growing unease, a shout into both the space of the text and the lighthouse at once. It is curious, too, that the narrator should note that he "observed" the sound of the word rather than heard it, the word "observe" connoting more of a visual than an acoustic field of perception.[29] This slight confusion of eye and ear points to a disorientation of the narrator's sensorium, one that reinforces his anxiety about his new surroundings as he tries to orient himself. The estrangement of eye and ear itself echoes a self-estrangement and displacement felt by the narrator, the loss of the positive valence of solitude, the fear of madness as a dissociation of self-identity, itself echoed in what he rejects as the "nonsense" of his writing.

In his claustrophobic self-estrangement, in the textual echo of the word "alone," the "I" that narrates after the shouted "alone!" would seem to be split between the narrating self and the "insulated" echo within those cylindrical walls, ones that share the same cylindrical form as early sound recording technologies, which produced echoes, repetition with a difference, from cylinders.[30] In being so alone, his own voice resounds with a singular otherness. In this passage, then, the narrator no longer speaks alone or "alone!" Rather, the narrator becomes doubled by his resonant solitude within the word "alone." He becomes estranged from and by the sound of his own voice in the stereophonic interior of the lighthouse.

The estrangement that occurs between the narrating self and the spatial interior in "The Lighthouse" closely resembles the way sound unsettles corporeality and psychic interiority furthermore in "The Tell-Tale Heart" and "The Black Cat." Both stories involve audiovisual interplay in which sounds and voices ultimately render what seems solid into something frighteningly permeable. In each tale, irony inflects the play of eye and ear, with the powers and dangers of the ear ultimately prevailing over the eye. In "The Black Cat," for example, hearing is prompted by touch, by the narrator tapping with a cane on the wall, a moment in the narrative that might be read in the context of medical advances with the stethoscope and the medical techniques of mediate auscultation, a kind of hearkening with the ear.[31]

In 1836 Poe himself, widely read in and knowledgeable of current scientific developments, published a review of the *British and Foreign Medical Review*. Although Poe does not mention the stethoscope in his review, the 1836 edition of this medical review included extensive descriptions of the stethoscope and auscultation, and it was edited by John Forbes, the English translator of Laennec's *Treatise on Mediate Auscultation* and Auenbrugger's treatise on Percussion as a medical diagnostic.[32] What Poe gleans from his reading of this medical journal furthermore bears, albeit obliquely, upon our exploration of nineteenth-century listening practices and the preservation of sound. Poe praises the state of medicine at the time for being "far advanced in a great and most salutary reformation, the progress of which is still onward."[33] He continues: "In nothing is this reform more conspicuous . . . than in the profession's now aiming to preserve health by timely precautions. . . . It is the art of preserving rather than the art of healing."[34] The state of acoustics in medicine at that moment was also, as Sterne argues, an "art" increasingly dependent on refined technologically mediated techniques of listening to the sounds of the body's insides, a practice that formed part of what Sterne calls "the cultural origins of sound reproduction."[35] In the medical journal that Poe reviewed, the elements of time, preservation, listening, and sound inhabit the text together in a way that speaks to nascent discourses on the emerging art of and need for sound preservation.

Several details at the end of "The Black Cat" encourage a reading of the concluding scene within this historical context of auscultative listening practices. René Laennec, the inventor of the stethoscope, in his 1819 treatise on the technology, draws from Leopold Auenbrugger's technique of percussion, of touching the patient's chest in such a way that the fingers could listen for sounds the ear could not detect on its own. To the extent that it functions as an auditory prosthesis between physician and patient, the stethoscope is an extension of this percussive technique. In "The Black Cat," when the police search the narrator's home, the narrator relates how he "rapped heavily, with a cane" on the wall.[36] The narrator will furthermore describe how, once the police hear the cat behind the wall, that very wall "fell *bodily*" (my emphasis). The wall doubles for the human body to be sounded for the secrets it holds about hidden interior health or sickness.

The narrator continues: "No sooner had the reverberation of my blows sunk into silence, than I was answered by a voice from within the tomb! [. . .] utterly anomalous and inhuman—a howl—a wailing shriek [. . .]."[37] Here, Poe grasps for words to evoke sheer sonority, which, at the same time escapes literary language and analogy.

Hence, Poe examines how such sonority articulates space—whether architectural, interpersonal, or psychic. In asking whether the sound signifies internal or external turmoil, he probes the limits of sound to orient self-possession. John Picker has argued that in "The Tell-Tale Heart," Poe "mocks the newfound power of the amplification of hidden bodily sound."[38] I would add that, if Poe does indeed mock these medical devices and procedures, one could argue that Poe also finds himself in competition with them; this new scientific practice of rational refined listening granted by the stethoscope would usurp the mystery of sound that is so often exploited by Poe in his stories. "The Tell-Tale Heart" and "The Black Cat" thus reclaim those sounds as a still fertile field for misapprehension, ambiguity, and insanity.

Poe's fictional narratives thus examine the fate of self-possession when these specialized listening techniques take one out of the sounds of the self into the internal sounds of another.[39] One could read this "strange and exceptional" progress of science in Poe's stories as a gross perversion of the aims of technology. In his fictional tales, Poe questions the progress in science and medicine that he celebrates in his article about the *British and Foreign Medical Review* and in texts such as *Eureka*. As Picker claims, "The Tell-Tale Heart" can be interpreted as a "mockery" of mediate auscultation and consequently as a tale of the mock macabre. However, by attending more closely to how scientific understandings of the human body, through acute listening to its sounds, were in flux in the 1830s and 1840s, we can see how Poe's story points to a commingling of the rational examination of bodily sounds (in the service of medical diagnoses aimed at anticipating sickness and hence preserving health) with the fear about being able to hear across previously stable acoustic divides, ones that are rendered newly marvelous and frightening in their porosity, producing insanity and horror of the medicinal macabre.[40] Poe would appear to be asking: How closely do we want to be able to listen to another's interiority? What kind of effect do the sounds of that interior space have on the one who listens so acutely? Auscultative listening, whether percussive or stethoscopic, unsettles self-identity. It offers Poe a narrative motif for his tales where extraordinary sound indexes ambiguity and anxiety about liminal states between life and death, sleeping and awakening.

Valdemar and the Collective "ear of humanity"

Poe's "The Facts in the Case of M. Valdemar" further explores the human body's instability when corporeality is probed in new (pseudo-) scientific and obliquely technological ways. Subject to new acoustic practices, the literal surface of the body can be made to sound out the more abstract contours of corporeality. The narrator of "Valdemar" is a mesmerist who is drawn to experimenting with the idea of whether mesmerism might be able to arrest death and dying. He tests this hypothesis on his gravely sick friend M. Ernest Valdemar with astonishing results, one being a series of remarkable utterances from the patient suspended between life and death—"Yes;—no;—I *have been sleeping*—and now—now—I *am dead*" (emphases in original)—together with the way those utterances issue not from Valdemar's lips but from his "swollen and blackened tongue," which vibrates each time it communicates.[41] The narrator's designation of Valdemar as a "sleep-waker" throughout the story both accentuates and complicates the idea of suspending death, rendered all the more dramatic by the story's rational tone of scientific reportage.

As an elaboration of a technological acoustic aesthetic in Poe's fiction, "Valdemar" centers on the negotiation of the body as a surface and container to be examined for meaning via a historical practice of listening.[42] At the same time, Valdemar's tongue forms part of the new graphic and acoustic technology of telegraphy, a technology that, in the story, troubles and unnerves the relations between writing and speech, life and death, and, as I want to emphasize, sound and voice.

To the extent we read Valdemar's tongue as a figure of electrical sound telegraphy, we might also consider the narrator's wonder and fright about its sound in the context of these new technological listening practices, in particular "audile technique," a means of listening closely to the telegraph's sounds to decipher the messages transmitted over the wire.[43] I do not mean to argue that Poe's narrator in this tale is a veiled telegraph operator masquerading as a mesmerist, but rather that Poe's text calls for dialogue with these emerging listening practices then in flux. Poe articulates a nascent fascination with ideas about the modernization of sound and listening. And hence the acoustic metaphor with which Barthes concludes his reading of "Valdemar," the "stereophony" he uses to describe narrative in general, is then perhaps not entirely aleatory or unmotivated by his reading of "Valdemar" and his singularly unnerving voice.

Indeed the language about voice and sound confounds the narrator of "Valdemar" in his attempts to find language adequate to describe voice and sound and to conceive of their relationship. Specifically, the "facts" of voice and sound appear to elude him (whereas life and death, sleeping and awakening seem strangely more given to "factual" reportage). Description of voice and sound leads the narrator into a complex succession of figurative language and expressions, as the very sound of Valdemar's voice profoundly shakes the narrator's tone of cool rationality. Extended attempts at description, part of the story's rhetorical and narrative suspense, create a temporal rift in the narrative that parallels the split between sound and voice.

The narrator says: "It would be madness in me to attempt describing" Valdemar's mesmerized voice.[44] And yet, he continues: "There are, indeed, two or three epithets which might be considered as applicable to it in part. I might say, for example, that the sound was harsh, and broken and hollow."[45] Hollowness suggests the connection between Valdemar's voice and his almost lifeless body as an empty, though perhaps in that respect, more resonant container.[46] Here we might see specifically how, with Valdemar's horrifying disembodied voice, the phonographic textuality of *Heart of Darkness* can be read as a response to both the technology and protophonographic motifs elaborated in Poe. Voice and sound acquire definition in the context of technological media, not only as literature responds to those media but as it shapes them.

The strangeness of the sound that Poe's narrator hears forces him to retract his words as he continues: "But the hideous whole is indescribable, for the simple reason that no similar sounds have ever jarred upon the ear of humanity."[47] In the shock encountered at hearing something seemingly altogether new, the verbal description itself appears to be immobilized. Voice approaches the status of the "facts" of the story in the way each collapses in on itself. Poe frames the narrative in the beginning as an attempt to redress a "garbled or exaggerated account . . . the source of many unpleasant misrepresentations," in effect as an attempt to filter out the noise surrounding the experiment on Valdemar.[48] The "facts," which the narrator professes to report, resemble Valdemar's voice in the way each resists description in parallel with figurative language. In the end, the facts and Valedemar's voice ultimately cannot do without such language. Each remains elusive, each needing the supplement of figurative language and the blurring of distinct sensory fields.

Despite the narrator's recourse to a tactile analogy (the voice sounding like something gelatinous to the sense of touch), the narrator still lingers on a split between sound and voice, uncertain how to resolve or even relate the two terms. He continues his meta-commentary by signaling this division in his previous attempts to describe: "I have spoken both of 'sound' and of 'voice.' I mean to say that the sound was one of distinct—of even wonderfully, thrillingly distinct—syllabification."[49] Wonder mingles with discord in this line, in the "jarring" effect upon the ear. Out of both the wonder about that discord and the discord of that wonder, each equally "jarring," a collective "ear of humanity" emerges, suggesting something like the perception of a new soundscape of technological modernity, the idea of a new stage of listening for humanity, while the human, as a category for soul and speech, comes under mesmerized telegraphic stress.

Jacques Derrida highlights this particular passage about sound, voice, and Valdemar's startling declaration "Now *I am Dead*" as one of the three quotations that form the epigraph to his *Speech and Phenomena: An Introduction to the Problem of the Sign in Husserl's Phenomenology*, and then again in the book's concluding chapter, "The Supplement of Origin." There, Derrida explains, as part of his examination of "supplementarity," how: "*Ma mort est structurellement nécessaire au prononcé du Je* [My death is structurally necessary for saying I]." He continues: "*L'énoncé 'je suis vivant' s'accompagne de mon être-mort et sa possibilité requiert la possibilité que je sois mort. Ce n'est pas là une histoire extraordinaire de Poe, mais l'histoire ordinaire du langage* [The Statement 'I am alive' is accompanied by my being dead, and its possibility requires the possibility that I be dead. This is not an extraordinary tale by Poe but the ordinary story of language]."[50] Derrida's insight here into the possibility of self-identity in language being a function of supplementarity, of the possibility of death residing behind the very ability to say "I," serves as a point of departure for Adam Frank's discussion of Poe's story. Frank's crucial question is: "But what difference does it make that this moment from Poe which assists Derrida in specifying a basic structure of language is both generally or ordinarily graphic and quite specifically telegraphic?"[51] For Frank, telegraphy critically animates both Valdemar's vibrating tongue and Poe's theory of mesmeric relations between writer and reader. Ultimately, Frank proposes one potential means for the realization of that mesmerizing theory: "Poe's writing ... is itself a medium that registers the 'indescribable' perceptions of telegraphic communication."[52] Poe's writing may indeed "register" telegraphic effects, but, lest that notion seem perhaps too technologically determinist, Poe's text also, as I want to emphasize, articulates its own literary acoustic field, its own sensory impressions in literary language and literary "stereophony," however much it strains to describe. It is in the narrative play of describable and indescribable sound that a singular poetics of "no similar sounds," which nevertheless do find some manner of similitude and expression, emerges.

With that stereophony, Poe helps to lay a foundation for a critical discourse on audiovisual apparatuses as forms of mass media, the aesthetics of listening remotely in place and in time from the source of the sound, at a distance that troubles not only expectations of presence and absence, but also life, death, and the corporeality of acoustic enunciation.[53] More than guarantee of scientific real, the narrator's attention to sound and voice in "Valdemar" reflects a self-consciousness about the use of language in the face of new graphic technologies and the specialized listening technique required to use such technologies and decipher their content. The narrator's creeping self-doubt about his powers to describe in language what he is capable of producing in mesmerism marks a fissure in his sense of self-identity as, if still surely a mesmerizing writer, a writer with doubts about his ability to write mesmerizing telegraphic voice and sound.

The Live Wire Imagination

The epigraph to Poe's "The Fall of the House of Usher" offers a means to gauge how technologically and telegraphically produced sound animates some passages in Poe's writings. The epigraph comes from the poem "Le Refus" by French poet and popular songwriter Jean Pierre de Béranger, whom Poe revered for the quality of "indefinitiveness" in his songwriting and for his "conception of sweet sound."[54]

> Son coeur est un luth suspendu;
> Sitôt qu'on le touche il résonne.
>
> (His heart is a suspended lute;
> As soon as one touches it, it resounds.)

Poe draws several details in the story from this epigraph: Roderick Usher suffers from a "morbid acuteness of the senses." That acuteness produces the auditory effect that "there were but peculiar sounds, and these from stringed instruments, which did not inspire him with horror."⁵⁵ The narrator additionally relates how he would listen "as if in a dream, to the wild improvisations of his [Usher's] speaking guitar."⁵⁶ As we saw with Cros, and as we will see with Villard (especially in Catulle Mendès's fictionalization of her life in his novel *La Maison de la Vieille*), musical improvisation figures centrally in the dreams about the needs for and possibilities of sound recording and reproduction technologies. Cros and his brother Antoine envisaged a machine to record and reproduce improvisations at the piano, while Stella d'Helys (Villard's cryptonym in Mendès's novel) often improvises at the piano in a house very much inspired by Poe's House of Usher, a place where artistic voices bloom and often meet with premature burial.

Usher's guitar speaks also, I would like to propose, through the medium of the letter, resonantly conveyed. Usher's letter to the narrator "arrives at its destination" in a singular fashion. The narrator's report of the letter's contents—"acute bodily illness [. . .] an earnest desire to see me [. . .] by the cheerfulness of my society, some alleviation of his malady"—is framed by a more insistent attention to the narrator's intuition about other qualities of the letter: "It was the manner in which all this, and much more, was said—it was the apparent *heart* that went with his request—which allowed no room for hesitation; and I accordingly obeyed forthwith what I still considered a very singular summons" (emphasis in original).⁵⁷ The emphasis on "*heart*" here directs our attention back to the epigraph and its "resonant" heart. The narrator's feeling about the heart demonstrates how Usher can impart the written letter with a kind of song or sound, the resonant heart going "with his request" as a kind of supplement to its literal content. These lute strings rest on the threshold of ideas about the means to write sound newly and the effects of that writing.

Poe's poem "Israfel" likewise draws from these lines by de Béranger. "Israfel" begins:

In Heaven a spirit doth dwell
"Whose heart-strings are a lute;"
None sing so wildly well
As the angel Israfel⁵⁸

These four lines remain relatively unchanged between the 1831 edition of the poem and the revised version published again in 1845, around the time of the invention and increasing use of the electric telegraph. In the later version, however, Poe makes some distinct changes to lines in the third stanza about Israfel's instrument that would suggest implicit comparison with the electric telegraph:

> And they say (the starry choir
>   And the other listening things)
> That Israfeli's fire
> Is owing to that lyre
>   By which he sits and sings—
> The trembling living wire
> Of those unusual strings.

How exactly are we to understand the wire in the poem as "living"? This evocative detail plays into networks of literary and neurophysiological analogies. In effect, something of a metaphorical electric wire joins the resonant lyre, guitar, and heart in Poe's fiction and poetry. Poe's "trembling living wire" draws from and, in a way, prefigures discourses that Laura Otis has explored in nineteenth-century networks between bodies and machines. She argues that distinct discourses analogizing organic nerves and inorganic wires took shape around the birth of telegraphic technology and continued to develop and be debated amongst writers, scientists, and inventors throughout the remainder of the nineteenth century.[59] Scientists came to question the value of metaphor and comparisons between networks of organic and inorganic wires, which in the end allowed physiologists and engineers alike to "model" functional communication systems. Technological and electrophysiological metaphors that took shape in literary texts participated in the advancement of scientific knowledge.[60]

Such metaphors, however, were not entirely new in the nineteenth century. James Kennaway, in his study, *Bad Vibrations: The History of the Idea of Music as a Cause of Disease*, notes: "Nerves had been compared to the strings of a musical instrument at least as far back as Galen."[61] Poe draws from this tradition, and from fears about musical overstimulation of the nerves, which originated in the seventeenth century and reached a certain peak at the dawn of the nineteenth. The element of electricity, however, together with the way analogies were increasingly drawn between communications networks and the human nervous system, distinguishes his metaphors from those of previous ages.[62] Even as Poe draws from eighteenth-century discourses on the metaphorical and literal impact of sound and music on human nerves, his metaphors connote a broader field of vibrations specific to nineteenth-century communication networks and changes in the material use of electricity, with an understanding of electrophysiology. With special attention to Poe's story "The Spectacles" (1844), Kieran Murphy has furthermore demonstrated how the nineteenth-century discovery of electromagnetism figured in Poe's writings, specifically how the interaction of electricity and magnetism together informed Poe's representation of the invisible forces animating human affections.[63]

Another example of such change in electrical communication networks appears in the writings of Jean-Georges Kastner, the French composer, musicologist, and ethnographer we met in this book's Introduction. He relates how resonant telegraph wires stressed the nerves of listeners in his *The Aeolian Harp and Cosmic Music: Study of the Relationships between Sonic Phenomena of Nature with Science and Art* (1856). Kastner's example instantiates broader currents in a modernization of listening present in the confluence of new technologies and their deployment in urbanization. He notes how electric telegraph wires could produce sounds similar to the aeolian harp and how these sounds were thought to stir up feelings of melancholy and malaise, which stressed the human nervous system. To illustrate this point, he provides a vivid anecdote about telegraph wires strung beneath the Pont d'Iéna in Paris, and how the wind blowing across them generated sounds similar to the aeolian harp: "This noise mingling with the murmur of the river's waters vividly strikes the observer [*impressionne vivement l'observateur*] and peoples his mind with fantastical memories. He (the observer) feels as though he is witnessing a scene out of a melodrama, and only the slightest step is required before he starts to perceive phantoms on the river quais."[64] Here the effect of such sounds, while more harmonious than discordant, generates the vision of phantoms on the quais; auditory signals spark a spectral, if not also hallucinatory, vision. These phantoms emerged in part, Kastner explains, out of a debate about the source of the sound, whether it was the result of electricity and the passage of messages over the wires, or an effect caused by the acoustic principles of the aeolian harp.[65] This question of the acoustic and acousmatic effects of the new technology mystified early listeners of a cityscape transformed visually and acoustically by newly installed telegraph wires in the middle of the nineteenth century.

Returning to "Usher," then, we can say that his letter reaches, and indeed touches, the narrator by pulling on the narrator's heartstrings in a way that drew from the literary scientific imagination of metaphorical networks between organic and inorganic communication wires.[66] In this way, a story like "Usher," which seems far from the overt issues of technological or urban modernity, is in subtle ways animated by them.

As much as Valdemar's tongue can be read as a figure of telegraphy, so too can Usher's letter to the narrator. This letter reaches its destination as a function of sound that touches, as much as a touch that sounds and resounds. This is not to say that Poe imagines Usher sending a veiled telegram, but that discourses on sound and electric telegraphy inflect his description of communication at a distance. With all the vocabulary of shuddering, murmuring, and quivering through electric vibrations in "The Fall of the House of Usher," it is as if, jolted by a metaphorical electricity, the story's heart, atmosphere, and text palpitate together in *re*sounding discord. The story represents and thematizes the corporeal affective relations between text, reader, and the listener it aims to provoke in its readers. The text becomes itself a percussive instrument, sounding out the insides of the reader.

Indeed Baudelaire would come to label Poe "the writer of nerves [*l'écrivain des nerfs*]."[67] In his first essay on Poe, Baudelaire adopts similar musical terms and analogies to characterize Poe's renderings of "the ends of seasons charged with trying splendors . . . when the southern wind softens and relaxes the nerves like the strings of an instrument . . . the contradiction established between nerves and spirit, and detuned man [*l'homme désaccordé*] on the verge of expressing grief through laughter."[68] Note how Baudelaire also invokes the tradition of likening human nerves to the strings of a musical instrument, like the aeolian harp and de Béranger's resonant lute. Baudelaire, however, brings out the possibility of discordant contradiction in this traditional analogy usually employed to evoke tranquility or the sublime in nature.[69] Debussy also offers an apt commentary on the singular acoustics of the House of Usher. In a letter to a friend, Debussy writes: "I have recently been living in the House of Usher which is not exactly the place where one can look after one's nerves—just the opposite. One develops the curious habit of listening to the stones as if they were in conversation with each other [. . .]."[70] Debussy evokes not only the element of auditory hallucination, but of the acoustic animation of the inanimate, of the "conversational" stones, akin to the nineteenth-century discourses on human nerves and electric wires.

Hence, Roderick Usher would appear to be one of the characters Baudelaire has in mind for the idea of a discordant or "detuned" man. The "detuning" of the text in "Usher" figures as a discordant analogue to the resonant lute of the epigraph. In this way, Poe's unnerved characters might no longer suffer only from physical and psychic nervousness, from the internal electrical impulses of the body, organic nerves touching the heart; they also suffer from the rewiring of those nerves with electromagnetic telegraphy and its *resonant* electricity through poetics continuous with a new soundscape of communication and sensory perception at a distance.

Gotham's *Tintamarre*

In Poe's urban imagination, the city can riot with sounds that disintegrate in their jarring discordance and loudness, spurring movement into other languages for recourse to description in words. Though Poe often uses French words and phrases in his stories, Poe's turns to French are not limited to the stories. In one of his newspaper articles, "Doings of Gotham," for example, he appeals to the French word *tintamarre*, meaning racket or din, to describe the overall effect of street noise in Brooklyn.[71] Poe reports: "The amount of general annoyances wrought by street-noises is incalculable; and this matter is worthy of our very serious attention."[72] Street noises are worthy in part, we find out, because they assault attention and interfere with communication, provoking madness in urbanites, taking those urbanites effectively out of themselves.

Though the tone of Poe's language in "Doings of Gotham" seems hyperbolic as he describes the sources of both visual and auditory blight in the city, his proposal at the end of the article for a new method of street paving seems comparatively more serious (especially as he writes about this topic in several other articles, and about street paving in an extended passage in "The Murders in the Rue Morgue"). It is possible, then, that even in his exaggerated tone of complaint about urban audiovisual blight, he is being a little serious as well. In the following passage about urban noise pollution, Poe stresses the nonhuman, unearthly noise of some "infernal machine":

> The street-cries, and other nuisances to the same effect, are particularly disagreeable here. Immense charcoal-wagons infest the most frequented thorough-fares, and give forth a din which I can liken to nothing earthly (unless, perhaps, a gong), from some metallic, triangular contrivance within the bowels of the "infernal machine." This is a free country, I have heard, and wish to believe if I can; but I cannot perceive how it would materially interfere with our freedom to put an end to these *tintamarres*.[73]

In one respect, Poe's use of *"tintamarre"* can be read as an example of what Jonathan Culler calls Poe's "perverse affinity for the French," a kind of rhetorical flourish in the article as Poe's tone builds toward an ironic and frenzied pitch.[74] On the other hand, it reflects a search for words adequate to conjuring up and representing such noise. Poe grasps at the sound of another language to capture the aural heterogeneity of urban life, and of New York in particular (Poe lived in several locations in Manhattan in the mid 1840s, and his last home was a cottage in Fordham). The departure from the use of the word "din" in English to its perhaps more onomatopoeic near-equivalent in French signifies a certain preoccupation with a vocabulary of noise and sound for Poe (as we saw for example in "Valdemar"), and in turn the sound of different languages in the city, the multilingual acoustic field that is so critical to the mystery in "The Murders in the Rue Morgue." This passage also illustrates an idea of acoustic space in the city together with the right to make noise. To whom does that space belong, we are led to ask, especially when Poe invokes freedom as both a challenge and something that might be challenged on this issue?

Poe's interest in the necessary material, and perhaps even the necessary language, to bury the unwanted noise he describes in this article might partly animate the desire of characters in his stories to bury unwanted sounds and voices. In that way, the immurements in "The Cask of Amontillado" and "The Black Cat" or the beating heart beneath the floorboards in "The Tell-Tale Heart" might be read, in part, as allegories of madness provoked by urban street noise, and the desire to suppress it. The nonhuman, unearthly sounds here might furthermore find their counterparts in the eerily uncanny human sounds and voices in "Berenice," "The Fall of the House of Usher," and "The Facts in the Case of M. Valdemar," or the animal sound of the Orangutan in "Rue Morgue." About Brooklyn, however, in this particular article, Poe continues to rail against both the human and nonhuman sounds of the street. Of the very materiality of the street and its pavement, he complains:

> The din of the vehicles, however, is even more thoroughly, and more intolerably a nuisance. Are we never to have done with these unmeaning round stones?—than which a more ingenious contrivance for driving men mad through sheer noise, was undoubtedly never invented. It is difficult to foresee what mode of street-pavement will come, finally, into vogue; but we should have *some* change, and that forthwith, or we must have new and more plentiful remedies for headache. . . . .[75]

In describing the very literal sound of the street itself, Poe calls the cobblestones "unmeaning," as if in the madness brought on by so many vehicles traversing this surface, "sheer noise" has the ability to strip away meaning. At the same time, however, this kind of madness serves as fodder for Poe's fictions, especially in the face of newly invented "ingenious contrivances," Poe's sarcasm here betraying a more genuine fascination with the scientific devices of the time.

As a point of comparison, both Baudelaire and Whitman draw analogies between poetic language and the particular material surface of the city street. In Baudelaire's poem "Le Soleil," for instance, the speaker makes an analogy between stumbling upon words the way he stumbles upon the surface of the street:

Flairant dans tous les coins les hasards de la rime,	In all corners uncovering the chances of rhyme,
Trébuchant sur les mots comme sur les pavés,	Stumbling on words as on cobble stones,
Heurtant parfois des vers depuis longtemps rêvés.	Colliding sometimes with long envisioned verse.

Baudelaire, in these lines, bridges the contingency of modern urban life with lyric poetry. Whitman, too, especially in "Song of Myself," draws attention to the actual sound of the street when he celebrates "the blab of the pave." The particular language of this urban sound serves, as Laure Katsaros has argued, as a connection between French and English, between New York and Paris.[76] Poe, in ironic contrast, at least in this newspaper article, favors the abolishment of these stones, so that the street might then literally speak less. He subsequently proposes one solution to the cacophony the stones and vehicles produce: the use of kyanized wood as a surface for the streets, which he believes will both be durable and will help reduce the noise. A grim humor marks this proposal for reducing street noise and the madness it creates, if read in relation to Poe's fictions of premature burial, murder, and madness. The frenzied tone of Poe's call for a suitable solution to street noises in this article mirrors the narrators' frenzied minds in his tales as they search for means to bury and conceal the sights and sounds of their adversaries. One thinks of the stones layered level by level in "The Cask of Amontillado" that muffle Fortunato's cries, and behind which is heard only the faint tinkle of his carnival bells at the story's end.

Poe's tone betrays a class-conscious elitism in his complaints over the vulgar cries of Brooklyn street vendors. But the seriousness of his tone remains in question here, as his point of reference is more about conversation and sociability than solitary artistic or philosophical contemplation. He turns to a reflection on the relation between noise and time for the broader urban population in general:

> It would be difficult to say, for example, how much of *time*, more valuable than money, is lost, in a large city, to no purpose, for the convenience of the fishwomen, the charcoal-men, and the monkey-exhibitors. How often does it happen that where two individuals are transacting business of vital importance, where fate hangs upon every syllable and upon every moment—how frequently does it occur that all conversation is delayed, for five or even ten minutes at a time, until these devil's-triangles have got out of hearing, or until the leathern throats of the clam-and-cat-fish vendors have been hallooed, and shrieked, and yelled, into a temporary hoarseness and silence! (emphasis in original)[77]

Poe highlights the struggle for audibility in an ever more concentrated space, the right to acoustic space and the questionable freedom to sound out, when one economy finds itself in conflict with another, monkey-exhibitors versus individuals "transacting business of vital importance." Time, fate, and syllables collide here similar to the way the human sounds and cries of the street vendors blend with the nonhuman technological sounds, such as the "devil's-triangles" of the charcoal wagons in the passage quoted previously. They all fuse into a jarring *tintamarre*, a disturbing sound of modern urban contingency.

Beyond the interruptions this noise causes, Poe generalizes to say that urban noise creates a new relation to time. In the urban space characterized by an accelerating pace of life, that pace finds itself slowed and arrested by the noise it creates as a byproduct of population density and speed. So much time, he says, is lost in delayed conversations, in so many important syllables left unheard. Poe's sentiments here illustrate what Christopher Prendergast, citing I. A. Richards, sees as the damaging effects of modern urban noise on the rhythms of poetry, "the new pervasive, almost ceaseless, mutter or roar of modern transport, replacing the rhythm of the footstep or of horses' hoofs."[78] If not only fate, but lyric poetry as well, both hang "upon every syllable and upon every moment," Poe's account demonstrates the effects of urban noise not only on time lost in everyday conversation in the city but upon poetry and spoken language in the city as well.

Poe's feelings for the cries of the street vendors in this passage contrast with, once again, composer Jean-Georges Kastner, who provides an account of street vendors in mid-nineteenth-century Paris. While Poe's vendors cry themselves into silence, Kastner tells of how Parisian street vendors are literally at risk of losing their voices *because of* the city's "*tintamarre*," as if that noise, "the din [*tintamarre*] of a busy city," were more the vendor's adversary than the noise of which the vendor's cry forms a part. Kastner even relates details of doctors treating cases of laryngitis among street vendors to support his point.[79] He then goes on to liken the contest between the street vendor and the city's "*tintamarre*" to the contest between an opera singer and an overloud orchestra, an example that adds a layer of complexity to period discourses and debates on the difference between music and noise as well as the particular modes of listening then in flux, both socially and phenomenologically speaking.

Poe's disdain for the vendors' "leathern throats" and his description of how they are "hallooed, and shrieked, and yelled into a temporary hoarseness and silence" share features with the horror of his stories. In this way he shares, too, a feeling for the city's noise—that it could be harnessed for poetic and literary purposes—that will come to define aspects of Baudelaire's poetry, noise as an element to be channeled into his poetics.

In "The Man of the Crowd," as the narrator sits observing the diverse multitudes passing by him outside the window of the London coffeehouse, he describes the particular visual features of the crowds and the individuals in the crowds. A reflection on the auditory accompanies the visual:

> ... beside these, pie-men, porters, coal-heavers, sweeps; organ-grinders, monkey-exhibiters and ballad mongers, those who vended with those who sang; ragged artisans and exhausted laborers of every description, and all full of a noisy and inordinate vivacity which jarred discordantly upon the ear, and gave an aching sensation to the eye.[80]

In one sense, "discord," as a distinctly aural phenomenon, forms part of the horrific opacity described in the story's opening paragraph, an iteration of that opacity, like the secret "essences of crime" that excite the narrator's attention. Discord might also be read as constituted by the clash of different languages that does not suffer itself to be understood in the London coffeehouse or street, something heard only as a noisy assault on the ear. Baudelaire translates "discordantly" with "par ses discordances" in French, effectively adding a plural element to the singular "vivacity." To the narrator's eye and ear, it is not only the old man with the dagger and diamond who stands out for his singularly bizarre behavior. Within the social taxonomy the narrator presents at the beginning of the story, he marks out a group that is, if not extraordinary, then at least strange: "Others, still a numerous class, were restless in their movements, had flushed faces, *and talked and gesticulated to themselves,* as if feeling in solitude on account of the very denseness of the company around" (my emphasis).[81] For these urban dwellers, the density of the urban crowd creates a void for language. The whole sensory field of the crowd seems to provoke this bodily response, owing to the "jostling" that occurs. The solitude they feel brings about an odd manifestation of interior thoughts, as if their silent internal reflections become strangely externalized and vocalized in the crowd, as if the crowd were acting passively like a percussive instrument, a stethoscope perhaps, to sound out their insides. These Londoners occupy their own private acoustic space, ironic in light of the story's epigraph: *"Ce grand malheur, de ne pouvoir être seul."*[82]

As Engels memorably formulated the visual experience of urban dwellers' discomfort with having to look at each other as strangers in the situation of mass public transit, so, too, can the question be posed for the aural experience of population density, the social norms for the acoustics of listening and being heard and overheard in particular urban spaces and situations.[83] Social and cultural codes emerged from the experiences of one heard talking to oneself in the space of the city street, or of overhearing, listening in on the speech of others, as we saw in this book's Introduction with Balzac's allusion to Rabelais and "frozen speech." And as we will discover with Whitman's omnibus rides in New York, Whitman takes that particular urban experience as an occasion, of all things, to declaim poetry into the passing city streets and crowds of people. This passage from "The Man of the Crowd" comments, in part, on those developing acoustical behavioral norms.

The narrator of Poe's tale continues about the group of people talking to themselves: "When impeded in their progress, these people suddenly ceased muttering, but redoubled their gesticulations, and awaited, with an absent and overdone smile upon the lips, the course of the persons impeding them. If jostled, they bowed profusely to the jostlers, and appeared overwhelmed with confusion."[84] Their "muttering" marks a sort of deformation of articulate language in the space of the city street, a turn to indistinct sound in the crush of bodies, looks, and words. Overwhelmed by the human density, articulate language finds itself immobilized, slipping away instead into pure sound or bodily gesture. The *perception* of these "muttering" Londoners begins to resemble the perception of the "voices heard in contention" by the witnesses in "Rue Morgue," the perception of nonsense and incomprehensibility in the sounds of a language, or what sounds like a language, absent its sense. Submission and submissiveness to the flow and "jostle" of the crowd involve recourse to "redoubled . . . gesticulations" as an alternative means of expression and communication, thwarted and abyssal as it might be, for this segment of the London population.

Through the stress on sound over sense in a language barely vocalized in this urban situation, Poe articulates a threat of immobilization at a historical moment when the increasing desire to circulate in urban space was taking hold. Walter Benjamin, in the *Arcades Project*, speaks of "immobilization" in relation to moments of intense repetition of words and phrases in Poe's writings (the monomania of the narrator in "Berenice," for example, in which so much of the suspense depends on the ability of intensely repeated sounds and words, once bereft of meaning or clear referent, to signify once again). In this way the horror of "The Man of the Crowd," while framed in terms of legibility, may involve a greater fear and horror of immobilization to the story, of an end to it, a horror that the story might itself, as a print commodity, be reduced to a kind of "muttering" into the void of urban clamor and industrialized print media. The man of the crowd, whom the narrator pursues, does not stop in the end. The narrator, however, must stop. Storytelling thus confronts the situation of talking to oneself in the city street like one of an anonymous crowd muttering indistinct sounds into a void.

Reflecting on "The Man of the Crowd" and transatlantic mass media in the first half of the nineteenth century, Edward Cutler concludes: "Poe was already a reflex of mass media; his "Man of the Crowd" is less a reflection upon urban experience than a reflex of extant mass urban print about the urban modern."[85]

Cutler's sense of the story (and of Poe) as a "reflex" betrays a sense of some homology between the story as a commodity in the mass urban print market and these "muttering" people in the crowd who "if jostled bowed profusely to the jostlers." Do we think, then, of their "reflex" and that of the story as one and the same? Do both "bow profusely" to the progress of transatlantic mass media and a certain mass of humanity?

I conclude this chapter by suggesting a way in which Poe, specifically with "The Fall of the House of Usher," did not "bow profusely" to such progress, but rather anticipated technological developments. "Usher" forms part of Poe's protophonographic imagination, in which the possibility of a seemingly magical process of sound reproduction encourages ideas of acoustic original and copy.

Near the end of the story the narrator, in a desperate attempt to soothe Usher, chooses to read aloud to him from a book he finds close at hand, "The Mad Trist" of Sir Launcelot Canning, not one of Usher's favorites, but sufficient, the narrator hopes, to alleviate his illness. When the narrator reads aloud to Usher, the narrator subsequently hears sounds in the house as uncanny echoes of sounds described in "The Mad Trist." The narrator hears, for instance, what he describes as "the exact counterpart of what my fancy had already conjured up for the dragon's unnatural shriek as described by the romancer."[86] The narrator's insistence that he "actually" hears can be read as a sign of an internal struggle about his perception of whether the sounds he hears are hallucinated or real, whether they resound within his own mind or from without. The notion of an "exact counterpart" opens up a discourse beyond plain verisimilitude, pointing to the concept of sound reproducibility, through which ideas of original and copy are constructed in an acoustic field. Like the narrator of "The Tell-Tale Heart," Usher suffers from a "morbid acuteness of the senses."[87] The acuteness of Usher's hearing at the end of the story enables him to reconstruct an alternate narrative from the mystery of sounds heard in the absence of their immediately known and visible source. What the narrator of "House of Usher" hears first as "low and indefinite sounds" and then as uncanny echoes of sounds described in the story that he is reading aloud, Usher, in contrast, hears as sounds relating to an alternate narrative, that of his still-living sister escaping from her premature burial. Usher eventually disabuses the narrator of his fancy about the apparent echo of sounds from "The Mad Trist" in the house, sounds the narrator reports that he "did *actually* hear" (my emphasis).[88] Usher thus explains, dispelling the illusion of "exact" inter- and intratextual echoes:

> *We have put her living in the tomb*! Said I not that my senses were acute? I *now* tell you that I heard her first feeble movements in the

hollow coffin. [. . .] And now—to—night—Ethelred—ha!ha!—the breaking of the hermit's door, and the death-cry of the dragon, and the clangor of the shield!—say, rather, the rending of her coffin, and the grating of the iron hinges of her prison, and her struggles within the coppered archway of the vault! (emphases in original)[89]

Implicit, among other things, in Usher's laugh is his recognition of the narrator's illusion. Usher does not laugh at a hallucination, but rather at a dream of a magically reproduced copy or "exact counterpart" in sound, less the unnerving similitude between sound fancied in the mind of the narrator and sound "actually" heard, than the possibility that such a process of reproduction could occur, and with such apparent exactitude.

In the way the narrator's fancy leads him to the mistaken perception of "actual" acoustic copies of a written text, of graphic signs, uncannily reproduced in sound, Poe articulates both a problem and possibility for representation. Debussy, for one, in his lengthy incomplete attempt to adapt Poe's "House of Usher" into an opera, struggled to recreate the effect of the narrator's alarm, his illusion of "actually" hearing the sounds described in "The Mad Trist," sounds "actually" heard but misperceived by the narrator as exact copies. Debussy's stage direction for his adaptation of this moment in the story is illustrative of this challenge: "As they are reading [silently], one hears the music Roderick Usher imagines." How might we as an audience intuit, in a live performance setting, that we hear what Usher imagines?[90]

Usher's ultimate declaration disrupts the narrative of acoustic original and copy, granting the power of echo not to the narrator who reads aloud, as something of a mediator between the textual description of sound and actual acoustic echo, but to Madeline, escaping from her tomb. Strangely, she makes no sound with her voice. Rather, it is all the mechanical movements about her exiting the tomb, the "rending" and "grating" of the material surfaces that reverberate throughout the house.

With "Usher," Poe elaborates, in addition to a fall, a corresponding rise, that of the germs of a discourse on sound fidelity in acoustic reproduction, echoes that arise out of graphic inscriptions and that are heard in actual acoustic space in a way that seems magical, astonishing, and horrifying. Poe's story is less an anticipation of the technology of mechanical sound reproducibility than an articulation of the idea of "actual" acoustic original and copy in an age before the invention of mechanical sound recording and reproduction.[91] The narrator's consumption of the acoustic illusion, as if it were reality itself, hinges on an idea of exceptional acoustic representation, if not also extraordinary reproducibility.

Poe, through the terror of his narrator, thus fancies something in the acoustic register akin to, as he describes in his daguerreotype article, "a more perfect identity of aspect with the thing represented." He fancies a distinctive field of listening, one characterized by the possibility of "actually" hearing sounds that were written in such a way they might be reproduced by extraordinary means, by someone or something other than the storyteller's voice or pen.

3
Tattered Sound
Baudelaire's Paris, Noise, and the Protophonographic

Baudelaire was in love with motion. More specifically, he was in love with movement of the sort produced by optical toys and mechanical devices for visual representation.

In *Baudelaire, l'irréductible* (2014), Antoine Compagnon concludes his exploration of Baudelaire's vexed relationship to photography by posing the provocative question: What would Baudelaire have thought about cinema, an art form unformed as such until roughly thirty years after the poet's death? Compagnon surmises that Baudelaire would have discovered in cinema the charm he found lacking in photography. Baudelaire would have appreciated cinema as an art form, especially because of its movement, the same kind of movement he so valued in "the optical devices he saw in opposition to photography: the magic lantern, the panorama, the diorama, the phantasmagoria, the kaleidoscope, the phenakistiscope, ancestors of cinema more than of photography," ancestors akin in their movement to the core of his poetry, always in movement.[1]

In this chapter, I entertain two related questions, one more particular, the other broader than Compagnon's question here about Baudelaire and the (proto-)cinematic. First, what would Baudelaire have thought about mechanical sound recording and reproduction technology? Second, what would Baudelaire have thought about the audiovisual modern to come and the kaleidophonic of his own time (in, among other places, ancestors and cousins of the phonograph such as the phonautograph and the flame manometer)?

Baudelaire's modernity involved, as I will uncover and emphasize here, the precinematic (in the form of these magical animation devices) and, often at the same time, the proto*phono*graphic field. These fields intersect in what I am calling the *kaleidophonic*. There are ideas latent in Baudelaire's writings, especially within what Ross Chambers has identified as the urban "poetics of noise," that connect with discourses on the protophonographic and emergent audiovisual modern at play in Baudelaire's era.

For one, the ragpicker's activity of collecting the material detritus of urban life offered a remarkable metaphor, one that was dear to Baudelaire, for the task of the modern artist and writer seeking to represent the modern city. But how to collect the intrinsically immaterial, the evanescent, the sounds and songs of the city that flit by and are not heard again?

In his prose poem, "Widows [*Les Veuves*]," Baudelaire evokes the raggedness of music heard by chance in urban space, "a rag of music [*un lambeau de musique*]" as he describes it, something the ragpicker, or any other urbanite of the time, would have had conceivable difficulty in recovering or fixing in place (Rimbaud, later on, recalling Baudelaire's urban prose poems, would discover his own "rags of music" in London with his poem "Bridges [*Les Ponts*]," specifically with the phrase "bits of castle concerts, remnants of public hymns [*des bouts de concerts seigneuriaux, des restants d'hymnes publics*]").[2] Those with highly trained or gifted musical ears could transcribe what they heard into musical notation. But there existed no acoustic technology analogous to photography that could capture and preserve the auditory field, in its totality, in quite the same way as the visual field for either Baudelaire or Rimbaud, at least when Rimbaud was still writing poetry.

By the end of the nineteenth century, however, phonographic technology would be used to record and systematically document such tattered sound, especially the distinctive calls and songs of street criers in cities, among other urban auditory phenomena.[3] French ethnographer and folklorist Alphonse Certeux, for example, in his 1893 book, *Les Cris de Londres*, describes how he and others dedicated themselves to collecting cries they feared were on the verge of being lost, cries "on the verge of disappearance."[4] In 1891, as Certeux reports, at a meeting of the Folk-Lore Society in London, members listened to audio recordings of urban street cries that were recorded with a phonograph. Hence, "rags of music" had, in those years, become newly mechanically collectible and preservable.

Roughly twenty years before that invention, however, the technology could still only be dreamed of, imagined as something like the photography of sound. Participating in this nascent acoustical imagination, Baudelaire's friend, the photographer Félix Nadar, writing in 1856, predicted that some day, and perhaps soon, there would be an invention that would function like an "acoustic daguerreotype [*daguerréotype acoustique*]."[5] Édouard-Léon Scott de Martinville, as we have seen, was another inventor using the photograph analogy as a touchstone for new acoustic technology; he described the plate on which sound was visualized in his phonautograph as "our daguerrean plate, or rather our negative [notre plaque daguérrienne, ou plutôt notre négatif]."[6]

As Nadar described his own idea, which he termed both a "daguerreotype of sound" and an "acoustic daguerreotype," the device would have the ability to reproduce "faithfully and at will all the sounds submitted to its objectivity [fidèlement à volonté tous les sons soumis à son objectivité]."[7] It would enable one to "see noise [voir le bruit]."[8] About the possible invention of such an instrument, Nadar posed the startling question: "Haven't you, like me, often dreamed about this instrument whose need is so widely felt? [N'avez-vous pas comme moi rêvé souvent à cet instrument dont le besoin se fait si généralement sentir]?"[9] Baudelaire, several years later, would employ a similar rhetorical form in his famous letter to Arsène Houssaye about his dream of prose poetry: "Who among us hasn't, in their days of ambition, dreamed of the miracle of a poetic prose [. . .]? [Quel est celui de nous qui n'a pas, dans ses jours d'ambition, rêvé le miracle d'une prose poétique [. . .]?"[10] Friends and dreamers alike, Nadar and Baudelaire, each deindividualize their dreams as they imagine broader communities of thought about these novel forms and devices.

Nadar is a key figure in this story as perhaps the closest historical connection between Baudelaire and the origins of mechanical sound recording. The photographer offers a means of bridging critical reflections on the place of urban noise in Baudelaire's writings, a topic of much recent scholarly interest, with the technological developments of the age.

Though Nadar's photographic portraits of the poet are iconic, his drawing and portraits in prose of the poet, decidedly more obscure, have their share of insights for our inquiry here, most notably an analogy Nadar draws about Baudelaire's appearance upon his first meeting the poet by chance in the Luxembourg Gardens (see Figures 18 and 19). Nadar writes that Baudelaire, appearing first in the distance as a "bizarre, spectral figure [une figure bizarre, fantomatique]," as he approached, dressed mostly in black (with blood red tie and pale pink gloves), with his meticulous fragmented gestures, called to mind the "successive silhouettes of the optical telegraph that appeared in broken succession on the towers of Saint-Sulpice, or, better yet, the angular gymnastics of the spider at the end of its thread in humid weather," gestures captured in Nadar's drawing.[11]

Nadar notes that this chance meeting occurred well before Edison's electricity, that is, before electric lighting illuminated Paris, as if to say that the encounter was perhaps only possible in the more tenebrous atmosphere of the gaslit city, or that it was all the more remarkable for the unspoken connection and understanding that was communicated at a distance, optically telegraphed,

TATTERED SOUND: BAUDELAIRE'S PARIS, NOISE, AND THE PROTOPHONOGRAPHIC 105

Figure 18. Félix Nadar. Charcoal drawing of Charles Baudelaire, circa 1857. Photo Credit: Snark / Art Resource, NY.

Figure 19. Félix Nadar. Photograph of Charles Baudelaire, circa 1855. © RMN-Grand Palais / Art Resource, NY.

if you will, between the poet and the photographer and his companions in the absence of brighter illumination. With Baudelaire still at a distance: "The understanding was already fully registered with our new friend despite his reserve, for so things came to pass back then well before the electricities of M. Edison: hardly a quarter of an hour, and the whole 'bench' was accompanying Baudelaire, in a swarm, back to his home [. . .]."[12] This narrative of Nadar's first encounter with Baudelaire provides a concrete, albeit very oblique, connection between the world of Baudelaire and the world of Edison, specifically of his electric light bulb. But what of Edison's phonograph? What of the broader world of telecommunications that is referenced here more specifically with the striking analogy Nadar draws between Baudelaire and the "optical telegraph"?

When Nadar imagines the invention of an "acoustic daguerreotype" device, it is remarkable and also somewhat puzzling that he tells of such a widely felt "need" for that kind of acoustic technology, though the phrase "so generally" could be read more as a rhetorical effect than an accurate measure of general societal feeling.[13] Jacques Perriault wonders whether Nadar overstates such a "need."[14] Still, in what circles, we are then led to ask, was that need, if it was truly felt, most acutely and most widely felt? What kind of functions, furthermore, would that need fulfill? Indeed, before launching into a few imagined functions in his 1856 text, Nadar exclaims: "What possibilities! [*Que de ressources!*]"

The work of Franco-German composer and urban ethnographer Jean-Georges Kastner (1810–1867), a dedicated collector of urban sound and music, articulated a few possibilities and evidenced an ethnographic "need" for the technology, something he himself imagined in 1856, the same year Nadar published his short text on the "acoustic daguerreotype," as offering "the possibility to imagine for sound rays [*rayons sonores*] what Daguerre imagined for light rays [*rayons lumineux*]."[15] Kastner, for his part, termed the idea "daguerreotypie musicale," a term that is significant for articulating a conception of musical preservation. Some media historians have tended to express surprise that music did not rank highly in the writings of Edison and his associates as something to be preserved by Edison's phonograph shortly after its invention in 1877. The prehistory of these devices, however, grants us a more complete idea of how their uses were shaped and imagined. The prehistorical imagination did very much involve music and, hence, offers a pointed retort to any claim that music and poetry had little to do with the origins and invention of mechanical sound reproducibility.

Beyond the question of just how generally such a need was felt, as Nadar articulated it, other questions can be posed, most importantly, about *how* particularly this need was felt and how particularly individuals dreamed of the instrument. How did scientific and literary discourses interact on this idea, whether conceived of as a distant ideal, a nearly attainable step in the progress of scientific research into acoustics, as it appeared to Nadar writing in 1856 and once again in 1864, or a new literary invention? Baudelaire, if not as explicitly as his photographer friend, if not exactly providing an analogous poetic image for the "acoustic daguerreotype," nonetheless articulated in his poetry an audiovisual field from which this "need" could spring (whether as a flower or a weed we will attempt to judge in what follows), such a need only beginning to bud when photography had already bloomed. In evoking the particular social dimensions of urban acoustic space in his poetry, Baudelaire dreams of another way of preserving sound in aesthetic modernity. The "lambeau de musique" forms part of a deeper undercurrent of the city's acoustic residue in Baudelaire's poetry and of grounds for aesthetic judgment on the possibility of the mechanical preservation of sound, this possibility something we might call a protophonographicity.

How, then, to evaluate an *anti*-protophonographicity in Baudelaire? A monster of a neologism for sure, the idea I seek to capture with the term is nonetheless fairly straightforward, beginning with something familiar both to our age and to Baudelaire's, that being a skepticism about and contempt for the idea of progress, here specifically in the realm of technological media.[16] With such anti-protophonographicity, I mean to designate contempt for the conditions of possibility of mechanical sound reproducibility—something like a countercurrent to the generally, or not so generally, felt "need" for the device, as Nadar spoke of the idea. If this contempt for acoustics (a suspicion of echoes) might be understood on a basic level as analogous to Baudelaire's contempt for photography (a suspicion of sunlight, the imperative to hide from the sun and glorify the "cult of obscurity"), then the kaleidophonic field, with its subtle and sometimes synesthetic mingling of image and sound, offers space for dialectical play in the tension between contempt and dreams.[17]

Beyond the manifold instances of pronounced urban acoustic shock and aural *flânerie* in *Les Fleurs du Mal* and *Le Spleen de Paris*, Baudelaire articulates an aesthetic of listening, a valorization of poetic listening as an alternative to discourses on the modernization and mechanization of sound and listening in Second Empire Paris. From the visual standpoint, in *Seeing Double: Baudelaire's Moderntiy* (2011), for example, Françoise Meltzer argues that Baudelaire presents the readers of his poetry with clashing unresolved contradictions, ones recorded primarily through visual channels beset by the optical shocks of modernity. He records without understanding, his poetry thus registering a deep incomprehensibility more characteristic of the kaleidoscope and its visual distortions than of the stereoscope and its synthesis of separate images into a single image with an illusion of depth.[18]

If Baudelaire shows contempt for photography and is unable to arrive at the synthesis of stereoscopic vision, the possibility of mechanical sound reproducibility presents a different aesthetic of echoes in modern life. The "recording'" of sound and acoustical shocks in Baudelaire's poetry can be read in the context of contemporaneous protophonographic imaginaries, a new consciousness of sound, and the possibility of imagining for sound what Daguerre had effected for light. Contained in Baudelaire's poetry, then, are the germs of possibility for aesthetic value in the process of recording interiority, suspended and potentially inscribed, in a new acoustic field, though one not necessarily mechanically framed.

In his essay "Le public moderne et la photographie" in the *Salon de 1859*, Baudelaire scorned the way photography came to be idolized along with the idea of technological progress, likewise incarnated by other modern inventions such as gas lighting, steam power, and electricity.[19] He disdained the way "vile society hastened, all at once like Narcissus, to contemplate its trivial image on the metal plate [*la société immonde se rua, comme un seul Narcisse, pour contempler sa triviale image sur le métal*]."[20] Society was thus itself metamorphosed into a "flower of evil," "un seul Narcisse," not by the whim of a slighted goddess or god, but by the mass appeal of photographic technology.[21] And this narcissistic society contemplated itself not in the stillness of mythic waters but on a metal plate, newly mechanically transformed.

But what of the idea of modern society, and specifically Parisian society, in the position of Echo, to draw from the other side of the myth (Ovid's version at least, the only one to pair Echo with Narcissus) that Baudelaire invokes, contemplating an acoustic reflection of itself, gathering less as "un seul Narcisse" than as a collective Echo in an acoustic daguerreotype? Would that echo be heard as a noisy clamor or as something more sonorous, even poetic? What kind of aesthetic judgment on the possibility of such acoustic reproducibility (of both a mythic past and an ephemeral present), of such a technological advance, is latent in Baudelaire's poetry and criticism?

One potential answer begins to take shape when we consider the distinctions that Baudelaire makes in his 1859 photography essay about the uses and aesthetics of photography. These distinctions reveal a more nuanced and complex, even if still contemptuous, sentiment about the technology. Specifically, Baudelaire opposes the bourgeois enthusiasm for image-making technology, along with the elevation of photography to the status of high art. At the same time, however, he grants that photography has other useful functions, though only as a "humble servant" to science and the arts. Chief among those uses is preservation: "To the extent photography can save from oblivion those crumbling ruins, books, engravings, prints, and manuscripts that time devours [*que le temps dévore*], precious things . . . that demand a place in the archives of our memory, it will be thanked and applauded."[22]

Here Baudelaire's thoughts on the preservational possibilities afforded by photography closely resemble what Nadar imagines in his 1864 text as similar possibilities for preservation afforded by "the Daguerreotype of sound [*le Daguerréotype du son*]": "something like a box in which melodies would be recorded and retained just as the dark room seizes and focuses images [*quelque chose comme une boîte dans laquelle se fixeraient et se retiendraient les mélodies, ainsi que la chambre noire surprend et fixe les images*]."[23] Nadar then offers the hypothetical example of a family that cannot attend an opera performance on the opening night of *Forza del Destino* or of *L'Africaine*. Thanks to acoustical preservation and reproducibility of the "daguerreotype of sound," this family might nonetheless have the ability to hear the opera performance at a later time and judge for themselves, with their own ears, that the tenor was perhaps overdoing it a little "[*Ne trouvez-vous pas que le tenor crie un peu trop?*]."[24]

Nadar and Baudelaire truly diverge, on one basic level, in the sense of hope versus pessimism about the fate of human progress. Whereas Nadar prefaces his idea about the daguerreotype of sound with a veritable faith in humanity's capacity for invention—"*il ne fallait défier l'homme de rien*"; "*tout est donc possible à présent*"—Baudelaire, in his second essay on Poe, fulminates against progress, namely the modern bourgeois worship of the idea of progress, which, the poet surmises, is responsible for science having lost more so than acquired insights into the physical world. Veritable discoveries and inventions, Baudelaire maintains, are not made but rather lost because of "incessant progress—the fatal, irresistible law of progress" (324).[25]

Ironies abound when Baudelaire and Nadar's texts are viewed side by side. Specifically, in Nadar's second text on the "daguerreotype of sound," he writes with false modesty when he implores the reader not to laugh so fast about the idea of a daguerreotype of sound while describing himself as an "ignorant" dreamer, a "man of imagination [*un homme d'imagination*]" in contrast to the scientist ("*un homme de science*").[26] In Baudelaire's essay about photography and the modern public, the poet complains precisely about a lack of imagination. The photographer, Baudelaire argues, has no imagination. At issue, then, is what exactly constitutes "imagination" for Nadar and Baudelaire.

However their definitions intersect or diverge, Nadar's imagination, in his first text on the acoustic daguerreotype, tends toward the ironic, as he forecasts the obsolescence of the popular press after such an invention even as he publishes his text in the popular press, in a periodical that featured magisterial illustrations by Nadar's friend Gustave Doré, among others (Baudelaire, too, occupied an ambivalent position with the gazettes of his day, as he both despised and depended on them).[27] Nadar details possible uses of the acoustic daguerreotype: "And when our government becomes parliamentary again, what an advantage for the rural or the Parisian subscriber who, instead of hearing about the meeting of the assembly through the ears of the periodical, always somewhat biased in its reporting, will find themselves in the position of having an exact account [*un compte rendu exact*] as faithful and impartial as mathematics [*fidèle et sans passion comme la mathématique*]."[28] Nearly forty years before Edward Bellamy's short story "With the Eyes Shut"(1889) and Albert Robida and Octave Uzanne's short story "The End of Books [*La fin des livres*]"(1894)—which were written *after* the invention of Edison's phonograph—imagined the challenge audio recording poses to print in the mediascape of the future, Nadar imagined audio competition and audio dominance over print media, at least in the journalistic and political context, in the Second Empire, as perhaps a tool to resist Emperor Napoléon, or "Napoleon le petit," as Nadar would mock him in the *Revue comique*.[29]

Irony emerges when the last detail of this idea, the "faithful and impartial" audio recording, is compared with Baudelaire's critique of photography, an image-making technology that Baudelaire scorns for being *too* faithful, too impartial in its visual account of reality, at least in the hands of lesser photographers who would, absent the poet's sensibility and oversight, photograph his mother with "all the wrinkles, all the imperfections, all the details of the face [. . .] very visible, very exaggerated."[30] Baudelaire wanted a photographic portrait of his mother more akin to an artful drawing than something rigid and exact. Nadar imagined the acoustic daguerreotype as a resource for the music critic with bad memory—"*quel secours pour le critique musical sans mémoire!*" Imagine, dear reader, Baudelaire in the possession of an artful audio recording of Wagner or Liszt, an "acoustic daguerreotype" with the audio equivalent of "le flou d'un dessin." Even if Baudelaire never wrote anything to the effect, Nadar, as we see here, halfway imagined it, not exactly for Baudelaire, but for the opera of his day.

With ideas such as Nadar's acoustic daguerreotype, the practices of listening in deep solitude or as part of a new multitude became susceptible to technological intervention, mechanical imitation, and reproducibility. Baudelaire found beauty in the solitude of private acoustic space within the public space of the city, or in retreating into the interior, both psychic and architectural, to make a dream world with its own acoustic atmosphere. Something like Nadar's "acoustic daguerreotype" could and would, however, threaten that space of listening. Such technology had the potential to create its own private acoustic spaces, toward which the public might clamor in like fashion to the way, as Baudelaire describes with contempt, "thousands of avid eyes stooped before the holes of the stereoscope as if they were the peepholes onto the infinite [*des milliers d'yeux avides se penchaient sur les trous du stéréoscope comme sur les lucarnes de l'infini*]."[31] The acoustic daguerreotype, like the purely visual daguerreotype, might then be aestheticized as a recorded object, a work of art. And the mechanical process of recording the soundscape of the city or the human voice as acoustic portrait would be valorized as an artistic undertaking.

For the Baudelaire writing on photography in 1859, this would be a bad thing. But the famous kaleidoscope comparison from Baudelaire's "Le Peintre de la Vie Moderne" essay in 1861 reveals a different, more ambivalent feeling about technology, visual technology in particular. Baudelaire still subordinates the kaleidoscope to the imagination of the artist, but in imagining a "kaleidoscope gifted with consciousness [*un kaleidoscope doué de conscience*]," Baudelaire, like Nadar, dreams of the possibilities of technological advances, a visual device "gifted" with something distinctly foreign.[32] For Nadar, that foreign element, lacking in photography, is sound. For Baudelaire, the foreign element, lacking in the kaleidoscope, is consciousness. The confluence of these two currents of thought provides a critical entrée into a new consciousness of sound in Baudelaire's poetry, a consciousness forged in and through the convergence of poetry, visual imagery, and urban crowds. These ideas of augmented visual technologies together offer a way of discovering latent acoustical subtexts and possibilities in Baudelaire's poetry.

In a letter of introduction that Baudelaire writes to James McNeil Whistler asking him to welcome Nadar to London, Baudelaire describes Nadar's ballooning adventures and projects: "One of my best and oldest of friends, M. Félix Nadar, is on his way to London with the aim, I believe, of telling the public about the adventures he has had with his great balloon, and also I presume, to share with the English public his convictions relative to a new mechanism [*un nouveau mécanisme*] that will replace the balloon."[33] Nadar, still injured from an earlier ballooning accident, was on his way to demonstrate his Géant balloon in an exhibition at the Crystal Palace.

At a most basic level, this passage from Baudelaire's letter to Whistler serves as an example of Baudelaire's knowledge of the progress of these machines, though without critical verdict or conviction about the novel "mechanism." (It is, however, interesting that this is how Baudelaire chooses to introduce Nadar to Whistler, Nadar as, first of all, a balloonist; Baudelaire neglects to mention Nadar's adventures in photography).

More specifically, however, the mention of a "new mechanism" (possibly Nadar's interest in helicopter-like mechanisms, inspired by children's toys, the kind of objects that interested Baudelaire in "La Morale du joujou," among other places) can again be contextualized alongside such ideas as Baudelaire's "kaléidoscope doué de conscience." Baudelaire's letter to Whistler dates from October 1863. The following year, Nadar published *Mémoires du Géant*, the sprawling account of his escapades and ambitions in aviation, with a brief discussion of a daguerréotype of sound. Might Baudelaire have ever dipped into this book, as it seems likely he had with Nadar's "Manifesto of aerial autolocomotion" (1863), and stumbled upon, "trébuchant sur les mots comme sur les pavés," mention of a device that could make an audio recording of the opera? In September 1864, in Brussels, Baudelaire watched Nadar take to the air in his Géant balloon. And two years later, Baudelaire's mother discovered several of Nadar's photographs in her son's pockets. The correspondence between poet and photographer, however, at least as of yet, offers no definitive answer to this question. One could imagine: If Baudelaire ever read either of Nadar's texts on acoustic daguerreotypy, would he have written to him calling such a thing an appalling or a magnificent idea? *Quelle idée atroce!* or, *Quelle idée épatante!* Nadar mentions that much of his correspondence with Baudelaire was stolen by thieves. One day, perhaps, a letter might come to light.

But in the meantime there are other ways.

Like Cros, Baudelaire also dreamed of photography in color. The two poets would have certainly shared enthusiasm for the movement and animation of devices such as the phenakistiscope. Just as Baudelaire imagined a "kaleidoscope gifted with consciousness" in relation to the rapid movement of the urban crowd, Cros imagined a phenakistiscope gifted with photography, in this way anticipating the movement of cinema to come.[34]

Though nothing like Cros's sustained work and scientific experiments over nearly two decades on color photography, the dream and idea of color photography occupied Baudelaire several times in his writings. Two instances have drawn the close attention of critics. One in particular merits our attention here.[35] Indeed Baudelaire's reflections on color and photography speak to the question of mechanical reproducibility of modern color. At the same time, as I want to emphasize, such reflections offer a window onto problems of lack and possibility in a novel technological development of the era. Antoine Compagnon suggests that Baudelaire, at least when writing in his *Salon de 1846*, shared with Sainte-Beuve the disappointment that photographic technology could not reproduce color.[36] When we consider Nadar's idea of an acoustic daguerreotype within the general euphoria and furor over the photographic means of representing modern life, it is possible to consider the disappointment about color beyond the purely optical realm of the daguerreotype. Instead, the lack of color springs more from a general critique of the relationship between representation and mechanical reproducibility, in which sound, color, and movement also had their place as elements waiting in the wings.

We can look more precisely at the particular language of such critique by turning to the idea of color photography in Baudelaire's *Salon de 1846*, where he took the painter Louis Lottier to task for the "marvelously cruel truth [*une vérité merveilleusement cruelle*]" of his Algerian landscapes. Baudelaire described these landscapes as "panoramas inundated with sun."[37] The poet critic continued: "One could say they were done with a daguerreotype of color [*on les dirait faits avec le daguerréotype de la couleur*]."[38] Ironically, some of the first known experiments in the history of color photography were Algerian landscapes photographed in the 1880s by Louis Arthur Ducos du Hauron, initially a competitor and then a friend of Charles Cros in the pursuit of color photography (see Figure 20).

A "daguerreotype of color," as Baudelaire imagined it here, is not quite the same thing as color photography as we have come to know it, a medium that is, to this day, often greeted with skepticism in the realm of fine art (and in this way Baudelaire *was* prescient about the critical response to photography as a

Figure 20. Louis Ducos du Hauron. Early color photograph of Algiers (detail). Circa 1884.

form of high art).³⁹ Baudelaire's "daguerreotype *of* color" more closely resembles Nadar's first description of mechanical sound recording as a "daguerreotype *of* sound" or Cros's conception of his pursuit as "the photography of colors [*la photographie des couleurs*]," the phrase Cros used most often in communications to the Académie des Sciences and in correspondence with Ducos du Hauron.

Art historian Laura Anne Kalba suggests that the early understandings and descriptions of color in photography as the photography *of* colors rather than photography *in* color speak in a way to certain modernist tendencies, exemplified, for instance, by photographer Alvin Coburn in the 1910s, toward abstraction in photography, an emphasis on "'design'—the form and structure underlying the image—over subject matter" or the desire to "depict color as such."⁴⁰ When Baudelaire critiques Lottier's landscapes for having been done as if *with* the daguerreotype of color, Baudelaire's sense of color and representation is more in line with this sense of depicting color as such.

This idea, the photography of color as such, paralleled the way scientists and inventors such as Scott, Lissajous, and Koenig were examining sound in those years: as a phenomenon to be visualized and studied. Nadar departed, in part, from that vein of thinking to envision the subject matter (opera performances, for example) that could be captured with such a mechanical procedure while still emphasizing the more abstract sense with something like the ability to "see noise." Baudelaire's practice of collecting photographs, of paintings and prints specifically—his wish to acquire photographs of Goya's works, for example—was closer to the former conception envisioned by Nadar, a mechanical means of capturing subject matter. At the same time, Baudelaire's critique of Lottier's landscapes partakes of the more abstract treatment of color as such, hence employing the same kind of discursive figures that structured both scientific and artistic thought on recording sound. What, we might ask, of a kaleidophone gifted with consciousness?

The Visualization of Parisian Noise

An early poem in *Les Fleurs du mal* meditates on the sound of the human heart. This poem is Baudelaire's "Le Guignon," a term signifying bad luck and misfortune, often associated with the bohemian artists of the nineteenth century.⁴¹ In this poem, a sonnet on the theme of solitude and artistic creation, the sound of the heart can signify life and the inevitability of death, both knowledge and a loss of the self, a kind of internal acoustic divide. In contrast to Poe's "The Tell-Tale Heart," where so much of the drama resides in the rising volume and frenzied displacement of the heartbeat, this poem describes a comparatively quieter and more desolate conflict about the heart and its beating. Specifically, the speaker draws an analogy between his heart and a muffled drum. This analogy parallels, in the poem, other figurations of loss and solitude, a forgotten gem and a secret fragrance from a regretful flower:

Pour soulever un poids si lourd,	In order to lift such a heavy weight,
Sisyphe, il faudrait ton courage!	Sisyphus, I would need your courage!
Bien qu'on ait du cœur à l'ouvrage,	Even though we might have the heart for it,
L'Art est long et le Temps est court.	Art is long and time is short.
Loin des sépultures célèbres,	Far from celebrated sepultures,
Vers un cimetière isolé,	Closer to an isolated cemetery,
Mon cœur, comme un tambour voilé,	My heart, like a muffled drum,
Va battant des marches funèbres.	Proceeds to the beat of funereal marches.
Maint joyau dort enseveli	Many a gem sleeps encased
Dans les ténèbres et l'oubli,	In darkness erased,
Bien loin des pioches et des sondes;	Far from pick axes and probes;
Mainte fleur épanche à regret	Many a flower emits with regret
Son parfum doux comme un secret	Its sweet perfume like a secret
Dans les solitudes profondes.[42]	In unknown solitary troves.

The images of secrecy and obscurity in the tercets cast into greater relief the veiled or concealed nature of the heart analogized as a drum in the second quatrain. Like the diffusion of the flower's aroma, a metaphor for lost and forgotten art, at the poem's end, the sound of the heart dissipates and is easily deadened and dampened.

In the space of the modern city, where it was distinctly challenging to remain audible even to oneself, the figure of the "tambour voilé" could signify just such a conflict about that hushed unsettled audibility.[43] Baudelaire adapted the image and another line from Henry Wadsworth Longfellow's poem "A

Psalm of Life" in *Voices of the Night*, a poem that Poe had cited in an early version of "The Tell-Tale Heart":[44]

> Art is long, and time is fleeting,
>   And our hearts, though stout and brave,
> Still, like muffled drums, are beating
>   Funeral marches to the grave.

A notable difference, however, in Baudelaire's translation from English to French, from "muffled" to "voilé," resides in the visual connotations of the word "voilé" in French.[45] Though "voilé" could be read more broadly as signifying murky or obscure, cousin to the "ténèbres" of the poem's next stanza, I want to linger on the visual connotations of the word, since this correspondence between sight and sound corresponds, in a way, with an attempt to visualize sound by Édouard-Léon Scott de Martinville, the inventor we met in this book's Introduction.[46] Scott literally veiled a drum in black soot as part of his procedure for writing sound with his phonautograph.[47] The device enabled sound to become visualized through a process of partially unveiling the drum (see Figure 21). In a similar fashion, scientist Jules Antoine Lissajous, whom Nadar cites in his discussion about the ability to see noise, analyzed sound vibrations and musical harmony with mirrors and tuning forks.[48]

Describing the abilities of the device in his scientific treatise "Fixation graphique de la voix" (1857), Scott relates how the device can help inaugurate the question of timbre as a new field of scientific research. In this respect, he finds a special discordance: "In the piercing cry, in the bitter sounds of instruments, the waves of condensation are irregular, unequal, not periodic." This discord reveals, as a question of timbre, what he describes as "the unwanted sounds of the voice, the muffled sounds [*les mauvais sons de la voix, les sons voilés*]."[49] Parallel pursuits for Scott and Baudelaire thus emerge in the obscurity of sound made visible, the deeply private and unknowable interiority of the soul with Baudelaire's metaphor of the heart as a "tambour voilé" in "Le Guignon," and the rational scientific description of timbre as a visualization of sound, of "les sons voilés" in Scott's phonautograph. Would we go so far as to translate "les mauvais sons de la voix" as the evil sounds of the voice?

For Scott, the rationality of scientific discourse is strained in the way he searches for a "langue propre à l'acoustique," but tends often toward poetic language and metaphor, especially in the way he relates his new technology to photography. Introducing his aim of visualizing sound, he says first, to recall, using the analogy of a writer's pen, that it is impossible, then invokes the chimera when he describes how, akin to the fixation of a light beam in photography, he wishes to preserve a "spectre sonore."[50]

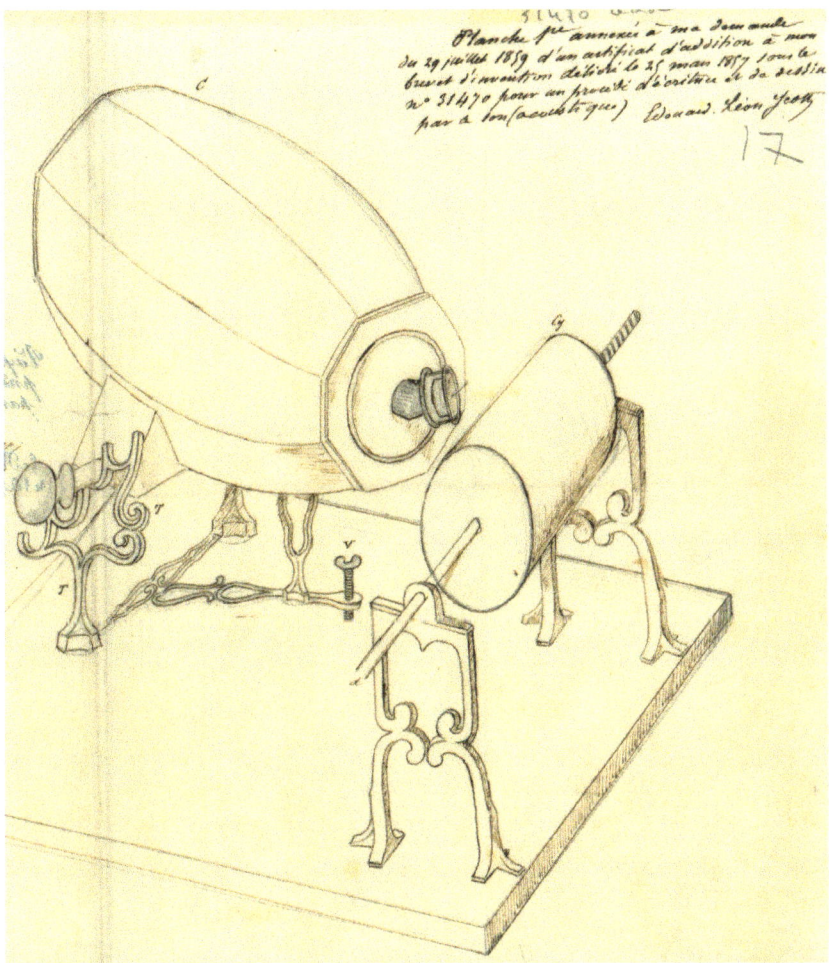

Figure 21. Édouard-Léon Scott de Martinville's drawing of his phonautograph (detail). From Scott, *Certificat d'addition*, 1859 (INPI ms. 31470). Courtesy Institut National de la Propriété Industrielle, Paris, France.

Scott's invention figured in the lineage of investigations into acoustics such as Ernst Chladni's tone figures (see Figure 22), Charles Wheatstone's kaleidophone, and Lissajous's curves, which all visualized sound waves in particular ways. Though Baudelaire's poem predates Scott's phonautograph, it is, nevertheless, striking how the image of the "tambour voilé," borrowed and subtly transformed from Longfellow (from "muffled drums" to "tambour voilé"), in its literary audiovisual connotations, parallels the technological translational process of the phonautograph, turning sound into a kind of vision. In that way,

118 TATTERED SOUND: BAUDELAIRE'S PARIS, NOISE, AND THE PROTOPHONOGRAPHIC

Figure 22. Ernst Chladni's figures of vibrating plates. From H. Holbrook Curtis, *Voice Building and Tone Placing* (New York: D. Appleton and Company, 1914), 219.

Baudelaire's poetic image, with its subtle synesthesia, begins to resemble Nadar's idea of an "acoustic daguerreotype" as a device to make noise visible. The lines traced in the black soot of Scott's phonautograph might then bear a poetic trace, while Baudelaire's "tambour voilé" beats "des marches funèbres" both to the rhythm of the poetic line and to the flow of acoustic technologies. As Clarence and Coeuroy argued, "poetry has always blazed a path for science to follow [*toujours la poésie a devancé la science*]."[51] The heart in Baudelaire's poem beats a funereal, shadowy murmur while also offering a figure for hearing the different acoustical registers of the sound of the human heart. Those sounds of life might be heard in the context of both the emergent nineteenth-century medical practice of auscultation and the nascent technological resistance to death of the human voice, the preservation and eventual reproducibility of the living voice as a trace sounded and resounded over time. In each case, translation, from English to French, from sound to sight, produces a deeper resonance. For Baudelaire, it can be heard in the synesthetic play of the phrase "tambour voilé." For Scott, the resonance was so deep that it was not until 2008 that the lines traced by his machine could be played back, translated back into audible sound and song.[52]

In his first essay on Poe, Baudelaire described writers like Poe cursed with obscurity as "men who wear the word 'guignon' written in mysterious characters in the sinuous folds of their face [*des hommes qui portent le mot* guignon *écrit en caractères mystérieux dans les plis sinueux de leur front*]."[53] Baudelaire's second essay on Poe offers one way of thinking about such "caractères mystérieux dans les plis sinueux" as evocative of acoustic obscurity, specifically as inaudibility. Reflecting on Poe's curse of being unappreciated by the general American public, Baudelaire juxtaposes so-called and so-perceived civilized and savage nations, identifying "civilized" society with "our lazy eyes and our deafened ears [*nos yeux paresseux et nos oreilles assourdies*]" and "savage" man with "eyes that could pierce the fog [*ces yeux qui percent la brume*]" and "ears that could hear the grass growing [*les oreilles qui entendraient l'herbe qui pousse*]."[54] American society, in what Baudelaire perceives as its bourgeois worship of progress, was deafened to the scope of Poe's imagination.

"Nos oreilles assourdies" can be read, in part, as a lament for the modern age and the encroachment of what Baudelaire fears as an "Americanization" of Paris, a loss of the beautiful in the wake of rampant capitalism and modern industry. Between the "guignon" invoked in the essay on Poe and the poem "Le Guignon," Baudelaire, however, demonstrates his special ability to hear through the deafening noise of modern society, to hear coming from an America that, as he describes, "chatters and rambles on with a stunning loquacity [*bavarde et radote avec une volubilité étonnante*]" the infrasounds of Poe's imagination.⁵⁵ In that way, by listening closely to Poe's works and the "lamentable tragédie que la vie d'Edgar Poe," Baudelaire can rescue him from the *guignon* of obscurity. Poe's sickness, which so fascinated Baudelaire, might then also be heard as a murmur that cannot make itself heard to the deafened ears of what Baudelaire regards as a society that rejects him. It is up to Baudelaire's critical literary poetic, and perhaps also microphonic or stethoscopic, ear to detect those transatlantic murmurs.

Just as Cros imagined deafness in the situation of modern everyday life with the devices he envisioned for his deaf students, Baudelaire, too, imagined a certain level of deafness as a kind of modern condition inflecting everyday life. In his poem "À une passante," deafness inflects everyday *urban* life, though that "deafening street" could also be read as a metaphor for modern society more broadly. In his "Notes nouvelles sur Edgar Poe," Baudelaire offers more explicitly a broader statement on deafness and modern society—indeed a condemnation of that society's eyes and ears.

For Cros, deafness might be overcome by modern technology while, in stark contrast, that modern technology, in Baudelaire's view, effectively created a deafened and deafening society. Noise that deafens, in this situation, could be read as a form of information saturation, most notably when it comes from print media, from the popular press Baudelaire abhorred even as he depended on it, or from photography and its excess of exactitude, detail, and concomitant lack of imagination, in Baudelaire's view.⁵⁶ How much of a presentiment of our own "information age," I am led to wonder, is present in Baudelaire's turn of phrase, in "our lazy eyes and our deafened ears"?

Sound and Blindness: "Les Aveugles"

Do deafened eyes tend toward blindness? In the distraction of eyes and ears, in their laziness, what fecundity is possible? Baudelaire celebrates a "fecund laziness" in "La Chevelure," a poem guided by smell more than any other sense. But deafness and sound have their part in the poem as well, its speaker sowing gems in his beloved's hair so she may never be deaf to his desire ("Afin qu'à mon désir tu ne sois jamais sourde!"), her hair metaphorized as a "resonant harbour *(Un port retentissant)*." How to dream of that resonance as a form of writing?

Theorist Philippe Lacoue-Labarthe, in his essay "L'Écho du sujet," conceives of phonography in relation to the writing subject as a form "of recording internal voices [*enregistrement des voix intérieurs*]."⁵⁷ Elaborating on this "acoustic sensibility," he tells of how it can work as a means to detect "the infrasounds of the unconscious [*les infrasons du processus inconscient*]."⁵⁸ While he presents these concepts in the context of autobiography and psychoanalysis (specifically psychoanalyst Theodor Reik's special acoustic sensibility and his theory and practice of "listening with the third ear"), Lacoue-Labarthe's theorization of phonography also offers a means of rethinking the lyric as a mode of writing the self. The possibility of this kind of recording for Baudelaire, for the lyric self, is threatened by what Georg Simmel describes in "The Metropolis and Mental Life" as the challenge of hearing oneself in the modern city.

Paris, for Baudelaire, as we find for instance in the poems "Les Aveugles" and "À une passante," could be as deafening as it was blinding. In "Le Crépuscule du Soir," the speaker will tell his soul, "Close your ear to this roar [*ferme ton oreille à ce rugissement*]," a command perhaps impossible to obey, one that involves the creation of a space both for introspection and an interior acoustic space in which the internal voices of the self, as Lacoue-Labarthe imagines, might be recorded. The "Sourde muette" of the prose poem Baudelaire had planned to write was a figure, who, in her deafness, in being gifted with an ear closed to the "rugissement" of everyday Paris, may have been equally gifted with clairaudience, a deeper hearing as ability to hear such internal voices of the soul or the "infrasons du processus inconscient." Though we have little more to go on than the title of this poem he planned to write, I want to highlight its singular feminine figure and how such muteness might be read as a figure for the ambivalent gesture of at once invoking and silencing feminine voices found in Baudelaire's poetry.[59] This silencing, conceived as a process effected over time, involves a vexed relationship with noise, the preservation of sound, and the potential for echo in a changing cityscape.[60]

In the tenth line of Baudelaire's "Les Aveugles," the speaker cries out, "O cité!" It seems as if he cries in competition with all the diverse sounds that constitute the urban din. Addressing the city in the familiar "tu" form, the speaker says, "While all around us, you sing, laugh, and roar [*pendant qu'autour de nous tu chantes, ris et beugles*]."[61] "Beugles," meaning roaring or bellowing, contrasts with the more ordered "singing" the city performs, whereas its "laughing" sits in between registers of ordered and disordered sound.[62] Positioned at the end of the poetic line, the word "roaring" puts the accent on disorder rather than the order in the urban soundscape. Whitman, as we will see, especially in "Song of Myself," invokes diverse and seemingly unmusical sounds of the city to resolve them into singing, only to dissolve that order back again into noise, though one that is less discordant than it is rapturous. This singing contrasts with Baudelaire in this way, and with Poe, and with something like the startling repetition in his poem "The Bells."

The spectrum of Baudelaire's language to characterize the heterogeneity and polysemy of urban sound invites reflection on the poetic assimilation of that kind of noise into its textuality, as Chambers has emphasized. In the sonnet "Les Aveugles," the city reduces the speaker of the poem to a stupor, one brought on by a kind of acoustic assault. His daze parallels but distinguishes itself from the condition of the blind, the object of the speaker's contemplation in the opening stanzas of the poem. Chambers has argued that poetic speech, emblematized in the "Je dis" that begins the concluding line of the sonnet, in a sort of contest with urban noise, must abase itself: "The din of the city . . . is a dangerous rival to poetic speech, but also its model."[63] Hence, the contest in "Les Aveugles," Chambers contends, signals a new "poetic diction . . . the speech of hébétude," the speech of stupefaction, which is one means, as Chambers maintains, of "incorporating" urban noisiness into a certain urban poetic aesthetics, a "noisy form of beauty."[64]

At the same time, the urban din, as represented in this poem, collapses distinctions and distance between self and other. And this momentary collapse plays into the expanse and limits of allegory in the poem, specifically the concluding tercet as an allegory of society at large and the speaker's fraught union with that society. Part of the distinction between the stupor of the blind and the stupor of the poet resides in the way sound and sight signify in the city. The poem implies a distinct relation between visuality and aurality with the rhyme between "beugles" and "ces aveugles," in the concluding tercets, in addition to the fraternal kinship expressed in the first tercet: ". . . le noir illimité / Ce frère du silence éternel." Blindness is fraternally bound with the effusion of sound in the city, a world of sound difficult and unsettling to imagine in and of itself. The text registers that lack of identification, the otherness and opacity of the blind world, through ambiguous naming of the collective.

For one, the very language of the poem implies different kinds of collectives, each conceived differently via visual and aural language and metaphor. In "Les Aveugles," the "pronominal agitation" of an apostrophe is split into two dialogues, the first between the speaker and his soul, and the second, between the speaker and the city.[65] The city's noise, as evoked in this poem, while troubling the relation between self and other, offers a possibility of the collective that is poignant in its ephemerality. Indeed, this is a strong contrast between Baudelaire and Whitman; for Whitman, and especially in his poem "Crossing Brooklyn Ferry," the soundscape of the crowd partakes more of the eternal than the ephemeral side of Baudelaire's dialectic of modernity.

The conflictual relation between self and other animates the poem's contemplation of the blind, a conflict that could be first located in the opening call, "*contemple*-les." The poem plays around the edges of that divide between observing subject and surveyed objects in parallel to the way it suggests degrees and depths of sensory acuity and dispossession.

The turn to the city, with the exclamation "O cité!" at the end of the second line of the first tercet, strikes a jarring note. The play of ambiguity and fragmentation of the speaker's self and the collective blind deepens at this juncture in the poem. Before addressing the city, the speaker had been addressing his soul. Speaking to the city, to seemingly all it encompasses, can be taken as a release from the mode of internal monologue.[66] He hears the city shouting back at him with its song, its laughter, and its roar. In this line a parallel movement from the individual to the collective urban masses occurs, because up to this point, the speaker was concerned with "them," with the blind. Suddenly, however, the city's sound encompasses us as well: "O cité! / Pendant qu'autour de *nous* tu chantes, ris et beugles" (my emphasis).

To whom, I want to ask, does "nous" refer? It is the one point in the poem when the speaker and the impersonal "on" that contemplates the blind appear to blur with the blind, with the objects of fascination and scrutiny. It is a point when self-other distinctions collapse. The city's soundscape activates momentary sympathy between the speaker and the blind, the evocation of an acoustic space that binds them together. Here the very diffusion of sound becomes coterminous with the sound and sense of "nous." Whether the ambiguity of "nous" is heard and understood as the speaker and the blind together as a collective body, signifies all of the urban population, or further implies union between the speaker and the reader, "nous" is a way of implicating the reader in this community.[67]

Notwithstanding the ambiguity of the phrase "autour de nous," it is difficult to imagine that the blind are still left at an imperious remove or distance from the speaker. If sympathy can be invoked to describe this sudden nearness, a sympathetic resonance, exactly how deep that sympathy runs nonetheless remains in question. The poem ultimately leaves open the question of whether this line about hearing the city's soundscape ought to be read as sympathetic in the sense of an understanding or an attempt to understand how the blind, how *they*, as radical other, understand, navigate, and live in the world, or whether in the ambiguity of "nous," in its indeterminate plurality, that opportunity for sympathy is somehow missed.

The line is perhaps where the speaker comes closest to playing the part of the multiple self as evoked in "Les Foules" but nonetheless falls short of entering unencumbered into a distinctly other world, as perhaps Cros was more capable of doing, given his experience teaching deaf students. For most of the poem, the speaker refrains from settling into the mind or body of the blind.

He remains fixated as an outside observer on their eyes rather than attempting to think of a world made only of sounds entirely bereft of vision, except in the one-line description of the urban soundscape.

In the concluding tercet, the condition of sensory deprivation, of blindness, becomes an allegory of sensory onslaught, of "hébétude," having pivoted on the representation of urban sound and the relation between sound and sight in the poem. In turning away from the blind to address the city, the speaker of "Les Aveugles" turns himself into an object of scrutiny, asking the city to reflect on him. In light of the poem's title, there is a touch of irony and malice when the speaker cries out for the city to *see*: "Look! I'm slogging along too! but, more stupefied than them, / I say . . . [*Vois! je me traîne aussi! mais, plus qu'eux hébété, / Je dis: . . .*]."

The ambiguity of who constitutes "*tous* ces aveugles" at the poem's end parallels the ambiguity of "nous" in the first tercet. The rhyme between aurality and visuality, between "beugles" and "aveugles," between noise and blindness, is telling. By the collective granted in noise, by its immersive quality, by the city that howls in the first tercet, the blindness of the poem's end no longer belongs exclusively to *them*, to the blind. It potentially applies to "us" as well, to a society at large, as in Baudelaire's condemnation of "our lazy eyes" in his essay on Poe.[68] Our eyes might be considered so lazy they are effectively blind. And it is remarkable, as several critics have noted, that "À une passante," which follows "Les Aveugles" in the "Tableaux Parisiens" section, offers a figure of deafness in the howling street: "La rue assourdissante autour de moi hurlait," where once again the immersive quality of sound is evoked with the expression "autour de."[69]

Sight, too, helps to unify, first in a dazzling excess of vision and then in collective blindness. The ephemeral moment, however, of the soundscape's unification, the "autour de nous," allows for the rich metaphorical and ambiguous play of the singular and the collective at the poem's end. This moment ultimately signals the threatening speed with which collectives can assemble and dissolve in the space of the modern city when that space is perceived acoustically. At the same time, the poem evokes the possibility of music as a rallying cry, both the danger and the salutary possibility of bodies together in resonance. The sounds of Paris in this poem might then be read as animating the ephemeral side of Baudelaire's elaboration of modernity, on the other side of which lurks something like Nadar's idea of an "acoustic daguerreotype," a device to arrest the flight of those sounds, rendering them if not eternal then at least into a conflicted echo of reality's present, "too much precision! [*trop d'exactitude!*]," as the poet would condemn of photography's mania to capture all, without a filter.

Between Noise and Music: Ambient Sound

Historian James Johnson has addressed a different kind of Parisian social formation in sound that is more refined than the city's "singing, laughing, and bellowing" in "Les Aveugles." In Johnson's social history of music's reception in Paris between 1750 and 1850, *Listening in Paris*, he argues that a decisive change occurred in the listening practices of Parisian concertgoers. They grew silent. They learned to stop making noise, to stop talking during musical performances and to start listening.

The social significance of this change he interprets as a bourgeois withdrawal into "unhappy passivity," the effect of a new propriety that contrasted with earlier modes of listening, such as the freedom of aristocratic concertgoers under the Ancien Régime to express their emotions and responses to the music in public.[70] The new behavioral norms quieted those public expressions and created what Johnson describes as a new "private sphere of feeling," one that could offer a "private space for inner communion" but was also often beset by boredom.[71] Greater silence in the audience might appear then to lead to greater introspection, but what, we might ask, of a deeper interior listening space?

Peter Szendy has proposed one way this might occur by subtly modifying the familiar thinking on the play of seeing and being seen in public concert and performance spaces (think, for example, of Cassatt's *In the Loge*). Instead of solely an occasion to see and be seen, the concert hall is also "a space where we come to look at those who listen, where we go to see people listening, or even to listen to people listening."[72]

Interior concert performance spaces, however, were not the only spaces in the nineteenth-century city for the development of changing listening practices and new interiorities that formed around those practices.[73] The urban crowd and public outdoor concerts, as featured, for example, in Manet's "Music in the Tuileries" and Baudelaire's prose poem "Les Veuves," also encouraged the formation of solitude, newly felt in an expanded acoustic field. Baudelaire recorded the conditions through which listening became newly interiorized in the city and took the opportunity to look intently at those listeners and listen to their listening.[74] Crowds formed via visual *and* auditory channels, through the language of both aural and visual experience. The city's soundscape shaped these possibilities for collective formation, dramatically so in the verse poem "Les Petites Vieilles" and the prose poem "Les Veuves." In the situation of physical social distance or distancing in the city, music could still touch.[75]

As with many of the prose poems in *Le Spleen de Paris*, "Les Veuves" recalls and develops themes, motifs, and language from certain verse poems in *Les Fleurs du Mal*, "Les Petites Vieilles" in particular. Central to each poem is an encounter with music in the space of the urban street or public park. The crowds in the poems, as well as the women of the two titles, those "singular beings" that fascinate the speaker, hear this music at a remove. The fragmented and displaced quality of the music comes across most vividly in "Les Veuves," in which the crowd gathered around the barrier set up around the public concert is described as "catching for free, at the whim of the wind, a rag of music [*attrapant gratis, au gré du vent, un lambeau de musique*]."[76] The crowd consumes music as a rag, second-handedly.

The listening experience created by this secondhand fragment of music fascinates the speaker in each poem, allowing for deep reflections on the dynamics of urban solitude and multitude as a function of listening and overhearing. These revealing differences between the poems offer ways of examining the representation of sound as it filters across divisions, both spatial and social, in public exterior space. Ultimately such divisions, as represented in the poems, enable us to ask how the idea of private acoustic space takes shape within public urban space.

In "Les Petites Vieilles," the women, subject to the shocks of urban traffic, tremble as if in resonant discord with its noise; Baudelaire describes them as "trembling with the moving roar of the omnibuses [*frémissant au fracas roulant des omnibus*]."[77] Whitman, in contrast, as we will see in the next chapter, takes the experience of riding the omnibus as a license to declaim, to roar within the city's "fracas." The American poet harmonizes with that noise.

The "fracas" made by the omnibuses in Baudelaire's poem is a sound associated with greater urban mobility but also danger, a symbol of the idea of progress Baudelaire challenges in, among other places, his essay "De l'idée moderne du progrès appliquée aux beaux-arts." When Baudelaire wrote this poem, ridership on Parisian omnibuses was soaring due in part to the changes afoot with the Haussmannization of Paris.[78] Indeed, the trembling of the women here seems akin to the dazed condition of the speaker in "Les Aveugles," and to the shock factor of the modern city that Benjamin sees as registered so profoundly in Baudelaire's poetry.

In the stanza following the one in which the women tremble with the sound of the omnibuses, Baudelaire develops the metaphor of their resonant bodies by likening the women to bells that ring at the will of a demon without pity. The women ". . . dansent, sans vouloir danser, pauvres sonnettes / Où se pend un Démon sans pitié!" The dancing, not willed by the women themselves, seems like a further variation of their trembling from the previous stanza, caused by the roar of the passing omnibuses. In this way, the demon could be read as an abstraction of those omnibuses and, by extension, the "evil" of modern progress, progress both in the literal spatial sense of the word and as a more abstract bourgeois idea of the sort reviled by Baudelaire.

The demon relates to a broader malaise about technological progress, the ambivalence about a city being shaped and reshaped by high capitalism, the spectacularization of modernization that turns urbanites into unwitting bells sounding its praises, however discordant. The image illustrates a conflict for art, an anticipation of the problems Baudelaire finds with photography and its encroachment on "the domain of the impalpable and the imaginary [*le domaine de l'impalpable et de l'imaginaire*]."[79] What becomes, then, of the artist's ability to dream willfully, to beat back against what Baudelaire sees as the bland reproducibility of "le vrai" through the camera? The demon of industry in "Les Petites Vieilles," urban mass transit, creates a debased form of dancing, reproducing the sound and movement of industry. This form of dancing arises from "l'obéissance involontaire forcée," as Baudelaire puts it in his essay on photography.[80]

In the prose poem "Les Veuves," the effect of dislocation, the unsettled resonance between bodies and social groups, becomes further pronounced and narrated in greater detail. Between "Les Petites Vieilles" and "Les Veuves," dislocations of social bodies emerge, "membres discords" and "êtres singuliers" that clash with multitudes both visually and acoustically. In the prose poem, Baudelaire emphasizes and develops the features of spatial marginality and dislocation in sound as a way of troubling both the signs of social division and distinction and the parallels that can exist across those boundaries. The urban crowd, if unnamed and secret in "Les Petites Vieilles," becomes an explicit player and locus of conflict in "Les Veuves."

If the invocation of a "family" of ruins partly mitigates the alienation evoked in "Les Petites Vieilles," in "Les Veuves," the widow's isolation is, in contrast, deepened and embittered. The prose poem furthermore lingers on the dimension of social and spatial marginality, the different social strata of "le peuple parisien." As in "Les Aveugles," the soundscape represented in "Les Veuves" frames and gathers an ambiguous social collective. The ambience, porosity, and diffusion of music in urban space highlight the situation of anxious social borders. The poem is less intent on the music itself than on how music filters through borders, unsettling both social borders and the kind of milieux that attract the attention of the poetic and philosophical mind.

Hence, after describing the first concert with one lone widow at a remove, the speaker is drawn to reflecting on "the crowd of pariahs that gather around the enclosure of a public concert [*la foule de parias qui se pressent autour de l'enceinte d'un concert public*]."[81] Though both spatially and socially excluded, pressed to the margins, the "pariahs" nevertheless constitute an audience for the concert, but one that is on the exterior of an urban spectacle for which it is necessary to pay for privileged firsthand access. On the outside of the concert space, they press against the "exterior barrier, catching for free, at the whim of the wind, a rag of music, staring at the shimmering blaze on the inside [*barrière extérieure, attrapant gratis, au gré du vent, un lambeau de musique, et regardant l'étincelante fournaise intérieure*]."[82] The aleatory quality of this activity and how the crowd listens in this poem, "attrapant gratis au gré du vent," resembles how the poet discovers poetic language in the city, as analogized in Baudelaire's "Le Soleil," where the poet is described as "stumbling on words in like fashion to the cobblestones [*trébuchant sur les mots comme sur les pavés*]."[83] In this way, as with the ragpicker analogy, a kinship exists between the poet and the pariahs, as with the old women in both "Les Petites Vieilles" and "Les Veuves."

After describing the situation of the public concert, the rich, well-dressed interior audience, and the "tourbe" on the exterior, the speaker proceeds in the following passage to recall the poem's opening ruminations on places fertile for poetic material: "It's always an interesting thing, this reflection of the joy of the rich in the depths of the eye of the poor. [*C'est toujours chose intéressante que ce reflet de la joie du riche au fond de l'œil du pauvre.*]"[84] While Baudelaire highlights the eye in the perception of this kind of "reflet," he also evokes the perception of an acoustic reflection or mirror in the phrase that follows. "But that day, across the crowd dressed in overalls and calico, I caught sight of a figure whose nobility created a dazzling contrast with all the surrounding coarseness. [*Mais ce jour-là, à travers ce peuple vêtu de blouses et d'indienne, j'aperçus un être dont la noblesse faisait un éclatant contraste avec toute la trivialité environnante.*]" If we understand "trivialité" as denoting sartorial coarseness, referring to "ce peuple vêtu de blouses et d'indienne," then "toute la trivialité environnante" appears to refer to the crowd of pariahs on the exterior. And yet the word "trivialité" has connotations of banality that speak beyond the merely literal or sartorial here, and hence reference the poem's reflections on the milieu of poetic and philosophical interest.

The "tourbe" on the fringes of the concert is the crowd, as we discover in the following paragraphs, that the widow with the air of aristocratic beauty and noble bearing joins, and against which she forms "such a dazzling contrast [*une tache si éclatante*]." In a way, it is difficult to locate "la trivialité environnante" precisely on either side of the divide. This indeterminacy, furthermore, is not merely the sign or the result of a contradiction in the speaker's thought. The logic that animates this indeterminacy, this apparent dereliction of interest in either side of the divide (because in the presence of the majestic widow, both sides are rendered, in a sense, "crude") resides in the woman's specialized ability to cut across social divides while at the same time accentuating them.

The clash of different exteriorities produces discord that remains unresolved and unassimilable to either side of this social divide. The widow becomes singular through her profound privacy and solitude and, in that way, like an echo of the music around her—the music around which the outcast crowd assembles.

Jean-Luc Nancy draws a distinction between the perception of a visual reflection and the perception of resonance, a distinction that helps to illuminate this moment in the poem: "Reflection requires a reflective surface, in principle external to the visible thing. Resonance is inside of sound itself: a sound is its own echo chamber."[85] The resonance of this widow's grief resides in her profound solitude, the absence of visual reflection in her eye. Though the speaker sees that she has "un œil profond," he does not find in her eye anything like the "ciel livide où germe l'ouragan," as in the "Passante" poem. Instead, "Les Veuves" suggests a need for her grief to be heard as an echo of "un lambeau de musique," through natural sound reproduction, an echo in deep solitude.

The music bestows a rhythm to the widow's act of listening. The slightness and the sweetness ("doucement") of her rhythmic nod signifies a harmony that can still spring from the grief and loss she endures while also signifying the tenuous hold she has on the music, on the "lambeau de musique," as if any more dramatic gesture would sever the attachment.

Visuality, evoked in the representation of ocular reflections from the speaker's point of view, provides the contrast, the source of division in this poem. Aurality (what we might think of as a point of listening), in the situation where the different social milieux overlap and lose their fixed bearings in sound, provides the figure of afflicted interpenetrating marginality that is at the core of the poem's meanings. The situation of the public concert, in the ways the concert is both heard and seen, undergirds the fluidity and mobility of the margin (when spatial margins become social margins become margins of the self, all serving as margins for the philosopher and poet). The visual and the aural both have their part to play in this spectacle. The specificity of the aural, though dependent on visual cues, lies in the diffusion and the impoverishment of the spectacle at a remove, the raggedness of music taken by the wind, song adrift and in tatters in a way that might have appealed, though perhaps not explicitly so, to T. S. Eliot and "O O O O that Shakespeherian rag."

In Baudelaire's poem, an analogy develops between the multiple poverties and riches perceived in the widow's "parfum de hautain vertu," her spectacular "éclatante" appearance, and the poverty upon which the poetic richness of a "lambeau de musique" depends. In "Les Petites Vieilles," the poet proclaimed the fecundity and poetic potential of "ruines" in their diversity. Recall Baudelaire's sentiments on photography and his feeling that it should be praised for preserving ruins for the contemplation of future generations. Here, however, he would prefer to leave these "ruines," their echoing, their acoustic preservation, and the exaltation of their aesthetic, to the widow, as seen through the poet's eye and heard with the poet's ear.

The rich ambiguous play of these phrases and motifs owes in part to the acoustic experience and acoustic space inflecting the linguistic expression, enabled by the raggedness of the "lambeau de musique," something to be encountered and contemplated differently if caught in the grip of a "daguerréotype acoustique" or the gramophone to come—"she smoothes her hair with automatic hand." In such a way, the newness of hearing and of being heard amidst crowds of the modern city conditions Baudelaire's poetics of urban acoustics, his "parrying" of the city's noise, if you will, in which there exists an aesthetics of deep listening, beauty and evil in the sounds that shape the play of solitude and multitude.[86]

Manet's "Music in the Tuileries" (1862) (see Figure 23), a painting that scholars have often paired with Baudelaire's "Les Veuves," offers a painterly angle on the audiovisual interplay in "Les Veuves."[87] Comparing the two works can help reveal the overheard acoustics of sociability and class in the situation of these public *plein air* concerts—the internal conflicts and divisions that, as Sima Godfrey has proposed, are present in "Music in the Tuileries."[88] Specifically, Godfrey argues that critics have overlooked the figure of a shadowy woman dressed in black, holding a child, at the very compositional center of the painting (a widow perhaps, as Godfrey proposes); hence, there is an important poetic intertext between the poem and the painting, in which Baudelaire is himself depicted, though hazily so.[89] Indeed the art critic Hippolyte Babou, who objected to the painting's indistinct modeling of faces and figures, its illegible "taches," would call that portrait "la tache Baudelaire," which we might translate as the Baudelairean blot or, harsher yet, the Baudelairean stain.[90]

Considered in this context, it is striking and ironic that Baudelaire describes the majestic widow in "Les Veuves" as "une tache si éclatante." As Godfrey argues, the radically provocative handling of paint in "Music in the Tuileries," which the critics considered offensive "taches," constituted Manet's means of grappling with the paradoxes of modernity, of rendering the movement and vitality of everyday urban life in paint.

A similar paradoxical movement animates Baudelaire's "tache si éclatante," something present in the specifics of his language and in his repetition of the word "éclatant(e)" to describe the widow at the end of the poem. Both "tache" and "éclatant" can signify a visual shock, a dazzling spectacular image or vision about which the speaker of the poem is explicit: "Singulière vision!" he calls the

TATTERED SOUND: BAUDELAIRE'S PARIS, NOISE, AND THE PROTOPHONOGRAPHIC 131

Figure 23. Édouard Manet. *Music in the Tuileries*. Oil on canvas, 1862. © National Gallery of Art, London / Art Resource, NY.

majestic widow. The word "éclatant," however, also has acoustic meanings and connotations, shared with the word "éclat" from which it derives.[91] The *Littré* dictionary gives one definition of 'éclatant' as "that which makes a great noise . . . by extension, the one who has sonority [*qui fait un grand bruit . . . par extension, qui a de la sonorité*]," and a definition of "éclat" as "sudden and violent sound or noise." There is yet another important meaning of "éclat," which the *Littré* dictionary gives as "a detached part of a solid body by a sudden, instantaneous force [*partie détachée d'un corps dur par une force subite, instantanée*]." Even as the widow makes for a startling contrast, a startling "tache éclatante," she becomes at the same time detached, a *tache détachée*. She becomes a "partie détachée d'un corps," a social body in both Baudelaire's poem and Manet's painting.

On this question of being sonorous, of having sonority, Jacques Derrida suggests in a brief reflection on the myth of Echo and Narcissus that Echo ". . . overflows with love. Her love overflows the calls of Narcissus, whose fall or whose sending she seems simply to reproduce."[92] Similarly, Baudelaire's majestic widow, overflowing with 'éclat,' overflowing with sound and song, "*si éclatante*," becomes singularly detached, like the "lambeau de musique." As she recedes into solitude, she gives back a sound, a sonority of music that has become detached in the experience of urban public spectacle. This is perhaps, in part, why we don't see any performing musicians depicted in Manet's painting, no explicit reference to the performance of music beyond the performance of social decorum shaped in the presence of that music. Music has been detached from the source and immediate space of its performance, and resides momentarily in the ears of all the elegant Parisians Manet has depicted. Composer Jacques Offenbach also appears in the painting, the composer whose music, as Siegfried Kracauer relates, was once described as reflecting "the gay tumult of the boulevards, like the shell that preserves within itself the roaring of the waves" (90).[93]

Rags of music mingle with the more fashionable dress of this worldly, elegant crowd assembled in the Tuileries, in which no rags are visible, only audible. For Baudelaire, the ability to hear the echo of these rags, these "infrasons," resides with the artist in the realm of the impalpable and the indefinite, the realm of the "taches." Indeed, one art critic, in 1863, described Manet's "Music in the Tuileries" as "un charivari de palette," a barb at the painter's palette, technique, and style in the form of an intriguing conjunction of noise and color, an idea of "seeing noise," akin to, once again, but different from Nadar's idea of the acoustic daguerreotype.[94]

These rags, "infrasons," or "sparks of contingency" are not, at least not yet, the stuff of an auditory imagination forged on the idea of an acoustic daguerreotype, on the idea of mechanical reproducibility to come. Baudelaire grants, instead, that special power of collecting song and poetic listening amidst the city's noise to the widow, the widow as an allegory of deep loss and modern urban life more broadly, as an echo of the possibility of sound recovered for art and poetry in an artful way in the city, a way of being sonorous and having sonority.

Coda, a Voice by Gas Light: "Mademoiselle Bistouri"

At the end of the third section of the "Painter of Modern Life" essay, Baudelaire describes the onset of night in the city: "But night has fallen. It is the bizarre and doubtful hour when the curtains of the sky are drawn, when cities become illuminated. Gas leaves its mark on the purple of twilight [*Le gaz fait tache sur la pourpre du couchant*]."[95]

Gas lighting technology was and is still known primarily, as in this passage, for its visual marks, its visible "taches" on the twilight and the nocturnal cityscapes of the nineteenth century, dramatically so in the Paris of Haussmannization. But, as Antoine Compagnon reminds us, gas lighting was not a uniquely visual phenomenon: "The sonority of the word is modern, foreign to the French language, and it figures in several terms with suggestive etymologies. That sonority intrigued Baudelaire."⁹⁶

In addition to the sonority of the word, gas was used to examine the sonority of speech itself at the time, namely in the scientific research of Rudolph Koenig (1832–1901), a Prussian instrument maker who immigrated to Paris to launch a career in the study of acoustics and voice visualization, inspired in large part by the theories and work of Hermann von Helmholtz; Koenig also worked with Scott on the phonautograph.⁹⁷ Among other devices, Koenig built an instrument called a "flame manometer" that worked with an array of mirrors and gaslit flames to visualize vocal figures, such as vowel sounds (see Figure 24). Koenig first demonstrated the apparatus to public audiences at the London Exposition of 1862. A speaking voice would modulate the heights and intensities of a flame by altering the amount of gas available to the burner.

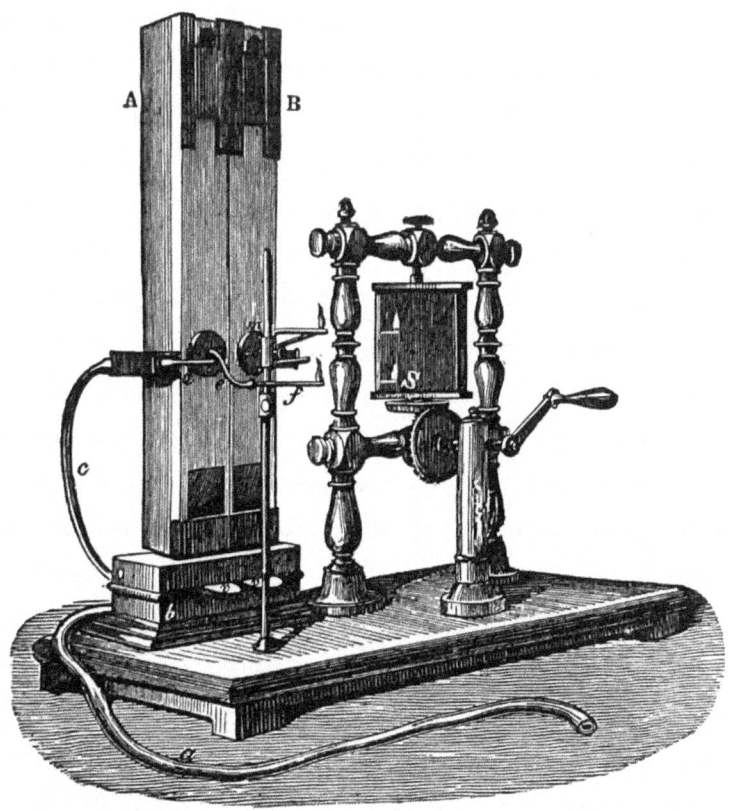

Figure 24. Rudolph Koenig's Flame Manometer. From H. Holbrook Curtis, *Voice Building and Tone Placing* (New York: D. Appleton and Company, 1914), 102.

If much recent scholarly attention to Baudelaire's "Mademoiselle Bistouri" centers on the text as the only poem in Baudelaire's oeuvre in which photography is explicitly named and invoked, how could we possibly read this poem in relation to sound technology and acoustics?[98] Here is one possibility. And it begins with this question: How might we read the narrator's experience of hearing a stranger's voice in the city street "aglow in flickering gaslight [*sous les éclairs du gaz*]"?[99] We can say that the gas lights the street, lights the narrator, lights the woman who has taken his arm, but what happens when we say that the gas lights the voice as well? That gas lights the woman's enigmatic question "Monsieur, are you a doctor? [*Vous êtes médecin, monsieur?*]" What, then, are the implications of a gaslit voice here, a gaslit spoken inquiry? Would it render the human voice less threatening, less mysterious because one is then more likely to see the source of that voice? Or would it be more mysterious because of the half-light play in the flickering intensities of the "éclairs"?

When we read the poem in the context of Koenig's gas flame manometer, we can situate the dialogue of the poem (and especially the voice heard by the speaker at the beginning) within an era when the nuances of human speech flickered in the gaslit mirrors of Koenig's machine in like fashion to the features of this woman "with wide-open eyes, light makeup, hair floating in the breeze with the strings of her bonnet," as I would emphasize "aglow in flickering gaslight [*sous les éclairs du gaz*]."

If so much of what follows in the poem speaks to the fetishization of doctors, photographs (specifically photographic portraits), and lithographic portraits, then Koenig's flame manometer (and the discourses on visualizing sound, the "graphical acoustics" and voice visualization studies, of which it formed part) allows for a reading of the voice heard in the street, the auditory encounter, to acquire a fetishistic quality as well. Before sight, touch and hearing are the sensory channels for the encounter with the "unhoped-for enigma [*énigme inespérée*]."[100] The enigma of the human voice heard by gaslight was in other circles (namely Koenig's) submitted to visualization and scientific investigation. In that context, gaslight serves as the source of illumination and knowledge, an unravelling of an enigma. In this poem, gaslight sets the stage for mystery and the deepening of the enigma.

Near the end of the poem, the speaker's question about Mademoiselle Bistouri's "peculiar passion" and her doleful response, "I don't know ... I don't remember," constitute the last, we presume, parting verbal exchange between the speaker and the mysterious woman. The detail that the woman averted her eyes as she spoke, "en détournant les yeux," accentuates the "air très triste" while separating sight from speech. Their encounter begins and ends with speech absent the meeting of the eyes. In the first instance, it is the urban situation, the play of the chance encounter, that produces or allows for this separation. In the second, the woman's averted eyes arise out of a heightened emotional state of fear or sadness, as the text would imply. The tension between sight and speech frames the encounter on both ends.

Here, then, in this field of audiovisual tension are lodged the strange encounter represented in the poem, the modern urban experience of the chance encounter in the street, strong emotions, and an evocation of contemporary explorations of the conditions, urban and technological, for distinctly modern ways of both separating and uniting speech and vision, speech and urban phenomena.

Mademoiselle Bistouri desires a more permanent visual form of the poem's speaker, a lasting tangible material visual portrait, but when she must answer to his most probing, penetrating, indeed surgical of questions, she cannot look at him. Now, we could examine her averted eyes in purely visual terms, in terms of a visual economy of desire and exchange. But the auditory expands the field of possibilities. Like Champfleury's daguerreotype story, we are left with a voice highlighted and suspended in the situation of visual photographic portraiture: her eyes are averted, and her voice is in an indeterminate suspended state. Her last words in the poem thus acquire a lingering ghostly eternal side. Mlle Bistouri's words hang in the air in a way that suggests a loss in Baudelaire's familiar poetic register of urban melancholy. At the same time, her words suggest a kind of danger and foreboding, a presentiment that her words, "I don't know . . . I don't remember," might be seized by some unknown agent or device, gazed at avidly, dissected under a flickering flame ("sous les éclairs du gaz") by gas that leaves a mark ("fait tache"), and then filed away like a photograph.

4

The Amazing Chorus

Whitman and the Sound of New York City

Recording Whitman: Performing for the Machine

Walt Whitman, in the lyric inspiration drawn from the modern city, depended on a certain sharing of voices, noises, and sounds to both lose and find himself within the urban crowd.[1] The poet, even as he sang his "Song of Myself," was in a way drawn out of himself.

Like poetic inspiration, but with different means and effect, technology could also draw poets and performers out of themselves; technology could literally and figuratively take their voices out of their bodies. In the Thomas Edison Archives, two letters, each dated February 14, 1889, attest to the possibility of acquiring a sound recording of Whitman with a then recently improved version of the phonograph.[2] In 1992, a sound recording came to light of what some believed to be Whitman's voice reciting four lines from his late poem "America," first published in 1888.[3] While debate and doubt about the authenticity of the recording persist in the absence of any written testimonials about such a recording from the poet himself or from his friend Horace Traubel, who kept scrupulous records of their daily interactions during the time of the presumed recording, the letters from the Edison Archive, though brief, speak to a broader cultural impulse to preserve the sound of the poet's voice for posterity.

Tyler Hoffman offers one distinctive angle for thinking about Whitman's relationship to mechanical sound reproducibility as a product of an idea and ideal of performance in Whitman's poetry and poetic readings, veritable performances of his writing, for example in his public readings during the Civil War.[4] Beyond Hoffman's biographical point that Whitman "came of age with the phonograph," I want to argue that Whitman textualizes listening and "sounding" in his poetry, thus articulating an aesthetic of acoustic recording and vibration born out of his encounter with the modern city.

The city becomes, for Whitman, a space of singular resonance, one that he could speak into and listen through, one that might preserve the poetry born out of such sounding.[5] Indeed Whitman often conceived of *Leaves of Grass* as something other than a book, something, instead, more like a living voice: "This is no book, but more a man, within whose breast the common heart is throbbing so much. These are no printed leaves, human lips O friend for your sake freely speaking."[6] Urban life, and particularly its acoustic qualities, offered Whitman a means to shape the "liveness" of that voice, those freely speaking human lips, together with the dream of acoustic reproducibility. Whitman conceived of voices buried in the streets of New York as still living, still vibrating, accompanied by deaths that differ in kind from the death in technology some associated with phonographic preservation in its early years.

Whitman was not the only poet or performer whose voice Edison sought to capture and preserve with the phonograph in those years. Alfred, Lord Tennyson used a phonograph to record himself reciting poetry in the early 1890s, as did one of the foremost Shakespearean actors of the era, Henry Irving.[7] A witness to Irving's first experience talking into the machine reported that he and other witnesses were surprised to hear something other than Irving's normal stage voice, that indeed the machine had "frightened [Irving] out of his own voice."[8] Irving's experience could be considered something of an acoustic analogue to Champfleury's "Legend of the Daguerreotypist," the irony in Irving's case being that a machine supposed to preserve the human voice frightened the person out of their normal speaking voice, leaving only the body and perhaps a shell of a voice behind. Faced with the phonograph, of Henry Irving, only a body remained! The phonograph could both take the living voice out of Irving while taking Irving out of his own living voice, thus destabilizing self-identity in the experience of a new medium.[9] We can imagine that Irving, faced with this strange new device, may have wondered: Who, beyond the witnesses to the event of this recording, will listen to my performance? And for how many ages hence? In such a way the phonograph, in this situation, from Irving's perspective, could be understood as a metonymy of disembodied future audiences. Irving's voice became disembodied in the encounter with a potentially mass disembodied audience.

I want to pause over Irving's reaction to performing for the machine, and ask: If we cannot know for sure of Whitman's own possible experience with Edison's phonograph, how else might we think of Whitman—the poet who famously described a certain acoustics of the urban crowd thusly: "A call in the midst of the crowd, my own voice"—in relation to sound technologies of the era? Throughout *Leaves of Grass*, the urban crowd returns the poet's voice with renewal, democratic en-masse individuality, providing a path to the soul of communal love and democratic community. In his encounter with the acoustics of urban life, Whitman's will to capture "all sounds," the exalted and the lowly, with a truly democratic ear, anticipates the phonograph's mechanical ability, later in the century, to capture the totality of the acoustic field.[10] Whereas Irving initially appeared to be "frightened out of his voice" and alienated by the phonograph, Whitman found in the sound of the urban crowd a means to both take leave of and return to his own voice.[11] In this way, Whitman helped to articulate a cultural impulse to preserve sound, of the kind that would, in turn, inspire the idea of recording him with the phonograph. Sounding within the city authorized and opened up a new possibility for the American poet of hearing and of being heard, of releasing the "living and buried speech ... always vibrating here" in the streets of New York City. The ways in which he releases that poetry and conceives of its urban vibrations are the central issues I examine here.

The "sounds of the city," as Whitman hears and registers them in his texts, frame urban space as a kind of training ground for the encounter with disembodied voices, indeterminate acoustics and shocking sounds in nineteenth-century New York. While Whitman wonders about the fate of the literary voice when confronted with the rising uproar of the urban crowd—as Poe, Baudelaire, and Cros also wondered—he discovers different modes of registering and negotiating that uproar in his texts. Whitman shares with Poe and Baudelaire an intense corporeal relationship to the sounds of his city while the rapturous nature of that relationship differs from Baudelaire's "ragged" urban sounds and Poe's unsettled thresholds of urban and technological listening. With Whitman, the city can itself be read as a kind of acoustic machine, a place of acoustic burial and retrieval that can be seized as a mechanism for greater poetic sounding.[12] Whitman draws sounds out of the city for accrual into his poetic language. Urban space absorbs sound and gives it back; the city, for the American poet, is ever resonant, ever full of acoustic life, as, once again, in this line from "Song of Myself": "What living and buried speech is always vibrating here."

Whitman and France

In his poem "Salut au Monde," Whitman declares, "I am a real Parisian."[13] This line is but one piece of his oeuvre animating scholarly inquiry into his importance for French poetics and a transatlantic urban imaginary between nineteenth-century Paris and New York. At mid-century, Parisians were often looking to New York while New Yorkers were often looking to Paris for comparative views on the daily life and aspirations of a growing metropolis.[14] Whitman was one of those New Yorkers thinking of Paris in comparison to the new American metropolis, and his connections with France are deep and manifold, from his attraction to the French language and use of French words throughout *Leaves of Grass* to the poems specifically dedicated to France and its history, as in "O Star of France [1870–1871]."[15] Despite the depths of this engagement with French thought, politics, and literature, Whitman came to know of Baudelaire relatively late in his career, and his knowledge of Baudelaire is both difficult to determine and generally thought of as marginal when compared to his knowledge of other French writers such as Rousseau and Hugo.[16] There is no mention of Whitman in any of Baudelaire's writings.

Whitman's representations of urban life often focus on the restless exchange of glances between city-dwellers, the vitality of crowds, and the intensely visual (perhaps even panoptic or ocularcentric, as some contend) qualities of urban life.[17] These are all compelling grounds for comparison with Baudelaire, as Laure Katsaros has recently explored. On urbanites' looks at each other, Baudelaire's "À une passante" and Whitman's "To a Stranger" are especially captivating in this comparative regard.[18]

At the same time, Whitman also sings of a distinctive urban acoustics, a kind of overhearing in a state of fluid immersion in the city streets, as when Whitman takes his own distinctive "bath of the multitude" in the crowds of Manhattan. How, then, does the acoustic "turbulence" of the urban crowd, which Whitman so often represents, inflect his language and relate to the visual spectacle of New York? Katsaros, for one, argues that Whitman's poetry has a powerful capacity to absorb the sounds of the city and that his language plays on both the harmony and dissonance of urban sound and poetic language. It is remarkable, she argues, that Whitman not only brings the city's noise into his poetry but also the slang, the very language of the street, hence eroding distinctions between high and low language. In this way, he redefines lyric poetry for the modern city, his sensitivity to the sounds of the city registered in the very sounds of his language.[19]

Such poetic effects, together with how Whitman conceives of listening and sounding out in the city, relate to discourses on sound preservation and the dream of reproducibility. In the way Whitman dramatizes rapt listening and poetic "sounding" within the city's "turbulent chorus," his urban lyric voice depends upon this noisy turbulence, the proximity between sounds of the modern city and his poetic language, and how these two are brought together.[20]

Sounding Out the City

In section twenty-six of "Song of Myself," the poet introduces an expansive catalog of sounds with this arresting declaration:

> Now I will do nothing but listen,
> To accrue what I hear into this song, to let sounds contribute
>   toward it.[21]

Though it may seem like a passive role, this resolution to do "nothing but listen," such intense attention to one sense over the others, can also be conceived in a more active light. It is a difficult activity to sustain, especially in the presence of overwhelming visual stimuli. Near the end of this section, for instance, the poet's body becomes drawn into the sounds, as he proclaims: "I hear the key'd cornet, it glides quickly in through my ears,/It shakes mad-sweet pangs through my belly and breast."[22] This intensely physical response to the sounds fashions the poet's body itself into a kind of resonant receptor for all sounds. Sounds make themselves felt across the expanse of the poet's body in vibration.[23] The catalog includes natural, rural, and urban sounds in a process of spirited fusion:

> I hear the sound I love, the sound of the human voice,
> I hear all sounds running together, combined, fused or following
> Sounds of the city and sounds out of the city . . . [24]

These lines feature as the epigraph to R. Murray Schafer's foundational *The Soundscape: Our Sonic Environment and the Tuning of the World* (1977), a book that has called attention to, among other things, the threat of noise pollution from modern industry in our sonic environment. In the soundscape of Whitman's poem, modern industry and technology find expression in both the visual and acoustic newness of a subject often depicted in *Leaves of Grass*, the drama of firefighters in the city, as the poet continues with: "The ring of alarm-bells, the cry of fire, the whirr of swift-streaking engines and hose-carts with premonitory tinkles and color'd lights." The speed associated with these sounds, the "ring" and the "whirr," together with the artificial illumination of the "color'd lights," reflects decisive changes in the pace and the "premonitory" dimension of the modern urban environment. Color and the sound of the "tinkles" are both indicative of the kind of speed and sometimes perilous commotion of the city, the dangers of stepping into urban space without a sensorium sufficiently adapted or attuned to such things as these auditory and visual signs.[25] These sounds also represent a new relation to time, something reflected in the mechanical industrial sounds cataloged in the next line: "The steam-whistle, the solid roll of the train of approaching cars." Such sounds give an impression of how speed is heard in the city, the particular kinds of aural indexes of time and rhythm that exist in the phenomenology of urban space. At the same time, "color'd lights" signal danger while also forming part of a nascent aesthetic of artificial illumination in and of vivid colors.[26] Whitman draws an urban tableau that could be described as kaleidophonic in its insistence on sound and light together in rapid motion.

The heightened use of alliteration and assonance in this section furthermore underscores the intensity and rapture involved in the poet's listening. He hears "the bravuras of birds," and sounds that are described as "fused or following." In another line he revels in hearing: "The heave'e'yo of stevedores unloading ships by the wharves . . ." This assonance, the "eave" of "heave'e'yo" and the "eve" of "stevedores," suggests an identification of the worker with the call that accompanies and indexes that labor. Hence, the call, or the written approximation of its sound, emerges in part out of the word "stevedore" itself. This poetic line thus enacts the process of "accrual" of sounds into song.

The catalog of sounds in this section of the poem parallels an earlier passage in section eight of the poem, one which represents the particular sounds of the urban street in demotic language, a language that seems born of the street itself: "The blab of the pave, tires of carts, sluff of boot-soles, talk of the promenaders,/The heavy omnibus, the driver with his interrogating thumb, the clank of the shod shoes on the granite floor, [. . .]."[27] In particular, the phrase "the blab of the pave" evokes the heterogeneity of the street's noise; speech mingles with noise. "Blab" and "sluff" are, as Katsaros notes, instances where Whitman allows urban sound to carve out a place in his poetic language. On this point, she suggests: "As he discovered the poetry distilled from the clashing sounds of the city, Whitman allowed his own voice to be overwhelmed by inanimate sounds, and by the 'awful din of the streets.'"[28] In this way, the language is stretched between the acoustic life of the city and the poet's self, akin to the way, in "Mannahatta," the poet discovers that what there is in the city, there is also in its "aboriginal name," this being "a word, liquid, sane, unruly, musical, self-sufficient."[29]

Poe was also one to stress the very sound of the Algonquin name of the island. In his "Doings of Gotham" series, Poe questions the use of "Manhattan" in place of "Mannahatta." He asks, "Why do we persist in *de-euphonizing* the true names?" (emphasis in original).[30] Poe himself uses "Mannahatta" throughout the article: "I have been roaming far and wide over this island of Mannahatta."[31] Whitman, in another poem titled "Mannahatta" in the First Annex, expands on the beauty of the Algonquin name: "My city's fit and noble name resumed, choice aboriginal name, with marvelous beauty, [. . .]."[32] Both Poe and Whitman share an impulse to preserve the memory of the aboriginal language by stressing the sound of one of its last vestiges, by celebrating the euphony of "Mannahatta." The two writers thus anticipate one of the early uses of the phonograph as an ethnographic tool to preserve the sounds of vanishing languages and voices speaking those languages.[33]

Whitman and Poe differ, however, on the point of affective response to city noise. To recall, Poe characterizes city noise (in Whitman's own Brooklyn, to be precise) as a source of frustration and madness, and by extension, one could argue, part of an urbanizing societal force that "de-euphonizes" the indigenous names and language, covering them over, burying them, along with any trace of Algonquin history.[34] The madness produced by that noise could also serve as a source of literary inspiration and creation for Poe, prompting him to wonder how such acoustical burial could be imagined and shaped into literary narrative. The unsettled burial of sound in stories such as "The Black Cat" and "The Tell-Tale Heart," as we have seen, conjoins anxieties about psychic and physical interiorities with urban spaces. Buried sounds and voices coincide most often with madness and murder, but also with ideas for new and strange ways of hearing. For Whitman, on the other hand, such noise, while also a source of poetic inspiration, generally calls for celebration. Instead of the "de-euphonizing" that Poe found in the transformation of Mannahatta into Manhattan, Whitman seeks a means of re-euphonizing the sounds and "buried speech" of New York.

There is a moment, however, in "Song of Myself" that offers a point of comparison between Whitman and Poe on the unsettled aesthetics of urban sounds and noises, when Whitman turns to an agonized side of the city more typical, as Alan Trachtenberg has remarked, of Baudelaire or T. S. Eliot, and, as I would add, of Poe as well. This, again, is the eighth section of "Song of Myself," one marked by jarring violent juxtapositions. It begins, for instance, with the speaker looking in on a baby sleeping in its cradle, shifts to young lovers climbing a hill, then suddenly veers toward violence and death with a suicide and pistol. The speaker then catalogs a multitude of urban sounds, "the blab of the pave" and "talk of the promenaders," together with "groans of over-fed or half-starved who fall sunstruck or in fits."[35] This catalog reaches an apex with the startling phrases: "What living and buried speech is always vibrating here, what howls restrain'd by decorum."[36]

In the final section of "Song of Myself," the poet announces what seems like the undoing of the "accrual" of sounds into song, the release of the "buried speech" and these "howls restrain'd by decorum." He declares: "I too am not a bit tamed, I too am untranslatable. / I sound my barbaric yawp over the roofs of the world."[37] Sounds escape in a process of more formidable sounding, in a "yawp," seemingly less refined than the "song" Whitman conceives, and more akin to the "blab of the pave," or to the city that bellows in Baudelaire's "Les Aveugles." A third element emerges between "sound" and "song," this third being a kind of noise, the "yawp," signifying tensions between language, noise, and sound. "Sound," here, employed as a verb, signifies a sonorous release as if in response to the question posed earlier in section twenty-five: "Walt, you contain enough, why don't you let it out then?"[38] The "yawp," then, is in one respect an instance of Whitman's affection for colloquial diction and the vernacular (in the same passage he also uses the word "gab" as slang for speech).[39] The sounding out of this "barbaric yawp" is a means for Whitman to rough up and revitalize poetic language, and in particular language drawn from the noise of the urban street, the fusion between what he catalogs as "sounds of the city, sounds out of the city."[40]

The "sounds of the city," in section eight of "Song of Myself," however, meet resistance on their way to becoming a "yawp" or a "howl." Whitman evokes latent unrest in urban acoustics for these effusions, a condition specific to the unsettled and troubled side of the city. In this section, the materiality of the built environment is itself made to sound out, to be a medium upon which the poet is meant to play. Even as Whitman will often describe what he hears from the city as a "chorus," in this particular section of "Song of Myself" the city seems more like a tense musical instrument equally ready to snap or fall into silence. For the sounds cataloged in this section and urban space, poetic "sounding" signifies less by "tending inward" and "tending outward," as described in section fifteen of the poem, than by setting off, in effect by touching the resonant material so that it might sound out on its own. Whitman represents the city as a space of singular resonance.

The city's crowds lead to a description of the space these crowds inhabit: "The impassive stones that receive and return so many echoes."[41] As if to allow those stones to resound, Whitman provides examples in the next line of some startling and dissonant echoes in the city: "What groans of over-fed or half-starv'd who fall sunstruck or in fits." The following line turns from the enunciation of echoes to reflection, once again, on the space of the city and how sound lives within it: "What living and buried speech is always vibrating here, . . ." This "vibration" might, in one respect, be read as an affirmation of the city as an eternally vibrant source for poetry. That celebratory tone is, however, immediately upset by what follows: "What howls restrain'd by decorum." Such "howls" connote the social inequities and strife evoked in this passage about the city, close in form and content to Whitman's lament for a dead prostitute in "The City Dead-House." Yet, the tone implies that, despite their discordance, these "howls" need to find an "openness" of voice, as in the "open voices" of the longer of Whitman's two "Mannahatta" poems, the antipode of the "howls restrained."[42]

The task falls then to the poet to unearth this speech, to act like the "impassive stones" and "return" the "howls" to the text of the poem and to the city as well. In "The City Dead-House," the speaker partly achieves this feat, effectively tuning out the city's "clangor" to discover echoes from the dead prostitute's body as a "house of life, erewhile talking and laughing."[43] Whether in so doing the poet becomes one with the resonant materiality of the city itself, or whether he stands aside and occupies another position, remains in question. In "The City Dead-House," the description of the prostitute's body as "that immortal house more than all the rows of dwellings ever built," and as "tenement of a soul," suggests unity, however fraught, between poetic text, human body, soul, and the built environment of New York.[44] But in section eight of "Song of Myself," that union of poetic self and urban environment remains hanging in the balance.

Eternal vibrations, which the poet describes at the end of the section as "resonance," could be read as metaphor for the poet's activity, his resistance to the "decorum" that would stifle the howl, his response to that social restraint. The poet, however, remains strangely apart from that vibration and resonance: "I mind them or the show or the resonance of them—I come and I depart."[45] In effect, by solely "minding" these things, by acting like something of a bystander, he resists becoming a resonant body himself; he does not himself vibrate with the sounds of these voices, these examples of urban discord.[46]

Though this "minding" could be read as a failure, like the kind of "evil" of passivity and muteness the poet describes in section six of "Crossing Brooklyn Ferry," it leaves open the possibility for the poet to act upon the city differently. Instead of being something like the ever-active resolute listener he becomes in section twenty-six of "Song of Myself," or the alembic through which all these sounds pass, are consumed, and in that way refined into song or roughed up into a "yawp," here he might function more like the force that enables or touches off the speech buried in the built environment. He presides over a city that he hears from a distance, within which he perceives the resonant potential of social unrest or rapturous material.[47] His task as listener then tends toward hearing the undertones. As "chanter" here, he does not sing so much as he exhales a breath alone, absent articulate language or music, across the resonant valves of the city, just as he would wish to impart, as life-giving substance, "one breath from my tremulous lips" to the dead prostitute in "The City Dead-House." The poet is like the wind that blows through the city at night, which, as Michel Chion describes in a meditation on the listener in the city, makes us hear the buildings and alleyways, the very materiality of the built environment, after the noise of the day has subsided.[48] Whitman modulates his singing voice from "blab" to "yawp" to pure exhalation to sound out the latent acoustic dynamics of life in New York.

Indeed, in Whitman's "That Music Always Round Me," the speaker declares, "I hear not the volumes of sound merely, I am moved by the exquisite meanings."[49] Within the chorus described in the poem, he hears "a transparent base shuddering lusciously under and through the universe."[50] Similarly, in "Sparkles from the Wheel," the speaker tells of how he joins a group of children in the city to observe a knife-grinder at work and describes "the attentive, quiet children, the loud, proud, restive base of the streets."[51] The poet reveals, however, that he needed to learn how to listen in this way. "That Music Always Round Me" begins with the speaker revealing "that music always round me, unceasing, unbeginning, yet long untaught I did not hear."[52] These poems, together with "Song of Myself," embody and bespeak a certain acoustic training. The poems textualize city space and sound as a kind of Benjaminian "training ground" for distinguishing between different registers of sound, to which the poet then lends musical terms, and upon which he plays with his breath and his language to suggest different possibilities of acoustic preservation, inscription, and recovery.

Omnibuses and Choruses: Sounding with Mass Transit

A passage in Whitman's *Specimen Days*, titled "Omnibus Jaunts and Drivers," suggests a different origin for such "sounding." Whitman seizes part of the city machinery, its emergent mass transit system, for a purpose other than pure mobility. The omnibus ride becomes a kind of mechanical device that blends deafening noise, panoramic spectatorship, and greater poetic "sounding out."

Whitman describes with evident fondness his experiences of riding up and down Broadway, Fifth Avenue, Madison Avenue, and Twenty-Third Street. Central to the experience he describes are the activities of intently listening (often to stories told by the omnibus drivers) and declaiming poetry. He tells of the "exhilaration" of "listening to some yarn (and the most vivid yarns ever spun, and the rarest mimicry)."[53] Of equal if not greater importance, however, were Whitman's own declamations along the bus routes. As if buttressed by what he describes as the "street-bass," he tells of how he often went "declaiming some stormy passage from Julius Caesar or Richard (you could roar as loudly as you chose in that heavy, dense, uninterrupted street-bass)."[54] That kind of "roaring" attests to a freedom in what might otherwise be perceived as an assault, the ever-present din. The declamation seems as if it is lost or drowned out, but in such a way that it enables the poet and his performances.

In another account of his omnibus declamations, Whitman conveys a sense of wonder: "How often I spouted this . . . on the Broadway coaches, in the awful din of the streets. In that seething mass—that noise, chaos, bedlam—what is one voice, more or less: one single voice added, thrown in, joyously mingled in the amazing chorus?"[55] A familiar jauntiness characterizes this account, the way the voice is "thrown in" and how, as a lone voice, it is susceptible to loss. Anonymity in an acoustic field, the sounds of nobody and everybody collide at once. Nonetheless, the tone of the passage suggests, at the same time, the possibility of sympathetic resonance, wherein the "single voice" and the "amazing chorus" amplify each other with reciprocal force. Individual sounds and voices dissolve in a process that results in greater collective amplitude.

Whitman's delight in the sensations of an omnibus ride, a notable development in the history of modern urban mass transit, contrasts with Baudelaire's representation of the conveyance in, for example, "Les Petites Vieilles," where the old women are described as "trembling with the rolling roar of the omnibuses [frémissant au fracas roulant des omnibus]."[56] Where Baudelaire represents the Parisian omnibus as a violent force to shake the human body with its rhythms and noise, Whitman exploits the omnibus as a device for amplifying poetry. He takes hold of the city with its modern conveyances and wide streets as a kind of mechanical device to speak through and into so that he might be transported—and so that he might transport others—in a distinctly other way. In this way, he resists the capitalist organization of urban space and mobility, the commodity logic mapped onto the city that dictates the paths traced by its residents.[57]

In the *Specimen Days* account of the omnibus rides, Whitman characterizes the noise of the street as a bass, as a comparatively low frequency, "heavy" and "dense." This "street-bass" could be understood as the support, a low sibilance, for the higher frequencies of Whitman's poetic declamations and the stories told by the omnibus drivers. Whitman demonstrates his sensitive and developed ear for the city street. In this evocation of low frequencies, we might hear the poet seeking to do away with distinctions between the high and the low, as Katsaros suggests about this anecdote. We might also think of the constitution of a new lyric self sounding by and on different frequencies, a way of thinking about a sonorous human body in Whitman's poetry, a loosening of contours around listening (or speaking) subjects and listened-to objects.[58]

Hence the noise of the street affects the poet in a way such that noise and speech are enfolded in each other, breaking down not only barriers between high and low but between subject and object. The aggressive quality of sonic assault that we find at times in Baudelaire, in a line such as "La rue assourdisante autour de moi hurlait," or in the "cri strident du vitrier," this sonic impact figures in Whitman's representations as something to be celebrated and redirected. For Whitman, noise acts as a kind of salutary, immersive force. While it may deafen or drown out, it also enables, activates, and conditions a voice and a body attuned to the sound and rhythm of the streets. The "barbaric yawp" of "Song of Myself" thus derives in part from Whitman's discovery of a license to "roar" and perform in the street's noise, a deep bodily, even tactile, connection with the urban soundscape. Noise buoys Whitman's poetic voice. Whitman himself appears to have anticipated such questions about the roots of his poetry when at the conclusion of the "Omnibus" reminiscence, he says in another parenthesis:

> (I suppose the critics will laugh heartily, but the influence of those Broadway omnibus jaunts and drivers and declamations and escapades undoubtedly enter'd into the gestation of *Leaves of Grass*.)[59]

To recall Ross Chambers's claim in Chapter 3 about Baudelaire's relation to urban noise, it being both "rival and model," we can say that, for Whitman, noise figures as a medium or texture to be inhabited, within which to "roar."[60] In that way, urban noise is perhaps more model than rival, though once again it could be described as both. The "street-bass" functions as rival in the sense that his declamations are drowned out, lost in a sea of voices and sounds, only to be recovered and reconstituted in his poetry. If there is an anxiety about being drowned out, Whitman responds with his own manner of absorbing noise into the text, so as to sound out more completely.

For Whitman, if the rivalry with noise exists, at least in his short prose pieces, it differs from the rivalry experienced by Baudelaire, not only in the jauntiness of Whitman's prose accounts (the poet's roar in a contest of decibels with the street) but in the way sound relates to life and death for each poet. Sounds of the modern city enliven and invigorate Whitman's language and verse while, for Baudelaire, urban sound can play upon the poetry as a "choc funèbre," deadening communication and assaulting life in urban space. Whitman parries this cacophonous shock by matching it, finding a place alongside it, in parallel, if not also within it.

Section forty-two of "Song of Myself," for instance, begins with the lines: "A call in the midst of the crowd, / My own voice, orotund sweeping and final."[61] Some ambiguity characterizes the relation between the call and the voice here. One might discern something like a momentary delay in self-recognition between the first and the second line, as if the speaker has become self-estranged in the crowd and does not immediately recognize his own voice as the call in its midst. A reading of the lines with this interpretation in mind might lay stress on the first two words of the second line, "My own," signaling something like a moment of self-possession, self-recognition, or a return to the self.[62]

However, the question and ambiguity of "owning" an individual voice in the crowd arises with another possible interpretation of the two lines: the speaker's "own voice" might signify a response to the call. This interpretation depends on a reading of the call in the "midst of the crowd" as that of another person, in the way Whitman's speakers often catch the glance of an individual in the crowd, as in the poems "To a Stranger" and "A Glimpse," or in "City of Orgies" when the speaker proclaims: "O Manhattan, your frequent and swift flash of eyes offering me love."[63] In this situation, stress could fall equally on "a call" and "my own voice" to emphasize the play of call and response.

Finally then, the "call"—whether emanating from the collective crowd or an individual within it—and the speaker's "own voice" could be heard as separate in the space of the text. The two are meant, however, to be heard and understood together as one and the same, in unity at least, if not in unison. Later in the same section the speaker declares: "This is the city, and I am one of the citizens, . . . Every thought that flounders in me the same flounders in them. / I know perfectly well my own egotism, / Know my omnivorous lines and must not write any less, / [. . .]."[64] The poet both speaks and hears himself through the crowd, while the crowd speaks and hears itself through the poet.[65] The noise of the crowd serves as the medium or texture of self-recognition, both as diffusion and unity, in the way that Whitman is ever configuring and reconfiguring the relation between the democratic individual and the democratic collective in *Leaves of Grass*.[66] The "omnivorous lines" themselves speak of the text's sonorous envelope in which the perception of a simultaneity of sounds and voices creates a distinctly acoustic field of self-other relations.

More so, perhaps, than an identification of the voice with the call or the voice as response to the call, it is the relay of vocal emanation and self-possession here amidst the noise of the crowd that speaks to the condition of modern urban life, where in the swift ceaseless current of bodies and voices, the two (the voice of the individual and the voice of the collective, if they can even be reduced to such stable positions with Whitman) are parried back and forth, unmoored from stable subject-object relations, immersed in dislocated auditory stimuli, amidst what the speaker calls in section thirty-three "the modern crowd as eager and fickle as any."[67] For Whitman, however, auditory and vocal dislocation do not signify loss or discordance in the way they do for Baudelaire. Whitman's voice amidst the New York crowd, if initially lost, if initially without perceptible source, is ultimately recoverable and reproducible. The poet qualifies his "own voice" as "sweeping, orotund, and final." Within a general democratizing sharing of voices, poetic voice blends with dislocated sounds and voices as an experience Whitman ultimately celebrates for its ability to gather together. For Baudelaire, on the other hand, acoustic dislocation and unstable resonances, as in "Les Veuves," and "Les Petites Vieilles," figure as social discordance, resulting in ambivalent and imperfect solitude, beauty in and of solitude of another sort.

Between Spectacle and Chorus:
Whitman's Urban Vision and Hearing

In Whitman's "Crossing Brooklyn Ferry," urban sensations are likened to material objects, "glories strung like beads."[68] Whitman's simile between overheard conversations in city streets and "beads" resembles Cros's simile in his poem "Inscription" between "beloved voices" and cameo portraits. Each poet finds a rapture and focused acoustic perception through love of others, a love that might be preserved by fixing sound in a material object. Whitman's expression of love for and within urban crowds, however, can falter when vocal resonance is blocked, when the kind of call and response activity I have examined in the previous sections falters. Urban "sounding out" in Whitman's "Crossing Brooklyn Ferry" offers a different perspective on eternal acoustic vibration in the city and the dangers of not fully achieving open resonance between self and others.

Philosopher William James has claimed, "Whitman felt the human crowd as rapturously as Wordsworth felt the mountains."[69] Whitman often celebrates the reciprocal and shared possibilities such intimacy with the crowd affords, together with the crowd as a modern phenomenon in and of itself, elevating it, as Larzer Ziff suggests, "out of the region of dark menace it inhabited in the minds of Poe and Emerson."[70]

This contrast between Whitman and Poe is especially pronounced on the level of sensory perception within the urban crowd. To recall, in Poe's short story "The Man of the Crowd," the narrator, surveying the crowd passing before him in London, marking out its constituents in a way not unlike Whitman's great catalogs, concludes with the maleficent effect it has on his senses: ". . . organ-grinders, monkey-exhibiters and ballad mongers, those who vended with those who sang; ragged artisans and exhausted laborers of every description, and all full of a noisy and inordinate vivacity which jarred discordantly upon the ear, and gave an aching sensation to the eye."[71] The eyes *and* ears of Poe's narrator suffer in equal measure. In contrast, Whitman's speaker in "Crossing Brooklyn Ferry," invoking those experiences of the city that serve as his "impalpable sustenance," calls upon "The glories strung like beads on my smallest *sights and hearings*, on the walk in the street and the passage over the river" (my emphasis).[72] In celebrating the glory of the multitude, the speaker emphasizes the sensory channels of vision and hearing in "the certainty of others, the life, love, sight, hearing of others" that he experiences crossing the ferry at sunset.[73] As opposed to the "discordance" and "ache" felt by Poe's narrator, Whitman's speaker finds "glories" and "certainty" in the crowd, a crowd that in this case adorns his senses with beads of rapture.

Whitman's hearings in "Crossing Brooklyn Ferry" differ from the majestic manner of hearing evoked in section three of his poem "Salut Au Monde." In that section, the poet surveys the sounds of the world, from the "continual echoes from the Thames" to "fierce French liberty songs," sonic phenomena that are comparatively more self-contained and focused than the "hearings."[74] In "Crossing Brooklyn Ferry," however, "hearings," in the plural, like the "beads" to which they are compared, suggest the aleatory and the fragmented. In their smallness, too, they further suggest a kind of sensory micro-perception, of the sort Jacques Rancière theorizes, a little mundane everyday impression. To recall from the Introduction, the kaleidophone employed small silvered beads of focused light to produce its "beautiful forms." As with the urban scenes of "Song of Myself," Whitman evokes urban experience in "Crossing Brooklyn Ferry" that could be described as both kaleidoscopic and kaleidophonic.

The idea of a "found voice" (akin to the way "found objects" became central to avant-garde artistic practices in the work of Duchamp and other modernist artists) may also help to describe the way speech is heard in this context.[75] "Hearings" become like objects in the city, their outlines at once sharpened in being found and blurred as they flow along with the great catalog of impressions. Whitman's openness to the "talk of the promenaders" or the discrete "hearings," perceived like stringed beads, in this way begins to resemble the experience of catching a "rag of music" ("*lambeau de musique*") in Baudelaire's "Les Veuves." While Baudelaire's "lambeau de musique" suggests a field of acoustic wreckage, a lament for "le vieux Paris," bearing the tatters of social division and class conflict to be remade into poetic beauty, Whitman's "hearings" exist already as a rapturous plurality of sounds and voices, both the poet's own and others'. The poet gathers these "hearings" together as reverence for what his city was becoming.

While Whitman's "talk of the promenaders" and his "hearing of others" also offer the poet acoustic debris to remake into poetry, these "beads" of urban experience ultimately contribute to the sense of timelessness, the generational bonds evoked in "Crossing Brooklyn Ferry." If in "Song of Myself" the restive strains of urban upheaval and misery are described as "always vibrating," the calls of the city sound out in "Crossing Brooklyn Ferry" as echoes across generations, as both audible pasts and futures. Voices "sound out" loudly enough to be felt across the body. The poet affirms: "I too had been struck by the float forever held in solution, / I too had received identity by my body."[76]

For Whitman, the flâneurial aesthetic is open to multisensory stimulation, marked by an openness to play between eye and ear. He pairs the aural and visual in "Crossing Brooklyn Ferry" with lines that emphasize the means of forging the "ecstatic community" within the crowd. As if his senses are also to be imagined as suspended in the "eternal float of solution," he commands: "Gaze, loving and thirsting eyes, in the house or street or public assembly! / Sound out, voices of young men! Loudly and musically call me by my nighest name!"[77] Gazing and sounding out here both connote a kind of embrace, as if the poet is searching for a means to touch and be touched both with his eyes and with his voice.

Though Whitman represents, here as elsewhere in his poetry, being with crowds as "rapturous" experience, especially through visual language and encounters, attention to the aural "turbulence" of the city reveals a curiously vexed side to this rapturous embrace of the modern urban crowd. In the concluding section of "Crossing Brooklyn Ferry," the poet's call for sounding out in the city marks a partial repetition of a line from the sixth section of the poem, this when the poet is "call'd by my nighest name by clear loud voices of young men as they saw me approaching or passing." Though he is hailed by these voices and by the "many I loved in the street or ferry-boat or public assembly," the poet does not respond. This silence in "Crossing Brooklyn Ferry" marks a departure from the rapturous declamatory mode instanced in section forty-two of "Song of Myself" or in the "Omnibus jaunts," in which the call and the uproar of the streets elicit a resounding response from the poet, sound matching sound.[78]

This lack of communication and lack of rapture amidst the crowd, when the rest of the poem hails the bonds across ages and generations, springs from the "dark patches" with which the section opens, and from the "evil" the poet confesses to know and by which he is seized. His silence despite being called, despite feeling "their arms on my neck as I stood, or the negligent leaning of their flesh against me as I sat," follows the poet's declaration: "I am he who knew what it was to be evil."[79] Evil in this instance thus involves a muteness and isolation from the crowd, contrasting with other moments in the poem when the speaker declares: "just as any of you is one of a living crowd, I was one of a crowd."[80] Here, the poet, who so often fuses "ecstatically" with the crowd, finds himself alienated within that crowd.

The poet's inability to respond to the call of the young men at this moment in "Crossing Brooklyn Ferry" springs partly from internal restraint, from what he describes as "dark patches." These "dark patches," in their capacity to silence the poet and sever him from contact with the crowd, recall the passage from "Song of Myself": "what howls restrain'd by decorum." Its lament for the sometimes brutal conditions and iniquities of modern urban life leads to howls that seethe within rather than sounding out in a "yawp."

The bonds of Whitman's ecstatic community in the city, here especially with the calls of young men, thus rely on an openness of sounds and voices, an ability to "sound out" in ways both turbulent and musical, an ability to release the "yawp" or the "howls."[81] Whitman's acoustic turbulence registers the urban chorus as sonic traces both inscribed in and released from the built environment as a medium, the city as itself a kind of technology that would always absorb and always reproduce his poetry. The city, conceived as acoustic space primed for eternal resonance, offered an alternative mode through which poetic emanation could resist the fixity of the printed book as something that Whitman believed, with his conviction that *Leaves of Grass* was more than a book of poetry, was too static, and perhaps also too silent, a medium.[82] Being "one of a crowd" with others could also mean "sounding out" with lips "freely speaking" and with a democratic ear for the "hearing of others." Whitman's eternal acoustic embrace of others in "Crossing Brooklyn Ferry," as he imagined future generations "ever so many hundred years hence," promised new forms of sounding out over time.

Transatlantic Noise

Baudelaire, in his first essay on Poe, called the United States "une grande barbarie éclairée au gaz" ("an uncivilized mass illuminated by gaslight").[83] In this contemptuous summation it is possible to hear, if only from afar, something of the noise of mid-nineteenth century America, the "barbarous" sound of foreign tongues, or at least the American sounds that fell upon Baudelaire's ear less mellifluously than the words of Poe. Baudelaire, here, speaks to a visual disenchantment, specifically from gas lighting, as symbolic of the changes new lighting technologies wrought upon cities and upon modernity more broadly.[84] He also speaks to commonalities in changes to France and America through technological progress and urbanization, namely the feeling that, with Haussmann's transformation of the French capital, the city was, in a way, becoming Americanized.[85] But what, I would like to ask, do the connotations of noise, the harsh sounds of a foreign language in the word "barbarie," mean for poetry in a transatlantic frame? What might we say about the American noise that grates on Baudelaire's ear, on the ear of the poet who called the "nevermore" rhyme in Poe's "The Raven" "one of the most sonorous rhymes of all"?

The audiovisual interplay in Baudelaire's phrase, "une grande barbarie éclairée au gaz" offers a means to imagine something like artificially illuminated noise, or perhaps even a kind of deafening illumination.[86] In one of Stéphane Mallarmé's prose poems, "Un Spectacle Interrompu" ("An Interrupted Spectacle"), Mallarmé describes the strange sound made by gaslight, heard in the audience's sudden hush at an urban circus performance, as "un bruit lumineux" ("a luminous noise"). If not exactly visible, noise is still luminous.

Between Baudelaire and Whitman, Baudelaire's description of America lit by gaslight, "une grande barbarie éclairée au gaz," calls for comparison with Whitman's famous declaration in "Song of Myself": "I sound my barbaric yawp over the roofs of the world." The contrast between the two is strong, between Baudelaire's contempt for a certain audiovisual coarseness of culture in the United States and Whitman's blithe reveling in the rough sounding "barbaric yawp," as well as the way he sounds it "over the roofs of the world."[87] Whitman celebrates the "barbarous" as a democratic ideal inclusive of all kinds of speech, sound, and noise, while Baudelaire is suspicious and disdainful of the way the industrial progress of American "barbarie," which Baudelaire viewed as its desensitizing democratic ideals, could alienate minds like Poe's, making him a stranger in his own land.[88] For Baudelaire, such American "barbarie," synonymous in this case with a certain idea of progress, deafened American society to the value of Poe's writings.

But the polysemy of the word "barbarie" and the way Baudelaire used it often in different contexts means that we can also find a point on which the French poet might have appreciated Whitman's "barbaric yawp," at least when brought to the level of the human senses. In "Notes Nouvelles sur Edgar Poe," as discussed in the previous chapter, Baudelaire offers a conception of the modern sensory world by contrasting an idea of so-called civilized nations and societies with a nostalgic idea of an Edenic "savage" world: "let us compare our lazy eyes and our deafened ears to those eyes that pierce the fog, to those ears that would hear the grass growing."[89] Our "civilized" eyes are lazy and our "civilized" ears are deafened in part, Baudelaire stresses, because of modern society's "ingenious inventions that deprive the individual of heroism."[90] The nineteenth century had its own "ingenious invention," its own technological prosthesis for listening to sounds as faint as the grass growing. The microphone was first invented in rudimentary form in 1827 by Charles Wheatstone, the inventor of the kaleidophone, and then further developed to greater public and literary recognition in 1878 by David Hughes. I highlight this passage from Baudelaire again here in part because of the image of grass, so dear to Whitman ("I bequeath myself to the dirt to grow from the grass I love"), and because this passage illustrates one aspect of Baudelaire's idea of the "savage" that is close to Whitman's idea of the "rough" and "barbarian" when compared on the level of the human senses.[91]

If meant to evoke scorn for American society and democracy in Baudelaire's first essay on Poe, "barbarie" takes on a different meaning in the fifth section, "L'Art Mnémonique," of Baudelaire's famous essay "Le Peintre de la vie moderne," a meaning that helps open up a particular transatlantic perspective on Whitman's worldwide "barbaric yawp." Baudelaire, who confesses that "this word *barbarousness* [. . .] has perhaps emerged too often from my pen," conceives of an aesthetic "inevitable, synthetic, child-like barbarousness that often remains visible in a perfect art (Mexican, Egyptian, or Ninevite), and which derives from seeing things in their immensity, from considering them above all in the effect of their whole."[92] Whitman's desire to sound his "barbaric yawp" derives from a similar grand synthetic embrace of the human sensory world, "of life immense in passion, pulse, and power," a life that, in its engagement with the city, does not entirely despair of deafening sounds, even while attending to the city's "smallest sights and hearings." Whitman could hear the grass grow even while reveling in the deafening sounds of New York.

Between the "smallest hearings" and the deafening roar, a novel sense of the acoustic spectrum of modern everyday life, right down to those most mundane "smallest hearings," emerged at the same time the human sensorium confronted the immensity of deafening noise.[93] Cros developed that sense at a school for the deaf, Baudelaire in Poe's works, Whitman while crossing Brooklyn Ferry.

5
Nina's Song
Music, Sound, and Performance in the Salon of Nina de Villard

An enigmatic watercolor by forgotten Impressionist painter Pierre Franc Lamy offers a window into the late stage of a daring bohemian artistic salon that spanned the Second Empire and Third Republic from 1863 to 1882 (see Figure 25). The muse and *maîtresse de maison* of that artistic milieu, the woman seated at the piano, mid-performance in this work, was Nina de Villard, known by some as "La muse du Parnasse contemporain."[1] If her name conjures up any associations for us today, if she enjoys any celebrity status, that status is to be found and concentrated in a different artwork, a painting by Manet known as *La Dame aux éventails* at the Musée d'Orsay, its title but a small part of a complex story of its subject's veiled identity (see Figure 26).

Such celebrity status in our day has more to do with the painting itself, with Manet, than with the sitter, her identity, and the intellectual world of the salon she animated. How, then, to define Villard's singular place in the literary, artistic, and musical avant-garde of the Second Empire and early Third Republic, when she presided over a salon that welcomed and inspired figures and movements as diverse as they were influential, from the Zutistes to the Parnassians to the Impressionists to the early days of Symbolism, such important vanguards of the Parisian intellectual world for a period of nearly twenty years? Villard published poems in the second *Parnasse Contemporain* in 1869, and after refusal to the third *Parnasse Contemporain*, she contributed to the *Dixains Réalistes* in 1876. A celebrated pianist, she performed to great acclaim in the Salle Pleyel, Salle Érard, and other esteemed venues. She and Charles Cros were lovers for nearly ten years. And yet this salon and its muse have now fallen into virtual obscurity.

Figure 25. Pierre Franc Lamy. *Le Salon de Nina de Villard (fan design)*. Watercolor, circa 1875–1877. © RMN-Grand Palais / Art Resource, NY.

Figure 26. Édouard Manet. *La Dame aux éventails (The Lady with the Fans)*. Oil on canvas, 1873. © RMN-Grand Palais / Art Resource, NY.

Though few in number, some scholars have illuminated Villard's role in the literature, visual arts, and—to a far lesser extent—music of the era. Sandrine Harismendy-Lony has argued that Villard merits a place at the table with the Zutistes as a central, if heretofore unacknowledged, voice in the *Album Zutique*. But the importance of her musicianship, the musicality and broader sonority of her salon, and their enduring impact on the musical landscape of Paris and the artistic avant-garde of the Belle Époque all remain to be probed for their own singular voices.

On the question of professional and social identity, in official documents Villard identified herself first and foremost as a pianist. Yet the scholarship has not looked very closely at her as a musician, in part, I might imagine, because there are few surviving manuscripts of her compositions, and no audio recordings.[2] And this is a veritable loss but also, as I suggest here, an opportunity. It is an opportunity to reconsider sound and music of that particular period and within her particular social world. How to recover the sound of that era? There are, for example, no explicit references to Villard's identity and reputation as a musician in the most famous image to survive of Villard, Manet's *La Dame aux éventails*. The painting's more overt exoticism is echoed in elements of other portraits of Villard in prose such as the *Japonisme* of Paul Alexis's *Madame Meuriot: Mœurs Parisiennes* (1890), where Villard appears engraved on Japanese paper as a Japanese divinity holding a lyre, or the "costume d'Algérienne de fantaisie" that journalist Maurice Dreyfous reported Villard having worn at their first meeting when he saw her as someone who seemed to run "in the company of Ariel, Puck, and Caliban."[3]

This chapter endeavors to recover Villard in other guises and to uncover traces of her sound in familiar and unfamiliar places to develop the following argument: If Villard has been effaced, exoticized, caricaturized, and oftentimes unsympathetically represented in several novels by misogynistic male writers, then sound and music are a most important terrain on which to recover her forgotten brilliance. With that knowledge, there emerges a more complete picture of the auditory culture of modernity, and of the milieu in which our present-day experiences with recorded sound and popular song were born. Analysis about the methods to recover her agency in musical performance and composition helps to expand and deepen the methodological tools necessary to reveal the hidden soundscape of the era. In particular, how do we reckon with the loss of Villard's musical works and performances at precisely the historical moment when such things were imagined as newly recordable and preservable?

A response to that question might begin by recognizing Villard's decisive role in constructing an acoustic space and an aesthetic that cultivated the birth of modern auditory culture. Her roles as muse and model, however, while important, limit the extent to which we can assess her own significance and that of the salon over which she presided. Across the twenty years of her salon's life, Villard became the architect of a social space with real and imagined acoustics that would, in turn, nurture a certain idea of performance and recording of modern life, a certain bohemian acoustical habitus. If Whitman was sometimes hailed as the "Prince of Bohemia," a title acquired during his years at Pfaff's in downtown Manhattan, and if Poe was labeled the "King of the Bohemians" and "*le bohème accompli*," Villard could lay equal claim to the title "Queen of la bohème Parisienne."[4] While her salon was, without a doubt, a temple of Parnassian poetry, the salon was also a veritable nexus for multiple artistic developments, for Impressionism in the visual arts and music, and for broader change in audiovisual culture.

Villard's salon was the milieu in which Cros's ideas took shape, Poe's reception in France was further celebrated and amplified, and in which Baudelaire was musicalized and rewritten in prose and verse forms. At the same time, her salon laid the groundwork for the next generation of avant-garde experimentation and new directions in modern music. As one early chronicler claimed, Villard's salon "set the stage for the Future [*on y préparait l'Avenir*]."[5]

This chapter contains three principal sections. To begin, after a brief reflection on listening, I examine two short stories authored by Villard about art, jealousy, and obsession. Second, I cover several *romans à clef* that contain fictionalized versions of Villard and her salon, the most significant and revealing being Catulle Mendès's *La Maison de la vieille* (1894), a book that Michael Pakenham and Jean-Jacques Lefrère have described as amounting to an act of cruelty, a "venomous" settling of scores, or, as Marie Boisvert recently paints it, a literary "massacre" of old friends.[6] I offer a different lens through which to read this novel, one that reveals the book's latent insights into the auditory culture of the age that Villard animated. Third, I probe the discourses on music, sound, and noise in her salon as an avenue into society's changing relations to sonic phenomena at the dawn of mechanical sound reproducibility, with special attention to composer Ernest Cabaner and to Villard's art criticism and poetry. Even in the absence of any surviving audio recordings or musical notation of her compositions, I conclude, the soundscape of that salon and the auditory abilities of its leader are not as forever lost or inaudible as we might think.

A Singular Listener and Listening

Histories of mechanical sound reproducibility commemorate singular instances of mechanical listening, moments in time marked by the emergence of the machine and its blueprints. Human listening as a distinctive practice and power, on the other hand, typically resists such precise location in time. When does human listening happen? The task to commemorate singular human listening poses distinctive challenges and, at the same time, opens up certain possibilities.[7] How do we remember someone who had a special power to listen? As Jean-Luc Nancy asks in a philosophical register: "What does it mean for a being to be entirely immersed in listening?"[8]

Some of Villard's contemporaries described her as a singular listener, the "confidante" of her generation. Maurice Dreyfous, for one, reported: "Nina was the sympathetic confidante of each of us; she understood everyone's dreams, joys, and pains, and to all she provided courage for the task."[9] In a similar vein, Marie de Grandfort, who was part of her circle, recounted that "no one knew how to listen like her, even in her last years . . . she heard everything [*elle entendait tout*] and was the first to understand the slightest nuances of what one was saying."[10] Grandfort proceeds to celebrate Villard's critical ability to hear poetry and literature, her ability to distinguish and, muse-like, to inspire genuine talent. It is worth pausing over the powers of her ear. Can we say that hers was an ear beyond sympathy, that it surpassed the common notion of a "sympathetic ear"?

As a "confidante" with a sympathetic ear and eye, Villard provided refuge and support for the likes of artists such as Paul Cézanne and writers such as early feminist Olympe Audouard, who sought to find their voices.[11] At the same time, Grandfort's phrase "she heard everything [*elle entendait tout*]" acquires heightened significance when considered in parallel with the emergence of mechanical sound recording technology at that historical moment. The description raises the following questions: Might we see Villard as a rival for the machine's ability to hear all, to capture every sonic nuance like the first generation of phonographs? Was she someone with her own microphonic ear, an ear that, as I argued about Baudelaire's reception of Poe, could detect the "infrasounds of the unconscious process"? Or, was she someone with her own proto-"third ear"? As muse to her generation, and in particular to Cros, Villard's singular listening ability pushed the limits of human hearing, and in turn inspired the possibilities of both human and mechanical listening.

More representative of her entwined listening powers and artistic agency is an account of the genesis of some of her musical compositions. As the phonograph would be used to gather and record urban street songs, Villard herself drew inspiration from songs she heard in city streets. One report recounts a trip to Italy during which she became taken with the melodies that flâneurs in Milan, Genoa, and Turin hummed in the streets.[12] Villard then transcribed and transformed these popular melodies into music for the concert hall, where she performed her own rendition of those melodies and, hence, provided material for humming once again, this time for the streets of Paris.

While it celebrates her agency in listening and in hearing, focusing on Villard as a listener risks restricting her to the status of muse. Ernest Raynaud, writing about Villard in the 1930s, claimed: "The *true* Nina breathes in the verses of the poets that she inspired" (my emphasis).[13] The inspiration that she provided as a muse surely merits attention but, at the same time, demands expansion into other registers. As Jean-Luc Nancy reminds us, there were multiple muses who, in turn, inspired different art forms.[14] Villard was both a distinctly plural muse and a visionary creator.

Verlaine once described Villard's salon as "nights entirely resonant [*toutes retentissantes*] with poetry and music."[15] Within that "resonant" quality, we might find Villard as an architect of resonance and a space designed to "resound fully." When poet Ernest Raynaud lamented the obscurity into which she fell after her death, he highlighted both figurative and literal acoustical dimensions. Villard had at one time stirred up [*remué*] all of Paris with her "noise [*bruit*]" and reputation, but then her melodies were forgotten, along with the "active role" she played in the "artistic and literary evolution" of a generation.[16] Raynaud's key phrase "active role" vests Villard with artistic agency. How then, we might ask, did her voice "resound" elsewhere and in ways other than in the poetry that she inspired and in which she still breathes? How did she usher in a new era of both figurative and literal echoing of "nights entirely resonant with poetry and music"?

The Bow and the Statue: Two Forgotten Tales

Within months of each other in the late summer and fall of 1869, Villard and Cros each published texts with the same title, "L'Archet [The Bow]." Cros's text was a poem, while Villard's was a short story whose conclusion contained an adaptation of Cros's poem.[17] In a kind of literary duet, with Villard the storyteller in prose and Cros in verse, they both meditated on the power of repeated sound and song and on the persistence of life in death via an audible medium, here, specifically, the sound produced by the singular hairs of a violin bow.[18] Elaborating on acoustic motifs from E. T. A. Hoffmann and Edgar Allan Poe, Villard and Cros conjured figures of ghostly music and artistic breakdown reminiscent of Balzac's Frenhofer of "The Unknown Masterpiece." If Balzac anticipated something like the Abstract Expressionism of Pollock in that tale, then Villard anticipated something like the riotous reception that greeted the first performance of Igor Stravinsky's *The Rite of Spring*.

To the extent they fictionalize their teller, this tale and another by Villard, titled "La Statue," offer important counterpoints to the numerous other literary works by other writers that used Villard and her salon as the basis of characters and settings in their fictional and poetic worlds.[19] In contrast to those works, "L'Archet" and "La Statue" provide an opportunity to discover Villard's own authorial self-projection into a fictional narrative, and her own literary vision of female artists and female artistry in the Second Empire.

Upon first glance, Villard's "L'Archet" reads as an autobiographically inspired work, Villard dividing herself between the narrator, who is an accomplished concert pianist, and the story's protagonist, Princess Claudine de N., also a pianist and an established *hôtesse de maison* for the Parisian aristocracy of "birth/name, talent, and grace."[20] To my knowledge, the only critical commentary about this story, a brief gloss in an essay by Michael Pakenham on Villard, describes the tale as "inspired by a poem of the same name by Charles Cros" in which "the heroine of the tale, a princess passionate about music, strangely resembles Nina de Callias."[21] While this interpretation is accurate, the strange resemblance also extends from author to narrator (and even, to a degree, to the object of the princess's affections, the elusive violinist Tristan Pâl as a commanding musical presence), and in this way provides a narrative strategy for self-observation, critique, and self-reflection. The narrator stands at a remove to observe her friend's passion both for music and for the strange violinist. The divide between characters is important, both as evidence of a complex autobiographical dimension to the tale (which stops short of outright confession) and as a reflection on the social dynamics of the two women. The two relate differently to the world of musical performance and an aesthetics of sonic rupture, with performances and musical instruments that sit precariously on the verge of breaking (hearts, minds, and fingers) and being broken.

In this way, Villard's story can be read as a partial rewriting of Hoffmann's short story "Councillor Krespel" (1816), as can Cros's poem, itself a reimagining of Hoffmann's tale.[22] Both Villard and Cros adapt and expand in different ways upon the German Romantic imagination's figure of the mad composer and the potential for violence in sound, music, and musical instruments—here, specifically, the violin bow. The deadly element of Hoffmann's story takes multiple ironic turns in Villard's retelling, when physical death morphs into social and artistic deaths, all still underpinned by violent acts.

By way of brief plot summary, Villard's "L'Archet" begins with a singularly unnerving performance by Hungarian violinist Tristan Pâl, who piques the interest of the narrator's close friend, Princess Claudine de N. . . . The princess subsequently invites the violinist to visit her salon, the center of Parisian high life, where he once again galvanizes his audience: "There, as at the concert the previous night, resonated these strange magnetic sounds, magnetizers [*résonnèrent ces sons étranges, magnétiseurs*]. Like the previous night, the women grew pale and the men were transfixed and seized by a sort of fear that they tried in vain to shake." To the dismay of the narrator and others to whom the princess openly pronounces her affections for the violinist, Claudine finds herself in a liaison where her desire far exceeds Tristan's. When Claudine arranges a coveted day alone with the violinist, Tristan arrives hours late and loses himself in musical theories. In a last attempt to curry his attention and affections, she seizes his violin bow from his hands in the hopes of a playful laugh and kisses. Met instead with his cold fury, she rips the hairs from the bow and throws the pieces into the fire. Tristan attacks her and then faints, after which the princess, physically and emotionally bruised, seeks help for the violinist before fleeing.

Months later the narrator visits the princess and her husband near Ems. There, Claudine learns about a concert Tristan is scheduled to give in Wiesbaden and becomes determined to reunite with her erstwhile lover. The narrator, full of misgivings but steadfast devotion to her friend, reluctantly agrees to accompany her. As the two women search for the violinist, the narrator lingers on the strange aspect of their presence and appearance there: "I saw that people were beginning to take notice of us at the neighboring tables; we must have had a strange air about us. Two women alone, she adorned in diamonds, me, because of a series of concerts I had just given, somewhat famous along the banks of the Rhine." Unable to find Tristan before the performance, the two finally take their seats in the concert hall only to witness a startling breakdown on stage: The acclaimed performer elicits "piercing cries, impossible shudders," followed by looks of disbelief and a "crazy laugh" from the audience that fills the entire room. He is subsequently chased off the stage to the sound of the audience's boos and hisses.

The tale concludes with an encounter sometime later between the narrator, the princess, and a wandering woman who sings a song with a strange melody. The song relates the unhappy fates of two lovers, a woman with fine blond hair who dies of sadness, and the paramour to whom she bequeaths her magnificent tresses with the request that he use them to make a violin bow of her hair with which he might charm his future lovers. At the song's end, after he has won the king's graces and seduced the queen with his music, the musician's dead lover returns as a green-eyed ghost to reclaim her hair and strip him of his musical talent by dispossessing him of the bow. When the narrator and the princess ask the woman where she learned the song, she replies that she heard it from a poor crazy man by the name of Tristan Pâl.

At the end of the story, at the end of the frame narrative for the poem, song signifies absence: absence of mind (Tristan has descended into madness), absence of talent (he can no longer perform as before), and absence of romance (the two are lovers no more). Yet the song also signifies a certain enduring presence, because Tristan Pâl, as the woman reveals, repeats the song without end. This endlessness of song echoes a particular theme in Tristan's song itself, specifically the passage in which the sound of the violin threads a line between life and death in sound: "Everyone experienced an intoxicating sensation / When listening. For in these sounds / The dead woman and her songs lived on [*Tous avaient d'enivrants frissons / À l'écouter. Car dans ces sons / Vivaient la morte et ses chansons*]." The story returns throughout to the detail of the vaguely disquieting, almost unnameable effect of musical performance on listeners, this "intoxicating sensation [*d'enivrants frissons*]" from the text in verse, an element that unifies the story in an undercurrent of subtle discord and the unnerving persistence of sound.

To introduce this foreboding element at the outset of the tale, the narrator relates: "I will always remember the almost mournful shiver [*frémissement presque douloureux*] I felt when, for the first time, I heard Tristan Pâl, the Hungarian violinist." The remarkable passage that follows, in which that performance is described, resembles a Baudelairean prose poem in its play of clashing oppositions, proto-Symbolist "correspondances" of Baudelairean motifs (magnificent palaces and deep woods, sweetness enmeshed with corruption), and a sense of implacable violence in the act of doubling:

> The bow, very slowly, set the string aquiver, and then produced the most unexpected of sounds—something immense and something subdued—a hollow sweetness joined with a magnetic power [*une douceur hypocrite unie à une puissance magnétique*]. One was led to imagine the lover and his mistress singing the same song in unison. The ear pricked up, the listener dreamed by turns of palatial splendors built by fairies, then suddenly veered with the more tender musical passages into the majestic woods, to the banks of lakes, where water sprites with green hair frolic [*où folâtrent les ondines aux cheveux verts*]; it was magical: one imagined the most loving nature a party to the most vicious luxury, and the two together creating marvels around two passionate souls.

Villard's language in this passage explicitly invokes Baudelaire, specifically the prose poem "Le Thyrse," which she may have had in mind.[23] Baudelaire dedicated that poem to Franz Liszt; at the end of the first section of Villard's story, the narrator relates that Liszt was one of several renowned pianists who had visited Princess Claudine's salon and performed on her piano.[24] Villard describes her water sprites using the same verb ("folâtrer" meaning to frolic, delight) that Baudelaire employs to describe the play of stems and flowers around the Thyrse of his eponymous poem. The marvels of nature and luxury around the two passionate souls in Villard's text resemble the "explosions of fragrances and colors" dancing around the hieratic stick. Pâl, who performs with "un mouchoir de dentelle—un mouchoir de femme évidemment" is himself possessed by the kind of "étonnante dualité" of Baudelaire's poem, specifically "the feminine element executing around the male its prestigious pirouettes [*l'élément féminin exécutant autour du mâle ses prestigieuses pirouettes*]."

Some of Villard's friends furthermore described her as a fairy-like spirit, and it is not too great a stretch to imagine her salon akin to the "palatial splendors built by fairies" of this passage, a space exerting a "magnetic power" in its distinctive audible character for those who knew how to hear it and could appreciate its sound. The princess reveals, in her initial invitation to Tristan Pâl: "I'm even something of a pianist myself, and I have in the past accompanied Vieuxtemps and Sivori [*je suis même un peu pianiste, et j'ai quelquefois accompagné Vieuxtemps et Sivori*]," here referring to two virtuoso violinists, Henri Vieuxtemps and Camillo Sivori, who had, as historical documents reveal, hailed Villard's talents as a concert pianist, that is, outside the more private realm of the salon, and in the more public performance space of the concert hall, where Villard often performed.

In the story, however, tension develops between the narrator and Claudine over the matter of accompaniment in piano and violin duets. As Claudine's romantic passion for the violinist grows, she suspects the narrator of betrayal when she discovers them playing music together: ". . . jealous of us all being around him. One evening she almost broke my fingers by slamming the piano shut because I had accompanied the violinist." Not only does this moment in the story reveal both romantic and artistic rivalry between two pianists—two women who perform music to varying degrees in both public and private spheres (indeed, it brings out that tension between the narrator, who performs more to public acclaim versus the private performing sphere of the princess, who is, in her words, more modestly "a little bit of a pianist")—but it also develops one of the story's central issues, the fragility and indeed the danger of musical performance in the face of threats to audibility. The passage reads as a more subdued version of a moment in Hoffmann's "Councillor Krespel" when Krespel's wife smashes his violin because of an inadvertent collision with his bow. The near-smashing of the narrator's fingers in Villard's tale reads as a small crack in the otherwise sisterly affection and devotion maintained by the two characters. But, minor as the detail may seem, it plays into the main themes of the tale about a musical and mental breakdown.

Indeed, there is something of Poe in the final concert in Wiesbaden, however attenuated the horror and Gothicism are by ironic understatement. A subtly subversive element, namely the "crazy laugh" that pierces the concert hall, dislocates Tristan's breakdown and situates it between performer and audience for an effect that undermines rational frames of reference and perception. Tristan awaits the end of the *tutti* before beginning his solo: "[. . .] and he began. Piercing cries arose, impossible shudders [*Ce furent des cris aigus, des frémissements impossibles*]; never have cats quarreling on rooftops been able to give an idea of the sort of concerto he performed. People looked at one another with disbelief, and then a crazy laugh took hold of the whole room [*un fou-rire s'empara de toute la salle*] [. . .]." The "cris aigus" would appear to originate within the audience, but the text leaves their source in a way ambiguous. Was the violin itself sounding *like* piercing cries? Were these cries in response to the violinist? Or were they one and the same, cries from the violin that elicited similar sounding cries from the audience? The narrator, to recall, began the story with the unforgettable "frémissement" she felt upon first hearing Tristan Pâl. Here, the shudder has become "impossible," its previously mournful quality undone to produce something beyond identifiable sentiment. If Tristan is identified as a poor crazy man at the story's end, the audience shares in that loss of nerve, in that craziness as the whole room is gripped by a "*crazy* laugh." Just who exactly *is* crazy, the story seems to be asking, to perform or to respond to the performance in that way? Villard demonstrates an attentiveness to the peculiar power of laughter in the modern era.

Hence, there is something both comical and frightening in the description of this sound, this concerto. There is something proto–chat noir-esque about it because the text harkens back to Poe and evokes an ineffability about the ghastly sound that is, if not otherworldly, as in Poe's "The Facts in the Case of M. Valdemar," then at least utterly unconventional. Words and analogy fail to capture the sound, as in "Valdemar" in the passage about unheard-of sounds grating on the ear of humanity.

Though the poem that follows the description of Tristan's Wiesbaden downfall narrates a sort of resuscitation of the dead—or seemingly dead—voices à la Poe and Hoffmann, the passage about the concert effectively mocks the concert and the concert-going public (read, the *bourgeois* concert-going public) to imagine sound that disconcerts otherwise. By juxtaposing the sound of professional demise, crazy and laughable, with the sound of fantastical demise and ghostly return, the story carves out a space for music to resound on another scale: in a singular, anti-bourgeois, anti-conventional—but perhaps still musical—fashion. Who, in the space of a proper concert hall, would dream of a concerto that sounded like cats' warring pitter-patter on city rooftops? This explosive concerto emerges from Poe's "Black Cat" shrieking behind a wall and Villard's rewriting of Hoffmann and Cros.

A superior musician, Villard presumably could have set the poem to music and thus altered lines to fit her musical accompaniment as poet and musician

Marie Krysinska, years later, would set Cros's poems to music for the Chat Noir cabaret.[25] In Villard's tale, more realist when compared to the fairy-tale setting of Cros's poem or Hoffmann's Romanticism, the very precariousness of musical performance that runs throughout the story, in turn, gives voice to an opposing force: the strange possibility of a more enduring record of singular sounds and performances, be that record in textual form (a short story, a song, or a poem) or in the element of an instrument (such as the hair of a violin bow). And this acoustic fragility and ephemerality differ from the violence done to, and by, a musical expression Hoffmann evokes in "Krespel" partly because Villard's tale is steeped in the quotidian details of her time and artistic milieu. The ghostliness and fairy-tale qualities of Cros's poem, situated as they are in Villard's narrative, are to be understood as the ravings of a madman, whom the princess renounces once and for all, in practically deadpan ironic statements to the narrator: "Is it possible that I once loved this man!" and "The poor devil."

To some degree, this rendering of Hoffmann's musical violence in a more realist setting and plot could be read as a reflection of the science of acoustics becoming less magical and more real, a more everyday manipulable element of the modern world.[26] More so, Villard's tale elaborates a different terrain on which modern acoustics might be built, a stage upon which sounds might contain the songs of the dead to be played and replayed on singular instruments that were, at least in 1869, yet to be imagined (and Cros was indeed busy imagining them). At that moment, these instruments would be present only in song or in the remnants of ancient oral traditions as in this quasi-mythical meeting of the two characters with the wandering woman who is able to reproduce Tristan Pâl's words and melody. The great irony is that with the advent of the phonograph, less than a decade away, something like Cros's poem would no longer need these vestiges of oral transmission to reach sets of happenstance ears, such as those of Claudine and the narrator. Machines, rather than serendipitous wanderers, would soon carry songs over every hill and valley.

This forgotten story claims an oblique, though enduring, acoustical resonance in one additional register. The violin, the Vieuxtemps Guarneri "del Gesù" of the Belgian Violinist Henri Vieuxtemps (1820–1881), one of the two virtuosos, whom Princess Claudine accompanies on piano in the story and is a real figure in music history, is today violinist Anne Akiko Meyers's instrument of choice for her concerts and recordings. How many nineteenth-century texts articulate an idea of phonography and also reference musical instruments that are still in use, still resonant today? In this way, as in many others, Nina de

Villard possessed a singular ear for what would endure and for how it could endure.

If Hoffmann's "Councillor Krespel" is a most important intertext for Villard's "L'Archet," Poe's tales of premature burial and the Pygmalion myth are the primary intertexts for Villard's "La Statue."[27] The story can be read as a "version" of Pygmalion, to quote J. Hillis Miller's term for the literary figure, and as a play on archetypal Parnassian motifs and aesthetics, such as the veneration of the classical statuary of antiquity. Villard's story, however, reverses the Pygmalion myth to end with the beloved woman becoming a statue and dying rather than the statue coming to life. Early on, the story hints at that possibility in a parodic moment characteristic of Villard's later parodies in verse in the *Dixains Réalistes* (1876), when the sculptor of this tale returns to his atelier late at night to contemplate an eerie seraglio of sculptures and pronounces ironically: "If only I were superstitious." In contrast to Pygmalion, who gives Galatea life, Pierre murders his beloved Eve de Brienne in a fit of jealousy by encasing her alive beneath a plaster cast.

The story plays furthermore with the silencing of the female voice, a common element of Parnassian poetry. As Gretchen Schultz has illuminated, such attitudes toward female voices and femininity as "imprisoned in marble and coldness" more broadly among male Parnassian poets is also an effect of the critical oversight about crucial contributions of female *Parnassiennes*, such as Villard, Louise Colet, and Léocadie Hersent-Penquer, to the poetic movement.[28] "La Statue" reproduces this experience in its protagonist, Eve, a gifted pianist who must regretfully abandon her musical ambitions for want of an instructor and because her widowed mother forbids her to go out in the city alone. Both "L'Archet" and "La Statue" address the travails of artistic identity, and of female artistic identity, in Second Empire Paris. Having given up music but still "an artist at heart" celebrated for her inspiration, Eve becomes the pupil and eventual lover of the reclusive sculptor Pierre Desyl and can continue to practice her artistic talents in the medium of sculpture for a time, with limited independence, however.

The story begins with a meditation on the architecture of sacred spaces and how they appeal to the human senses, particularly for those of an artistic mind who cannot fail to be seized by the "poetry of sacred buildings." The passage recalls Baudelaire's sonnet "Correspondances"—specifically the fragrances that sing "les transports des esprits et des sens"—and foreshadows the Symbolist aesthetics that would blossom among the poets who frequented Villard's salon, Mallarmé chief among them. Villard's narrator describes the resonant lament of Hebrew song in synagogues, the vapor of incense mixing with the fragrance of flowers in gothic cathedrals, and the sound of church organs and harmoniums that accompany choruses of singing women. In its evocation of resonant harmonious spaces, the story's opening contrasts with its violent end, in which Eve is encased in plaster that silences her cries.

The opening scene, in which the music and fragrances of the church transport the sculptor Pierre into "a sort of vague ecstasy similar to that felt under the influence of haschisch," is later replayed in the profane setting of a worldly Parisian salon where, quite literally, "de confuses paroles," those of a conversation between Eve and her friend Mina, reach Pierre's ear, revealing Eve's liaison with a journalist and upending Pierre's world. In this scene, it is as if Villard imagines a narrative loosely inspired by Baudelaire's "Correspondances," in essence setting the poem at a party of Parisian high society.

The description of the mansion's ballroom, "The ballroom is a virgin forest [*La salle de bal est une forêt vierge*]," recalls the opening line of Baudelaire's poem, "Nature is a temple where living columns [*La nature est un temple où de vivants piliers*]." Indeed the orchestra in the ballroom plays hidden behind a flowerbed of magnolias and camelias, and, with a hint of discord, offers up a "promenade en musique," while Pierre grows "intoxicated on perfumes and colors [*s'enivrait de parfum et de couleur*]," echoing Baudelaire's "*Les parfums, les couleurs, et les sons se répondent.*" Sounds mingle with the "warm atmosphere of the party," as Pierre subsequently overhears his mistress's voice and her ensuing conversation with her friend Mina.[29]

The story's overall arc is a movement that begins with open resonance in the blossoming and expansion of artistic spirit but eventually—and violently—closes that resonance in the plaster beneath which Eve suffocates. As in "L'Archet," Villard examines violence against the female voice and body through relationships with material objects. With respect to sound, the story effectively marks a transition point between the motifs of Parnassian poetry and those of Symbolism. The story identifies sacred architecture as a religious space and an artistic temple that amplifies the resonance of women's voices. This contrasts with the more familiar limitations imposed by marriage, invoked in Eve's repeated refusal of Pierre's proposals to marry. It similarly challenges the nineteenth-century art-and-literary world's patriarchal order that reduces women to models, as Eve served for Pierre, rather than recognize them as makers, a role to which Eve aspired as a concert pianist, and which she briefly assumes upon claiming a degree of independence from Pierre.

Like the incense that infuses the church, music suggests infinite expansion early in the story but is suffocated by the end. The story ultimately asks what alternatives there are from serving only as a model for male artists, from being modeled so stiffly as to become literally a statue.[30] Villard's salon and her artistic visions for sculpture and music provided manifold escapes from the bleakness of this story's end. At the same time, writings that Villard published shortly before these two stories articulate a sense of female artistic independence, and of musical independence in particular.

Several months prior to publishing these stories, Villard was writing as visiting correspondent and music critic in Baden, Germany, for the French paper *La Chronique universelle*. Her reports from this period recount her artistic interests and experiences. In particular, she wrote about her views on prominent female musicians, actresses, and singers on stage. These same reports may be read as veiled political statements about female political and artistic agency under the Second Empire. Villard celebrates, for instance, the "superb passion" of actress Madelaine Brohan in one piece. In another, she praises the vocal development and stage presence of French soprano Marie Battu: "I remember having seen her debut at the *Italiens*. At the time, she was just a young girl with a profoundly melancholy air. Already an exquisite method but a weak voice that recalled, in its dawning, the last days of the great Frezzolini. Today she is altogether radiant, confident in herself, and in the public she commands: her voice has acquired depth and brilliance [*de l'ampleur et de l'éclat*]. Her talent has only grown [. . .]."[31] Another entry extolls the virtues of women who perform in diverse public settings, from actress Léonide Leblanc to opera singer Suzanne Lagier to travel writer and journalist Olympe Audouard, who gave lectures in Spa, Belgium, and fought for women's rights in France.[32]

In the same series, Villard hailed the achievements of two female pianists, Marie Wieck and Marie Jaëll. Wieck, the half-sister of Clara Schumann, performed a Chopin concerto and Lizst's *Soirée de Vienne* with "deeply classical and solid expression," according to Villard.[33] Jaëll and her husband performed a Schumann piano duet with "stunning precision." Villard's music criticism complements her published fiction by carving out a space of audibility for female voices, femininity beyond conventional gender stereotypes in the artistic sphere, and women on the stages of concert halls and theaters. And like Audouard, whose political journalism met with censorship and rebuke for its protest of the limits on women's legal rights in France, Villard's reports also carved out a space for female voices in the political arena of the press.[34] In this way, in the mass press, Villard helped provide Audouard a stage from which to fight for gender equality, while Villard's salon offered a more private setting in which to do the same.[35]

As Chapter 3 illustrated, Nadar imagined a future in which audio recording and reproduction might supplant print media as a more faithful medium for political reporting. Both Villard and Audouard would die before audio recording was a practical possibility for the press. But Villard's reportage on prominent female musical voices, which skillfully included and implicitly promoted Audouard's feminist platform, reimagined connections between the concert stage and the mass press in the service of newfound resonance for women. Villard thus engaged musical performance, and the reportage of it, as an alternative political sphere from the press explicitly read and designated as political, the media platform where Audouard was censored, where her designs for a political journal were thwarted by Second Empire state censors akin to the way Villard's Eve de Brienne was encased in plaster in "La Statue."

A House Everywhere Audible

Catulle Mendès's novel *La Maison de la vieille* [*The House of the Old Woman*] (1894) is both a searing betrayal of Villard and, at the same time, of interest primarily for what it betrays, even in caricatural form, of her time and milieu. I follow the critics who have noted this paradoxical quality about the novel (a fiction that could be read practically as historical testimony) in search of what the novel reveals despite itself, namely a deeper truth about the historical milieu amidst the gross fictional parodies of real-life figures. The novel has a cast of more than two hundred characters, many identified with their historical counterparts by scholars, others invented or of as yet unidentified inspiration.[36] Jean-Didier Wagneur, for one, calls it a tale told by "a cynical libertine haunting spiritualistic revues to conjure up the very shadow of the age."[37] The novel verges on pornography and ends in tragedy.

In its day in the Belle Époque, the novel functioned in part to settle old scores. In this way, it bitterly responded to the kinds of stories Villard published and to other ways she dared to transgress gender norms in the male-dominated literary world.

The house of its title (ever ambiguously suggesting both a proper home and a brothel) could be likened to a cauldron from *Macbeth*, as Wagneur describes it (and as metaphorized in the novel's prologue, as a "sorcerer's cauldron" [106]).[38] The crucible of ideas and of artistic and political ferment that was Villard's house is ultimately transformed, in Mendès's hands, into a ghastly and ghostly cauldron. Stella d'Helys, the novel's masked Nina de Villard character and its protagonist, dies a gruesome death at the novel's end. If Rimbaud ever poured real acid into Cros's drink, this novel represents acid in prose hurled at Villard's memory and legacy. And if Manet's *La Dame aux éventails* is the most revealing portrait of Villard in paint, Mendès's book is the most developed, but not necessarily most faithful, literary portrait of Villard in prose. Despite its caricatural tendencies, the novel is nevertheless vivid, complex, and well worth our attention both for its window onto a generation of artists and as a literary work.

Awash, first of all, in ideas about sound, music, and, in a few places, audiovisual media, the novel offers one way to recover the acoustics of Villard's salon, her milieu, and her band, as well as the ideas and literary imagination those acoustics inspired. In doing so, the book raises many questions. What, I would like to ask, does the novel tell us about the status of ephemeral performance at the dawn of recorded sound amidst the fervent crucible of that invention and the elaboration of that possibility? At the same time, what does the novel reveal about Villard as the architect of that space? Might we extract something like a more resonant temple for art, the kind she imagined at the beginning of "La Statue" and which she forged in both concert hall and home, out of the carnivalesque mockery of her house reconstructed and then demolished in Mendès's prose? If the literary portrait of Villard in this novel is painted in shades of scorn, with little consideration for the veritable art she produced, practiced as a musician, and cultivated among others, are there cracks in that portrait that *do* reveal a certain visionary nature, both in the character of Stella d'Helys (Villard's cryptonym in the novel) and in the house and milieu of the novel?

Here I propose to focus on those questions in the context of two particular elements of the novel: First, I look at how Mendès anticipates Proustian effects relating to memory and sound, projection and visual media, the magic lantern specifically. Then I examine how Mendès looks back to Poe and how the novel offers a reception of Poe in the French context less familiar than the reverence found among Baudelaire, Mallarmé, Manet, Valéry, Gauguin, and Debussy, among others.

To call the novel as a whole pure caricature would be too reductive. Cruel as the book often is, there are nuances to its characterization of Stella, especially in the context of music and acoustics. Describing, for instance, her first "awakening" to dreams of artistic glory, the narrator initiates a metaphor that will be pursued throughout the novel, one that contributes to the identification of Stella with her house and the house with Stella. The narrator likens her to a luthier's room: "When she began to learn music [. . .] the sound—of a harpsichord that was, however, old and badly out of tune, with two or three dead notes [*notes mortes*], broken by scales and exercises—penetrated her, moved her, sent her into ecstasy, rendered her herself, within, entirely sonorous [*la pénétra, l'émut, l'extasia, la fit elle-même, au-dedans, toute sonore*], the way a breath of air would move luths, harps, and viols on a wall to vibrate, when entering a luthier's room; henceforth she would come to love melodious noise forever" (156). Stella becomes both a musician and, in this metaphor that develops throughout the novel, a space of resonance, less an instrument herself that could be played upon like a violin and more like a room that harbors multiple instruments.

The foreboding note in this passage, specifically the out-of-tune harpsichord with broken keys, reaches its thematic closure in a detail that, as in Villard's own "L'Archet," recalls Hoffmann. Following the deaths of Stella and her mother at the end of the novel, amidst the general tumult of the house as it is emptied of its contents, the narrator reports: "An object, in falling, sounded like a lament; it was the worn-out box of a stringless violin" (499).

But before the stringless violin, among many other objects, can mark Stella's tragic end, Stella comes to adore playing plaintive and bizarre melodies (156); is moved to tears by Schubert (157); performs on the piano in the Salle Érard and Salle Pleyel concert halls (315); plays Chopin waltzes at home to the delight of her guests (317, 328); improvises Mazurkas and battle cries for the communards (318, 410); feels slighted by an editor who refused to publish a waltz she had composed (354); imagines, between improvising and composing at the piano, who will listen to her compositions (354); and finally, in her declining mental state, composes waltzes that amount to "melancholy pieces in carnival attire" (452). Across these passages, Stella emerges as a character who is, as Mendès describes her early in the novel, *"toute sonore,"* entirely resonant with the sounds around her, both harmonious and discordant. Such characterization approaches the idea Jean-Luc Nancy imagines in the beginning of *Listening*, the question of a being entirely "immersed in listening."

Near the end of the novel, as a kind of culmination of this *"toute sonore"* effect, Stella has a chance encounter in a bar (*un débit de liqueurs*) on the avenue de Clichy with a character she met as a child at the beginning of the novel. The sound of his name kindles a vague memory she cannot at first pinpoint in what reads like a proto-Proustian passage: "A sound caused Stella to shiver [*tressailir*]. A sound that awakened in her something past and long forgotten [*elle ne savait de quoi de très ancien*]—something very sweet, something very luminous. It was in her being as if in a room long since closed [*close*] where now a window opens that allows in air and the dawn, blue and rose colored. What was it that she had heard?"[39] In this passage, note how Stella is likened to a house when compared to a closed room, especially with the adjective *"close,"* which alludes to the history of her house as a brothel (*une maison close*) and to the brothel-like prostitution of art that Mendès and others accused Villard of having entertained.[40] The narrator continues: "A pleasant noise [*un bruit aimable*], auspicious, it seemed to her, uttered by the resurrection of a friendly echo [*proféré par la résurrection d'un amical écho*]." Unlike in Proust, however, this episode does not prompt an outpouring of happiness in the resurrection of childhood memory via the eventual recognition of the sound, of what exactly it was she had heard. Instead, it is bitterness in the realization that Stella was not blessed but effectively cursed by the childhood encounter now resuscitated in this sound. The "amical echo" will soon turn plangent as Stella "searched in the recesses of herself [*fouillait au fond d'elle*] just as one looks for an object lost in a drawer encumbered with all manner of things. Suddenly, the name that the barman had spoken and that she had only half heard, reformed in its entirety in her hearing [*se reforma tout entier dans son ouïe*]."

The sound she had "half heard" was the name of a gifted but ill-fated writer, Lysis Arbois, author of "*Les Aventures du Chevalier Azur dans le pays des Fées*" that Stella adored as a child, a book she discovered during her musical awakening and which served as inspiration for her earliest musical improvisations at the piano. Early in the novel, Stella's mother, at her urging, takes her to visit the writer at his home, where they offer him a sum of money so he can pay off his debts and avoid being evicted. At this meeting, Stella is surprised (she wondered whether the author and the gallant Chevalier Azur of his book might be one and the same person) and horrified (only Stella's mother knows about the author's dire financial situation) by the gloom of his life. In a tender moment, the writer recognizes the artist's dream in young Stella, the search for the ideal, but also the artist's curse, "le guignon" (as we saw with Baudelaire and Poe), in her case wings that might elevate her only so high that her "fall would be all the more painful" (170).

In the later episode, when Stella again finds herself face-to-face with the author, the "friendly echo" that resonates within her seems suggestive of a happy interiority awakening to the dawn. That echo turns bitter, however, when the two characters finally recognize each other's identity and the circumstances under which they first met, with Stella as a hopeful, naïve child, Arbois as an already failed cursed writer struggling to support his young family. Stella, for her part, before Arbois has entirely remembered her, attempts to produce the same effect on him by uttering a word that would unearth a memory of their long-forgotten first meeting. She says "Azur," referring to the hero of Arbois's book, which gives Arbois a start. And then she recounts the end of the tale, the poisoning of a flower by a "cruel sorcerer" (*un cruel enchanteur*), the part of the book, the unhappy ending, that as a child, after a certain point in time, she had ceased to read and in turn had repressed. It all surges back to both her and the author as Stella points to the drinks they are getting drunk with and says: "The cursed flower [*la vilaine fleur*], with the poison, it's this, isn't it?"

Mendès often lays it on thick in this novel, but this is a powerful moment, both in its tragic thematic tightness (it follows the nightmarish resurfacing of another painful memory for Stella) and in its evocation of a chance meeting amidst a Gothic cityscape. Powerful as this moment in the narrative is, it almost reads at the same time as a self-parody of the novel itself, as a *roman à clef* in which characters' identities are like the sound of the name Stella only half hears at first. The novel's cryptonymic antagonisms thus have a certain acoustic frame to them, one that Mendès literalizes and plays with throughout the story. The novel's keys are the clues to its characters' true identities, while the keys to the house belong to Stella's mother, the "vieille" of the title. Throughout the novel, those keys ring out with a "bruit tintinnabulant de clés à la ceinture" (495) whenever the old woman appears. One could argue that the novel, in its cryptonymous aspect, is like the rattling noises of so many keys dangling against the old woman's belt. The novel itself, then, becomes an echo chamber of names and identities evoked in ways meant to sear the however dim or however vivid memories of these bohemian companions and raucous nights with the sense of failed resonance. This is how, among other figures, Cros is portrayed in the novel. Mendès, though, has him die much earlier in history, during the Prussian siege of Paris (i.e., in 1871, when Cros, in fact, died in 1888). He also conflates Cros somewhat with his friend Nadar: Cros devises an ingenious balloon that will liberate Paris but is, in the end, still bested by a Prussian balloon of inferior design.

Another motif near the conclusion of the novel deserves attention for its audiovisual connection and strange anticipation of an effect in Proust. This is the magic lantern.

In the chapters immediately preceding the encounter with Lysis Arbois, during which Stella's descent into alcoholism is related, she becomes increasingly tormented by hallucinations, which can be read in part as the twisted distortions of Arbois's evocation of the young artist's dream, "l'exaltation vers les chimères" (474): "As if her eyes and her ears were no longer made of flesh, she did not see, did not hear any more except with her soul; if a brutal clamor obliged her to leave this ideal ceiling behind [*redescendre de l'idéal plafond*] to return to waking life, she would drink several more [. . .]" (439). As she soars amidst the chimeral memories of her aspirations, she sees herself as an actress in theaters on a distant star, as a singer, and as a poetess, accompanied by "music never heard before [*des musiques jamais ouïes*]." Within the frame of the novel's plot, these projections onto the blank canvas of the ceiling sit midway between nostalgic reminiscence of childhood dreams, the salon at its pinnacle with her career as a pianist at its apex, and the nightmarish hallucinations that will follow and eventually lead to her demise. The long passage about her hallucinations concludes with this startling finale, in which the imaginary ceiling (*le plafond idéal*) of her dreams merges with the actual ceiling in her salon in a moment that briefly anticipates an epochal sea change in media and representation, historically speaking, soon to take place: "The ceiling was like a blank canvas where the magic lantern that she had inside her was projecting her splendidly visible images, melodiously speaking [*ses images splendidement visibles, mélodieusement parlantes*]" (439). Roughly one year after this novel appeared, the Lumière brothers would project their first films.

Magic lanterns had been projecting images for centuries, and it would still be decades before those projected images would become "melodiously speaking," but three details in this passage merit closer attention. First, the verb "*projetait*" in the imperfect tense suggests a continuous sequence of image and sound—more like cinema, the innovations in the projected animation of Émile Reynaud's *Praxinoscope à Projection* (see Figure 27), and what Proust would describe with Golo and Geneviève de Brabant—rather than the single image succession of discrete magic lantern slides.[41] Second, the space of this projection is a domestic one, defamiliarized and in ways unsettling as in Proust. Simultaneously, it is a half-hallucinated surface that is also partly public because this room served as the gathering place for so many of Stella's salon habitués. Only she sees the projection, but she imagines it in a space that is in so many ways theatrically and performatively charged. It is a space that is, indeed, also acoustically charged, where the images can also become "melodiously speaking."[42] It is not insignificant that Mendès should situate the magic lantern

Figure 27. Louis Poyet. "Nouveau Praxinoscope à projection de M. Reynaud." *La Nature* 492, (Nov. 4, 1882), 357.

projection in this space. As Jonathan Crary has argued, the transformation of the nineteenth-century observer allowed for the emergence of a new optically constructed space. Here, this space that is both optically and acoustically minded suggests the emergence of an early cinematic observer.[43]

Finally, dual interiority—architectural and psychic—defines the space in which the lantern is situated. Stella possesses the lantern inside herself (*qu'elle avait en elle*), and this metaphor echoes the one established earlier in the novel of Stella's psychically interior resonant room as a luthier's space. In the sense that I described earlier of the novel forecasting Villard's veritable artistic visions despite itself, even as the novel dwells in what it perceives as her failure, it is as if she becomes the unconscious bearer of revolutionary aesthetic practices and representational techniques, namely the protocinematic with the supplement of projected images that speak, a dawning that is different from the bitter dawn in the Clichy bar sequence. In such a way, in the literary distortion of the memory of Villard's salon, in that memory becoming Stella's salon, the audiovisual frame of Villard's salon and its milieu assumes a protocinematic aspect that inherits the real visionary nature of Nina de Villard. And if Villard was a true and most influential muse of her generation who contributed to the protocinematic imaginary, she figures within the prehistory of what some have called cinema's function as "the muse of the twentieth century."[44]

Return to the "House of Usher"

Though Jean-Didier Wagneur's comparison of Mendès's novel to Poe's "House of Usher" comes across as fairly offhand, I want to take that comparison seriously. It is, after all, a character named *Edgar* Alfred who unwittingly, wanting to protect Stella from her inner demons, precipitates her death. Wagneur argues: "If Mendès refuses hagiography . . . he transforms this dwelling into a 'House of Usher' whose crack, essentially mental, will precipitate its downfall."[45] The mental crack to which he refers is primarily the madness and alcoholism that afflict Stella at the end of the novel. At the same time, amidst the macabre and ghostly motifs that define this rewriting of Poe's "House of Usher," Mendès reimagines the uncanny echoes heard in Poe's tale to explore a different feeling about such unnerving echoes, specifically how Poe's House of Usher might sound in fin de siècle Paris. Whereas Debussy struggled to adapt "House of Usher" into an opera, Mendès drew inspiration from the story while satirizing the reverence Villard and her cohort felt for Poe. At the same time, Mendès provided a feeling for what Poe's haunted house could sound like in an urban setting, if not exactly onstage as an operatic work, then as a house haunted by shattered dreams resounding through the streets of Paris.

Though the "house of the old woman" is located near the outskirts of the city—as was the second primary location of Villard's salon when it moved to the rue des Moines—the house nonetheless remains audible throughout the city. In the novel's prologue, the narrator pronounces: "In lending an ear, people could hear, from every corner of Paris, the house of the old woman laugh and cry out" (106). In contrast to this noisiness, an early chapter begins with a lengthy meditation on urban brothels and their quiet shadowy appearance to those who pass by not knowing what they are: "They remain mysterious, these houses, and they isolate themselves. [. . .] Children and young women can look and listen without peril. These dwellings are closed, more closed than prisons and cloisters; and they are silent. The rare noises that escape from them—a faint ritornello played on a piano or the refrain of a song quickly faded—are so distant that one may not even hear them" (136). After they move into the former brothel, Stella and her mother, however, suspicious but as yet uninformed, share a vague sense of unease: "The emptiness of the house, the silence of the house, seemed to them full of dirty memories" (143). An eerie silence hangs about the house in its interior for those who sense but do not yet know its true history.

As if to banish this silence and these anxieties related to the house's past, Stella and the old woman animate the dwelling so that it becomes more like the description in the novel's prologue, a house audible in every corner of Paris, a place so loud that in its wildest of moments the narrator likens it to a "wall of sound [*une muraille sonore*]" (390). And it is with this kind of description, this wall of sound, that Mendès plays up the irony by freely adapting "House of Usher," together with the spirit of Poe's tales of premature burial, and by bringing murder into the narrative, recalling a story like Poe's "The Cask of Amontillado," which involves death by immurement.

During a particularly spirited party at Stella's, Henry (painter Franc Lamy), one of Stella's lovers, locks Evariste Myriem (poet Germain Nouveau) in an outdoor shed in the freezing cold, where he subsequently freezes to death. His cries, the kind that with Poe make the skin crawl, become here dramatic and suspenseful but at the same time also the stuff of farce and grotesque satire.

Henry, the murderer, upon leaving the scene, explains his early departure from the party by complaining that people are making "too much noise" (385). Such noise effectively drowns out Myriem's cries for help until Lafilède (composer Ernest Cabaner) begins to search for him in a sequence that recalls Poe's tales of premature burial, "The Tell-Tale Heart," and the kind of sounds heard in "House of Usher" before the narrator learns about Roderick's sister. Upon finding Myriem, Lafilède's cries likewise fail to penetrate the "wall of joyous tumult; they would have awakened the dead from the cemetery before they would reach the living of the house" (391).

Poe-esque horror metamorphosed into farce here is, in one respect, how Mendès perceives Villard and her generation as so much forgotten noise. It is also how Mendès skewers and renders grotesque the memory of the eccentric composer Ernest Cabaner. In his eccentricity, Cabaner was often likened by his contemporaries to Poe.[46] But Cabaner also lodged Rimbaud and likely even taught him to play piano for a time during Rimbaud's Parisian sojourns (Rimbaud is also thought to have once masturbated into a glass of milk by Cabaner's bedside as a joke). Hence this sequence in Mendès's novel is important for the memory of the strange composer and his connection to poets of that generation as rendered through a farcical reimagining of Poe. Lafilède (Cabaner, who was also a great supporter of the Impressionists), with his musical ear, hears the poets of that generation as if they are locked away and dying from the cold. This is how Mendès both updates and adapts Poe for his "contemporary novel" (the subtitle of *La Maison de la vieille*), and at the same time imagines an eccentric ear as having once listened to the works of his contemporaries, as if they were voices buried in the snow too faint to rise above the party's "wall of sound."

Origins and Legacies of the Chat Noir

If, as Nadar claimed, the need for sound recording occupied the minds of so many in the mid-nineteenth century, couldn't we expect to find this idea explicitly articulated in Villard's salon, in the place where so many artistic, political, and scientific theories were entertained, in the very salon frequented by Cros, the French inventor of mechanical sound recording? Such explicit evidence may have gone the way of lost photographs of Villard by acclaimed photographers Etienne Carjat and by Nadar himself, photographers who so frequently crossed paths with Villard that scholars presume they must have taken her portrait at some point or another. What became of those photographs? Some things simply get lost.

We could imagine that after a particularly spirited poetic recitation or theatrical or musical performance, those present might have remarked: Wouldn't it be superb to hear that particular performance again? Or, a regular habitué who happened to be absent that night really should have been there to hear it (as when Verlaine writes to Villard expressing his regret for having missed her birthday party during which she gave a lively performance: "The rhinoceros, so I have heard, was performed by you with the kind of brio, beware, that will provoke my artistic jealousy! [*Le rhinocéros, paraît-il, a été dit par vous avec un brio qui, prenez-y garde, va susciter ma jalousie d'artisssse!*]"). Cros, they might have said, is going to build a device so we won't have that problem of missing a performance in the future, so that the "brio" of Villard's reading could be replayed and preserved for the absent ones and for future generations.[47]

A scene such as this does play out in Paul Alexis's novel *Madame Meuriot* (1890), in a chapter inspired by Villard's salon, when Gray (cryptonym for Cros) explains his theory of how to "photograph sound [*photographier le son*]"[48] to capture the entirety of a musical performance, everything from the singer's raspy voice to the audience's applause. Gray's interlocutor in explaining this theory is the painter Édouard Thèkel, a character inspired by Manet. This is one instance where the textual record does precisely situate the dream of mechanical sound recording within the space of Villard's salon, and, interestingly, in dialogue with painting and one of the most modern of painters as well.

By indirectly examining the history of invention and expanding the line of inquiry out from the particular line of a phonographic or paleophonic machine to the broader preservability of performance within Villard's salon performance culture, we probe the horizon of audiovisual possibility skirting the eruptions of explicit blueprint or built device. Villard, for example, was recognized for her passion for the work of musician and composer Charles de Sivry, a devoted habitué of her salon, known for "the most beautiful efforts to recover early music [*les plus beaux travaux de reconstitution de la musique antique*]."[49] Such work of resuscitating early music, which Villard encouraged and provided space to take shape in her salon, would have conceivably played into the "paléo" side of Cros's "paléophonic" designs. Some scholars have expressed surprise that music did not initially occupy a higher position in Edison's thinking about potential uses of phonographic technology. Hence, it is important to examine the dynamic musical life of Villard's salon, the salon frequented by Cros, Edison's rival, as a counterpoint historical context for Edison's list. We need to account for the importance of sonic events in a salon at the vanguard of currents in both modern music and scientific thought.

Novelists of Villard's generation and more recent scholarship alike have recognized Villard's salon as a kind of precursor of the Chat Noir cabaret and journal.[50] Villard cultivated a popular bohemian performance aesthetic together with a particular attitude to listening specific to the bohemian salon. These elements would prove visionary for directions in modern music, one being the kind of music performed at the Chat Noir cabaret with, for example, pianist and composer Erik Satie, who performed at the Chat Noir for roughly ten years. The connection lies less in a pianistic sense—the virtuoso aesthetic of Villard's early reputation as a concert pianist would not necessarily apply to Satie at the Chat Noir—but more in the area of cultivated attitudes to performance and listening that would ultimately bear on revolutionary representational techniques in the field of audiovisual media such as Satie's contribution to *Parade* (1917) or the music he composed for *Entr'acte* (1924), an early synchronization of a musical score to film.

These aesthetic practices, these ways of performing and consuming performances in a kind of bohemian attitude in a space that was in ways both public and private (a habitus or attitude of a more informal quotidian nature than the postures assumed in formal concert halls like the Salle Pleyel, where Villard also performed) took shape in the same intellectual milieu that, in the figure of Cros, would produce revolutionary thought in the mechanical recording and reproduction of sound and color.[51] About the unconventional attitudes of "Nina's band," Villard's friend, the journalist Maurice Dreyfous, penned this revealing description:

> It was a strange bunch [*une drôle de troupe*], I assure you, that group following our friend Nina, nearly everywhere and especially in the Salles Pleyel, Herz, and other concert halls where she played piano with much success amongst the most renowned artists of the era [. . .] when great artists, like Sivori and Vieuxtemps, saw Nina and her band arrive, they said to each other, "Things are going to heat up in here [*ca va chauffer*]." [. . .] from her fingertips she evoked the soul of Chopin on the piano keys. The arrival of this hirsute, bearded, and questionably dressed troupe appeared quite out of place [*détonait*] in these rather elegant, rigid, proper and reserved assemblies.[52]

I would argue that that band and its milieu encouraged, if not outright invented, a modern form of sociability in its distinctive attitudes to listening.

On the other hand, one could argue, as the Goncourt brothers did, that such a raucous salon and such bohemian attitudes only hindered deep listening or true work from taking place ("a sort of intellectual haschisch-tinged drunkenness [. . .] prevented work from happening"), that someone like Cros couldn't build working devices in such an environment, that he, or any true inventor, needed a space more like the laboratory (together with the money, time, and equipment) afforded him by one of Cros's scientific patrons such as the Duke of Chaulnes. This is true in Cros's case, but only to a certain extent. And here is where Villard's spirit and that of her salon remain of capital importance, specifically and somewhat ironically in its deepest, most diabolical, and bohemian nature. Cros met with opposition to his experiments at the chateau of the Duke of Chaulnes because some in the duke's family, principally the duke's mother, the Duchess of Chevreuse, viewed such experiments with sound reproducibility as sacrilege.[53] Villard and her milieu, on the contrary, inheriting a taste for the diabolical from

Poe and Baudelaire, would only have ever encouraged mechanical sound reproducibility or color photography as so much irreverent pathbreaking activity to challenge and upset the establishment. These pursuits were perhaps all the more revolutionary as scientific theory developed for the public domain, as Cros sometimes presented his work (and given the communard sympathies of Villard and her circle), rather than as capitalist enterprise, as with the case of Edison, the "wizard of Menlo Park," who thwarted the sorcerers and sorceresses of the rue Chaptal and the rue des Moines.[54] More indicative of the audiovisual revolution to come than the scientific patronage the Duke of Chaulnes offered Cros would have been the patronage Jules Carpentier provided Cros in efforts to develop color photography. Years later, after Cros's death but likely inspired partly by his theories, Carpentier would become a principal engineer of the Lumière brothers' cinematographe, their first movie camera.[55] And so the technological audiovisual media competition and rivalry continued.

At the same time, the spirit of Villard's salon can be seen as a link in the lineage of musical performance that would come to underlie influential currents in the musical and artistic avant-garde of the early twentieth century. In suggesting a genealogy from Villard and her salon habitués to Satie at the Chat Noir and in his later dadaist guises, I do not mean to emphasize or suggest so much connection along strictly musical or even pianistic lines as much as the kind of performance aesthetic and milieu, continuity, and development in that context, from Villard's bohemian salon to Chat Noir provocation and avant-garde experimentation.

Villard's salon, moreover, deserves recognition as a fertile milieu for ideas about intermedial aesthetics, of which the synesthetic frame is only one among several possible frames for inter-arts relations of this era. From a musicological perspective, Villard's salon has been overlooked as a critical nexus in the cultivation of seminal trends in musical modernity, not only important trends but trends that clashed or at least would come to clash as opposing poles. As an early and ardent supporter of Wagner (in that respect sharing enthusiasm with Baudelaire and Cros for the German composer), Villard recognized one current that would come to define musical modernity of the era. At the same time, the germs of a starkly different musical trajectory coexisted with Wagnerism in Villard's salon, this other line pointing toward Satie's conception of music, which came to be at odds with Wagner's.

The largely forgotten composer Ernest Cabaner, "Tronche," as Rimbaud called him, Lafilède in Mendès's novel, as we saw in the previous section, most incarnates that other element of the musical life of Villard's salon.

In addition to frequenting Villard's salon, Cabaner contributed to the *Album Zutique*, housed Rimbaud for some time, and was an early proponent of Cézanne's radical vision in painting (indeed, the Impressionists, after Cézanne enlisted the help of Zola, staged a benefit show and sale of their works to offer financial support to an ailing impoverished Cabaner). The poet François Coppée, recalling his impressions of Cabaner, doubted whether "a creature as fantastical as him had ever emerged from the mind of Hoffmann, of Edgar Poe or Achim von Arnim."[56]

Cabaner stands beside Villard, who is seated at the piano, in the watercolor of Villard's salon by the mostly forgotten Impressionist painter Pierre Franc Lamy, the murderer in Mendès's novel (see Figure 25). As a composer, Cabaner might anticipate Satie more in his mystique and the fictional characters he inspired in several novels than in what little survives of his music, though there is at least one musical program that situates Cabaner as a musical ancestor of Satie and the School of Arcueil.[57]

In the way Satie would come to include everyday noises, such as a typewriter, as musical elements in his compositions for *Parade* (1917), Kabaner, the Cabaner character in Paul Alexis's novel *Madame Meuriot*, would seem to have paved the way with the vision of his "great modern opera . . . in which the principal noises of reality will be reproduced [*où seront reproduits les principaux bruits de la réalité*]," a passage imbued with more than a touch of sarcasm.[58] The idea of reproducing the noises of reality draws out, almost to absurdity for the era, Cabaner's musical theories, which Verlaine described as "sometimes abracadraba-esque [*abracadabrantes*]."[59] "Reproduced" is a key word in that passage because it highlights the profound interest of the era for "reproducing reality."[60] Indeed, Alexandra Kieffer has recently demonstrated how the reception of Debussy's music of a slightly later period, circa 1902–1910, involved an intense debate among music critics in the Parisian press about the "rendering" of sonic realities, often the sounds of nature, in music.[61] Music critical discourses on Debussy involved differing conceptions of music as sound, an attention to music's "sonic materiality," with the result that Debussy's listeners often found themselves presented with distinct challenges in making his music intelligible.[62] With the reception of Debussy's opera *Pelléas et Mélisande*, for instance, some critics appealed to noise and the nonmusical as a way of negotiating a tension between, as Kieffer explains, music as a historically bound system and, on the other hand, music as "sonic materiality [. . .] outside all history and all convention."[63]

The passage from Alexis's novel, however, leaves open the specific question of how exactly the noises of Cabaner's imagined modern opera would be reproduced, whether by traditional musical instruments, by playback of phonographic recordings, or by the very noisemakers themselves. Absent that word, if the modern opera were to be quite simply made of "the principal noises of reality," the passage would have more closely presaged the innovations of futurist "art of noises" and then of the *Musique Concrète* to come with the GRM in the 1950s and 1960s, a musical and theoretical movement which did precisely that, record and reproduce the noises of reality for musical composition.[64]

Cabaner's song *Le Pâté* became one of the principal musical refrains of Villard's salon, a song described by Léon Valade in a poem of the *Album Zutique* as " a splendid thing [chose *épatante*]," the popular refrain of an entire generation.[65] The irreverent playfulness and humor of this musical "hit" would find a close echo in the title of Satie's *Trois Morceaux en forme de Poire*, an archetypally humorous title Satie chose after, as one story goes, Debussy chided him for a lack of form in certain other compositions. In Alexis's *Madame Meuriot*, characters request to hear Kabaner's *Le Pâté*, lyrics and music, its title undisguised but parodied all the same in the novel. Such parody arises because, after *Le Pâté*, Kabaner continues to play a piece with the title *La Mortadelle* (a kind of sausage) at which one character exclaims "musical charcuterie . . . we will dine on it!" (311). Kabaner responds, with the kind of humor Satie would come to adopt with *Trois Morceaux* and other compositions such as *Le Water-Chute*: "Why not? Charcuterie after pastry! Then I'll turn to musical groceries [*l'épicerie musicale*], when I compose *The Gherkin* and maybe even the *Prune of Agen*." The irony here is that Alexis mocks the legacy of Cabaner and Villard with a kind of humor that will form part of the veritable musical avant-garde to come. Kabaner concludes that "musical charcuterie" is excellent preparation for his modern opera of contemporary noises, for *"les principaux bruits de la réalité."* This passage reads like a prehistory of musical noisiness as farce. Historical developments, musical ones to be precise, are prophesized here as farce before they are repeated as farce. Jacques Attali was one, with his wide-ranging *Bruits* (Noise, the political economy of music) (1977, 1985) to emphasize music's specific power to offer premonitions of historical developments.

In Alexis's sarcasm, if these noises speak to Cabaner's incomprehensibility, both in sound and in music theory, the novelist further provides a frame for inter-arts relationships with the character Poldex (likely a cryptonym for Cézanne), who is a painter. He is the only one who understands Kabaner. Cabaner, to recall, was known for his ardent support and passion for Cézanne's vision (and, indeed, it was in Villard's salon where the two met and recognized the audacity of each other's art). By mocking Cézanne through Cabaner/Kabaner, Alexis offers an acoustic parallel for critical accounts of the time judging Cézanne under the banner of incomprehensibility, an answer to the question of what would have sounded as shocking and incomprehensible in the acoustic realm as a Cézanne painting in the visual field at that historical moment.

Cabaner's contemporaries further left vivid accounts of the "unforgettable" sound of his performances.⁶⁶ In particular, his voice, "like a cracked clarinet" or a "lamentable rip [*une déchirure lamentable*]," marked by a lisp, sung with "an air that could summon the devil upon earth, a melody more solemn than a Bach fugue" with lyrics of patent ridiculousness about a delicious pâté, a strange combination that Pakenham and Lefrère conclude must have produced "irresistible comedy."⁶⁷ The cracked and torn quality of his voice could have only contributed to the comparisons with Poe. Cabaner, it would appear, could have walked straight out of the house of Usher into the house of Villard; the diabolical summoning recalls Baudelaire. Indeed, an 1880 letter from Cabaner to composer Emmanuel Chabrier details how Cabaner "applied" Baudelaire's poem "La Beauté" to music by arranging it with a Bach fugue.⁶⁸ It should be noted that Cabaner says he is "applying" the poem to the fugue when the poet Théodore de Banville praises Cabaner for finding the melody contained *within* the verses: Cabaner, "marvelous harmonist, uncovers the melody within our poets' stanzas rather than pasting [*plaquer*] those stanzas onto dance tunes."⁶⁹ In this way, attention to Cabaner and Villard provides a means of gauging one way in which Baudelaire sounded and resounded amongst the generation of poets and artists of the latter half of the Second Empire and the early Third Republic. It provides a particular way in which Baudelaire was heard in Villard's circle—Baudelaire set to Bach. These historical documents allow us to imagine, at the dawn of mechanical audio recording, how Baudelaire was heard in the Belle Époque: "La Beauté" accompanied by the strains of Bach arranged by an eccentric composer, who appropriately enough in his air and general appearance made everyone think of Poe, and who developed his thinking about Bach in dialogue with Chabrier, another habitué of Villard's salon.⁷⁰

Looking ahead, before Debussy would set Mallarmé's *L'après-midi d'un faune* to music, Cabaner set Mallarmé's *Hérodiade* to music, a work attested to but now lost.⁷¹ One wonders how Mallarmé, who was also known to have spent time in Villard's salon, might have heard Cabaner's music for *Hérodiade* or if the notes ever reached his ears. Such a historical record is crucial, nevertheless, because it shows how Villard's salon served as a transitional space for the development of Impressionism in music. Debussy's setting of Mallarmé's poetry to music is well known, indeed legendary, but Cabaner's music for Mallarmé's poetry is not. Nor is Debussy's setting of Cros's poem "L'Archet" to music, which followed in the footsteps of Cabaner's music for "L'Archet."⁷² Indeed, composers central to the musical ambiance and thought of Villard's salon—Charles de Sivry and Henry Ghys—gave piano lessons to the next generation of composers, de Sivry to Debussy and Ghys to Ravel.

It is important to note that Cabaner was also a synesthete.[73] As a synesthete, he inspired bizarre means of representing sound, one being his own particular notational system, likened by one of his contemporaries to a Balzacian search for the absolute: By one account, Cabaner had invented a "particular system of 'intentional notation,' which is to say that in order to indicate the subtlest inflections of singing and the clarity of the interpreter, he imagined special typographic signs [. . .] that were unintelligible to anyone but himself. He had hoped to go even further, and ultimately indicate sounds with letters: not by juxtaposed vowels and consonants."[74] Such an account offers context and some help in deciphering the very strange dashes of color at the center of Franc Lamy's watercolor of Villard's salon (see Figure 25), where Villard is at the piano and Cabaner stands to her side. These strokes of different colors evoke Cabaner's synesthesia together with a sense of his "intentional notation," his search for an alternate typographic system for sounds based on color, Baudelairean "correspondances" of sound and color, hearkening back even to Castel's ocular harpsichord, in a sense (Figure 4). At the same time, the patches of color might suggest the transcription of the sounds Villard is producing at the piano together with the sense of Villard as someone who *could* interpret Cabaner's arcane system.

Indeed, Cabaner authored a curious poem, "The Sonnet of Seven Numbers [*Le sonnet des sept nombres*]," which he dedicated to Rimbaud. The poem may have predated and influenced Rimbaud's famous "Voyelles" sonnet. In the manuscript of Cabaner's poem, Cabaner used different color inks for different sections of the poem. It is also known that Rimbaud was once heard humming a strange melody composed by Cabaner, the music for Cabaner's poem "Souffles de l'air," which was dedicated to Charles Cros.[75] Rimbaud's singing of the poem serves to index Cabaner and Villard's resounding musical hum throughout Paris, the veritable influence of Villard's salon as a resonant space that intersected acoustically with some of the most important artistic movements of the time.[76] Indeed, the manuscript of Cabaner's "Le sonnet des sept nombres," for instance, with its startling approach to color, after Cabaner's death, found its way into the hands of a certain Doctor Gachet, *the* Doctor Gachet whom Van Gogh knew and painted at the end of his life at Auvers.[77]

Rimbaud, Cabaner, and Gachet's stories aside, there is a different historical and theoretical context for the strange patches of color in Lamy's painting that evoke new and burgeoning attitudes to sound. Villard was often acclaimed for her touch on the piano, a quality that viewers of Lamy's painting in her circle would have recognized, a dimension that adds yet another sense to the synesthetic play of the image. Indeed, music critics often praised her for possessing the spirit of Chopin in her playing, specifically in her touch. Early in her career as a pianist, Villard studied with the renowned piano teacher Henri Herz, who had another pupil, Marie Jaëll. Jaëll became an acclaimed concert pianist and author of theories of music performance, including a method involving images of fingerprints on piano keys to aid in the search for a particular pianistic touch (see Figure 28).[78] Indeed, the photographic reproductions of these fingerprints could be conceived as yet another means, as Cros and others envisioned the future of phonography, of photographing sound.

Villard and Jaëll crossed paths at least once in August 1869 when Villard saw Jaëll and her husband perform piano duets in Baden. In the published review, to recall from earlier in this chapter, Villard hailed the "ravishing" performance of Schumann's variations for two pianos for its "remarkable precision [*étonnante précision*]."[79] Even if the 1869 concert marked the only time that Villard and Jaëll were present together in the same room (and I would hazard they met in other circumstances, and that Jaëll, who lived in Paris, very well could have performed in Villard's salon), the very title of one of Jaëll's later publications, *A New State of Consciousness: Color Added to Tactile Sensations* [*Un nouvel état de conscience: la coloration des sensations tactiles*] (1910), offers striking context for a genealogy that could be drawn from Villard and Jaëll's lessons with Herz to Rimbaud's piano lessons with Cabaner (with colors

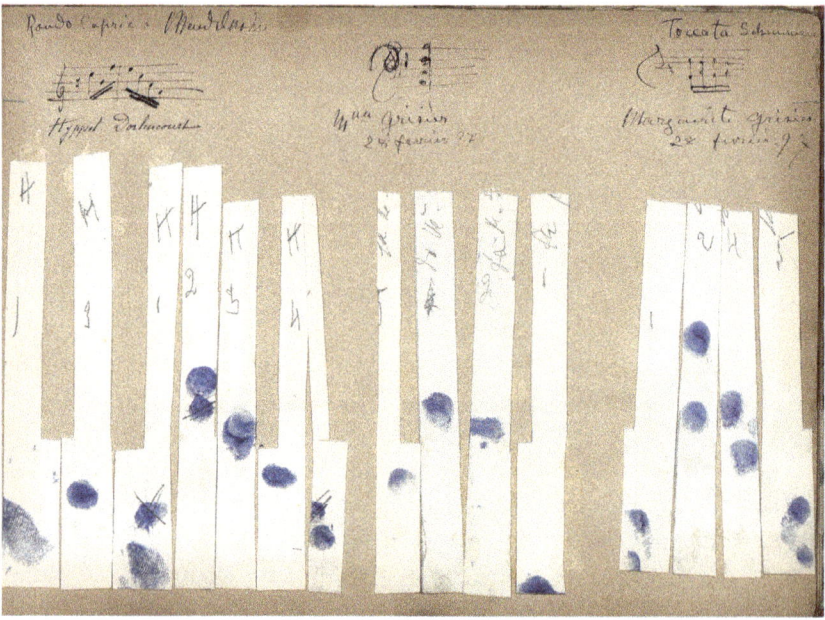

Figure 28. Fingerprints of Marie Jaëll's students, circa 1897 (Fonds Marie Jaëll, ms. 560-1). Courtesy Bibliothèque Nationale et Universitaire de Strasbourg.

possibly even painted on the keys of Cabaner's piano) to Villard's salon music to Jaëll's music theories.

Theories about the relationships between color and sound were not new to this period (recall once again Castel's "clavecin oculaire" from the eighteenth century), but Lamy's painting helps us to see Villard's salon as a critical nexus in developing those theories and practices, expanding the synesthetic field into a phonographic field registering the color of sound as imprint. Such expansion of the synesthetic field likewise offers an unexpected angle on a poem as canonical as "Voyelles," beyond even the enigmatic and startling intertext of Cabaner's "Sonnet des sept nombres." To that intertext we can add Lamy's painting of synesthetic performance, the musical life of Villard and her salon, and the music theory of Marie Jaëll, all of which ultimately offer a broader kaleidophonic field of the era to contemplate. In the way Harismendy-Lony argues Villard's poetic voice deserves attention, specifically with respect to the *Album Zutique*, I thus want to highlight Villard's importance, beyond her role as muse, as an architect of intersensory and intermedial relationships, in the spirit of the broader multisensory experience of nineteenth-century mass culture.

Still within the field of sound and color relationships, though an explicit statement of Cros's desire to preserve Villard's voice and music with his "paleophonic" technology has not been found, there is evidence of Cros's attempt to reproduce her image mechanically, specifically in the medium of color photography. A photographic print from Cros's experiments in color photography circa 1876 features, among other still-life objects, a ceramic portrait of Villard on a plate likely made by Charles's brother Henry (see Figure 29).[80] Henry was primarily a sculptor who worked in the medium of polychrome wax sculpture. At once an important intertext for Manet's images of Villard (her hair and vest in the ceramic resemble her hair, with feathered comb, and her vest in the *La Dame aux éventails* painting), the photographic print further demonstrates the breadth and depth of intermedial experimentation and research in Villard's salon. It is indicative of the desire to represent the modern world anew with diverse means and materials, from color photography to polychrome wax sculpture to sound recordings.

And it is in these materials where Villard, gazing out of this still-life photograph, commands a particular outlook on the media in which modern life could be newly recorded. Specifically, Henry Cros sought novel techniques of achieving a broad palette of color in wax sculpture. In this wax medium, the poet Jules Laforgue saw an opportunity for the sculptor to represent subjects drawn from modern life—subjects for instance one might find walking the streets of modern Paris, such as prostitutes, ragpickers, jockeys, and dancers.[81]

Figure 29. Charles Cros, trichrome photograph, 1876. Collection Bibliothèque Centrale of the Muséum d'histoire naturelle, Paris. From Cros, *Inédits*, plate III.

After the tinfoil medium of Edison's first audio recordings, wax became in the mid-1880s the principal material in which sound was recorded on early phonographic cylinders. Hence, in wax in the 1880s, color and sound would come to be inscribed in uncommon ways in a common substance.

Villard articulated her visionary critical statement on the direction that wax, as an important material of modernity, would take in the public eye when she authored a penetrating review of the 1881 Impressionist Exhibition and highlighted Degas's *Petite Danseuse de quatorze ans*, a sculpture that was initially modeled by the artist in wax. In her review, Villard presages an art of the future—specifically a novel means of recording modern life:

> [. . .] such subtleties of her chin, eyelids, and straps on her foot presage future dignities [*font présager les royautés futures*].
>
> Before this statuette I felt one of the most violent artistic impressions of my life: For a long time I had been dreaming of this.
>
> When seeing virgins in village churches, saints in painted wood, covered with ornaments, fabrics, and jewels, I would say to myself: How is it that a great artist hasn't had the idea to apply these altogether naïve and charming approaches to a powerful modern work, and here it is I have found my idea realized [*et voilà que je trouve mon idée réalisée*] [. . .].
>
> All around me people were saying: It's just a doll. What difficulty one finds when trying to convince the public to look without anger at something it has not already seen the day before.
>
> But the artist should take comfort: The misunderstood work of today will perhaps one day be in a museum, admired respectfully as the original formula of a new art [*la première formule d'un art nouveau*].[82]

Villard thus demonstrates the powers of her vision for the future of art and media. In this way, she both assumes and transcends the role of muse to become a visionary art critic and figurative architect of a space in which these "formulas" for new art and media forms could flourish.

I close this chapter with a reflection on Villard as an architect and concertmaster, specifically in the improvisatory spirit and bohemian habitus she inspired, which involved a distinctive attitude toward creating new art forms and the specific materials for their making. Her poem "Impromptu" (by one account composed on-the-spot near the end of her life) speaks to this attitude.[83] Like the divine poet of Baudelaire's prose poem "Loss of Halo," which Villard's poem appears to invoke, the divine figure of Villard's poem, a Venus of the boulevards, a Venus with "black hair [*franges* noires]," to emphasize, delights in mingling with the world of the modern city. Just as the speaker of Baudelaire's poem attempts to help the seraphic poet of yore recover his lost halo on the streets of Paris, the Parisians of Villard's poem would like to construct altars to worship Venus's beauty. To this wish, she responds that it bores her and that she would instead prefer the "poor mortals" speak "argot in her company."

On lui voudrait bien dresser des autels,	For her we can envision pedestals,
Mais elle répond que cela l'ennuie	But she says that's sheer ennui
Et qu'elle permet aux pauvres mortels	And that she'd rather us poor mortals
De parler argot en sa compagnie.[84]	Speak argot as company at her party.

In this situation, "argot" suggests the beauty of the quotidian, of everyday life, namely the urban boulevards and their everyday language as material for art.

At the same time, the "argot" implies a disdain for bourgeois etiquette and formality; "argot" evokes the bohemian qualities of Villard's circle and her salon that were widely chronicled, attitudes to noise and noisemaking cherished as the disruptive spirit of novel art forms.[85] The imperative became to upset, first of all literally, the slumber of the bourgeois interior as a literal and figurative means of upsetting moribund slumbering art forms. The noise of her parties and concerts was famous for upsetting the quiet decorum of the bourgeois apartment building. Indeed, in a review of one of Villard's concerts, domestic and public performance spaces are juxtaposed: "The piano, so hated, so dreaded when heard from the neighbor living above, even during the course of normal evening gatherings, or, still worse, during a concert, the piano has an altogether welcome effect in a theater space."[86] In composer Charles de Sivry's account of his first visit to Villard's salon, he related that: "We must play Wagner both to annoy the bourgeoisie and in the spirit of revolution [*embêter les bourgeois et par esprit de révolution*]," and then he concluded about the music making: "The effect of the rehearsal was bizarre. Everyone was making jokes the whole time; it was in the end very funny."[87]

Such radical comportment inflected the broader spirit of spontaneity, quick wit, and the search for the shape of art and media to come, a climate in which the music of both Wagner and Cabaner could be heard and celebrated. And it is finally in this way that we might consider the dreams and methods of writing sound in this era inflected by a taste for the radically new in the unheard-of provocations that took shape in Villard's salon. The imperative to "speak argot" in Villard's "Impromptu" poem harmonized with the imperatives to write sound and color in wax, to see how sound and color could newly inhabit this material substance, to model profane modern everyday life in wax in the shape of sacred icons. Similarly, argot spoken between goddess and "poor mortal Parisians" harmonized with the way starving artists, political radicals, and princesses and princes alike sat side by side on the floor or crouched on the stairs of Villard's salon, the way, as de Sivry related, jokes were told over the choruses of *Lohengrin*.[88]

Conclusion
Pyrophonica and the Rhythms of Inspiration

In a short essay titled "What I Am [*Ce que je suis*]" (1912), Erik Satie—a longtime pianist at the cabaret that was animated by Cros in its early days, the cabaret successor of Villard's salon, the cabaret whose name was borrowed from a short story by Poe, a tale translated and often recited by Baudelaire, the poet who intimately knew the same Norman port town kissed by "the poetic waters of the Seine and the stormy waters of the Channel," Honfleur, where Satie was born—explicitly articulates an idea of kaleidophonic recording.[1] Specifically, a half-imagined instrument, a "kaleidophone-recorder" assisted him, so he says, in his composing. Satie begins the short text by responding to critics' attacks on him and his music with irony and his own characteristic wit: "Everyone will tell you that I am not a musician. It's true."[2] The eccentric composer then outlines alternative classifications of the various activities he pursues. "Pyrophonia," for instance, concerns sonic explosions. The idea prefigures the thundering of Dada soon to come at the Cabaret Voltaire while hearkening back to something like Baudelaire's "deafening street" in Paris.[3] "Phonometrography," Satie continues, involves close scientific inspection of sounds and music, a "repugnant" B-flat, for example, or an "ordinary" F-sharp that weighs precisely 93 kilograms (heavy, yes, for an F-sharp). Satie imagines, or at least partly imagines, devices to assist him in accomplishing these tasks: a "phonomètre" to measure all of Verdi and all of Beethoven; a "phono-peseur" to record their weight; and a "phonoscope" to peer, as one would with a microscope, into the hidden visual structures of musical notes (similar but not quite the same idea as the microphones at play in something like Francis Ford Coppola's 1974 film *The Conversation* or Brian de Palma's 1981 *Blowout*—Satie is really talking about *seeing* into a sound).[4]

Man Ray once remarked that Satie was the only composer he knew who had eyes. One can read this text and these imaginary instruments both as characteristic of Satie's humor ("without batting an eyelid too much") and as a response to the scientificity of certain artistic schools and of music critics' attempts to classify, in Satie's view, absurdly so. Satie redirects the absurdity and takes it a step further.

But are statements like these all entirely comic? Are they altogether ironic? This is a question Daniel Albright has posed of Satie's writings, and of this text in particular, especially as Albright claims: "For Satie, music was not expression, but a barrier against expression [. . .] a barrier against sound itself."[5] More specifically about "What I am" and Satie's self-description as a "phonometrographer," Albright has argued: ". . . it is impossible not to regard it as a piece of frivolity [. . .] a caricature of Satie's real method of stressing the self-containment and heft of sounds, the acoustic substrate that doesn't develop, doesn't cue emotions, but just lies there, furnishing the ear."[6] Though emotions *are* there sometimes with Satie ("like a nightingale with a toothache") and the word "furnishing" begs further comment (more on that in a moment), for now, I want to emphasize Albright's interpretation that this text offers something like a "caricature" of Satie's method and close attention to the "self-containment of sounds." I linger on the question of method here because Satie, in "What I Am," goes on to reveal that he composed his "pièces froides" with the help of a "kaleidophone-recorder." The instrument is most likely an imaginary one, this "kaleidophone-recorder," like the phonoscope or the strange secret castles and cast iron flying machines Satie drew in meticulous calligraphic script on note cards in private.[7] However, Man Ray's remark about the power of the composer's eyes should give us pause.

A kaleidophone transforms sounds into beautiful visual forms. It is, after all, about audiovisual play with a "philosophical *toy*," as Wheatstone conceived it. Satie, with aphoristic verbal play, sees his method of composing in the lineage of a real device, the kaleidophone, which he modifies by imagining it endowed with the element of recording. It is possible Satie mocks the idea of needing an instrument like a kaleidophone-recorder for composing (because he already composes that way, gifted with a visual artist's eyes, on his own, *without* using any scientific instrument). At the same time, he provides insight into the audiovisual play presiding over the composition of his "pièces froides," their critical reception, and the broader Parisian intermedial artistic milieu in which he was such an important figure. And if what Satie is really doing with this text, whether caricatural or serious, is stressing the very possibilities latent in focusing microscope-like and phonoscope-like on the "self-containment" of sounds, he is simultaneously *expanding* the field of acoustical aesthetics in a way that we might find later exemplified in such things as Russolo's futurist "Art of Noises [L'Arte dei rumori]" (1913), the noises Satie himself incorporated as musical sound in *Parade* (1917), the innovations of the GRM and *musique concrète* in the 1950s and 1960s, or the audio sampling and experimentation in the sound art and electronic music of today.[8]

The last scientific device Satie imagines in "What I Am" recalls Cros's similarly satirical text "The Journal of the Future" (1880). Satie says that it is thanks to a "motodynamophone" that he has *written* so much. The machine allows even a mediocre "phonometrist" to "notate more sounds than the most expert musician [*le plus habile musicien*], given the same amount of time and effort." The absurdity here, which can in one sense be read as a revolt against bourgeois temporal rhythms imposed on artistic pursuits, also characterizes Satie's remarkable "Musician's Day" text, in which Satie details how, among other daily activities, he is regularly "inspired" from 10:23 to 11:47 in the morning and then again from 15:12 to 16:07 in the afternoon, an interval he calls "*autre inspiration*." Similar to the way Villard's bohemianism irritated the Goncourt brothers and her other detractors, Satie's *montmartrois* bohemian side would continually frustrate Cocteau. In these ways, Satie imagines himself, again satirically so, in a position akin to the writers of the *Chat Noir* journal of the future as Cros imagined it, writers who, aided by so many technological inventions, could turn out poetry faster than Victor Hugo. Furthermore, Satie's phrase "le plus habile musicien" is the same one Kastner uses in *Les Voix de Paris* (1857) when describing the challenge of transcribing the acoustic signature of a city, the challenge of finding the last note in Paris's "polymorphic canon." Where to begin, where to end in the "sonic chaos" of nineteenth-century Paris? In Kastner's *Les Voix de Paris*, "le plus habile musicien" is overwhelmed by the urban "polymorphic canon"; in Satie's "What I Am," "le plus habile musicien" is outpaced by the modern machine. Even as Satie pokes fun at the idea that technological devices have surpassed the ears and hands of the most gifted musicians, he seems comparatively serious when he ends the text by declaring that the future belongs to "philophony."

For futurist painter Luigi Russolo, the future belonged to noise. Inspired by Filippo Marinetti's poetry and Balilla Pratella's music, Russolo opened his 1913 manifesto by declaring: "Ancient life was altogether silent. It was only in the nineteenth century, with the invention of machines, that noise was born." More precisely, Russolo was interested in breaking out of what he considered the restrained and limited spectrum of pure sounds into the "infinite variety of sound-noises." Where Satie mostly imagined acoustic devices, Russolo took the step of actually building devices for noisemaking concerts with the assistance of painter Ugo Piatti (see Figure 30). Russolo gave these noisemakers names,

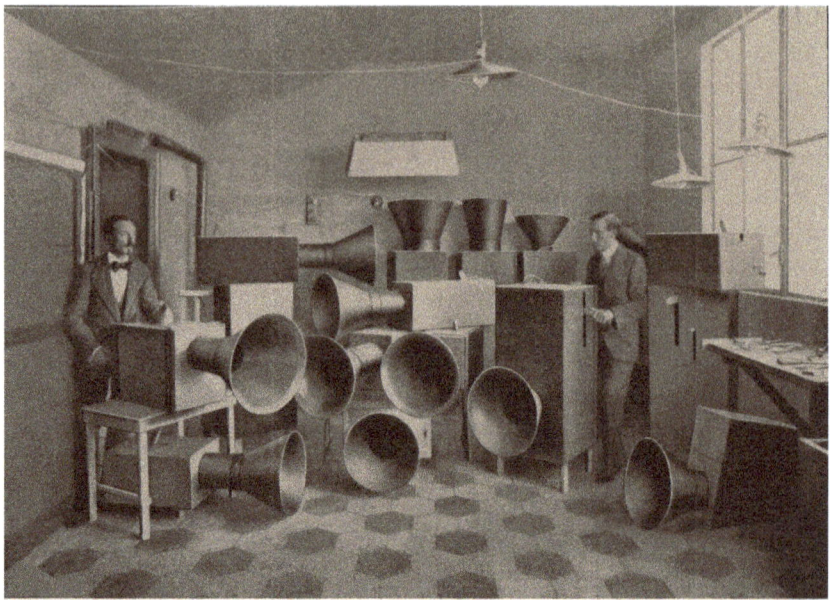

Figure 30. Luigi Russolo and Ugo Piatti with their "Intonarumori," Milan, 1913. Courtesy Heritage Image Partnership Ltd. / Alamy Stock Photo.

such as "ululatori," "stropicciatori," and "gorgogliatori," contributing in effect to both poetic and musical discourse. Russolo concluded his 1913 manifesto by imploring: "We must evermore enlarge and enrich the domain of sounds."[9]

With this book, my aim has been to respond to that kind of call. I've sought to articulate a response to such an imperative to "enlarge and enrich" the sonic domain, the "spectre sonore" understood in this way more as range than specter, here specifically with the nineteenth-century auditory imagination, the birth of kaleidophonics along with a machine-age nineteenth-century noise.

How, then, do these nineteenth-century phenomena bear on auditory phenomena in modernist literature and avant-garde aesthetics?[10] Without positing a strict genealogy between the texts I have examined and Russolo's "art of noises" or Satie's "What I Am," I still want to claim that such futurist noise-making and such protodadaist farcical playfulness and irreverence have origins in those literary texts, from the jarring sounds of Poe's "Valdemar" to Baudelaire's "deafening street" to Cros's paleophonic interplanetary love affairs to Whitman's "barbaric yawp" to the resonant nights of Villard's salon, as well as in the strident technologies the futurists were championing at the dawn of the twentieth century. Where Kastner discovered music within (and sometimes despite) the noise of nineteenth-century Paris, Russolo called for a transformation of music *by* the "art of noises." And where Dickens, in the passage from *The Old Curiosity Shop* cited in this book's Introduction, spoke of "detecting" differences within urban noise, Russolo imagined a similar activity while also aiming to "orchestrate" those noises into an artistic work, its acoustic palette located in the growth of modern machines and cities. Russolo suggests: "Let us cross a great modern capital city together, our ears more attentive than our eyes, and we will vary the pleasures of our sensibility."[11] For anyone who has tried to maintain ears more attentive than eyes or to "do nothing but listen," as Whitman proclaimed in "Song of Myself," this is in fact a difficult activity to sustain for any extended period of time in a city. Such difficulty lends support to Georg Simmel's claim in his influential essay "The Metropolis and Mental Life" (1903) that stimulation of urbanites' vision tends to dominate stimulation of urbanites' ears in the context of urban social life.[12] In this way, I would add, such a claim should also alert us to the distinct challenge of assessing activities of the ear, its attentiveness or lack thereof in large cities. The dominance of the visual in urban life might also key us into what some have termed an "acoustical unconscious."[13] Russolo's call still remains an ongoing question for the growing convergence between studies of nineteenth-century visual and auditory culture: How do we expand and enrich our inquiry into acoustic phenomena?

One critical edge we gain from probing the acoustic field in nineteenth-century literature is a deeper understanding and appreciation of the interactions between nineteenth-century media and literature, of how literature itself involved theories, narratives, and metaphors of such technological change. I have argued that in the decades before the invention of sound recording and reproduction technologies, these writers were already directly and obliquely posing the kinds of questions about sound reproducibility that would occupy writers and inventors for decades after the invention of the phonograph. How would urbanites contend with the shock of disembodied voices in an ever more densely populated space? How, in the heightened presence or absence of physical closeness, could sound still touch, still bring people together? How could the sound of languages spoken by threatened populations and cultures be preserved?[14]

Ivan Kreilkamp has, for instance, cited a journalist's opinion from 1888 as evidence of optimism for what the newly invented phonograph could provide to late Victorian literature: The phonograph "will be, in many respects, a source of joy to novelists as an entirely new source of startling disclosures and unexpected *dénouements*."[15] On the other hand, I have argued, for one, that Poe's *dénouements* both drew from and shaped the social and cultural forces that would give rise to phonographic technologies and concepts such as Satie's "furniture music," new roles hence for music in everyday life. The nineteenth-century audiovisual imagination provided grounds and codes to critique the possibilities and dangers of these new devices together with their place in an increasingly urbanizing society.

A literary prehistory of modern audiovisual technologies lends itself more to discovering diverse theories and ideas about technologies and less to focusing exclusively on the technologies that have won out over others. Such is one advantage of exploring the prehistory of these media. On this point, Haun Saussy has claimed that one methodological pitfall of media theory is the risk that such theory follows "the self-description of the winners. A successful technology overtakes its predecessors and rivals; it defines the age; it is totalitarian."[16] As an alternative to the dangers of this totalitarian perspective that Saussy has identified, I have argued that theories of technology and media in the aesthetic field offer insights that we might not otherwise discover in histories of the "winning" technologies, the success stories, the history that gets written in, on, and by the "winning" media. And this critical move involves more than purely asserting that there is value and interest in exploring impasses and dead ends of history. Instead, I have sought to expand our methodological and historical purview in ways that take account of multiplicity in the convergence of media and literary studies. This convergence involves an openness to the multiple possibilities and shifting textualities of media technologies as represented in the literature of this historical period. And this is why I have had more recourse to terms such as "kaleidophonic," "sound recordings," and "sound reproducibility" than to *the* phonograph. Though I don't dispute the epistemological break in the mediascape that occurred with Edison's phonograph and Bell's telephone, it is nevertheless crucial to continue to probe how the practices and technologies of phonography became multiple in the nineteenth century. And these plural phonographies (plural, in part, because they were also conceived as paleophonies, paleographies, and acoustic daguerreotypes) would remain plural after the invention of Edison's phonograph, as they had been plural before.

My goal has thus been to stretch the domain of media studies and sound studies in the nineteenth century so that, for one, scholars in these areas might take more note of the period between 1830 and 1880, of literature and transatlantic dialogue in these years, for the development of modern mass audiovisual media.[17] My point, however, is not simply that we need to look further back in time or beyond the inventors and engineers for the origins of such mass media formations. Instead, I have aimed to demonstrate how we can read a range of works for a great multiplicity of ideas, representations, and narratives about how sound and listening were radically transformed, or modernized, as some might say, in the nineteenth century. The conditions of possibility as shaped in literature offer an alternative perspective on the perceived newness of modern relations to sound, a means of gauging the force of acoustical shock in the modern era, in modern cities, and in the face of modern acoustical media.

Such ideas contributed to new conceptions of an audible present. In anticipation of and response to that acoustic media sphere, the artistic imagination offered its own sonic cocoon or envelope in which one could find refuge and resources. My emphasis has been on the aesthetics and representations of such ideas: on how strange and exceptional plots and narrative *dénouements* in Poe, literary fantasies in Cros, metaphors in Baudelaire, poetic language in Whitman, and attitudes to listening and noisemaking in Villard's salon could create literary spaces for the emergence and aesthetics of these technological devices so that literature, in competition and in confluence with new media and new inscriptive technologies, was not wholly unprepared for shocks of the acoustic new and the broader audiovisual modern. Authors could say they had a hand in imagining and creating the machines and their social preconditions, again not always explicitly (except in the case of Cros) but in implicit and oblique ways in their texts. The literary prehistory of modern audiovisual technologies (the multiple *means of* dreaming about the recording and reproduction of sound, often in dialogue with color and image) served, in part, as literature's protective layer, its shield against the acoustic shock of the modern city.[18] That prehistory achieved (and in ways still achieves) this feat by always dreaming. Satie's "kaleidophone-recorder" serves, I would argue, as a case in point of this still dreaming activity; the composer resisted being entirely up to date with every scientific tool to appear in the capitalist marketplace by using irony to undo stable temporal frames and the activities typically associated with musical and scientific instruments.

At the same time, such a spectral layer (to recall Scott, Nadar, Balzac, and the daguerreotype), once stripped away by an audio recording device or a camera, would also serve to orient the direction of those devices. However firmly grafted onto or loosely clinging to the media, such layers altered, gradually but decisively, the trajectories of those media. In a way, Satie literalizes these impulses with his "furniture music," in the way such music was conceived, as Satie specified, "to neutralize the street noises."[19] But the music did other things too; it reimagined the space and place of everyday soundscapes. For example, his musical furniture, as described in one of Satie's private advertisements, could be consumed off the rack or tailor made (*"confection et sur mésure*").[20] And as Satie accomplished with René Clair's short film *Entr'acte* in 1924, music, in the form of a film score, could also be tailored to fit the moving image.

I have not taken for granted James Lastra's claim that "there was hardly a writer in the nineteenth century . . . who did not speculate in similar terms" as Félix Nadar on the idea of a device that might do for the ear what photography did for the eye.[21] We might still ask if such an idea was truly occupying so many minds, both literary and scientific (my feeling is that Lastra overstates that point, as Jacques Perriault has also wondered about Nadar's claim to the same effect in the nineteenth century). But the more important question, as I have stressed, is *how* precisely such an idea occupied those minds. My contention has been that such ideas came to be represented in the confluence of technological and urban imaginaries, in the mechanizing tendencies of modern urban life.[22]

The idea of an "acoustic daguerreotype" has been a frequent touchstone throughout this book. I have intended that idea to serve less as an example of literary premonition or corollary to what existed for photography with texts such as Tiphaigne's *Giphantie* (1760), and more as an example of dialogue between media. This one example indexes the expansive imagination that fear of and desire for those technologies could inspire. Scholars have commented on this audiovisual dialogue between technologies by noting that Edison's phonograph, soon after its invention, was often compared to photography, which had been around for nearly forty years.[23] While these types of comparison are revealing, they can be all the more so when considering similar comparisons that occurred *before* the technical realization of the phonograph, in the writings of Nadar for one, and, as I have revealed, in the writings of Scott and Kastner, among others (that is, more or less, explicitly in their writings). An important part of my argument has been that we can discover similar discourses and comparisons operating under other guises in literary texts, as in Champfleury's "Legend of the Daguerreotypist" (1863).

While media scholars may often use the term "remediation" to describe the understanding of new media in terms of older preexisting technology, a term more apt for the example of the "acoustic daguerreotype" as it was written and conceived in the 1850s and 1860s might be pre-mediation or, better yet, pre-remediation, understanding of an anticipated, not yet invented technology in terms of a preexisting technology.[24] And this involves more than literary fantasies that approximate the mechanics or ability of the technological devices, though those literary expressions can be as revealing as they are startling (e.g., with Rabelais and Tiphaigne de la Roche, as discussed in the Introduction, and with

CONCLUSION: PYROPHONICA AND THE RHYTHMS OF INSPIRATION 201

Cyrano, as discussed in Chapter 1). These literary representations are more revealing in the way they articulate the uses, fears, and wonder (to specify a few of the dimensions I have examined in this book) about new media and their perceived newness. The elaboration of such possibilities and affective responses in an ostensibly silent medium, in literature and poetry as it appeared on the printed page, a very ancient technology for textualizing sound, promised its own defense against modern acoustic shocks and collisions while also creating a space to redirect those intrusions toward poetic and literary purposes. Ross Chambers argued, for example, about noise in Baudelaire's poetics, where urban noise could be both rival and model for poetry, involving a poetic attunement to urban discordance, to its noise.[25]

Lisa Gitelman, for instance, invokes the example of the acoustic daguerreotype in her discussion of phonograph demonstrations to public audiences in the years immediately following Edison's invention, in 1878–1879, when members of the audience collected scraps of the tinfoil on which sound was written and reproduced by Edison's machine.[26] Edison's first version of his phonograph inscribed sound on bands of tinfoil, a surface which could only be replayed a limited number of times before it was worn through. Scraps of this tinfoil metamorphosed into souvenirs for audience members who came to listen to demonstrations of the phonograph. Here was, in a sense, something like Baudelaire's "lambeau de musique" materialized, a metaphor made into material form as a scrap of tinfoil. Gitelman's comparison between the tinfoil as a souvenir of the event, of what those audience members had heard, and the idea of an acoustic daguerreotype is revealing. However, her approach to that idea differs from mine and the context within which I have examined it.

Indeed there might be something of a temporal dialectic between these two approaches. We think of the acoustic daguerreotype as, most broadly conceived, an analogy, a conception of one form sound recording could take, or, as Saussy has emphasized, one medium manifesting itself in relation to other media. Gitelman thinks of the acoustic daguerreotype as a way in which audiences, who were listening to the phonograph for the first time, could have made an analogy between the photograph as a souvenir and the scrap of tinfoil as a souvenir, a tinfoil record of sounds past, proof that the demonstration of the phonograph actually happened.[27] Hence, the idea of an acoustic daguerreotype in this context suggested a more tangible objecthood—something audiences could more easily grasp *like* a photograph.

In contradistinction, the idea of an "acoustic daguerreotype" in the 1850s and 1860s, as I have examined it, involved this question: How might sound that was still fugitive in that present be inscribed and recorded in the future? How would one do with sound what Daguerre had already done with light? Gitelman, on the other hand, considered the idea in 1878 in relation to the sounds inscribed on the tinfoil artifact. How did the audience at phonograph demonstrations conceive of this artifact, the souvenir of the mechanical demonstration, as remediation, a tangible record of how sound was newly recorded and reproduced by Edison's phonograph? That record was not replayable by those collectors who took their tinfoil souvenirs home with them from the phonograph demonstrations. These souvenirs resisted being read, were illegible as recorded sound, and were instead legible only as a "harbinger" of a new acoustic commodity still decades away, a commodity of mass-produced sound recordings available for consumer playback on improved devices such as the gramophone, the audio device more closely associated with literary modernism, as in *Ulysses* or "The Waste Land."

Though it may be easier to conceive of this book crystallizing around the phonograph and the telephone as mechanical devices, I prefer to maintain, as other scholars have, the terms "phonographies" or "sound reproducibility" as indicative of broader imaginaries for what was involved in discourses about ways of modernizing listening and sound. At the same time, my focus on the acoustic field of the modern city helps deepen our inquiry into what scholars such as Emily Thompson and Kata Gellen have called the "soundscape of modernity," in which they argue that a fundamentally new conception of the relation between sound and space arose in architectural practice, as Thompson argues for the period 1900–1932 in America, and in modernist literature, as Gellen argues specifically with Kafka.[28] Julie Napolin, too, like Gellen, among others, has helped us tune our sensibilities to the sonic in modernist literature, with a focus on narrative and the unconscious.[29] As complement to the study of those dramatic shifts in modernist literature and architecture, I have offered a means of covering the terrain leading up to the newness of those pivotal collisions between modernist sound, space, and literary text by demonstrating how the nineteenth-century city encouraged new acoustic collisions between media, elements of aesthetic modernity that might be described as kaleidophonic.

A particular conception of audiovisual relations in modernity enhances theories of visual modernity and vice versa. For instance, scholars of the history of photography and scholars of the history of phonography in the nineteenth century could be having more conversations about where their fields intersect. Sound and auditory culture, however, are more than substitutes or new players alongside visual culture. I would refrain from saying that any claims about the singularity of the visual field in the nineteenth century are always already audiovisual. Such a viewpoint, while provocative, seems too extreme. On the other hand, I have argued that undercurrents of acoustic figures (such as echo, disembodied voice, and acousmatic sound, to name a few) offer alternative means of critiquing the growth of mass media, mass culture, and the imbrication of the two.[30] Cros's literary representation of the telephone as a device for mass mechanical data collection would be one salient example of such a means of political and social critique.

Although I have dealt with poetry at length here, my emphasis has been less on the specific sounds of words—the way, for instance, Mallarmé's poetry approached pure sound ("Ses purs ongles très haut dédiant leur onyx"), or the way he and other symbolists invoked musicality as an ideal toward which their poetry aspired. I have addressed, but again with less emphasis, the way orality in the nineteenth century involved poetic declamations, public reading tours, reading aloud, and historical changes in literacy. As a complement to these "soundings" of literature and media, my emphasis has been most decidedly on representations and theories of sound in literary texts as connected to discourses on urban and technological audiovisual change.

The nineteenth-century city, though perhaps a noisier place than cities had ever been in ages past, was also a place where there was an impulse to shape that noise into the form of sounds beautiful and strange. It was a space to do other things with sound, to record it, reproduce it, and push beyond it, eventually into something like Russolo's "noise-sounds."

If noise has, at least for now, lost the kind of aesthetic potential it had with Russolo, if it became, as Jacques Attali argued in the 1970s, a figure of the "political economy of music," or, as Michel Serres proposed shortly thereafter in *Genesis* (1982), a figure of the multiple as a "new object for philosophy," then perhaps the future now belongs to something different. With sound studies as a field of scholarly inquiry continuing to expand, perhaps the future belongs to the archaeophonists just as much as it still belongs to, as Satie put it, philophony, a mode in which, as Attali found with music, prophecies might still be found or in which they might still find us.

Acknowledgments

Remarkable scholars, librarians, archivists, friends, and family members have all supported me in this endeavor, and I wish to acknowledge them here. At Northwestern University, where this book began its journey, Michal Ginsburg provided sharp insights, steadfast guidance, careful editing, and inspiration. I cannot thank her enough. Chris Bush likewise offered inspiration and support at critical junctures in the research and writing process. Sam Weber helped to inspire both the beginnings of this book (with a suggestion that I explore theories of the acoustic) and its later stages, when I benefited so much from the vibrant discussions of the Paris Program in Critical Theory. Alexander Weheliye graciously helped to introduce me to sound studies while guiding me in various research endeavors. I also wish to thank my professors and former colleagues at Northwestern in the Comparative Literary Studies Program and the Department of French and Italian who helped in ways both big and small (and, oftentimes, the seemingly small suggestions and words of encouragement grew over time): Jörg Kreienbrock, Alejandra Uslenghi, Peter Fenves, Thao Nguyen, Scott Durham, Doris Garraway, Nasrin Qader, Topher Davis, and Jane Winston. Jacob Wilkenfeld, Robert Ryder, and Matt Gilmore deserve special thanks for the conversations and suggestions that guided me in the early stages of discovering the topic of this book.

In Paris, my research and thinking on this project benefited greatly from conversations with Peter Szendy, Isabelle Alfandary, Ronald Rosbottom, Jennifer Cazenave, Haun Saussy, and Françoise Meltzer, in addition to a workshop at the University of Chicago Center in Paris. I thank the Société des Professeurs Français et Francophones d'Amérique (SPFFA) for their generous support of my research in Paris with a Bourse Jeanne Marandon.

At Amherst College, the Center for Humanistic Inquiry provided me with a vibrant scholarly community and helped me discover new directions in the research for this book. Thank you to Reed Gochberg, Adrianna Link, Caterina Scaramelli, Elizabeth Kolenda, and especially to Martha Umphrey, all of whom contributed to creating a forum for the exchange of ideas from which this book benefited immensely. I am grateful to the staff of Frost Library and to the professors, friends, and scholars who helped make the fellowship year so rewarding for me: Christian Rogowski, Laure Katsaros, Dale and Lorna Peterson, Raphael Sigal, Rosalina de la Carrera, Paul Rockwell, Ronald and Betty Rosbottom, Anouk Alquier, Christopher Grobe, and Tom Zanker.

Several institutions, archivists, and librarians are also to be thanked for their generous support. At the Bibliothèque nationale de France, Pascal Cordereix, Bruno Sebald, and Xavier Loyant all helped guide my research and were very generous with their time, particularly with my exploration of the Collection Charles Cros. Hélène Virenque and Eric Walbecq, with the assistance of Jean-Didier Wagneur, helped me track down some particularly elusive texts. I wish to thank Jean-Paul Thibaud and Anthony Pecqueux at CRESSON at the École Nationale Supérieure d'Architecture de Grenoble for their valuable thoughts and suggestions on sound, architecture, and cities. The team at the Bibliothèque Historique de la Ville de Paris deserves thanks for providing me with a delightful and inspiring place to conduct research and write. The staff at the archives of the Académie des Sciences in Paris, especially Isabelle Maurin-Joffre, offered me marvelous support in exploring their Charles Cros dossier. Jallal Aro at the Phono Museum in Paris likewise offered me valuable insights into the history of sound recording and was most gracious with his time.

Warm thanks are in order for Dale Peterson, who, in guiding me through my first long scholarly endeavor, helped prepare me for others to come.

I am grateful to the readers for Fordham University Press—Andrea Goulet and the anonymous reader—who offered thoughtful comments and suggestions on the manuscript. I also wish to express my gratitude to Tom Lay, Eric Newman, and Mildred Sanchez for their editorial prowess in helping this book become a reality.

Heartfelt thanks to my colleagues in the French and Francophone Studies program at William & Mary for their kindness, encouragement, and support: Michael and Angela Leruth, Magali Compan, Giulia Pacini, Nathan Rabalais, Katherine Kulick, Kate Conley, and Déborah Lee-Ferrand. I would also like to thank my colleagues in the Department of Modern Languages and Literatures, especially Robert Leventhal, Sergio Ferrarese, Silvia Tandeciarz, Noel Blanco Mourelle, and Michael Hill. Additionally, I wish to thank the Faculty

Research Committee at William & Mary, Dean Maria Donoghue Velleca, and the Office of the Dean of Arts and Sciences for their support in the form of two summer research grants. Thank you to Sarah Adams for help with editing.

To the friends who supported this undertaking, a hearty thanks: Matt Gilmore, Elizabeth Benjamin, Tera Lee Hedrick, Terah Walkup, Vincent Valour, Jennifer Croft, Corine Tachtiris, Brian Hochman, Saein Park, Caroline Vial, Miklos Gosztonyi, Amr Kamal, Denis Dapo, Casey Drosehn, Sidne Koenigsberg, Robert Dumitrescu, John and Jenny Lee, Emily Marker, Semyon Khoklov, James Mckay, Matthieu Moerlen, Vincent Lendower, Maïté Marciano, and Sima and Larry Smith.

Finally and most of all to family, my parents, Geri and Bill, my brother Todd, his wife, Emily, and their sons, Wesley and Nico, and to my wife, Amy, and our sons, Leo and Ethan, words cannot express how grateful I am to you.

Notes

Introduction: Acoustic Spectra

1. On Scott and his phonautograph, see Haun Saussy, *The Ethnography of Rhythm: Orality and Its Technologies* (New York: Fordham University Press, 2016), 89–93.

2. See Édouard-Léon Scott de Martinville, "The Phonautographic Manuscripts of Édouard-Léon Scott de Martinville," translated and edited by Patrick Feaster (Bloomington, Ind.: FirstSounds.org, 2010), 25. Feaster translates the phrase as "sound spectrum."

3. Scott de Martinville, "Phonautographic Manuscripts."

4. Scott de Martinville, 26–27.

5. See Saussy, *Ethnography*, especially Chapter 3, 97, where he argues that it is important to account for the medium-specificity of these inventions. If we consider them only as "imperfect anticipations" of media technologies to come, we miss valuable historical insights about the human senses.

6. On Tiphaigne and *Giphantie*, see François Brunet, *Photography and Literature*, (London: Reaktion, 2009), 23–24.

7. See Lisa Gitelman, *Scripts, Grooves, and Writing Machines: Representing Technology in the Edison Era* (Stanford, Calif.: Stanford University Press, 1999), 22.

8. On the illustrated book, see Juliet Wilson-Bareau and Breon Mitchell, "Tales of a Raven: The Origins and Fate of *Le Corbeau* by Manet and Mallarmé," *Print Quarterly* 6, no. 3 (1989): 262. On the color photograph, see Ariane Isler-de Jongh, "Manet, Charles Cros, et la photogravure en couleurs." *Nouvelles de l'estampe* 68 (1983); and Brett Brehm, "Media Environments: Manet, Cros, and the Colours of Spring," *History of Photography* 44, no. 1, (2020): 50–64.

9. Goncourt Journal, March 18, 1886. Cited in Louis Forestier, "Pavane pour un visage défunt," in *La Dame aux éventails: Nina de Callias, modèle de Manet* (Paris: Réunion des musées nationaux, 2000), 20.

10. Benjamin Steege has similarly characterized Hermann von Helmholtz, whose prominence as a scientist was coupled with a humanistic involvment in the arts and music especially, as "discipline-transcending" in the nineteenth century. See Benjamin Steege, *Helmholtz and the Modern Listener* (Cambridge: Cambridge University Press, 2012), 8–9.

11. The story was originally published in Champfleury's collection *Les Bons contes font les bons amis*. It has been translated into English and included in Jane Rabb, ed., *Literature and Photography: Interactions 1840–1990: A Critical Anthology* (Albuquerque: University of New Mexico Press, 1995), 10–14.

12. See Saussy, *Ethnography*, 83–84, especially his claim: "To say that 'the phonograph opened the possibility of X' is not only to name an event in history but also to mediate among the languages proper to several phases of technical consciousness (the semantic field prior to the phonograph; that field plus the phonograph; the field, including the phonograph and its derived technologies, from which we speak today, and so forth)."

13. On anxiety about the daguerreotype, see Rabb, *Literature and Photography*, 10.

14. Félix Nadar, *Quand j'étais photographe* (Charlieu: La Bartavelle–Éditeur, 1993), 8–9.

15. "A Visit to Plumbe's Gallery," in *The Gathering of the Forces*, ed. Cleveland Rogers and John Black, vol. 2 (New York: Putnam, 1920), 116. Cited in Laure Katsaros, *New York–Paris: Whitman, Baudelaire, and the Hybrid City* (Ann Arbor: University of Michigan Press, 2012), 32.

16. Walter Benjamin, "First Sketches," in *Arcades Project*, trans. Howard Eiland and Kevin Mclaughlin (Cambridge, Mass.: Harvard University Press, 1999), paragraph C. 5, 831.

17. Marcel Proust, *In Search of Lost Time, Volume III: The Guermantes Way*, trans. C. K. Scott Moncrieff and Terence Kilmartin (New York: The Modern Library, 2003), 94.

18. See Gerhard Richter, *Walter Benjamin and the Corpus of Autobiography* (Detroit: Wayne State University Press, 2000) and the chapter titled "Benjamin's ear," for a discussion of sound more generally in Benjamin's autobiographical writings. The phrase "soundscape of modernity" is the title of Emily Thompson's book about modern architectural acoustics in America.

19. For some prominent texts in sound studies, see, among others, Jonathan Sterne, *The Audible Past: Cultural Origins of Sound Reproduction* (Durham, N.C.: Duke University Press, 2003); John Picker, *Victorian Soundscapes* (New York: Oxford University Press, 2003); Peter Szendy, *Listen: A History of Our Ears*, trans. Charlotte Mandell (New York: Fordham University Press, 2008); Szendy "The Auditory Re-Turn," in Van Maas, *Thresholds of Listening*; Gitelman, *Scripts, Grooves, and Writing Machines*; and Steege, *Modern Listener*. On the more specific terrain of Parisian soundscapes, see, among others, Emma Dillon, *The Sense of Sound: Musical Meaning in France, 1260–1330* (New York: Oxford University Press, 2012), chap. 2; Aimée Boutin, *City of Noise: Sound and Nineteenth-Century Paris* (Urbana:

University of Illinois Press, 2015); and Jean-Paul Thibaud, "The Sonic Composition of the City," in *The Auditory Culture Reader*, ed. by Michael Bull and Les Back (Oxford: Berg, 2004). Prominent works in the field of visual culture studies include the scholarship of Jonathan Crary, Vanessa Schwartz, and Jeannene Przyblyski.

20. The phrase "disenchanted night'" is the title of Wolfgang Schivelbusch's study of nineteenth-century lighting technology. And the phrase "luminous noise" is from Mallarmé's prose poem "Un Spectacle Interrompu," which I discuss briefly in Chapter 3 of this book. The "panacoustic" is theorized by Szendy in *All Ears: The Aesthetics of Espionage*, trans. Roland Végső (New York: Fordham University Press, 2016), which I consider more closely at the end of Chapter 1.

21. Like Sterne's emphasis on the "cultural origins of sound reproduction," I focus on the cultural conditions that made mechanical sound recording possible in the nineteenth century. My approach differs from Sterne's, however, in the way I examine the conditions that made specific imaginings of sound reproducibility possible in the nineteenth century, namely the literary and artistic genealogy. Sound reproducibility had been imagined for centuries, but I argue that the nineteenth-century imagination, its own particular set of dreams about sound reproducibility, especially in the literary domain, was distinct from prior eras. Sterne places justifiably great emphasis on the nineteenth-century innovation of the tympanic mechanism, the "vibrating diaphragm that allowed telephones and phonographs to function," as both a crucial mechanical step and "an artifact of changing understandings of human hearing" (Sterne, *Audible Past*, 7). As Sterne relates, Emile Berliner, inventor of the gramophone, situated Charles Cros's ideas on the vibrating diaphragm as the last conceptual link in a chain of inventions leading to Berliner's gramophone (77–80). I argue, in turn, that Cros, as inventor-poet and all-around polymath, provides evidence for both the importance of the tympanic mechanism and the artistic world, of which Cros was so much a part, for nineteenth-century histories of sound and listening.

22. For the argument about the modernization of vision, see Vanessa Schwartz and Jeannene Prsyblsyki, eds., *The Nineteenth-Century Visual Culture Reader* (New York: Routledge, 2004), 71. For an account of Hermann von Helmholtz's profound influence on the fields of acoustics, music theory, and the shape of the modern listener in the nineteenth century, see Steege, *Modern Listener*. For commentary on the problematic progress narrative often freighted in the term "modernization" in the history of sound and listening, see Sterne, *Audible Past*, 9–10. The modernization of listening and the modernization of sound are different though related subjects, each with distinctive histories. My emphasis is on the interaction of the literary with new media technologies. Modernized listening would designate particular practices developing both in advance of and in reaction to technologies such as the telegraph and telephone, while modernized sound would designate something like the specificity of mechanized sound in the nineteenth century as, for example, something like the steam-engine sounds in Emile Zola's *Au bonheur des dames* or the audio recordings in Jules Verne's *Le Château des Carpathes*.

23. For scholarship on listening subjects and the urban soundscape in earlier historical periods, see, among others, Dillon, *Sense of Sound*. See also musicologist Mylène Pardoen's Projet Bretez, a multimedia recreation of the soundscape of eighteenth-century Paris, specifically the quartier du Grand Châtelet. Emily Thompson has pioneered exploration and cataloging of the soundscape of early twentieth-century New York City in a project called "The Roaring Twenties."

24. For a discussion of Schopenhauer, see Françoise Meltzer, *Seeing Double: Baudelaire's Modernity* (Chicago: University of Chicago Press, 2012), 117–18. For a discussion of Proust's cork-lined room, see Christopher Prendergast, *Paris and the Nineteenth Century* (Oxford: Blackwell, 1995), 126.

25. Walter Benjamin, *The Writer of Modern Life: Essays on Charles Baudelaire*, ed. Michael Jennings (Cambridge, Mass.: The Belknap Press of Harvard University Press, 2006), 80.

26. Jean-Georges Kastner, *Les Voix de Paris* (Paris: G. Brandus, Dufour et cie, 1857), 20.

27. For critical discussion of Kastner and *Les Voix de Paris*, see Vincent Milliot, *Les Cris de Paris ou le Peuple Travesti: les représentations des petits métiers parisiens (XVIe–XVIIIe siècles)* (Paris: Publications de la Sorbonne, 1995), 42–43, 284; Boutin, *City of Noise*, 39, 90; and Jacek Blaszkiewicz, *City Myths: Music and Urbanism in Second Empire Paris*, PhD diss., Rochester, NY: University of Rochester, 2018, chap. 4. For reflections on an "auditory turn" in the humanities, see Peter Szendy, "The Archi-Road Movie," in *The Senses and Society*, vol. 8 (London: Bloomsbury Publishing, 2013), 58.

28. For the notion of a period ear, see Anthony Pecqueux, "Le son des choses, les bruits de la ville," in *Communications* 90 (Paris: Seuil: École des Hautes Études en Sciences Sociales – Centre Edgar Morin, 2012), 6; and Alain Corbin, *Les Cloches de la Terre: Paysage Sonore et Culture Sensible dans les Campagnes au XIXe siècle* (Paris: A. Michel, 1994).

29. Milliot, *Les Cris de Paris ou le Peuple Travesti*, 42–43.

30. Alphonse Certeux, *Les Cris de Londres* (Paris: Chamuel, 1893), 167. See also Erika Brady, *A Spiral Way: How the Phonograph Changed Ethnography* (Jackson: University Press of Mississippi, 1999); and Brian Hochman, *Savage Preservation: The Ethnographic Origins of Modern Media Technology* (Minneapolis: University of Minnesota Press, 2014).

31. For a discussion of Fournel and Mainzer's attention to street cries, see Boutin, *City of Noise*.

32. For Azoulay, see John Attridge "'La vaste rumeur d'autrefois': Noise, Memory, and Mediation in *À la recherche du temps perdu*," in *Modernism/Modernity*, vol. 4, no. 3 (2019). For Pernot, see Pascal Cordereix, "Les enregistrements du musée de la parole et du geste à l'exposition colonial," Paris: Presses de Sciences Po, *Vingtième Siècle. Revue d'histoire*, 2006.

33. Szendy, "Archi-Road Movie," 58; and Szendy, "The Auditory Re-Turn: The Point of Listening," Keynote Address, "Thinking Hearing—The Auditory Turn in the Humanities," University of Texas at Austin, October 2, 2009, 7–8n4.

34. On the question of sensory separation in the nineteenth century, see Jonathan Crary, *Techniques of the Observer: On Vision and Modernity in the Nineteenth Century* (Cambridge, Mass.: MIT Press, 1990), especially chap. 3.

35. For a discussion of audiovisual spectacles in Paris in the first half of the nineteenth century, see John Tresch, *The Romantic Machine: Utopian Science and Technology after Napoleon* (Chicago: University of Chicago Press, 2012), chap. 5, especially 135–52. Tresch highlights spectacles in Paris such as the diorama, panorama, Hector Berlioz's innovations in musical technologies, and operas of attractions such as Giacomo Meyerbeer's 1831 *Robert le diable*. Tresch emphasizes that these spectacles were "frequently improved with the assistance of scientists who sought to understand and control the properties of light and sound"(143) and that scientists such as Ernst Chladni, with his geometrical figures, "studied the interactions of sound and light in ways that straddled experiment and performance" (144).

36. See Charles Wheatstone, "Description of the Kaleidophone or Phonic Kaleidoscope; a New Philosophical Toy, for the Illustration of Several Interesting and Amusing Acoustical and Optical Phenomena," *Quarterly Journal of Science, Literature, and Art* 23 (1827): 344–51." This text is reproduced with commentary in Nicholas J. Wade, ed., *Brewster and Wheatstone on Vision* (London: Experimental Psychology Society, 1983), 205–12.

37. For a description of the mechanics of Wheatstone's kaleidophone and variations on the device by others, see Wheatstone, "Description of the Kaleidophone"; and Robert J. Whitaker, "The Wheatstone Kaleidophone," *American Journal of Physics* 61 (1983): 722–28.

38. Crary, *Techniques*, 116. For commentary on the kaleidoscope, including Marx and Engels's "attack on Saint-Simon" and their skepticism of the kaleidoscope's multiple images, see Crary, *Techniques*, 114.

39. See Yoshiko Terao, *Le fixe et le fugitif: Tiphaigne, Diderot, Mical, Castel et leurs machines audiovisuelles*, Thèse doctorale, Université Lumière Lyon 2, 2016; and Shelby McCloy, *French Inventions of the Eighteenth Century* (Lexington: University Press of Kentucky, 2015), 131–32. McCloy calls Castel's "clavecin oculaire" a precursor of Wheatstone's kaleidophone and Wilfred's Clavilux. Keely Orgeman likewise situates Wilfred's Clavilux in the lineage of color organs and calls Castel, whom Wilfred himself invoked as inspiration for his work, an ancestor. See Orgeman, "A Radiant Manifestation in Space: Wilfred, Lumia, and Light," in *Lumia: Thomas Wilfred and the Art of Light* (New Haven, Conn.: Yale University Press, 2017), 23n6. Orgeman, however, highlights the particular absence of sound in Wilfred's works together with the artist's insistence on the very silence of his works, however much they might seem to appeal to the interplay of color and audible music (23).

40. Castel as cited in Terao, *Le fixe et le fugitif*, 197.

41. Jean-Luc Nancy, *Listening*, trans. Charlotte Mandell (New York: Fordham University Press, 2007), 3. Roberto Casati and Jérôme Dokic, *La Philosophie du Son* (Éditions Jacqueline Chambon, 1998).

42. See, among others, Jean-François Augoyard, in Olivier Balaÿ, *L'Espace Sonore de la Ville au XIXe siècle* (Bernin: A la Croisée, 2003), 14; Jacques Perriault, *Mémoires de l'ombre et du son: une archéologie de l'audio-visuel* (Paris: Flammarion, 1981), 202; Thomas Baumgartner, ed., *Le Goût de la Radio et Autres Sons* (Paris: Mercure de France, 2013); Allen Weiss, "Radio Icons, Short Circuits, Deep Schisms," in *Experimental Sound and Radio* (Cambridge, Mass.: MIT Press, 2001), 1–7; and Franc Schuerewegen, *A distance de voix: essai sur les "machines à parler"* (Lille, France: Presses Universitaires de Lille, 1994), 13. Perriault argues: "What was at the origin of the concept of phonography? [. . .] a whole tradition of storage of speech [*stockage de la parole*], that Rabelais was the first to evoke: the speech and rumbling of a battle that unfreezes [*les paroles et les rumeurs d'une bataille qui 'dégèlent*]" (Perriault, *Mémoires de l'ombre et du son*, 202).

43. For the Chinese legend, see André Coeuroy and G. Clarence, *Le phonographe* (Paris: Kra, 1929), 11–12. For the island explorer, see Coeuroy and Clarence, 8. Shane Butler, likewise looking, or rather listening, back thousands of years, has recently explored the "Ancient Phonograph" in his eponymous book. Butler begins his book with Edison while arguing that the question of writing the voice was "an ancient one" that was entertained in the "role of sound in Greek and Latin literature." He ultimately examines a certain idea of "the voice in classical literature" (See Shane Butler, *The Ancient Phonograph* [New York: Zone Books, 2015], 27).

44. Coeuroy and Clarence, 12.

45. Augoyard, in Balaÿ, *L'Espace Sonore*, 14.

46. For a discussion of "archaeophony," see Alec Wilkinson, "A Voice from the Past: How a Physicist Resurrected the Earliest Recordings," *New Yorker* (May 19, 2014): 50–57; and Boutin, *City of Noise*, 134.

47. See Aimée Boutin, "Aural Flânerie," *Dix-Neuf* 16, no. 2 (July 2012): 149–61.

48. See Michel Chion, *La Voix au Cinéma* (Paris, 1972); and Boutin, "Aural Flânerie," for reflections on acoustic/aural *flânerie*.

49. Perriault, *Mémoires de l'ombre et du son*, 201. Franc Schuerewegen highlights a similar confluence of literature and science in the concept of telecommunications. Schuerewegen invokes Charles Cros and George Bernard Shaw as illustration of this confluence between literature and science, between the writer and the engineer, and as a reminder that writing is itself a *tekhnè*. He asserts that literary writing is not without its own form of *"ingéniosité"* (Schuerewegen, *A distance de voix*, 12). On the question of connections between machines, science, and romanticism in Paris in the first half of the nineteenth century, see Tresch, *The Romantic Machine*, where he highlights cases in which romanticism and mechanism, so often seen in opposition, were in fact "entwined" (3).

50. Laura Otis, *Networking: Communicating with Bodies and Machines in the Nineteenth Century.* Ann Arbor: University of Michigan Press, 2001, 84. For scientific thought in Poe's *Eureka* and a startling connection with twentieth-century physics, see Tom Siegfried, *Strange Matters: Undiscovered Ideas at the Frontiers of*

Space and Time (New York: Berkley Books, 2002), 130–37. He makes the provocative claim: "It seems that the first scientist to really appreciate the possibility . . . that the universe may in fact be expanding, was the Russian mathematician Alexander Friedmann. And I think I know why Friedmann was the one. It had something to do with his taste in literature" (130).

51. Jacques Rancière, *Le Partage du Sensible: esthétique et politique* (Paris: La Fabrique-éditions, 2000), 50: "On the one hand the technical revolution comes after the aesthetic revolution. But also regarding the aesthetic revolution, it is first of all the glorification of the ordinary, the everyday—which is pictorial and literary before becoming photographic or cinematographic."

52. For recent exploration of Poe's legacy in another vein, specifically in French crime fiction, see Andrea Goulet, *Legacies of the Rue Morgue: Science, Space, and Crime Fiction in France* (Philadelphia: University of Pennsylvania Press, 2015).

53. Michael Baxandall, *Painting and Experience in Fifteenth-Century Italy* (Oxford: Oxford University Press, 1972), 29–109. See also Corbin, *Les Cloches*; Mark Smith, ed., *Hearing History: A Reader* (Athens: University of Georgia Press, 2004); Balaÿ, *L'Espace Sonore*; and Pecqueux, "Le son des choses."

1. Paleophonics: Charles Cros's Audiovisual Worlds

1. On the recordings of Tennyson with Edison's phonograph, see John Picker, *Victorian Soundscapes* (New York: Oxford University Press, 2003), 123–25; Ian Christie, "Early Phonograph Culture and Moving Pictures," in *The Sounds of Early Cinema* (Bloomington: Indiana University Press, 2001), 5; and Jason Camlot, *Phonopoetics: The Making of Early Literary Recordings* (Stanford, Calif.: Stanford University Press, 2019), chap. 3. On Apollinaire as a "poète phonographiste," see Marc Battier, "What the GRM Brought to Music: From Musique Concrète to Acousmatic Music," in *Organised Sound* 12, no. 3 (2007): 189–91; and Brian Kane, "*Acousmate*: History and De-Visualised Sound in the Schaefferian Tradition," *Organised Sound* 17, no. 2 (2012): 181–82. On the relation between Segalen and phonography, see Christopher Bush, *Ideographic Modernism: China, Writing, Media* (Oxford: Oxford University Press, 2010), 77–83.

2. Cros relied on the financial support of several different patrons for his scientific research. Some of Cros's contemporaries and some scholars would claim that his inability to build was more a lack of practical will, too much the personality of a Renaissance man who had strayed into an inhospitable century.

3. On Berliner's debt to Cros, see Élizabeth Giuliani, "La réception du média," in *Revue de la Bibliothèque nationale de France,* Naissances du disque, n. 33, 2009, 12; Xavier Sené, "L'Impression du Son," in *Revue de la Bibliothèque nationale de France,* Naissances du disque, n. 33, 2009, 25; and Jonathan Sterne, *The Audible Past: Cultural Origins of Sound Reproduction* (Durham, N.C.: Duke University Press, 2003), 77–80. On Villiers's debt to Cros for *L'Ève Future,* see Louis Forestier, *Charles Cros: L'Homme et l'Oeuvre* (Paris: Lettres Modernes Minard, 1969), 157.

4. André Breton, *Anthologie de l'humour noir* (Paris: Jean-Jacques Pauvert, 1966), 160.

5. See, for example, James Lastra, *Sound Technology and the American Cinema: Perception, Representation, Modernity* (New York: Columbia University Press, 2000), 18.

6. On this collaboration, see Nathalie Boulouch, *Le Ciel est bleu: Une histoire de la photographie couleur* (Paris: Éditions Textuel, 2011); Ariane Isler-de Jongh, "Manet, Charles Cros, et la photogravure en couleurs," *Nouvelles de l'estampe* 68 (1983); and Brett Brehm, "Media Environments: Manet, Cros and the Colours of Spring," *History of Photography* 44, no. 1 (2020): 50–64.

7. Friedrich A. Kittler, *Gramophone, Typewriter, Film*, trans. with an Introduction by Geoffrey Winthrop-Young and Michael Wutz (Stanford, Calif.: Stanford University Press, 1999), 22. In a similar vein, though more specifically on the concept and etymology of telecommunications, Franc Schuerewegen juxtaposes Cros and Edison and claims that Edison seems to have been more "media-minded" than Cros. See Schuerewegen, *A distance de voix: essai sur les "machines à parler"* (Lille, France: Presses Universitaires de Lille, 1994), 12n7.

8. See Picker, *Victorian Soundscapes*, chap. 4, for a discussion of how the gramophone is typically associated with early and high modernist literature, with Joyce and Eliot especially. See also Ivan Kreilkamp, *Voice and the Victorian Storyteller* (Cambridge: Cambridge University Press, 2005), for a discussion of Joyce, *Ulysses*, and the phonograph. Joyce makes the same analogy between photograph and phonograph as Cros does in his poem "Inscription," the idea of hearing voices of the dead again and preserving them.

9. See, for example, Timothy Taylor, ed., *Music, Sound, and Technology in America: A Documentary History of Early Phonograph, Cinema, and Radio* (Durham, N.C.: Duke University Press, 2012), who begins his account with Edison's ideas for what the machine could do. Taylor is surprised that music ranks only fourth in Edison's first list and that it did not rank higher.

10. See, for example, Lastra, *Sound Technology*, and Erika Brady, *A Spiral Way: How the Phonograph Changed Ethnography* (Jackson: University Press of Mississippi, 1999).

11. Charles Cros, *Inédits et Documents*. Recueillis et présentés par Pierre E. Richard, Éditions Atelier du Gué, Éditions Jacques Brémond, 1992, 180.

12. On the irony that Scott's phonautograph recordings were made to resound with the help of optical technologies in 2008, see Alec Wilkinson, "A Voice from the Past: How a Physicist Resurrected the Earliest Recordings," *New Yorker*, May 19, 2014, 50–57. See also Haun Saussy, *The Ethnography of Rhythm: Orality and Its Technologies* (New York: Fordham University Press, 2016), 89–93; and Sterne, *Audible Past*, 45–51.

13. See Jacques Perriault, *Memoires de l'ombre et du son: une archéologie de l'audio-visuel* (Paris: Flammarion, 1981), 268.

14. Cros, *Inédits*, 51.

15. Kittler, *Gramophone*, 22. Deafness, it should be noted, was also significant in Bell's invention of the telephone. See Sterne, *Audible Past*, 36–41, on the relation between Bell and deafness. See also the section devoted to sound reproducibility and deafness in the *Sound Studies Reader*. See also Lastra, *Sound Technology*, 28–31, and my note below about the parallel between Cros and Bell on deafness.

16. See Perriault, *Memoires*, 134–38; and Jonathan Rée, *I See a Voice: Deafness, Language, and the Senses: A Philosophical History* (New York: Holt Paperbacks, 2000), 207–18, esp. chap. 19.

17. See Cros's writings about language pedagogy written during those years in Cros, *Inédits*, 34–35 ("Parallel between the way a speaker learns a foreign language and the way a deaf person must learn his native tongue"), and Cros, 37–39 ("Parallel between the way a speaking child begins in the mother tongue and the way a deaf person needs to learn this same language").

18. Quoted in Perriault, *Memoires*, 134–35.

19. See Haun Saussy, "Interplanetary Literature," *Comparative Literature* 63, no. 4 (Fall 2011), 438–47.

20. Quoted in Perriault, *Memoires*, 137.

21. See Lastra on Alexander Graham Bell (*Sound Technology*, 28–35). Note also the parallels between Cros and Bell in their exposure to ideas about speaking machines and automata (cf. Cros, *Inédits*, 51). Lastra notes how Bell was profoundly influenced by his father's search for, as Bell Jr. described it, "a universal alphabet, capable of expressing the sounds of all languages in a single alphabet" (28). Cros, while teaching deaf students, would write about his own search for such an alphabet, with his "study of all the known sounds that compose the languages of the globe" (Cros, *Inédits*, 51).

22. See Forestier, *Charles Cros*, 75; and Antoine Cros, *L'Organographie plessimétrique*, Paris, 1884.

23. Cros, "Sténographie Musicale," in *Inédits et Documents*, Recueillis et présentés par Pierre E. Richard, Éditions Atelier du Gué, Éditions Jacques Brémond, 1992, 58–65,

24. Forestier, *Charles Cros*, 156. See also Antoine Cros's memoirs, in which he details their ambitions for designing player piano technology.

25. Such a device was in part realized in 1864 by the Comte du Moncel, who would later serve as one of Edison's representatives in Paris at the time of the phonograph's invention. In the same year, Cros and his brother Antoine devised a similar procedure, which they attempted to patent but abandoned partly because of competing technologies from Du Moncel and others.

26. Cros, *Oeuvres Complètes*, Bibliothèque de la Pleiade, édition établie par Louis Forestier et Pierre-Olivier Walzer (Paris: Gallimard, 1970), 158–59.

27. Cros, *OC*, 158–59.

28. Cros, 158–59. Translations of Cros's texts in this chapter are mine unless otherwise indicated.

29. Cros, *Inédits*, 64.

30. This description comes from the novel *La Maison de la Vieille* (1894) by poet and novelist Catulle Mendès (1841–1909), which I discuss at length in Chapter 5. For this quotation, see Mendès, 251. Mendès exaggerates and alters much about Cros's biography and person in the novel, but the racial element aligns with other nonfictional accounts by one of Cros's contemporaries, an editor who described him as "le type d'un Hindou" or a fakir. Beyond the intrigue of these and several other descriptions of Cros's physiognomy, there is no known evidence to suggest that Charles or members of his family were multiracial. The descriptions of Charles, sometimes verging on derogatory caricature, are all the same important to take into account as potential factors that shaped Cros's recognition in his own lifetime, his outsider status in ways, and his historical recognition, or lack thereof.

31. Cros, *Coffret*, "Plainte."

32. See Breton, 160: ". . . la surprenante orchestration de certains de ses poèmes en prose ('Sur trois aquatintes de Henry Cros') qui préparent les *Illuminations*. . . ." See also Forestier, *Charles Cros*.

33. See Forestier, *Charles Cros*, Lockerbie, and Juin on the history and chronology of this period, the relationship between the poets, and the aesthetic affinities and connections between their poetry. The quotation about the dream of the "art of tomorrow" is from Cros's poem "Excuse" in *Le Coffret de santal*.

34. Cros, *OC*, 160.

35. Cros, 88.

36. Cros, 167.

37. Schuerewegen argues that Verne's novel offers a certain phonographic conception of history. He says that, for Verne, the phonograph has immobilized History to the extent that the future can henceforth no longer be anything other than "a mechanical repetition of the past," of what the subject chooses to repeat of the past (Schuerewegen, *A Distance*, 42).

38. Cros, *OC*, 47.

39. Cros was deeply involved in developing new models of the telegraph in the 1860s. He exhibited his model of a telegraph at the 1867 Universal Exhibition in Paris. See Perriault, *Memoires*, 140–55; and Cros, *Inédits*, 69–103.

40. Cros, *OC*, 557: "C'est dans le cours de ce travail sur l'ouïe que j'ai imaginé le phonographe." Cros's *Principes de mécanique cérébrale* was mostly written in the early 1870s but was not published until 1879, after the invention of the phonograph. Cros's footnote here shows him taking part in examining his own path to imagining the phonograph.

41. See Jonathan Crary, *Techniques of the Observer: On Vision and Modernity in the Nineteenth Century* (Cambridge, Mass.: MIT Press, 1990), 133, for discussion of phenakistiscope. Crary argues that the phenakistiscope was a device by which the human observer was turned into a tool for the technique of illusion, becoming "simultaneously the magician and the deceived."

42. See Perriault, *Memoires*, 262. Another photographic portrait of Cros, at an apparently slightly younger age, also thought to have been taken by Nadar, is in the

collection of the Phono Museum in Paris. My thanks to Jallal Aro at the museum for showing me this portrait from their archives.

43. Cros's investigations into color photography may have also brought him into contact with the photographer before their meeting for Cros's portraits in 1879 and spurred conversation about scientific innovation and possibilities such as mechanical sound reproducibility.

44. See Brehm, "Media Environments."

45. This kind of manipulation of a technological device similarly animates Franc Schuerewegen's inquiry into the nineteenth- and early twentieth-century literary imagination about telecommunications technologies. Schuerewegen calls the treatment of particular technological objects such as the telephone and phonograph in literary texts from a range of authors as a sort of "opération de détournement ou, si l'on veut, de *dérivation*, comme si l'objet technologique était chaque fois malicieusement, perversement détourné de son but, de sa fonction première, et utilisé *autrement*" (A *distance de voix*, 16, emphases in original).

46. See again, Saussy, "Interplanetary Literature."

47. Cros, OC, 373–34.

48. Cros, 374.

49. Cros, 375.

50. Cros, 375.

51. Cros, 376.

52. See Forestier, *Charles Cros*, 89–93; and Gérard Bobillier, *L'Homme inachevé* (Lagrasse: Verdier, 2012), 24–25, for what we know of Cros's activities during the Commune and of his sympathies and alliances with the Communards.

53. For a discussion of the uses of photography during and after the Paris Commune, see Jeannene Przyblyski, "Revolution at a Standstill: Photography and the Paris Commune of 1871," *Yale French Studies* 101 (2001): 54–57. She furthermore highlights the creation in 1874 of the *Service Photographique de la Préfecture*, which was "charged with the task of photographing all suspected criminals detained in Paris," and she argues that "the Commune stood squarely behind these anxieties" (57).

54. Alphonse Allais, "La Mort de Charles Cros," *Le Chat Noir*, August 18, 1888. See also Cros, *Inédits*, 69–80. For one of Cros's own articulations of this idea referenced by Allais, see chapter 5, "Des actions mécaniques de la lumière," of Cros's text, "Principes de mécanique cérébrale" (Cros, OC, 551). Cros's brief description is, I would argue, a forgotten point of origin in the history and development of the wireless telephone.

55. Alexander Graham Bell, "The Photophone," *Science* 1, no. 11 (Sept. 11, 1880): 130–34.

56. Alexander Graham Bell, "An Interview with Alexander Graham Bell," *Records of the Columbia Historical Society, Washington, D.C.*, vol. 48–49, 1946–1947, 181–89.

57. Letter from Alexander Graham Bell to Alexander Melville Bell, February 26, 1880 (MSS51268), US Library of Congress, Digital Collections.

58. Alexander Graham Bell, "Application of the Photophone to the Study of the Noises Taking Place on the Surface of the Sun," *Science* 1, no. 25 (Dec. 18, 1880): 304.

59. Bell, "Application of the Photophone."

60. See also Lastra, *Sound Technology*, esp. chap. 1, on these kinds of analogies in the prehistory of cinema.

61. Cited in Perriault, *Mémoires*, 134. See also Félix Nadar, *Mémoires du Géant* (Paris: E. Dentu, deuxième édition, 1865), 272.

62. See Wolfgang Schivelbusch, *Disenchanted Night: The Industrialization of Light in the Nineteenth Century*, trans. Angela Davies (Berkeley: University of California Press, 1988).

63. Art historians *are* beginning to look at paintings of the period for their sound. Among others, see Asma Naeem, *Out of Earshot: Sound, Technology, and Power in American Art 1860–1900* (Berkeley: University of California Press, 2019).

64. See commons.princeton.edu/josephhenry/photophone.

65. See also Cros's "Sonnet Astronomique" for an example of the interplay between his poetry and his scientific investigations, as expressed in the papers given at the Académie des Sciences. Kittler also notes that "Inscription" is a poem to "honor his inventions" (*Gramophone*, 22). In this vein, for an illuminating reading of Cros's "Hiéroglyphe," see also Jongh, "Manet, Charles Cros," 9. See also Saussy, "Interplanetary."

66. Cf. Perriault, *Mémoires*, 129–76.

67. Quoted in Forestier, *Charles Cros*, 148 (Maupassant to Flaubert, December 26, 1879).

68. Kittler, *Gramophone*, 80: "Technology triumphs over mnemotechnology. And the death bell tolls for poetry, which for so long had been the love of so many."

69. Cros, OC, 167.

70. See Kittler, *Gramophone*, 55; and Taylor on how the reproducibility of musical performances was surprisingly not one of the principal applications envisaged for the phonograph in its early years, at least by Edison and his associates. Again, as I want to stress, the prehistory also needs to be considered. Nadar had the idea of the audio recording and reproducibility of opera performances in 1864, as I discuss in detail in Chapter 3.

71. On repetition, resonance, and reflection, see Philippe Lacoue-Labarthe, "L'Écho du Sujet," in *Le Sujet de la Philosophie* (Paris: Aubier: Flammarion, 1979), 250.

72. In the months after the unveiling of Edison's device, Cros would submit plans and methods for perfecting phonographic inscription to the Académie des Sciences, designs for achieving greater sound fidelity by reducing the distorted "polichinelle" sound of recorded voices, in this way making those voices easier to love.

73. See Allen S. Weiss, *Breathless: Sound Recording, Disembodiment, and the Transformation of Lyrical Nostalgia* (Middletown, Conn.: Wesleyan University Press, 2002), for the argument that death is central to the nineteenth-century imagination about sound reproducibility.

74. See, for example, the first stanza of "Hieroglyphe" for the enfolding of love and death. See Jongh, "Manet, Cros," 9–10, who offers a compelling reading of the poem's connection to Cros's trichrome color photographic method.

75. On patents and phonograph technology, see Alexander Weheliye, *Phonographies: Grooves in Sonic Afro-Modernity* (Durham, N.C.: Duke University Press, 2005); and Lisa Gitelman, *Scripts, Grooves, and Writing Machines: Representing Technology in the Edison Era* (Stanford, Calif.: Stanford University Press, 1999).

76. Perriault, *Mémoires*, 144–46.

77. See Perriault, 144–46. To cite another example, Emile Berliner, in designing his gramophone, found himself in conflict with Bell's patents. On that topic, see Sené, "L'Impression du Son," 24–25.

78. This was May 7, 1869, at the Société Française de Photographie. Alexander Graham Bell and Elisha Gray also found themselves in conflict about credit for invention of the telephone, as they both applied for patents on their work on the same day, within hours of each other.

79. Quoted in Forestier, *Charles Cros*, 149.

80. See Giuliani, "La réception du média," 12; and Sterne, *Audible Past*, 77–80.

81. Hubert Juin for one argues: "His scientific adventure did not take aim at commercialization, but was rather a Faustian project." But this claim is in part belied by numerous scientific papers authored by Cros claiming rights to commercial exploitation of technological improvements and principles. See, for example, Cros *Inédits*, 71–72 and 199–213, for explanation of the "pli cacheté" procedure at the Académie des Sciences. Inventors could deposit a sealed envelope with details of their work at the Académie. This was done when the inventor wished to lay claim to the priority of their work at a certain date, while oftentimes still wishing to improve upon and develop the work detailed in the sealed envelope (before fully unveiling it to the scientific community and public).

82. For a reading of Cros's monologues, their performance history, and the context of technological invention, see Greg Kerr, "Laughing Matter: Charles Cros, from Paléophone to Monologue," *Nottingham French Studies* 59, no. 1 (March 2020): 34–50. Sound recordings of Coquelin Cadet's performances survive and are available at the Bibliothèque nationale de France. Some are also available for listening online at phonobase.org.

83. Cros's official title while teaching at the Institut des Sourds Muets was "répétiteur."

84. Cros, *Inédits*, 208–9.

85. Emile Berliner, in 1889, would begin to develop a toy version of the phonograph. See *De Fil en Aiguille: Charles Cros et les Autres*, exh. cat., Paris: Bibliothèque Nationale de France, December 15, 1988–April 1, 1989, 93.

86. Cros, *Inédits*, 209.

87. As the editors of the Pléiade edition of Cros's poetry have indicated, the poem's central image of a dead woman's voice living on in a musical instrument owes a debt to the Romantic imagination, in particular the stories of E. T. A.

Hoffmann, "Rath Krespel" among others. I will have more to say about this poem in Chapter 5.

88. Cros, *Inédits*, 206. Cros describes how thread can be used as the container of sound. About these "phonogrammes filiformes" he proposes: "ils seront l'image exacte du temps qui s'écoule, pendant que la nature ou l'homme font du bruit, parlent ou chantent."

89. See Pierre Liénard, "Conserver les sons," in *De Fil en Aiguille: Charles Cros et les Autres*, exh. cat., December 15, 1988–April 1, 1989, 21–26; and Christie, "Early Phonograph Culture."

90. Liénard, "Conserver les sons," 22.

91. I want to argue that Cros very likely knew this text by Cyrano. Forestier, in his biography of Cros, makes reference to Cyrano as an author with whom Cros would have felt a close kinship (510).

92. Bruno Sebald, "L'édition du disque," in *Revue de la Bibliothèque nationale de France*, Naissances du disque, n. 33, 2009, 31.

93. For discussion of the original Greek meaning of "ptyx," see Henry Weinfield, *Stéphane Mallarmé: Collected Poems* (Berkeley: University of California Press, 1994), 217.

94. One could begin a study of the soundscape of the modern department store by noting the likelihood that Cros, as Forestier proposes, wrote this scientific treatise on paper purchased at the Bon Marché (Forestier, *Charles Cros*, 158).

95. Kittler, *Gramophone*, 21.

96. Kittler, 22.

97. Kittler, 23.

98. Breton, 119–20.

99. Kittler, *Gramophone*, 70, 86.

100. Cros, *OC*, 238. This prose work resembles others, titled *"Fantaisies en prose,"* by Cros in his first collection, *Le Coffret de santal*. "Le meuble" and "L'heure froide," have the most developed feel of a short narrative, and in this way resemble "Le Journal de l'avenir," while a work such as "Le vaisseau-piano" is closer to Rimbaud's prose poems of *Illuminations*.

101. Bobillier, 55; and Forestier, *Charles Cros*, 195.

102. Bobillier, 55.

103. Cros, *OC*, 236, 238.

104. Perriault, *Mémoires*, 138, n119. See also Ambroise Firmin-Didot, *Observations sur l'orthographe ou l'Ortografie française*, 1868, esp. 326–28, critique de la phonographie; and Collin, *Observations sur la réforme orthographique* 14, Avallon, 1873 — cited in Emile Littré, *Dictionnaire de français "Littré"* (1863–1877), Softissimo, 2010.

105. For a discussion of connections between utopian visions, technology, romanticism, and the arts in France in the first half of the nineteenth century, see John Tresch, *The Romantic Machine: Utopian Science and Technology after Napoleon* (Chicago: University of Chicago Press, 2012). Tresch argues that in Paris

in the period between "the fall of one Napoleon and the rise of another . . . debates about the impact of technology were at the center of cultural and political life" (*Romantic Machine*, 3).

106. See Cros's prose poem "Effarement" for a similar vertiginous transition between dream world and reality, one that recalls Baudelaire's "Rêve Parisien."

107. Cros, *OC*, 236

108. Cros, 236.

109. Ernest Raynaud, *La Bohème sous le second empire: Charles Cros et Nina* (Paris: L'Artisan du livre, 1930), 9.

110. Cros, *OC*, 235.

111. See Peter Szendy, *All Ears: The Aesthetics of Espionage*, trans. Roland Végső (New York: Fordham University Press, 2016). See also Kittler, *Gramophone*, 67, for another moment when the phonographic apparatus is imagined as a means of surveillance.

112. On Edison, the phonograph, and surveillance, see also Lastra, *Sound Technology*, 19–20.

113. See Dominique Villemot, "Chronique des années 1876 à 1938," in *De Fil en Aiguille: Charles Cros et les Autres*, exh. cat., Paris: Bibliothèque Nationale de France, December 15, 1988–April 1, 1989, 83. In *All Ears*, Szendy provides a theory of the panacoustic through readings of Foucault, Bentham, and the panopticon. Ultimately Szendy's broader concerns involve the place of the listener and of listening in representation.

114. Cros, *OC*, 238.

115. See Forestier, *Charles Cros*, on the idea of the "journal parlé" as an anticipation of the problems and possibilities of mass communication. Cf. also Apollinaire's reaction to being recorded on a phonograph in 1913 for the "archives de la parole": "Plus de livres . . . des disques!"("No more books . . . only disks!"), in *Gil Blas*, December 25, 1913. For a similar literary imagining of this kind of phenomenon, see Gitelman's reading of Bellamy (*Scripts*, 65–66).

116. One could read this idea of "le journal parlé" in the phonograph as an anticipation of radio, dependent in part on the portability sketched out in Cros's plan for a "petit phonographe." The story is, however, vague about how "les traces reproduites à des millions d'exemplaires" necessarily reach subscribers to the journal. For this reason, Forestier suggests that the "journal parlé" is less an anticipation of radio than of mass distributed sound recordings on disc.

117. Cros, *Inédits*, 197, for his text about reducing voice distortion, called "la voix de polichinelle," in Edison's phonograph recordings. Proust lingers on this kind of acoustic distortion in *The Guermantes Way*, in the passage about speaking with his grandmother on the telephone.

118. In-text page numbers in this concluding section of the chapter refer to the English translation of Robida's novel, *The Twentieth Century*, trans. Philippe Willems (Middletown, CT: Wesleyan University Press, 2004).

119. On Proust and the Théatrophone, see John Attridge, "'La vaste rumeur d'autrefois': Noise, Memory, and Mediation in À *la recherche du temps perdu*," *Modernism/Modernity* 4, no. 3 (2019).

120. Cf. Willems's introduction to the novel, *xxx–xxxv*.

121. To the extent Robida was pioneering with his illustrated books, that publishing venture was also inaugurated in a way by Cros. Art historians have characterized Manet and Cros's collaboration on *Le Fleuve* (1874) as "the first modern illustrated book." See Juliet Wilson-Bareau and Breon Mitchell, "Tales of a Raven: The Origins and Fate of *Le Corbeau* by Manet and Mallarmé," *Print Quarterly* 6, no. 3 (1989): 262.

2. Poe's *Tintamarre*: Transatlantic Acoustic Horizons

1. See Jane Rabb, ed., *Literature and Photography: Interactions 1840–1990: A Critical Anthology* (Albuquerque: University of New Mexico Press, 1995), 4.

2. See Simon Schaffer, "The Leviathan of Parsonstown: Literary Technology and Scientific Representation," in *Inscribing Science: Scientific Texts and the Materiality of Communication*, ed. by Timothy Lenoir (Stanford, Calif.: Stanford University Press, 1998). About Rosse's telescope, Schaffer argues that literary representations played an important role in the dissemination of scientific technology and knowledge to the public.

3. Charles Baudelaire, *Oeuvres Complètes, II*. Texte établi, présenté et annoté par Claude Pichois, Bibliothèque de la Pléiade, Paris: Gallimard, 1975–1976, 749.

4. Edgar Allan Poe, *Poetry and Tales*, ed. Patrick F. Quinn (New York: Library of America, 1984), 1340.

5. Poe, *Poetry*.

6. For a recent scholarly account of Poe's *Eureka*, see David N. Stamos, *Edgar Allan Poe*, Eureka, *and Scientific Imagination* (Albany: State University of New York Press, 2017). For Poe and the history of physics, specifically about *Eureka*, see also Tom Siegfried, *Strange Matters: Undiscovered Ideas at the Frontiers of Space and Time* (New York: Berkley Books, 2002), 130–37.

7. See Poe's "The Philosophy of Composition" for his discussion of "undercurrents of meaning," in Poe, *Essays and Reviews*, ed. G. R. Thompson (New York: Library of America, 1984), 24.

8. See Schaffer, "The Leviathan," 208–10, on the mechanization and industrialization of mirror making for large reflecting telescopes in the 1830s and 1840s.

9. Rabb, *Literature and Photography*, 5.

10. Poe, *Poetry*, 1319.

11. Roland Barthes, "Textual Analysis of a Tale by Poe," in *On Signs*, ed. Blonsky, Marshall (Baltimore: Johns Hopkins University Press, 1985), 96. On the idea of a "point d'écoute" in a narrative, see Peter Szendy, *All Ears: The Aesthetics of Espionage*, trans. Roland Végsó (New York: Fordham University Press, 2016).

12. On the historical origins of stereophony and the development of binaural listening, with the stethoscope in particular, in the nineteenth century, see Jonathan Sterne, *The Audible Past: Cultural Origins of Sound Reproduction* (Durham, N.C.: Duke University Press, 2003), 155–56.

13. Poe, *Poetry*, 839.

14. See Dennis Pahl, "Sounding the Sublime: Poe, Burke, and the (non)sense of language," *Poe Studies* 42, no. 1 (2009): 41–60. Pahl argues that the role of sound in Poe can be examined through Edmund Burke's aesthetics of the sublime.

15. Baudelaire, *OC II*, 335.

16. Jonathan Rée, François Bonnet, and John Picker ("Aural anxiety") each focus on "The Tell-Tale Heart." Other compelling scholarly works on Poe and sound include: Adam Frank on "The Facts in the Case of M. Valdemar"; Allen Weiss on death and sound in Poe as prefiguration of radio and phonography; and Lindon Barret on race and sound, with a focus on "The Purloined Letter."

17. For discussion of the acousmatic as a cultural and musical listening practice, see Brian Kane, *Sound Unseen: Acousmatic Sound in Theory and Practice* (New York: Oxford University Press, 2014). Kane highlights important junctures in the historical practice of "acousmatic listening," an idea that became central for *musique concrète* and Pierre Schaeffer, and one that has been theorized in film studies most prominently by Michel Chion, who adapts the term "acousmatic" into the neologism "*acousmètre*" to describe the audibility of a voice in film absent the image of the speaker on screen. See Chion, *La Voix au Cinéma* (Paris, 1972), 25–33. Kane offers an important critique of Schaeffer's theory of acousmatic experience. For more commentary on acousmatic sound and Chion, see Carolyn Abbate, "Debussy's Phantom Sounds," *Cambridge Opera Journal* 10, no. 1 (March 1998): 67–96.

18. On this particular point about audio technologies and the acousmatic experience of sound, see Kane's discussion of Michel Chion's approach to the acousmatic (Kane, *Sound Unseen*, 4–5). See also Sterne, *Audible Past*, 19–21, and chapter 5. Kane differs from Sterne's approach to the acousmatic in important ways, however. Where Sterne pairs schizophonia with acousmatic listening, Kane emphasizes critical differences, one being the historical context of the two concepts relative to audio technologies. See Kane, *Sound Unseen*, 245,n7.

19. Kane, "*Acousmate*: History and De-Visualised Sound in the Schaefferian Tradition," *Organised Sound* 17, no.2 (2012): 183–84.

20. Kane, "History and De-Visualised Sound," 186.

21. Kane, 180.

22. According to Walter Benjamin, the "strange and exceptional" was one of the main themes of Poe's aesthetic. See Walter Benjamin, *Arcades Project*, trans. Howard Eiland and Kevin Mclaughlin (Cambridge, Mass.: Harvard University Press, 1999), 234.

23. Kane, in a brief reading of "The Tell-Tale Heart," calls this mysterious sonic element an "auditory undecidability" (Kane, *Sound Unseen*, 159).

24. Here I draw on Kane's reflections about acousmatic experience, specifically when he asserts: "Modern audio technology does not create acousmatic experience; rather, acousmatic experience, first discovered in the Pythagorean context, creates the conditions for modern audio technology. Radio, records, the telephone, and the tape recorder exist within the horizon first opened by the Pythagorean veil" (Kane, *Sound Unseen*, 4–5). For a definition of acousmaticity, see Kane, *Sound Unseen*, 225. On the specificity of nineteenth-century urban apartment living and how ghost stories often dramatized the acoustics of such experience, see Sharon Marcus, *Apartment Stories: City and Home in Nineteenth-Century Paris and London* (Berkeley: University of California Press, 1999).

25. Ivan Kreilkamp, *Voice and the Victorian Storyteller* (Cambridge: Cambridge University Press, 2005), 200.

26. See Jonathan Crary, *Techniques of the Observer: On Vision and Modernity in the Nineteenth Century* (Cambridge, Mass.: MIT Press, 1990), and *Suspensions of Perception: Attention, Spectacle, and Modern Culture* (Cambridge, Mass.: MIT Press, 1999). See also Helmut Müller-Sievers, *The Cylinder: Kinematics of the Nineteenth Century* (Berkeley: University of California Press, 2012), 3.

27. Poe, *Poetry*, 924.

28. Poe, 925.

29. On concepts of the nineteenth-century observer, see Crary, *Techniques*, 6.

30. Müller-Sievers, *The Cylinder*, 3, 88–89. See also Sterne, *Audible Past*.

31. On auscultation, see among others, Sterne, *Audible Past*; Szendy "The Auditory Re-Turn (The Point of Listening)," Keynote Address, "Thinking Hearing—The Auditory Turn in the Humanities," University of Texas at Austin, October 2, 2009"; and Jonathan Rée, *I See a Voice: Deafness, Language, and the Senses: a Philosophical History* (New York: Holt Paperbacks, 2000), 53.

32. See Sterne, *Audible Past*, chapter 2, 120, 126, for Forbes's significance in bringing the practice and ideas of Laennec on mediate auscultation to the English-speaking world.

33. Critical notices, *Southern Literary Messenger*, vol. II, no. 7, November 1836.

34. *Southern Literary Messenger*.

35. Sterne, *Audible Past*, 102. He argues: "Every movement of the organs in the human thorax could be tracked by listening to the body with the aid of an instrument, and those movements could be rendered meaningful. *This* was Laennec's innovation, not the physical composition of a simple device to accomplish the task."

36. Poe, *Poetry*, 605.

37. Poe, 606. On Laennec and the phenomenon of pectoriloquy, see Sterne, *Audible Past*, 126.

38. John Picker, "Aural Anxieties and the Advent of Modernity," in *The Victorian World*, ed. Martin Hewitt (London: Routledge), 605.

39. See Szendy, "The Auditory Re-Turn," on *egophony* and the idea of a "sonority of the ego."

40. On this point, see also James Kennaway, *Bad Vibrations: The History of the Idea of Music as a Cause of Disease* (London: Routledge, 2016), 8.

41. Poe, *Poetry*, 840. Valdemar suffers from phthisis, a pathology that was diagnosed by auscultation, among other methods, in the early nineteenth century. Auscultation, as applied to cases of phthisis, is detailed in an article in the medical journal Poe reviewed in 1836, 22–23. The authors of the article describe the necessity of being able to distinguish several distinctive sounds when auscultating the phthisic patient: "the *gargouillement*, or *râle caverneux*, . . . resonance of the voice when a cavity has formed . . . metallic tinkling . . . aegophony (vox tremula similis voci caprarum)."

42. Adam Frank highlights the element of sound in "Valdemar" in dialogue with what Frank calls a "telegraphic imaginary." Frank proposes that Valdemar's tongue conjures up mid-nineteenth-century discourses on the relation between mesmerism and electromagnetic telegraphy, which had its own distinct sound effects.

43. On listening practices associated with electric sound telegraphy in 1840s America, see Sterne, *Audible Past*, chapter 3, in which he proposes that telegraph operators over the course of the decade began to practice a form of what he calls "audile technique."

44. Poe, *Poetry*, 839.

45. Poe, 839

46. On Kurtz as a voice without a body, see Kreilkamp, *Victorian Storyteller*.

47. Poe, *Poetry*, 839.

48. Poe, 833.

49. Poe, 839–40. Frank reads the "thrillingly distinct syllabification" as a figure of the "telegraphic transmission's precision and tap-tap distinctness."

50. Derrida, La *voix et le phénomène: introduction au problème du signe dans la phénoménologie de Husserl* (Paris: Presses Universitaires de France, 1967), 108.

51. Adam Frank, "Valdemar's Tongue, Poe's Telegraphy," *ELH* 72, no. 3 (Fall 2005): 638.

52. Frank, "Valdemar's Tongue, 654.

53. On the relationship between Poe and mass media, specifically mass urban print media of the first half of the nineteenth century, see Edward Cutler, *Recovering the New: Transatlantic Roots of Modernism* (Hanover: University Press of New England, 2003). He focuses on the "transatlantic interplay of print and urban transformation at mid-nineteenth century that gave rise to later modernist practice" (21).

54. Poe praises de Béranger several times in his essay "Song-writing" from the *Marginalia*.

55. Poe, *Poetry*, 322.

56. Poe, 324.

57. Poe, 318.

58. Poe, 62.

59. See also Müller-Sievers, *The Cylinder*, 178, on Siegert and the inventors of phonography and telephony, who "used entire animal and even human organs as interfaces." Cf. also Sterne, *Audible Past*, chapter 1, for a discussion of those practices as well, namely the ear phonautograph of Alexander Graham Bell and

Clarence Blake. Frank also highlights these analogies between organic nerves and inorganic wires in his discussion of "Valdemar" and telegraphy.

60. See Laura Otis, "The Metaphoric Circuit: Organic and Technological Communication in the Nineteenth Century," *Journal of the History of Ideas* 63, no. 1 (Jan. 2002): 106–7.

61. Kennaway, *Bad Vibrations*, 27. He examines "the idea of 'sympathetic vibration' between music and literally vibrating nerves."

62. Kennaway, 15.

63. Kieran Murphy, *Electromagnetism and the Metonymic Imagination* (University Park: The Pennsylvania State University Press, 2020). Murphy offers compelling analysis of the link between nineteenth-century scientific discoveries in electromagnetism and the metonymic imagination. With Poe's "The Spectacles" in particular, Murphy highlights the opening of the story and its reference to magnetism and electricity in Poe's phrases "ethical magnetism or magnetoesthetics" and "electric sympathy" (24–25).

64. Jean-Georges Kastner, *La Harpe d'Éole et la Musique Cosmique, études sur les rapports des phénomènes sonores de la nature avec la science et l'art* (Paris: G. Brandus, 1856), 105.

65. Cf. again "Valdemar" and the narrator's uncertainty about sound and voice.

66. As noted above, cf. Murphy for instances where metonymy and electromagnetism converge in nineteenth-century literary and scientific discourses, as Murphy highlights in the writings of Poe, Balzac, and Villiers. Murphy contends: "Whereas electric imagery tended to emphasize metaphorical relations founded on resemblance, electromagnetic imagery underscored metonymic relations based on contiguity" (5).

67. Baudelaire, *OC II*, 316.

68. Baudelaire, 317. Cf. also Baudelaire's prose poem, "Le *Confiteor* de l'Artiste" where "les nerfs criardes" in the poem evoke the tactility and corporeality of sound.

69. See Kennaway, *Bad Vibrations*. On the Romantic poets' use of the Aeolian harp analogy, see John Picker, *Victorian Soundscapes* (New York: Oxford University Press, 2003), 7.

70. See Abbate, "Debussy's Phantom Sounds," 81.

71. From the June 12, 1844, entry in *Doings of Gotham*. See Phillip Lopate, ed., *Writing New York: A Literary Anthology* (New York: The Library of America, 2008), 101; and for use of French in Poe's stories, see esp. "Purloined Letter," and "The Murders in the Rue Morgue." For a discussion of Poe's influence on Baudelaire and the less frequently posed question of the significance of the French language for Poe, see Jonathan Culler, "Poe and Baudelaire," in *Zeitschrift für französische Sprache und Literatur*, Bd. 100, Sprachwissenschaft-Literaturwissenschaft-Semiotik, Wechselwirkungen in Theorie und Praxis, 1990.

72. See Lopate, *Writing New York*, 102.

73. Lopate, 101.

74. Culler, "Poe and Baudelaire," 73.

75. Lopate, *Writing New York*, 102.

76. See Laure Katsaros, *New York–Paris: Whitman, Baudelaire, and the Hybrid City* (Ann Arbor: University of Michigan Press, 2012), 24. On Whitman's alteration of the French word '*pavé*' here, Katsaros offers a key insight on sound and language that supports her broader claims about a transatlantic poetic urban imaginary between New York and Paris. Whitman turns to French for a certain exuberance of language and, as Katsaros argues, to imply connection between New York and Paris.

77. Lopate, *Writing New York*, 102.

78. Christopher Prendergast, *Paris and the Nineteenth Century* (Oxford: Blackwell, 1995), 129.

79. Jean-Georges Kastner, *Les Voix*, 82–83: "il faut compter pour quelque chose le bruit incessant des voitures et le tintamarre d'une ville affairée contre lesquels il lutte du matin au soir, à grand renfort de poumons."

80. Poe, *Poetry*, 391–92.

81. Poe, 389.

82. Poe, 388. See Alexander Weheliye, *Phonographies: Grooves in Sonic Afro-Modernity* (Durham, N.C.: Duke University Press, 2005), esp. 108–13, on the idea of how sound articulates space and, in the case of the city, a "modern urban spatiality." See also Henri Lefebvre, *Rhythmanalysis: Space, Time, and Everyday Life* (London: Continuum International Publishing, 2004), on the concept of "rythmanalyse" for acoustic rhythms in urban everyday life.

83. See the quotation from Engels in Benjamin's essay "On some motifs in Baudelaire."

84. Poe, *Poetry*, 389.

85. Cutler, *Recovering the New*, 121. He argues that Poe's "Man of the Crowd" and Baudelaire's "Sept Vieillards" allegorize both the "condition of the modern age" and "their own standing as print commodities in an era of mass production" (115). These specific points about Poe and Baudelaire serve to illustrate Cutler's broader argument that the "cult of the new," which is so important for modernism and modernist aesthetics, had its origins in massified urban culture of the nineteenth century, especially in the transatlantic popular press. Like Cutler, whose study focuses on Poe, Baudelaire, and Whitman, I am especially interested in these transatlantic connections in aesthetic modernity, connections that have also been highlighted by Katsaros on the urban element in Baudelaire and Whitman. See also Benjamin ("On some motifs in Baudelaire"), who highlights this phrase about jostling in Poe's story. On the question of "reflex" and Poe, cf. Frank, "Valdemar's Tongue," 642 and the relation between Poe's texts and nineteenth-century discourses on reflex physiology and how the reader could physically experience something represented in a narrative.

86. Poe, *Poetry*, 333.

87. Poe, 322.

88. Poe, 333.

89. Poe, 334–35.

90. See Robert Orledge, "After *Pelléas*: The Poe Operas (*Le diable dans le beffroi, La chute de la Maison Usher*," in *Debussy and the Theatre* (New York: Cambridge University Press, 1982), 102–27; and Abbate, "Debussy's Phantom Sounds," 67–96.

91. See Sterne (*Audible Past*) where he argues in his chapter "The Social Genesis of Sound Fidelity": "'Original' sounds are as much a product of the medium as are copies—reproduced sounds are not simply mediated versions of unmediated original sounds. Sound reproduction is a social process. The possibility of reproduction precedes the fact" (219).

3. Tattered Sound: Baudelaire's Paris, Noise, and the Protophonographic

1. Antoine Compagnon, *Baudelaire: l'irréductible* (Paris: Flammarion, 2014), 167 (my translation). For a brief summary of critical accounts of Baudelairean movement, see Françoise Meltzer, *Seeing Double: Baudelaire's Modernity* (Chicago: University of Chicago Press, 2012), 68.

2. Whidden's translation. See also Seth Whidden, *Arthur Rimbaud* (London: Reaktion, 2018), 103. Whidden writes about that section of the poem: "It is all too much to take in, and so it becomes noise."

3. For discussion of street cries amidst the noise of nineteenth-century Paris, see Aimée Boutin, *City of Noise: Sound and Nineteenth-Century Paris* (Urbana: University of Illinois Press, 2015).

4. Alphonse Certeux, *Les Cris de Londres* (Paris: Chamuel, 1893), 167. These preservational efforts were showcased and discussed during several conventions held under the auspices of La Société des traditions populaires in Paris. On the use of the phonograph as a tool of ethnography more broadly, see Brian Hochman, *Savage Preservation: The Ethnographic Origins of Modern Media Technology* (Minneapolis: University of Minnesota Press, 2014); and Erika Brady, *A Spiral Way: How the Phonograph Changed Ethnography* (Jackson: University Press of Mississippi, 1999).

5. Félix Nadar, "Les Histoires du mois," in *Musée français-anglais*, n. 24, December, 1856, 7, first column on left. This text is available on Gallica, https://gallica.bnf.fr/ark:/12148/bpt6k8920146/f6.item. See also Jacques Perriault, *Mémoires de l'ombre et du son: une archéologie de l'audio-visuel* (Paris: Flammarion, 1981), 133, where the citation from Nadar is correct, but the source is mistakenly noted as *Musée franco-anglais* instead of *"français,"* as it should be.

6. Édouard-Léon Scott de Martinville, "Fixation Graphique de la voix" (Paris: Impr. de J. Claye, 1857).

7. Nadar, "Les Histoires." Translations from French to English in this chapter are mine unless otherwise indicated.

8. Félix Nadar, *Mémoires du Géant* (Paris: E. Dentu, deuxième édition, 1865), 272.

9. Nadar, "Les Histoires."

10. Baudelaire, *Oeuvres Complètes, I*, Texte établi, présenté et annoté par Claude Pichois, Bibliothèque de la Pléiade (Paris: Gallimard, 1975–1976), 275–76.

11. Félix Nadar, *Charles Baudelaire, Intime, Le Poète Vierge* (Paris: A. Blaizot, Éditeur, 1911), 38–39.

12. Nadar, *Charles Baudelaire*, 39.

13. Nadar, "Les Histoires," 7.

14. Perriault, *Mémoires*, 133.

15. Jean-Georges Kastner, *La Harpe d'Éole et la Musique Cosmique, études sur les rapports des phénomènes sonores de la nature avec la science et l'art* (Paris: G. Brandus, 1856), 117.

16. See Baudelaire, "Notes nouvelles sur Poe"; and Ross Chambers's comment (*An Atmospherics of the City: Baudelaire and the Poetics of Noise* [New York: Fordham University Press, 2015], 179) that Baudelaire vividly articulates his contempt for the idea of progress in his essays on Poe.

17. On Baudelaire and the "cult of obscurity," see Compagnon, *Baudelaire*, chapters 3 and 4.

18. One example of that incomprehensibility to his vision was his failure to see the greatness of Manet. See especially Meltzer, *Seeing Double*, 75.

19. For his reflections on the idea of progress and these particular inventions, see Baudelaire's "Exposition Universelle 1855: Méthode de critique, De l'idée moderne du progrès appliquée aux beaux-arts. Déplacement de la vitalité" (Baudelaire, *Oeuvres Complètes II*, Texte établi, présenté et annoté par Claude Pichois, Bibliothèque de la Pléiade [Paris: Gallimard, 1975–1976], 575).

20. Baudelaire, *OC II*, 617.

21. My reference here is to Ovid's version of the Echo and Narcissus myths in *The Metamorphoses*, in which Narcissus is turned into a flower.

22. Baudelaire, *OC II*, 618–19.

23. Nadar, *Mémoires du Géant*, 1864, 271–72. See also Perriault, *Mémoires*, 133–34.

24. Nadar, 272.

25. Nadar, "Les Histoires" 7. Baudelaire, *OC II*, 324.

26. Nadar, *Mémoires du Géant*, 272.

27. On Baudelaire and the press, see "Un poète journaliste," in Antoine Compagnon, *Baudelaire: l'irréductible* (Paris: Flammarion, 2014).

28. Nadar, "Les Histoires," 7.

29. Stéphanie de Saint Marc, *Nadar* (Paris: Gallimard, 2010), 230.

30. Baudelaire's letter to his mother in Baudelaire, *Correspondance II*, 554.

31. Baudelaire, *OC II*, 617.

32. Baudelaire, 692.

33. Baudelaire, *Correspondance II*, 326.

34. Cros worked on color photography with Jules Carpentier, who would years later become the engineer of the Lumière Brothers's cinematographe.

35. For discussion of the other appearance of color photography in Baudelaire's writing, see Compagnon, *Baudelaire*, 101–3.

36. Compagnon, 95.

37. This is in part XV, "Du Paysage" of the *Salon de 1846* (Baudelaire, *OC II*, 484).
38. Baudelaire.
39. For years, color was neglected in particular studies of media, surprisingly, even with something like television, as Susan Murray has recently examined in *Bright Signals: A History of Color Television* (Durham, N.C.: Duke University Press, 2018).
40. Laura Anne Kalba, *Color in the Age of Impressionism: Commerce, Technology, and Art* (University Park: Penn State University Press, 2017), 196.
41. Cf. Dictionnaire Littré, http://littre.reverso.net/dictionnaire-francais/definition/guignon. For reflections on the term and its usage by Baudelaire and others, see also Charles Baudelaire, *Les Fleurs du mal*, présentation par Jacques Dupont (Paris: Flammarion, 2006), 268,n1.
42. Baudelaire, *OC I*, 17.
43. On the idea of literally and figuratively being able to hear oneself in the modern city, see Georg Simmel's essay "The Metropolis and Mental Life" in Georg Simmel, *Simmel on Culture: Selected Writings*, ed. by David Frisby and Mike Featherstone (London: Sage Publications, 1997).
44. See Jacques Dupont edition of *Les Fleurs du Mal*, 34–35, 268, for a discussion of lines that Baudelaire has adapted from Henry Wadsworth Longfellow's "A Psalm of Life"; and Thomas Gray's "Elegy Written in a Country Churchyard." See also Graham Chesters, "A political reading of Baudelaire's 'L'Artiste Inconnu' ('Le Guignon')," *Modern Language Review* 79, no. 1 (Jan. 1984): 64–76, for a discussion of this aspect of the poem.
45. See, for example, the way Baudelaire uses the word in "Le Balcon": "Les soirs illuminés par l'ardeur du charbon, / Et les soirs au balcon, voilés de vapeurs roses."
46. For accounts of the phonautograph in the history of science, see Perriault, *Mémoires*; Jonathan Sterne, *The Audible Past: Cultural Origins of Sound Reproduction* (Durham, N.C.: Duke University Press, 2003), esp. 31, 35–36, 38, 45–46; and Haun Saussy, *The Ethnography of Rhythm: Orality and Its Technologies* (New York: Fordham University Press, 2016), 89–93. For an account of developments in acoustics in the nineteenth century, from the perspective of the dawn of the twentieth, see James Loudon, "A Century of Progress in Acoustics." *Science* 14, no. 365 (Dec. 27, 1901): 987–95.
47. Perriault explains: "Scott de Martinville utilisa la gravure sur un tambour enduit de suie pour rendre compte des vibrations de la parole. Un pavillon canalisait la voix vers une membrane qui agitait l'aiguille de ce phonautographe." Perriault, *Mémoires*, 138.
48. Nadar, *Mémoires du Géant*, 272.
49. Édouard-Léon Scott de Martinville, "The Phonautographic Manuscripts of Édouard-Léon Scott de Martinville," translated and edited by Patrick Feaster (Bloomington, Ind.: FirstSounds.org, 2010) 35.
50. See Laura Otis, *Networking: Communicating with Bodies and Machines in the Nineteenth Century* (Ann Arbor: University of Michigan Press, 2001), for reflections on how science and literature have a symbiotic relationship in metaphor,

how metaphors developed in the confluence of the two fields can both enhance scientific knowledge and enrich literary expression.

51. See André Coeuroy and G. Clarence, *Le phonographe* (Paris: Kra, 1929), 12.

52. For a discussion of the discovery of Scott's recordings, see François Bonnet, *Les Mots et les Sons: un archipel sonore* (Paris: Éditions de l'éclat, 2012); and Jody Rosen, "Researchers Play Tune Recorded Before Edison," *New York Times*, March 27, 2008, Arts Section. To listen to this recording, visit http://www.firstsounds.org/sounds/1860-Scott-Au-Clair-de-la-Lune.mp3.

53. Baudelaire, *OC II*, 296.

54. Baudelaire, "Notes nouvelles sur Edgar Poe," in *OC II*, 326. The Pléiade editors believe the expression "ears that would hear the grass growing" may be inspired by Poe's poem "Al Aaraaf." I would imagine the line they have in mind is in Part II: "Young flowers were whispering in melody [. . .]." The editors wonder whether Baudelaire had in fact read that poem, and suggest another source, a fairytale character that Mme. de Staël alludes to in *De l'Allemagne*.

55. Baudelaire, 320.

56. On Baudelaire and the popular press of his age, see Compagnon, *Baudelaire*, esp. chapter 2.

57. Philippe Lacoue-Labarthe, "L'Écho du Sujet," in *Le Sujet de la Philosophie* (Paris: Aubier: Flammarion, 1979), 253.

58. My emphasis on Lacoue-Labarthe's "infrasons du processus inconscient" draws inspiration from recent theories of an "acoustical unconscious," which are inspired by Walter Benjamin's theory of an "optical unconscious" in his "Short History of Photography" essay. See Robert Ryder, *The Acoustical Unconscious: From Walter Benjamin to Alexander Kluge*, (Berlin: De Gruyter, 2022); and Veit Erlmann, *Reason and Resonance: A History of Modern Aurality* (New York: Zone Books, 2010).

59. This conflicted "silencing" is a feature of Baudelaire's poetry that, as Kamuf argues, involves a "pluralized femininity" whose presence hinges on a problematic of feminine voice and silence. See Peggy Kamuf, "Baudelaire's Modern Woman," *Qui Parle* 4, no. 2 (Spring 1991): 1–7; and Kamuf, "Baudelaire au féminin," in *Signature Pieces: On the Institution of Authorship*, (Ithaca, N.Y.: Cornell University Press, 1988), 123–44.

60. Among others, Prendergast, Chambers, and Boutin have each offered insightful explorations of noise and Baudelaire's phenomenology of the urban sensory environment. Prendergast, focusing on urban noise and lyric harmony, argues that such noise threatens the integrity and rhythm of the poetic line (Christopher Prendergast, *Paris and the Nineteenth Century*, [Oxford: Blackwell, 1995], 129). Chambers, considering Baudelaire's "atmospherics of the city," argues that art came to form an "alliance, in modernity, with the power of noise" (Chambers, *Atmospherics*, 161). Boutin argues that Baudelaire, in a poem such as "Le Mauvais vitrier," embraces "strident dissonance," in turn influencing an allied poetic and ethnographic impulse exemplified by attention to urban street cries (Boutin, *City*, 103–4, 133–34).

61. Baudelaire, *OC I*, 92.

62. See Baudelaire's essay "De l'Essence du Rire" for Baudelaire's own reflections on the different levels of meaning and expression involved in laughing (Baudelaire, *OC II*, 525).

63. Ross Chambers, "Baudelaire's Street Poetry," *Nineteenth-Century French Studies* (Summer 1985): 253. See also William Sharpe, *Unreal Cities: Urban Figuration in Wordsworth, Baudelaire, Whitman, Eliot, and Williams* (Baltimore: Johns Hopkins University Press, 1990), 55.

64. Chambers, *Atmospherics*, 48.

65. This vexed representation of the collective arises out of what Paul de Man calls "pronominal agitation" in Baudelaire's poetry, the "*je-tu* apostrophes or dialogues," found throughout *Les Fleurs du Mal*, the fracturing of the lyric self in the experience of the urban crowd for example. See Paul De Man, "Anthropomorphism and Trope in the Lyric," in *The Rhetoric of Romanticism* (New York: Columbia University Press, 1984), 243.

66. See Ross Chambers, "Seeing and Saying in Baudelaire's 'Les Aveugles,'" in *Pre-Text, Text, Context*, ed. by Robert Mitchell (Columbus: Ohio State University Press, 1980).

67. On self-other relations in the context of poverty and the poor in Baudelaire's poetry, specifically the implications of the collective "we" implied in the title of a poem such as "Assommons les pauvres," see Patrick Greaney, *Untimely Beggar: Poverty and Power from Baudelaire to Benjamin* (Minneapolis: University of Minnesota Press, 2007), xviii.

68. For the notion of the auditory self as "porous membrane" in contradistinction to a distinctive, removed, Cartesian point, see Steven Connor, "The Modern Auditory 'I,'" in *Rewriting the Self: Histories from the Renaissance to the Present*, ed. by Roy Porter (London: Routledge, 1996), 203–23.

69. On connections between "Les Aveugles" and "À une passante," see, among others, Sharpe, *Unreal Cities*, 57.

70. James H. Johnson, *Listening in Paris: A Cultural History* (Berkeley: University of California Press, 1996), 228.

71. Johnson, *Listening in Paris*, 235–36.

72. Peter Szendy, *Listen: A History of Our Ears*, trans. Charlotte Mandell (New York: Fordham University Press, 2008), 113–14.

73. For an architectural history of how changes in concert hall acoustics shaped perception, see Emily Thompson, *The Soundscape of Modernity: Architectural Acoustics and the Culture of Listening in America 1900–1933* (Cambridge, Mass.: MIT Press, 2002).

74. On the urban crowd and relations between multiplicity, atomization, and collectivity, see Vanessa Schwartz, *Spectacular Realities: Early Mass Culture in fin-de-siècle Paris* (Berkeley: University of California Press, 1998). Schwartz suggests that the urban crowd in fin de siècle Paris formed as a "new collectivity" around the "spectacularization of reality," those primarily visual forms of entertainment and

emergent mass culture such as boulevard culture, panoramas, and dioramas, among other entertainments.

75. For a discussion of how sound can articulate space in the city, see Alexander Weheliye, *Phonographies: Grooves in Sonic Afro-Modernity* (Durham, N.C.: Duke University Press, 2005), esp. 107–8, 136. For concepts of music and formation of social groups in the nineteenth century, see James Kennaway, *Bad Vibrations: The History of the Idea of Music as a Cause of Disease* (Routledge, 2016).

76. Baudelaire, OC I, 294. Proust uses the word "lambeau" to describe the little phrase's exit at the marquise de Saint-Euverte's soirée: "[. . .] quand la phrase se fut enfin défaite, flottant en lambeaux dans les motifs suivants qui déjà avaient pris sa place [. . .]." See Marcel Proust, *Du côté de chez Swann*, préface d'Antoine Compagnon (Paris: Gallimard, 1988), 347. Scott Moncrieff and Kilmartin translate "en lambeaux" as "fragmentary echoes."

77. Baudelaire, OC I, 89.

78. On the omnibuses and urban mobility, see Harvey, *Paris*, 113: "Haussmann engineered the consolidation by merger of all the omnibus companies in 1855 into one private monopoly—the Compagnie des Omnibus de Paris—thereby increasing the number of passengers moved from 36 million in 1855 to 110 million by 1860." See also Masha Belenky, *Engine of Modernity: The Omnibus and Urban Culture in Nineteenth-Century Paris* (Manchester: Manchester University Press, 2019). Belenky examines the impact of omnibuses on the cultural imagination of nineteenth-century Paris. She argues that the omnibus became a "laboratory of social relations" and, as such, a "super-topos" of literary and artistic representation (Belenky, 165).

79. Baudelaire, *Salon de 1859*, "Le public moderne et la photographie" (Baudelaire, OC II, 619).

80. Baudelaire.

81. Baudelaire, OC I, 293.

82. Baudelaire, 294.

83. See also Victor Fournel, as quoted in Benjamin's *Arcades Project*, who relates his experience hearing a fragment of conversation in the street. Such a quotation has given rise to the notion of a particular acoustic *flânerie* in recent scholarship (see Aimée Boutin, "Aural Flânerie," *Dix-Neuf* 16, no. 2 [July 2012]: 149–61).

84. Baudelaire, OC I, 294.

85. Jean-Luc Nancy, "Ascoltando," in Peter Szendy, *Listen: A History of Our Ears*, trans. Charlotte Mandell (New York: Fordham University Press, 2008), x.

86. On the idea of "convertibility" of multitude and solitude as expressed in Baudelaire's prose poem "Les Foules," see Kamuf, "Baudelaire's Modern Woman," 4.

87. See Prendergast, *Paris*, 181; and T. J. Clark, *The Painting of Modern Life: Paris in the Art of Manet and his Followers* (Princeton, N.J.: Princeton University Press, 1999), 64. Clark and Prendergast each highlight the contrasts between the two works. They claim that Manet's painting does not exhibit the same kind of interest in the marginal figures upon which the speaker casts his gaze in Baudelaire's poem. Instead, they argue, "Music in the Tuileries" offers a view of bourgeois adherence to

rules of social decorum, the performance of Second Empire leisure and sociability, the performance of class.

88. Sima Godfrey, "Strangers in the Park: Manet, Baudelaire, and *La Musique aux Tuileries*," in *Baudelaire and the Poetics of Modernity*, ed. by Patricia A. Ward (Nashville: Vanderbilt University Press, 2001), 45–60.

89. Godfrey argues that critics have missed an intriguing poetic intertext between "Les Veuves" and "Music in Tuileries," this being the presence of a marginal, isolated woman at the center of the painting. She argues furthermore that art historians have smoothed over "the painting's internal conflicts" and that Baudelaire's poetry, specifically the prose poems, not only his essays and art criticism, may offer art historical knowledge and insight, in the same way Manet's paintings can offer insights into the poetry.

90. The critic was writing in *La Revue Libérale* in 1867, cited in Godfrey, "Strangers in the Park," 55–56.

91. Contrast this "éclat" with the more purely visual "éclair" of the widow in "Passante": "Un éclair . . . puis la nuit!—Fugitive beauté."

92. Jacques Derrida, "Preface: veni," in *Rogues: Two Essays on Reason* (Stanford, Calif.: Stanford University Press, 2005), xii.

93. Siegfried Kracauer, *Jacques Offenbach and the Paris of His Time* (New York: Zone Books, 2002), 90.

94. Cited in Godfrey, "Strangers in the Park," 55.

95. Baudelaire, *OC II*, 693.

96. Compagnon, *Baudelaire*, 190.

97. On Koenig, see Saussy, *Ethnography*, 116; Patrick Feaster, *Pictures: One Thousand Years of Educed Audio: 980–1980*, Dust-to-Digital, 2013, 99–102; and David Pantalony, *Altered Sensations: Rudolph Koenig's Acoustical Workshop in Nineteenth-Century Paris* (Dordrecht: Springer, 2009).

98. For recent readings of "Bistouri" and photography, see Compagnon, *Baudelaire*, 103–5; Elissa Marder, "Baudelaire's Feminine Counter-Signature: 'Mademoiselle Bistouri's Photographic Poetics" in *Nineteenth-Century French Studies* 46, no. 1–2 (Fall–Winter 2017–2018): 1–25; and Marit Grøtta, *Baudelaire's Media Aesthetics; the Gaze of the Flâneur and Nineteenth-Century Media* (London: Bloomsbury Academic, 2015), 62–66.

99. Baudelaire, *OC I*, 353.

100. On Koenig and graphical acoustics, see Pantalony, *Altered Sensations*, 41–50.

4. The Amazing Chorus: Whitman and the Sound of New York City

1. My approach here is in part guided by Jean-Luc Nancy's meditation on Plato's *Ion*, in which Nancy thinks of "the differentiation between singular voices" as a kind of "sharing of voices." In this way, Nancy suggests, the inspired poet is drawn out of a certain sense of self. Jean-Luc Nancy, "Sharing Voices," in *Transforming the*

Hermeneutic Context: from Nietzsche to Nancy, ed. Gayle L. Ormiston and Alan D. Schrift (Albany: State University of New York Press, 1989), 236–37.

2. See The Thomas Edison Papers, February 14, 1889, Letter Alfred Ord Tate to Sylvester Baxter, General Letterbook Series: LB-028 (Jan.–Apr. 1889); and The Thomas Edison Papers, February 14, 1889, Letter from Thomas Alva Edison to Jesse H. Lippincott, General Letterbook Series: LB-028 (Jan.–Apr. 1889).

3. See Ed Folsom, "The Whitman Recording," *Walt Whitman Quarterly Review* 9, no. 4 (Spring 1992): 214–16; and Larry Don Griffin, "Walt Whitman's Voice," *Walt Whitman Quarterly Review* 9, no. 3 (Winter 1992): 125–33. To listen to the recording, visit http://www.whitmanarchive.org/multimedia/index.html.

4. Tyler Hoffman, "Walt Whitman 'Live': Performing the Public Sphere," *Walt Whitman Quarterly Review* 28 (2011): 198. Hoffman furthermore reveals what would seem like Whitman's articulation of a need for a phonographic device in one of his conversations with Traubel, Whitman's desire to "talk into a machine" instead of writing with a pen, because of physical fatigue near the end of his life. It may be too quick, however, to assert that Whitman had a veritable "fascination with the phonograph," given the doubts that linger about the recording.

5. Here I draw from Alan Trachtenberg's argument that, for Whitman, the city is both "material place and mode of perception" (Trachtenberg, "Whitman's Lesson of the City," in *Breaking Bounds: Whitman and American Cultural Studies*, ed. by Erkkila, Betsy and Grossman, Jay [New York: Oxford University Press, 1996], 163).

6. Quoted in Tyler Hoffman, *American Poetry in Performance: From Walt Whitman to Hip-Hop* (Ann Arbor: University of Michigan Press, 2011), 20. See also Laure Katsaros, *New York–Paris: Whitman, Baudelaire, and the Hybrid City* (Ann Arbor: University of Michigan Press, 2012), 36.

7. For a discussion of Tennyson, see John Picker, *Victorian Soundscapes* (New York: Oxford University Press, 2003), chap. 4. For a discussion of Irving, see Wes Folkerth, *The Sound of Shakespeare* (London: Routledge, 2002), 1–7. To listen to the recording of Irving, visit http://www.youtube.com/watch?v=7Z4gXiNKR4s.

8. Folkerth, *The Sound of Shakespeare*, 2. Apollinaire had a similar experience in 1913 when reciting poetry to the phonograph for the first time for the "Archives de la Parole," inaugurated in 1911 by linguist Ferdinand Brunot at the Sorbonne in Paris.

9. See Lisa Gitelman, *Always Already New: Media, History, and the Data of Culture* (Cambridge, Mass.: MIT Press, 2006); Gitelman examines how new media generate and are themselves shaped by new social protocols.

10. The quote about capturing "all sounds" is from Whitman's "Proud Music of the Storm."

11. Trachtenberg describes a similar dialectic in Whitman's urban imaginary, his rapt attention to seeing the city "processionally" as Whitman's means of, Trachtenberg argues, "remaining within the float even while disentangling oneself from it" ("Whitman's Lesson of the City," 173).

12. See Katsaros, *New York–Paris*, 89; and Walter Benjamin, *The Arcades Project*, trans. Howard Eiland and Kevin Mclaughlin (Cambridge, Mass.: Harvard University Press, 1999), for the idea of machinery and "the mechanistic aspects of the human body." See also Edward K. Spann, *The New Metropolis: New York, 1840–1857* (New York: Columbia University Press, 1981), 164. Spann cites Charles Loring Brace, a social reformer concerned with the plight of New York's poor in the 1850s, who described urbanites as "mere machines of society, wound up to work fifteen hours a day."

13. Whitman, *Complete Poetry and Collected Prose*, ed. Justin Kaplan (New York: The Library of America, 1982), 293.

14. See, among others, Spann, *New Metropolis*, 157.

15. Betsy Erkkila claims that "Whitman was the first major American writer to find important sources and analogues for his own work in the literature and philosophy of France," and furthermore that "Whitman looked to France as a model in his attempt to liberate American sensibility . . . into a new moral and political consciousness" (Erkkila, *Walt Whitman among the French: Poet and Myth* [Princeton: Princeton University Press, 1980, 4]).

16. See Katsaros, *New York–Paris*, 1–12; and William Sharpe, *Unreal Cities: Urban Figuration in Wordsworth, Baudelaire, Whitman, Eliot, and Williams* (Baltimore, Md.: Johns Hopkins University Press, 1990), 190nn12–13. Whitman came to Baudelaire seemingly only late in his career, and the American poet mentions Baudelaire only once in his writings.

17. See Dana Brand, *The Spectator and the City in Nineteenth-Century American Literature* (New York: Cambridge University Press, 1991), 185, for the argument that Whitman finds himself caught up in "the panopticism of his age." For the claim that "Song of Myself" is a mostly "ocularcentric" poem, see Edward Cutler, *Recovering the New: Transatlantic Roots of Modernism* (Hanover: University Press of New England, 2003), 147–48.

18. On this comparison, see Katsaros, *New York–Paris*, 47.

19. Katsaros, *New York–Paris*, 21–25.

20. See Trachtenberg, "Whitman's Lesson of the City," for a discussion of William James's reflections on Whitman's "rapt attention" in the city (164–66).

21. Whitman, *Poetry*, 214. This and subsequent references are to the 1891–1892 "deathbed" edition of *Leaves of Grass*. This activity is echoed in a later poem, "Proud music of the storm," in which the speaker says, "Give me to hold all sounds, (I madly struggling cry,) / . . . Utter, pour in, for I would take them all!"

22. Whitman, 214.

23. See Adrienne Janus, "Listening: Jean-Luc Nancy and the 'Anti-Ocular' Turn in Continental Philosophy and Critical Theory," *Comparative Literature* 63, no. 2 (2011): 191. And for another conception of a "phonographic body" in the nineteenth century, see Anthony Enns, "The Phonographic Body: Phreno-Mesmerism, Brain Mapping and Embodied Recording," in *Sonic Mediations: Body, Sound, Technology* (Newcastle: Cambridge Scholars, 2008), 18–20, who argues that the early to mid-nineteenth-century practice of phreno-mesmerism, in its ability to turn the body

into a kind of machine for storing and reproducing acoustic information, prefigured certain abilities of the phonograph.

24. Whitman, *Poetry*, 214.

25. For a discussion of learning to adapt to signs of danger in the modern city, see David Bell, "Balzac and the modern city: mapping Paris in *Old Goriot*," in *Approaches to Teaching Balzac's Old Goriot*, ed. by Michal Ginsburg (Modern Language Association of America, 2000), 84. See also Peter Bailey, "Breaking the Sound Barrier," in *Hearing History: A reader*, ed. by Mark Smith (Athens: University of Georgia Press, 2004), 30.

26. On technologies and cultures of vivid color in the nineteenth and early twentieth centuries and their connections with art and literature, see Laura Anne Kalba, *Color in the Age of Impressionism: Commerce, Technology, and Art* (University Park: Penn State University Press, 2017); and Nicholas Gaskill, *Chromographia: American Literature and the Modernization of Color* (Minneapolis: University of Minnesota Press, 2018).

27. Whitman, *Poetry*, 195.

28. Katsaros, *New York–Paris*, 25.

29. Whitman, *Poetry*, 585. The self-sufficient musicality of a word is something Mallarmé will develop in his poetry. See Erkkila, *Poet and Myth*, for connections between Mallarmé and Whitman.

30. Phillip Lopate, ed., *Writing New York: A Literary Anthology* (New York, NY: The Library of America, 2008), 92.

31. Lopate, *Writing New York*.

32. Whitman, *Poetry*, 613.

33. See, as I have noted elsewhere, Erika Brady, *A Spiral Way: How the Phonograph Changed Ethnography* (Jackson: University Press of Mississippi, 1999); and Brian Hochman, *Savage Preservation: The Ethnographic Origins of Modern Media Technology* (Minneapolis: University of Minnesota Press, 2014).

34. See Katsaros, *New York–Paris*, 23–25. She contrasts the persistence of history in Whitman and Baudelaire's representations of their changing cities: "Baudelaire noticed all the scars in the cityscape, no matter how carefully they had been smoothed over by urban planners. He exhumed the rougher layers of the past underneath . . . But Whitman's hidden "Mannahatta" exists in a time that predates the beginnings of history. The Algonquin past has been so thoroughly annihilated that it is not even buried underneath the surface of the modern metropolis: it is simply gone" (23).

35. Whitman, *Poetry*, 195.

36. Whitman, 195. See Trachtenberg's commentary on this section of the poem and his comparison of it to moments in Baudelaire. Also see Whitman's "Mannahatta" and the phrase "open voices" for something like the antipode to the "howls restrained by decorum."

37. Whitman, *Poetry*, 247.

38. Whitman, 213.

39. See Louise Pound, "Whitman and the French Language," *American Speech* 1, no. 8 (May 1926): 421–30. See also OED, and the reference from Robert Louis Stevenson quoting this line from "Song of Myself."

40. Other scholars have made use of the expression "sounding out the city," namely Michael Bull and Adrien Curtin. While in dialogue with these scholars, my use of the expression derives more from the language of Whitman's poetry, especially when in "Crossing Brooklyn Ferry" he calls for young men to "sound out."

41. Whitman, *Poetry*, 195.

42. For the "open voices" line, see Whitman, *Poetry*, 586.

43. Whitman, 495.

44. Whitman, 494.

45. Whitman, 195.

46. My understanding of the poet as himself a resonant body is informed by Jean-Luc Nancy's concept of a *"corps sonore,"* in *Listening*, trans. Charlotte Mandell (New York: Fordham University Press, 2007); and, in part, from Enns's "The Phonographic Body" (cited above).

47. See Betsy Erkkila, "Whitman and the Homosexual Republic," in *Walt Whitman: The Centennial Essays*, ed. by Ed Folsom (Iowa City: University of Iowa Press, 1994); and my discussion of "Crossing Brooklyn Ferry" below for the sociopolitical valences of seeking "open voices" in the city as freedom to respond to a certain repressive societal "decorum."

48. Michel Chion, *Le Promeneur Écoutant: essais d'acoulogie* (Paris: Plume, 1993), 31–34.

49. Whitman, *Poetry*, 564.

50. Whitman, 564.

51. Whitman, 515.

52. Whitman, 563.

53. Whitman, 703.

54. Whitman, 703.

55. Horace Traubel, *With Walt Whitman in Camden* 2 (1907; rpt. New York: Rowman and Littlefield, 1961), 246. For a discussion of this anecdote, see Katsaros, *New York–Paris*, 24–25.

56. As noted in Chapter 3, on the development of the omnibus in Paris under Haussmann, see David Harvey, *Paris: Capital of Modernity* (Routledge, 2005). On the omnibus as an "engine of modernity" in the literary imagination and visual culture of nineteenth-century Paris, see Masha Belenky, *Engine of Modernity: The Omnibus and Urban Culture in Nineteenth-Century Paris* (Manchester: Manchester University Press, 2019). Additionally, see Spann, *New Metropolis*, 285–95, for insights into the competing economic interests at play in the development of mass transit systems to alleviate congestion and traffic jams in lower Manhattan in the nineteenth century.

57. Again, see Spann, as noted above, for discussion of the complex economic forces at play in shaping the paths of the omnibuses through New York.

58. For the concept of a "corps sonore," see Nancy, *Listening*: and Janus, "Listening: Jean-Luc Nancy," 194.

59. Whitman, *Poetry*, 703.

60. Ross Chambers, "Baudelaire's Street Poetry," *Nineteenth-Century French Studies* (Summer, 1985): 253.

61. Whitman, *Poetry*, 234. Several scholars have pondered the relation between the call and the voice in this line. For the echo interpretation, see Sharpe, *Unreal Cities*, 71. Cf. also Katsaros, *New York–Paris*, 13–33; and Trachtenberg, "Whitman's Lesson of the City," for readings of this line. Trachtenberg views it as "self-interpolation" (170).

62. Larzer Ziff interprets Whitman's frequent merging with the urban crowd as a return to the self (Ziff, "Whitman and the Crowd," *Critical Inquiry* 10, no. 4 (June 1984): 589).

63. Whitman, *Poetry*, 279.

64. Whitman, 236.

65. See Katsaros, *New York–Paris*, who makes a similar argument in general about Whitman's relation to the urban crowd.

66. Ziff, "Whitman and the Crowd," 586.

67. Whitman, *Poetry*, 223. See Mary Esteve, *The Aesthetics and Politics of the Crowd in American Literature* (New York: Cambridge University Press, 2003). Esteve argues that simultaneity is a crux of radical empiricism, and something that is central to the representations of urban modernity in nineteenth-century American literature (8).

68. Whitman, *Poetry*, 308.

69. See Katsaros, *New York–Paris*, 9. Ziff has argued: "When Whitman merges into the crowd, he does so as a gesture of joy and strength, a return to himself" (Ziff, "Whitman and the Crowd," 589).

70. Ziff, 586.

71. Edgar Allan Poe, *Poetry and Tales* ed. Patrick F. Quinn (New York: Library of America, 1984), 391–92.

72. Whitman, *Poetry*, 308.

73. Whitman, 308.

74. Whitman, 288.

75. For notion of a "found voice," see Michael Bull and Les Back, eds., *Auditory Culture Reader* (Oxford and New York: Berg, 2004), 348. For audiovisual relations and the flâneur, see Steven Connor, "The Modern Auditory 'I,'" in *Rewriting the Self: Histories from the Renaissance to the Present*, ed. Roy Porter (London: Routledge, 1996), 210. Consider also the concept of a "collage" of "found sounds" in the hip hop tradition of the late 1980s and early 1990s, as Brian Foo has emphasized in his "Citizen DJ" project for the United States Library of Congress.

76. Whitman, *Poetry*, 310.

77. Whitman, 312.

78. See also Whitman's "A Broadway Pageant" for this line: "I chant aloud over the pageant."

79. Whitman, *Poetry*, 311.
80. Whitman, 309.
81. See Erkkila, "Whitman and the Homosexual Republic." Erkkila examines how in Whitman's "Calamus" poem "the dream of democracy will give rise to a city—and ultimately an American republic—in which men loving men can live and love and touch openly" (159).
82. See Katsaros, *New York–Paris*: "Whitman always considered his poetry as a form of performance instead of literature. He repeatedly claimed, in print and in person, that *Leaves of Grass* was no book, but a living voice and a living body" (36). See also Hoffman, "Walt Whitman 'Live,'" for this characterization of Whitman's ambivalence about the printed word: "For Whitman, there was to be no divide between the book of poems and his own body and its voice" (191).
83. Charles Baudelaire, "Edgar Poe, sa vie et ses oeuvres," in *Oeuvres Complètes, II*, Texte établi, présenté et annoté par Claude Pichois, Bibliothèque de la Pléiade (Paris: Gallimard, 1975–1976), 297.
84. See Wolfgang Schivelbusch, *Disenchanted Night: The Industrialization of Light in the Nineteenth Century*, trans. Angela Davies (Berkeley: University of California Press, 1988). Cf. also Charles Cros, "Plainte": "Vrai sauvage égaré dans la ville de pierre,/A la clarté du gaz je végète et je meurs."
85. See Katsaros, *New York–Paris*, Introduction, and 61–62, in which she argues that Baudelaire despaired of the way Haussmann effectively "Americanized" Paris by disrupting the city's private sphere. See also Huysmans, *À Vau-l'eau*, in which the Paris of that novella is compared to "un Chicago sinistre."
86. See also Baudelaire's "Les yeux des pauvres" and the passage about the gaslight in the café that is "aveuglant." Compare this phrase also with Rudolph Koenig's flame manometer machine, discussed at the end of Chapter 3, for analyzing the sounds of human speech with gaslight.
87. On the contrast between Whitman's and Baudelaire's sentiments on democracy, see Katsaros, *New York–Paris*, 4–5. She argues that Baudelaire's aristocratic conception of beauty contrasts with Whitman's democratic conception of beauty. The "orgue de barbarie" was a motif often employed, in diverse ways, by symbolist poets such as Mallarmé and Laforgue. Laforgue translated several of Whitman's poems into French and was planning a translation of *Leaves of Grass* into French at the time of his death. In the context of Victorian England, see Picker, *Victorian Soundscapes*, chap. 2, for a discussion of hostility toward the barrel organ in London.
88. Baudelaire initiated the great French obsession with translating Poe. Whitman declares, however, in the line before he sounds his "barbaric yawp," that he is "untranslatable." Laforgue, as noted above, would be the first to translate Whitman into French.
89. Baudelaire, *Oeuvres Complètes, I and II*, Texte établi, présenté et annoté par Claude Pichois, Bibliothèque de la Pléiade (Paris: Gallimard, 1975–1976), 326.

90. Baudelaire, *OC II*, 325. On the microphone in the nineteenth century, see Picker, *Victorian Soundscapes*, 3–4. Baudelaire's argument here furthermore helps to expand scholarly consideration of the relationship between deafness and sound recording technology in the nineteenth century (see my discussion in Chapter 1 on Charles Cros, Edison, Bell, and deafness).

91. "Song of Myself," section fifty-two (Whitman, *Poetry*, 247).

92. Baudelaire, *OC II*, 697.

93. My thinking here and my allusions to the sensorium and micro-perceptions draw, in part, from Jacques Rancière's *Le Partage du sensible: esthétique et politique* (Paris: La Fabrique-éditions, 2000).

5. Nina's Song:
Music, Sound, and Performance in the Salon of Nina de Villard

1. For terminology of "salonnière" and "maitresse de maison," see Marie Boisvert, *La Dame aux éventails: Nina de Villard, musicienne, poète, muse, animatrice du salon*, PhD diss. University of Toronto, 2013, 45–46.

2. Boisvert, *La Dame aux éventails*, 143, 12.

3. Paul Alexis, *Madame Meuriot: Mœurs Parisiennes* (Paris: Bibliothèque Charpentier, 1890), 296; Maurice Dreyfous, *Ce que je tiens à dire: un demi-siècle de choses vue et entendues, 1862–1872* (Paris: Librairie Paul Ollendorff, 1912), 36.

4. For Whitman and the bohemians, See Joanna Levin and Edward Whitley, eds. *Whitman among the Bohemians* (Iowa City: University of Iowa Press, 2014); and Laure Katsaros, *New York–Paris: Whitman, Baudelaire, and the Hybrid City* (Ann Arbor: University of Michigan Press), 2012, 16. For the Poe citation, see Anthony Glinoer, *La Bohème: Une figure de l'imaginaire social* (Montréal: Les Presses de l'Université de Montréal, 2018), citing Barbey d'Aurevilly, 242.

5. Ernest Raynaud, *La Bohème sous le second empire: Charles Cros et Nina* (Paris: L'Artisan du livre, 1930), 72. Translations from French to English in this chapter are mine unless otherwise indicated.

6. Boisvert, *La Dame aux éventails*, 270. Jean-Jacques Lefrère and Michael Pakenham, *Cabaner, poète au piano* (Paris: L'Échoppe, 1994), 13, 62.

7. On the idea of commemorating listening and assigning a certain signature to an experience of listening, see Peter Szendy, *Listen: A History of Our Ears*, trans. Charlotte Mandell (New York: Fordham University Press, 2008).

8. Jean-Luc Nancy, *Listening*, trans. Charlotte Mandell (New York: Fordham University Press, 2007), 4.

9. Dreyfous, *Ce que je tiens à dire*, 38.

10. Emile Goudeau, *Dix ans de bohême* (Paris: A la Librairie Illustré, 1888), 117.

11. I will have more to say about Audouard later in the chapter. For recent scholarship about her, see Rachel Nuñez, *Between France and the World: The Gender Politics of Cosmopolitanism*, PhD dissertation, Stanford University, 2006.

12. *Revue du monde nouveau: Littéraire, Artistique, Scientifique*, vol. 1, no. 2, April 1, 1874, 152–53. The text is anonymous, but scholars believe Cros is likely its author.

13. Raynaud, *La Bohème sous le second empire*, 76.

14. Jean-Luc Nancy, *Les Muses* (Paris: Éditions Galilée, 2001), 11: "Il y a les Muses, et non la Muse. Leur nombre a pu varier, ainsi que leurs attributs, toujours les Muses auront été plusieurs. C'est cette origine multiple qui doit nous intéresser."

15. Paul Verlaine, *Œuvres en prose complètes*, ed. Jacques Borel (Pléiade. Paris: Gallimard, 1972), 519.

16. Raynaud, *La Bohème sous le second empire*, 72. See also Glinoer, *La Bohème*, 164, for a note about the double meaning of "bruit" in a context like this, meaning both noise and reputation.

17. Though Villard's story, as Michael Pakenham notes, draws inspiration from Cros's poem, the context of the relation is more complex than inspiration alone (see Michael Pakenham et al., *La Dame aux éventails: Nina de Callias, modèle de Manet*, exh. cat. [Paris: Musée d'Orsay, 2000, 62]). The tale concludes with Cros's poem, altered and, in places, abbreviated. I believe that the version of the poem published with Villard's story is most likely Villard's variation on Cros's poem. No scholar, to my knowledge, has commented on this version of one of Cros's most celebrated poems. The Pléiade editors of Cros's collected works do not note it. As a poem and as a song that was performed, "L'Archet" became one of the most enduring and recognizable audible presences in Villard's salon. Cros dedicated his poem to Richard Wagner, and Claude Debussy later set the words of Cros's poem to music. Though Cros has always been credited as the author of the poem, this story offers a means of discovering Villard's role in shaping the mystique and sonic imagination about the poem and its musical accompaniments that would become touchstones for a generation of artists in her salon.

18. The story was published *en feuilleton* in the periodical *La Réforme politique et sociale* November 25–27, 1869, not in *La Chronique universelle*, as noted in Pakenham, *La Dame aux éventails*, 62. My thanks to Hélène Virenque and Eric Walbecq at the Bibliothèque Nationale de France, and to Jean-Didier Wagneur for helping me find this publication.

19. On the effacement of Villard's true social reality under layers of representation by, for the most part, men, see Sandrine Harismendy-Lony, *De Nina de Villard au Cercle Zutique: violence et representation*, PhD diss., University of California, Santa Barbara, 1995. Gérard da Silva has more recently reinterpreted Manet's painting of Villard as an homage to her communard sympathies. See Gérard da Silva, "Manet, Nina ou la Commune au coeur de l'Art," in *Intempestives: La Commune, Enjeu Vivant* (Paris: L'Harmattan, 2010), 9–37.

20. Because these stories were published under the name Nina de Callias, it is reasonable to assume those in her social circle could have read the tales and recognized their author or other historical figures in particular characters. Scholars have read the acidic treatment of Villard and her circle in novels such as Mendès's *Maison de la vieille* as a form of public settling of scores in literary form. Hector

Callias's request that Manet not exhibit his painting of Villard, the painting we know as *La Dame aux éventails*, with his name attached to it involves this kind of arena of cryptonymic hostilities fought on the printed page and publicly exhibited canvas.

21. Pakenham, *La Dame aux éventails*, 62.

22. See Louis Forestier, *Charles Cros: L'Homme et l'Oeuvre* (Paris: Lettres Modernes Minard, 1969).

23. Arsène Houssaye, who, in his capacity as director of the literary section of *La Presse*, published many of Baudelaire's prose poems, frequented Villard's salon and served as a witness at Villard's marriage to Hector de Callias in 1863. Houssaye himself published a poem in prose, "La Chanson du vitrier," that he dedicated to E. T. A. Hoffmann. Villard shared Baudelaire's admiration for Liszt and his music. Baudelaire's "Le Thyrse" was first published in the *Revue nationale et étrangère* on December 10, 1863. A letter from Baudelaire to Liszt from 1861 further testifies to Baudelaire's veneration of the Hungarian composer (Pléiade edition of Baudelaire's correspondence, vol. 2, 162).

24. Incidentally, Villard's own piano would have been the kind of instrument Baudelaire imagined in his poem singing Liszt's praises, as both Villard and Cros were, in their day, recognized for certain talents of improvisation at the piano. Cros in particular, as reported by Verlaine, improvised when it came to recitations of the poem "L'Archet."

25. Forestier, *Charles Cros*, 208.

26. On realism and the bohemian imagination, specifically the writing of "la vie de bohème," see Glinoer, *La Bohème*, 240. On the science of acoustics in the nineteenth century, particularly to changes in acoustic perception and the modern listener in the context of Hermann von Helmholtz's work on acoustics, see Benjamin Steege, *Helmholtz and the Modern Listener* (Cambridge: Cambridge University Press, 2012).

27. This story was published *en feuilleton* in *La Réforme politique et sociale*, November 30–December 3, 1869. For the importance of sculpture in Villard's life and circle, see "Henry Cros: Le Moyen Âge et la couleur" in Pakenham, *La Dame aux éventails*, 111.

28. Gretchen Schultz, *The Gendered Lyric: Subjectivity and Difference in Nineteenth-Century French Poetry* (West Lafayette, Ind.: Purdue University Press, 1999), 140–47, 154–62. For the quotation, see Schultz, 140.

29. As with "L'Archet," a biographical reading of this tale might interpret Villard as divided between two female characters, Eve and Mina, who are both friends and rivals. Pierre could be read as a cryptonym for Hector de Callias, Villard's husband from whom she had obtained a legal separation (divorce was not legal at that time in France.)

30. See Glinoer, *La Bohème*, 58–59, on the social restrictions women were subject to when they aspired to become artists and mix with the bohemian world of arts and letters dominated by men hostile to womens' artistic careers.

31. *La Chronique universelle*, "Courrier de Bade," August 10, 1869.

32. On Audouard, see Nuñez, *Between France and the World*, 108–95. See also Pakenham, *La Dame aux éventails*, 61.

33. *La Chronique universelle*, "Courrier de Bade," August 10, 1869.

34. On censorship of Audouard's political journalism, see Nuñez, *Between France and the World*.

35. Pakenham, *La Dame aux éventails*, 61.

36. Pakenham, 76; Pakenham, Introduction in Catulle Mendès, *La Maison de la vieille: roman contemporain* (Seyssel: Éditions Champ Vallon, 2000), 94.

37. See Jean-Didier Wagneur's essay in Pakenham, *La Dame aux éventails*, 79–80.

38. In-text page number references are to Catulle Mendès, *La Maison de la vieille: roman contemporain* (Seyssel: Éditions Champ Vallon, 2000).

39. Mendès, *La Maison de la vieille*, 469. Also, cf. another proto-Proustian moment in Paul Alexis's novel *Madame Meuriot* (293) involving Villard.

40. See Wagneur, "La légende de Nina," in Pakenham, *La Dame aux éventails*, 80, who reports that several writers, among which Edmond de Goncourt, saw Villard's salon as a place for the prostitution of art. See also the passage in "L'Archet," when Tristan discovers Eve's liaison with the journalist, a liaison he sees as a certain prostitution of art.

41. On Reynaud's praxinoscope projections, see Jonathan Crary, *Suspensions of Perception: Attention, Spectacle, and Modern Culture* (Cambridge, Mass.: MIT Press, 1999), 259–67.

42. See also Nathalie Boulouch, *Le ciel est bleu: Une histoire de la photographie couleur* (Paris: Éditions Textuel, 2011), 31, who finds a reflection of Cros's color photographic theories and practices in the "miraculeusement photochromée" projected images of the android of Villiers's *L'Ève future* (1886). Villiers frequented Villard's salon and was a close friend of Cros.

43. See Crary, *Techniques of the Observer: On Vision and Modernity in the Nineteenth Century* (Cambridge, Mass.: MIT Press, 1990), 126.

44. Vanessa Schwartz, *Spectacular Realities: Early Mass Culture in* Fin-de-Siècle *Paris* (Berkeley: University of California Press, 1998), 200n1: Miriam Hanson and Susan Barrows claim that cinema can be conceived as the "muse of the twentieth century."

45. See Wagneur's essay in Pakenham, *La Dame aux éventails*, 80.

46. Lefrère and Pakenham, *Cabaner*, 18, 48.

47. Pakenham, *La Dame aux éventails*, 129.

48. Alexis, *Madame Meuriot*, 313, for this passage of dialogue about the possibility of sound recording. Several aspects of Thékel's character call Manet to mind.

49. Dreyfous, *Ce que je tiens à dire*, 39.

50. Glinoer, *La Bohème*, 164.

51. Mathilde Mauté describes Villard as among other things "très bonne musicienne," and of the soirées/réunions, Mauté reports: "ces réunions n'étaient ni mondaines ni protocolaires, mais essentiellement artistiques et fort intéressantes." See Mauté (Ex-Madame Paul Verlaine), *Mémoires de ma vie* (Paris: Champ Vallon

Éditions, 2014), 30. On the question of bohemian sociability, see Glinoer, *La Bohème*, 190.

52. Dreyfous, *Ce que je tiens à dire*, 61.

53. Forestier, *Charles Cros*, 154–55, 158. Charles's brother Antoine's grandson related that the duchess, upon hearing of Charles's designs for the paleophone, protested that only God could create speech and that it was blasphemy for Charles to attempt it with science and a machine (158).

54. Charles Cros, *Inédits et Documents*, Recueillis et présentés par Pierre E. Richard, Éditions Atelier du Gué, Éditions Jacques Brémond, 1992, 197–98, where Cros, referencing the photographic procedures of Niépce and Daguerre and their public domain status rendered by the French state, protests that phonographic technology should follow the same principle: "Principe et appareil sont donc dans le domaine public. Avis aux constructeurs de tous pays." Cf. also Raynaud, *La Bohème sous le second empire*, 9.

55. See Brett Brehm, "Media Environments: Manet, Cros, and the Colours of Spring," *History of Photography* 44, no. 1 (2020): 50–64."

56. Lefrère and Pakenham, *Cabaner*, 18.

57. Lefrère and Pakenham, esp. 43–49. As one example of musical kinship between Cabaner and Satie, baritone Francis Dudziak and pianist Pascal Devoyon include works by Cabaner in their album titled *Erik Satie et l'école d'arcueil* (2002).

58. Alexis, *Madame Meuriot*, 311. Simon Shaw-Miller makes an important distinction about Cocteau and Satie, namely the distinction between noises like music and noises as music. Concerning Satie's use of "found sounds, such as the typewriter, the revolver, and sirens" in *Parade*, Shaw-Miller argues that Satie is not, as Cocteau would have it, imitating these sounds. Rather, these sounds *are musical sound*. See Simon Shaw-Miller, "'The Only Musician with Eyes': Satie and Visual Art," in *Erik Satie: Music, Art, and Literature*, ed. Caroline Potter (London: Routledge, 2013).

59. Boisvert, *La Dame aux éventails*, 232.

60. See, among others, Schwartz, *Spectacular Realities*.

61. Alexandra Kieffer, *Debussy's Critics: Sound, Affect, and the Experience of Modernism* (New York: Oxford University Press, 2019). On the relationship between Debussy's music and sonic realities, see especially 103–6. The question of "sonic realism" likewise animated the depiction of bell peals in Ravel's piano music around the same time. See Kieffer, "Bells and the Problem of Realism in Ravel's Early Piano Music," *Journal of Musicology* 34, no. 3 (Summer 2017): 432–72." For a consideration of Debussy and the soundscape of Paris with attention to everyday street sounds and Parisian visual culture, see Laura Kalba, "Hearing Voices: A Study of the Soundscape and Visual Culture of Debussy's Paris," in *Debussy's Paris: Art, Music, and Sounds of the City* (Northampton, Mass.: Smith College Museum of Art, 2012), 14–31.

62. Kieffer, *Debussy's Critics*, 20.

63. Kieffer, 85. On the invocation of noise in the critical reception of Debussy's *Pélleas*, see especially 119–24.

64. See Marc Battier, "What the GRM Brought to Music: From *Musique Concrète* to Acousmatic Music," in *Organised Sound* 12, no. 3 (2007): 189–202.

65. Lefrère and Pakenham, *Cabaner*, 30–33.

66. Lefrère and Pakenham, 32: Alphonse Allais says: "[. . .] with a voice that those who have heard it will never forget."

67. Lefrère and Pakenham, 30–31.

68. Cabaner's interest in Bach is evidenced in a letter from Cabaner to the composer Emmanuel Chabrier (illustration just before page 33 in Lefrère and Pakenham, *Cabaner*). For Baudelaire's "Beauté" and Bach reference, see Lefrère and Pakenham, 108. The transcript of the letter, dating from 1880, is in Lefrère and Pakenham, 111–12.

69. Lefrère and Pakenham, *Cabaner*, 44.

70. See the recently created "Baudelaire song project" by Helen Abbott, among others, at baudelairesong.org. Of all the cataloged musical settings of Baudelaire's poetry, this is the only known one, to my knowledge, involving Bach.

71. Lefrère and Pakenham, 33.

72. Cabaner's musical notation for this poem does survive and is available on Gallica. Since his music was published several times and often performed, it is conceivable Debussy knew of and had heard Cabaner's rendition.

73. On Cabaner's synesthesia and a portrait of the composer by Manet, see Therese Dolan, "Manet's Synesthetic Portrait: Composing Cabaner," in *Perspectives on Manet*, ed. Dolan (Farnham: Ashgate, 2012).

74. Lefrère and Pakenham, *Cabaner*, 96n120.

75. Lefrère and Pakenham, 37.

76. Lefrère and Pakenham, 37.

77. Lefrère and Pakenham, 51.

78. About Villard's time studying with Henri Herz, see, among others, da Silva, "Manet, Nina," 26. See also Julia Kursell, "Visualizing Piano Playing, 1890–1930," in *Grey Room* 43 (Spring 2011): 66–87.

79. *La Chronique universelle*, "Courrier de Bade," August 10, 1869. See also Cros's short-lived *Revue du monde nouveau*, vol. 1, no. 1, April 1, 1874, 69–70, which has an unattributed brief review of a performance by Jaëll (authored by Villard?), coupled with another review comparing Manet and Liszt, and a score of Cabaner's music and poetry, "Souffles de l'air" incidentally, all in the same issue.

80. See Boulouch, 28–29; and Emmanuelle Héran's essay in Pakenham, *La Dame aux éventails*, 114.

81. See Pakenham, *La Dame aux éventails*, 115. If Laforgue ever visited Villard's salon (to my knowledge there is no direct evidence), it is possible Whitman's free verse may have been heard and appreciated there, as Laforgue translated and drew inspiration from the American poet. See also Schwartz, *Spectacular Realities*, esp. chs. 3 and 5, the section "cinema endures, wax does not," in which she concludes: "the institutional connection between the wax museum and film [. . .] provides a context in which we can locate cinema's emergence in and from the broader

fin-de-siècle visual culture [. . .] without that context, cinema might have been simply another gadget and not the emblem of modern life that it became" (199).

82. Pakenham, *La Dame aux éventails*, 115–16.

83. Goudeau, *Dix ans de bohême*, 116–17, citing Marie de Grandfort about the situation in which "Impromptu" was written.

84. Gretchen Schultz, ed., *An Anthology of Nineteenth-Century Women's Poetry from France* (New York: Modern Language Association of America, 2008), 206.

85. See, among others, Schultz, *Gendered Lyric*, on Villard's as the most bohemian of salons (141).

86. *Revue du monde nouveau: Littéraire, Artistique, Scientifique*, vol. 1, no. 2, April 1, 1874, 152–53.

87. Mauté, *Mémoires de ma vie*, 33.

88. Raynaud, *La Bohème sous le second empire*, 74. See also Mauté recording the account she had from her brother about his first visit to Villard's salon (*Mémoires de ma vie*, 32–33).

Conclusion: Pyrophonica and the Rhythms of Inspiration

1. The quotation is from Satie's "Hidden Corners of My Life," which was grouped together with "What I Am" in the collection *Memoirs of an Amnesiac (fragments)*.

2. See Erik Satie, *A Mammal's Notebook: The Writings of Erik Satie*, ed. Ornella Volta (London: Atlas Press, 2014), 108; Satie, *Mémoires d'un amnésique*, présentés et annotés par Raoul Coquereau, Éditions Ombres, 2010, 15.

3. On soundscapes as warfare and modernist aesthetics of noise, specifically in the German context, see Tyler Whitney, *Eardrums: Literary Modernism as Sonic Warfare* (Evanston, Ill.: Northwestern University Press, 2019).

4. Incidentally, scientist and mathematician Jules Antoine Lissajous, whom we met in Chapter 3, in 1857 employed a device he called a "phonoptomètre" to examine sound vibrations by means of an arrangement between a microscope and a tuning fork. Satie may have been far more informed about the progress and history of scientific research in acoustics than the humor of "What I Am" might lead us to believe.

5. Daniel Albright, *Untwisting the Serpent: Modernism in Music, Literature, and Other Arts* (Chicago: University of Chicago Press, 1999), 191

6. Albright, *Untwisting the Serpent*, 192–93.

7. See Joseph Auner, "Weighing, Measuring, Embalming Tonality: How We Became Phonometrographers," in *Tonality 1900–1950: Concept and Practice*, ed. Felix Wörner, Ullrich Scheideler, and Philp Ripprecht (Stuttgart: Franz Steiner Verlag, 2012), for a discussion of the instruments Satie invokes in "What I Am" and of the broader implications of Satie's phonometrography for twentieth-century music and tonality.

8. See Simon Shaw-Miller, "'The Only Musician with Eyes': Satie and Visual Art," in *Erik Satie: Music, Art, and Literature*, ed. by Caroline Potter (London:

Routledge, 2013). Shaw-Miller argues that Satie's noises in *Parade* (e.g., the typewriter, revolver, and sirens) are not conceived as mimetic but rather musical in their own right, in a sense as protodadaist "found sound." See also Marc Battier, "What the GRM Brought to Music: From *Musique concrète* to Acousmatic Music," in *Organised Sound* 12, no. 3 (2007): 189–202, on the GRM; and Auner, who also draws connections between Satie's phonometrography, Russolo, and Schaeffer's *Musique concrète*.

9. Luigi Russolo, *L'art des bruits: manifeste futuriste 1913* (Paris: Éditions Allia, 2013), 25.

10. For a discussion of auditory culture in modernist and twentieth-century literature, see Kata Gellen, Tyler Whitney, Angela Frattarola, and Philipp Schweighauser, among others.

11. Russolo, *L'art des bruits*, 17.

12. Benjamin quotes this passage from Simmel in the *Arcades Project*. See Walter Benjamin, *The Arcades Project*, trans. Howard Eiland and Kevin Mclaughlin (Cambridge, Mass.: Harvard University Press, 1999), 433.

13. On the "acoustical unconscious," see Robert Ryder, *The Acoustical Unconscious: from Walter Benjamin to Alexander Kluge* (Berlin: De Gruyter, 2022); and Veit Erlmann, *Reason and Resonance: A History of Modern Aurality* (New York: Zone Books, 2010).

14. See, among other texts, "Voix Mortes: Musiques Maoris"; and "Dans un monde sonore" in Victor Segalen, *Segalen et Debussy* (Monaco: Éditions du Rocher, 1961). See also Erika Brady, *A Spiral Way: How the Phonograph Changed Ethnography* (Jackson: University Press of Mississippi, 1999); and Brian Hochman, *Savage Preservation: The Ethnographic Origins of Modern Media Technology* (Minneapolis: University of Minnesota Press, 2014).

15. Ivan Kreilkamp, *Voice and the Victorian Storyteller* (Cambridge: Cambridge University Press, 2005), 190. Jules Verne's *Le Château des Carpathes* (1892) offers a case in point in the French context.

16. Haun Saussy, "Interplanetary Literature," *Comparative Literature* 63, no. 4 (Fall 2011): 444. And this point would appear to draw, in part, from Benjamin's theses on history, particularly the notion that history gets written by the winners (especially as articulated in theses VI and VII).

17. Media historian Lisa Gitelman, for instance, identifies 1877–1914 as a particularly formative and critical moment in the development of modern mass media, a historical period shaped by the growth and expansion of phonographic technologies. Whereas Gitelman has examined the question of "representing technology in the Edison era," here the focus has largely been on the literary prehistory of acoustic technologies and discourses about modernized sound and listening in the era before Edison, with an emphasis on the transatlantic perspective.

18. Here I draw from Walter Benjamin's reading of Freud in "On Some Motifs in Baudelaire," in *Illuminations*, ed. Hannah Arendt (New York: Shocken, 1968).

19. See Albright, *Untwisting the Serpent*, 191.

20. See Satie, *A Mammal's Notebook*, 213.

21. James Lastra, *Sound Technology and the American Cinema: Perception, Representation, Modernity* (New York: Columbia University Press, 2000), 16.

22. Deleuze was one to emphasize the mechanizing tendencies of the nineteenth-century city and their effect on urban dwellers, "crushed" like Bartleby in Melville's eponymous tale. See "Bartleby, ou la formule," in Gilles Deleuze, *Critique et clinique* (Paris: Minuit, 1999).

23. Emily Thompson, "Machines, Music, and the Quest for Fidelity: Marketing the Edison Phonograph in America, 1877–1925," *The Musical Quarterly* 79, no.1 (Spring 1995): 135: "As a storage device, the phonograph was initially compared to the camera."

24. See Lisa Gitelman, *Scripts, Grooves, and Writing Machines: Representing Technology in the Edison Era* (Stanford, Calif.: Stanford University Press, 1999), 224, for a discussion of Bolter, Grusin, and McLuhan on "remediation" as a "representation of one medium in another." See Christopher Bush, *Ideographic Modernism: China, Writing, Media* (Oxford; New York: Oxford University Press, 2010), 25, for the term "premediative," Bush's term that responds to Gitelman's arguments. Bush explains: "'Premediation' would describe the estrangement of older and existing cultural forms, their figuration or reconceptualization in terms of new media, as in 'the Victorian Internet.'" See also Haun Saussy, Preface in *The Ethnography of Rhythm: Orality and Its Technologies* (New York: Fordham University Press, 2016), XIII: "Conditions of . . . appearance as a figure of thought" and the claim that "a medium manifests itself always and only in relation to other media."

25. Ross Chambers, *An Atmospherics of the City: Baudelaire and the Poetics of Noise* (New York: Fordham University Press, 2015), 133.

26. Gitelman, *Always Already New: Media, History, and the Data of Culture* (Cambridge, Mass., MIT Press, 2006), chap. 1, esp. 39–40.

27. Gitelman, 38. Gitelman notes that she is surprised this analogy between souvenir photograph and souvenir tinfoil scrap was *not* more frequently articulated in early accounts of phonograph demonstrations, when audiences were collecting these tinfoil souvenirs.

28. Kata Gellen, *Kafka and Noise: The Discovery of Cinematic Sound in Literary Modernism* (Evanston, Ill.: Northwestern University Press, 2019).

29. Julie Napolin, *The Fact of Resonance: Modernist Acoustics and Narrative Form* (New York: Fordham University Press, 2020).

30. On this point, I would emphasize additionally that transatlantic dialogue in the nineteenth century is critical for the field of sound studies to consider; Edward Cutler, in *Recovering the New: Transatlantic Roots of Modernism* (Hanover: University Press of New England, 2003), similarly emphasizes the importance of the transatlantic in the growth of the mass popular press in the nineteenth century.

Bibliography

Abbate, Carolyn. "Debussy's Phantom Sounds." *Cambridge Opera Journal* 10, no. 1 (March 1998): 67–96.

Adorno, Theodor. "The Form of the Phonograph Record." Translated by Thomas Levin. *October* 55 (Winter 1990): 56–61.

Albright, Daniel. *Untwisting the Serpent: Modernism in Music, Literature, and Other Arts.* Chicago: University of Chicago Press, 1999.

Alexis, Paul. *Madame Meuriot: Mœurs Parisiennes.* Paris: Bibliothèque Charpentier, 1890.

Alis, Harry. *Hara-Kiri.* Paris: Paul Ollendorff, Éditeur, 1882.

Allais, Alphonse. "La Mort de Charles Cros." *Le Chat Noir,* August 18, 1888.

Andrews, Malcolm. "Walt Whitman and the American City." In *The American City: Literary and Cultural Perspectives,* edited by Graham Clarke, 179–97. New York: St. Martin's Press, 1988.

Anzieu, Didier. *The Skin Ego.* Translated by Chris Turner, esp. "The Sound Envelope," 157–74. New Haven: Yale University Press, 1989.

Armstrong, Tim. "Player Piano: Poetry and Sonic Modernity." *Modernism/Modernity* 14 (Jan. 2007): 1–19.

Attali, Jacques. *Noise: The Political Economy of Music.* Translated by Brian Massumi, Foreword by Fredric Jameson. Minneapolis: University of Minnesota Press, 1985.

Attridge, John. "'La Vaste rumeur d'autrefois': Noise, Memory, and Mediation in À la recherche du temps perdu." *Modernism/Modernity* 4, no. 3 (2019).

Augoyard, Jean-François, and Henry Torgue, eds. *Sonic Experience: A Guide to Everyday Sounds.* Montreal: McGill-Queen's University Press, 2006.

Auner, Joseph. "Weighing, Measuring, Embalming Tonality: How We Became Phonometrographers." In *Tonality 1900–1950: Concept and Practice,* edited by

Felix Wörner, Ullrich Scheideler, and Philp Ripprecht, 25–46. Stuttgart: Franz Steiner Verlag, 2012.
Bailey, Peter. "Breaking the Sound Barrier." In *Hearing History: A Reader*, edited by Mark Smith. Athens: University of Georgia Press, 2004.
Balaÿ, Olivier. *L'Espace Sonore de la Ville au XIXe siècle*. Bernin: A la Croisée, 2003.
Barrett, Lindon. *Blackness and Value: Seeing Double*. 185–213. New York: Cambridge University Press, 1999.
Barthes, Roland. "The Grain of the Voice." In *Image, Music, Text*. 179–90. London: Fontana Press, 1977.
———. "Textual Analysis of a Tale by Poe." In *On Signs*, edited by Marshall Blonsky, 84–97. Baltimore: Johns Hopkins University Press, 1985.
Battier, Marc. "What the GRM Brought to Music: From *Musique Concrète* to Acousmatic Music." *Organised Sound* 12, no. 3 (2007): 189–202.
Baudelaire, Charles. *Correspondance, I and II*. Texte établi, présenté et annoté par Claude Pichois avec la collaboration de Jean Ziegler, Bibliothèque de la Pléiade. Paris: Gallimard, 1973.
———. *Les Fleurs du mal*, présentation par Jacques Dupont (Paris: Flammarion, 2006).
———. *Oeuvres Complètes, I and II*. Texte établi, présenté et annoté par Claude Pichois, Bibliothèque de la Pléiade. Paris: Gallimard, 1975–1976.
Baumgartner, Thomas, ed. *Le Goût de la Radio et Autres Sons*. Paris: Mercure de France, 2013.
Baxandall, Michael. *Painting and Experience in Fifteenth-Century Italy*. Oxford: Oxford University Press, 1972.
Belenky, Masha. *Engine of Modernity: The Omnibus and Urban Culture in Nineteenth-Century Paris*. Manchester: Manchester University Press, 2019.
Bell, Alexander Graham. "Application of the Photophone to the Study of the Noises Taking Place on the Surface of the Sun." *Science* 1, no. 25 (Dec. 18, 1880): 304.
———. "An Interview with Alexander Graham Bell." *Records of the Columbia Historical Society, Washington, D.C.*, vol. 48–49, 1946–1947, 181–89.
———. "Lecture Photophone," *Science* 1, no. 25 (Dec. 18, 1880): 304.
———. Letter to Alexander Melville Bell, February 26, 1880 (MSS51268). US Library of Congress, Digital Collections.
———. "The Photophone." *Science* 1, no. 11 (Sept. 11, 1880): 130–34.
Bell, David. "Balzac and the Modern City: Mapping Paris in *Old Goriot*." In *Approaches to Teaching Balzac's Old Goriot*, edited by Michal Peled Ginsburg. New York: Modern Language Association of America, 2000.
Benjamin, Walter. *The Arcades Project*. Translated by Howard Eiland and Kevin Mclaughlin. Cambridge, Mass.: Harvard University Press, 1999.
———. "A Short History of Photography." In *Selected Writings, Volume 2, Part 2: 1931–1934*, edited by Marcus Bullock and Michael W. Jennings. Cambridge: Mass.: The Belknap Press of Harvard University Press, 1996.

———. "On Some Motifs in Baudelaire." In *Illuminations*, edited by Hannah Arendt. New York: Shocken, 1968.

———. *The Writer of Modern Life: Essays on Charles Baudelaire*. Edited by Michael Jennings. Cambridge, Mass.: The Belknap Press of Harvard University Press, 2006.

Blaszkiewicz, Jacek. *City Myths: Music and Urbanism in Second Empire Paris*. PhD diss., University of Rochester, 2018.

Bobillier, Gérard. *L'homme inachevé*. Lagrasse: Verdier, 2012.

Boisvert, Marie. *La Dame aux éventails: Nina de Villard, musicienne, poète, muse, animatrice du salon*. PhD diss., University of Toronto, 2013.

Bonnet, François. *Les Mots et les Sons: un archipel sonore*. Paris: Éditions de l'éclat, 2012.

Boulouch, Nathalie. *Le Ciel est bleu: Une histoire de la photographie couleur*. Paris: Éditions Textuel, 2011.

Boutin, Aimée. "Aural Flânerie." *Dix-Neuf* 16, no. 2 (Jul. 2012): 149–61.

———. *City of Noise: Sound and Nineteenth-Century Paris*. Urbana: University of Illinois Press, 2015.

———. "Sound Memory: Paris Street Cries in Balzac's *Père Goriot*." *French Forum* 30 (Spring 2005): 67–78.

Brady, Erika. *A Spiral Way. How the Phonograph Changed Ethnography*. Jackson: University Press of Mississippi, 1999.

Brand, Dana. *The Spectator and the City in Nineteenth-Century American Literature*. New York: Cambridge University Press, 1991.

Brehm, Brett. "Media Environments: Manet, Cros, and the Colours of Spring." *History of Photography* 44, no. 1 (2020): 50–64.

Brenni, Paolo. "Le triomphe de l'acoustique experimentale: Marloye et Koenig." *La Revue* 12 (Sept. 1995).

Breton, André. *Anthologie de l'humour noir*. Paris: Jean-Jacques Pauvert, 1966.

Brunet, François. *The Birth of the Idea of Photography*. Translated by Shane B. Lillis. Cambridge, Mass.: MIT Press, 2019.

———. *Photography and Literature*. London: Reaktion, 2009.

———. "Poe à la croisée des chemins: réalisme et scepticisme." *Revue française d'études américaines* no. 71, sciences et savoir dans la littérature américaine au XIXe siècle (Jan. 1997): 44–50.

Burton, Richard. "Metamorphoses of the Ragpicker." In *Baudelaire and the Second Republic*, esp. 220–75. Oxford: Clarendon Press, 1991.

———. "The Protean Self: 'Les Sept Vieillards' and 'Les Petites Vieilles.'" In *Baudelaire in 1859: A Study in the Sources of Poetic Creativity*. 105–128. Cambridge: Cambridge University Press, 1988.

Bush, Christopher. *Ideographic Modernism: China, Writing, Media*. Oxford: Oxford University Press, 2010.

Butler, Shane. *The Ancient Phonograph*. New York: Zone Books, 2015.

Calas, Marie-France. "Enregistrement sonore et lieux de mémoire." In *De Fil en Aiguille: Charles Cros et les Autres*, exh. cat., Paris: Bibliothèque Nationale de France, December 15, 1988–April 1, 1989, 69–73.
Camlot, Jason. *Phonopoetics: The Making of Early Literary Recordings*. Stanford, Calif.: Stanford University Press, 2019.
Casati, Roberto, and Jérôme Dokic. *La Philosophie du Son*. Éditions Jacqueline Chambon, 1998.
Castel, Louis-Bertrand. "Clavecin pour les yeux, avec l'art de peindre les sons, et toutes sortes de pièces de musique." *Mercure de France*, Paris, Guillaume Cavelier, novembre 1725, 2552–77.
Certeux, Alphonse. *Les Cris de Londres*. Paris: Chamuel, 1893.
Chambers, Ross. *An Atmospherics of the City: Baudelaire and the Poetics of Noise*. New York: Fordham University Press, 2015.
———. "Baudelaire's Street Poetry." *Nineteenth-Century French Studies* (Summer 1985): 244–59.
———. "Seeing and Saying in Baudelaire's 'Les Aveugles.'" In *Pre-Text, Text, Context*, edited by Robert Mitchell. Columbus: Ohio State University Press, 1980.
Champfleury, Jules. "The Legend of the Daguerreotypist." In *Literature and Photography: Interactions 1840–1990: A Critical Anthology*, edited by Jane Rabb. Albuquerque: University of New Mexico Press, 1995.
Charbon, Paul. "Naissance du transport et de la conservation du son." In *De Fil en Aiguille: Charles Cros et les Autres*, exh. cat., December 15, 1988–April 1, 1989, 31–46.
Chesters, Graham. "A Political Reading of Baudelaire's 'L'Artiste Inconnu' ('Le Guignon')." *The Modern Language Review* 79, no. 1 (Jan., 1984): 64–76.
Chion, Michel. *Le Promeneur Écoutant: essais d'acoulogie*. Paris: Plume, 1993.
———. *La Voix au Cinéma*. Paris, 1972.
Christie, Ian. "Early Phonograph Culture and Moving Pictures." In *The Sounds of Early Cinema*. 3–13. Bloomington: Indiana University Press, 2001.
Clark, T. J. *The Painting of Modern Life: Paris in the Art of Manet and His Followers*. Princeton, N.J.: Princeton University Press, 1999.
Coeuroy, André, and G. Clarence. *Le phonographe*. Paris: Kra, 1929.
Compagnon, Antoine. *Baudelaire: l'irréductible*. Paris: Flammarion, 2014.
Connor, Steven. "The Modern Auditory 'I.'" In *Rewriting the Self: Histories from the Renaissance to the Present*, edited by Roy Porter, 203–23. London: Routledge, 1996.
Corbin, Alain. *Les Cloches de la Terre: Paysage Sonore et Culture Sensible dans les Campagnes au XIXe siècle*. Paris: A. Michel, 1994.
Cordereix, Pascal. "Les enregistrements du musée de la parole et du geste à l'exposition coloniale." Paris: Presses de Sciences Po, *Vingtième siècle: revue d'histoire* 92, no. 4 (2006): 47–59.
Crary, Jonathan. *Suspensions of Perception: Attention, Spectacle, and Modern Culture*. Cambridge, Mass.: MIT Press, 1999.
———. *Techniques of the Observer: On Vision and Modernity in the Nineteenth Century*. Cambridge, Mass.: MIT Press, 1990.

Cros, Charles. *Le Caillou mort d'amour: et autres contes.* Édition établie et annotée par Isabelle Péchoune. Toulouse: Éditions Ombres, 2006.

———. *Inédits et Documents.* Recueillis et présentés par Pierre E. Richard. Villelongue d'Aude: Éditions Atelier du Gué, Éditions Jacques Brémond, 1992.

———. *Oeuvres Complètes.* Bibliothèque de la Pleiade, édition établie par Louis Forestier et Pierre-Olivier Walzer. Paris: Gallimard, 1970.

Culler, Jonathan. "Poe and Baudelaire." In *Zeitschrift für französische Sprache und Literatur*, Bd. 100, 61–73. Sprachwissenschaft-Literaturwissenschaft-Semiotik, Wechselwirkungen in Theorie und Praxis, 1990.

Curtis, H. Holbrook. *Voice Building and Tone Placing.* New York: D. Appleton and Company, 1914.

Cutler, Edward. *Recovering the New: Transatlantic Roots of Modernism.* Hanover: University Press of New England, 2003.

Cyrano de Bergerac. *Voyage aux états et empires de la lune.* Pomport: Cyrano, 2012.

Da Silva, Gérard. "Manet, Nina ou la Commune au coeur de l'Art." In *Intempestives: La Commune, Enjeu Vivant.* 9–37. Paris: L'Harmattan, 2010.

De Gerando, *De l'education des sourds-muets de naissance.* Paris: Mequignon Aine, 1827.

De Man, Paul. "Anthropomorphism and Trope in the Lyric." In *The Rhetoric of Romanticism.* 239–62. New York: Columbia University Press, 1984.

———. "Rhetoric of Temporality." In *Blindness and Insight.* 187–228. Minneapolis: University of Minnesota Press, 1971.

De Saint Marc, Stéphanie. *Nadar.* Paris: Gallimard, 2010.

Deleuze, Gilles. *Critique et clinique.* Paris: Minuit, 1999.

Deleuze, Gilles, and Félix Guattari. "De la Ritournelle." In *Mille Plateaux.* Paris: Les Éditions de Minuit, 1980.

Derrida, Jacques. *La voix et le phénomène: introduction au problème du signe dans la phénoménologie de Husserl.* Paris: Presses Universitaires de France, 1967.

———. "Preface: veni." In *Rogues: Two Essays on Reason.* xi–xv. Stanford, Calif.: Stanford University Press, 2005.

Dillon, Emma. *The Sense of Sound: Musical Meaning in France, 1260–1330.* New York: Oxford University Press, 2012.

Dolan, Therese. "Manet's Synesthetic Portrait: Composing Cabaner." In *Perspectives on Manet*, edited by Therese Dolan. Farnham: Ashgate, 2012.

Dreyfous, Maurice. *Ce que je tiens à dire: un demi-siècle de choses vue et entendues, 1862–1872.* Paris: Librairie Paul Ollendorff, 1912.

Duval, Georges. *Le Carnaval parisien: Le Quartier Pigalle.* Paris: C. Marpon et E. Flammarion, éditeurs, 1884.

Edison, Thomas Alva. "The Phonograph and Its Future." *North American Review* 126 (May–Jun. 1878): 527–36.

Eliot, T.S. "From Poe to Valéry." *The Hudson Review* 2, no. 3 (Fall 1949): 327–42.

Enns, Anthony. "The Phonographic Body: Phreno-Mesmerism, Brain Mapping, and Embodied Recording." In *Sonic Mediations: Body, Sound, Technology.* 13–26. Newcastle: Cambridge Scholars, 2008.

Erkkila, Betsy. "To Paris with My Love: Walt Whitman among the French Revisited." *Revue française d'études américaines* 2, no. 108 (2006): 7–22.
———. *Walt Whitman among the French: Poet and Myth*. Princeton, N.J.: Princeton University Press, 1980.
———. "Whitman and the Homosexual Republic." In *Walt Whitman: The Centennial Essays*, edited by Ed Folsom, 153–71. Iowa City: University of Iowa Press, 1994.
Erlmann, Veit. *Reason and Resonance: A History of Modern Aurality*. New York: Zone Books, 2010.
Esteve, Mary. *The Aesthetics and Politics of the Crowd in American Literature*. New York: Cambridge University Press, 2003.
Feaster, Patrick. *Pictures of Sound: One Thousand Years of Educed Audio: 980–1980*. Atlanta, Ga.: Dust-to-Digital, 2013.
Feld, Steven. "Waterfalls of Song: An Acoustemology of Place Resounding in Bosavi, Papua New Guinea." In *Senses of Place*. Santa Fe: School of American Research Press, 1996.
Folkerth, Wes. *The Sound of Shakespeare*. 1–11. London: Routledge, 2002.
Folsom, Ed. "The Whitman Recording." *Walt Whitman Quarterly Review* 9, no. 4 (Spring 1992): 214–16.
Forbes, John, and John Conolly, eds. *The British and Foreign Medical Review or International Journal of Practical Medicine and Surgery*, no. 2 (Apr. 1836).
Foucault, Michel. "Message ou bruit." In *Dits et Écrits: 1954–1988*, I. Paris: Gallimard, 1994, 557–60.
———. *Naissance de la clinique*. Paris: Presses Universitaires de France, 1963.
Fournel, Victor. *Les Cris de Paris*. Paris: Les Éditions de Paris, 2003.
Forestier, Louis. *Charles Cros: L'Homme et l'Oeuvre*. Paris: Lettres Modernes Minard, 1969.
———. "Charles Cros ou l'ambition de l'unité." In *De Fil en Aiguille: Charles Cros et les Autres*, exh. cat., December 15, 1988–April 1, 1989, 11–20.
———. "A propos de Rimbaud et Charles Cros." *Revue d'Histoire littéraire de la France*, no. 2 (Apr.–Jun. 1964): 296–98.
———. "Pavane pour un visage défunt." In *La Dame aux éventails: Nina de Callias, modèle de Manet*. 9–40. Paris: Réunion des musées nationaux, 2000.
Frank, Adam. "Valdemar's Tongue, Poe's Telegraphy." *ELH* 72, no. 3 (Fall 2005): 635–62.
Frattarola, Angela. "Developing an Ear for the Modernist Novel: Virginia Woolf, Dorothy Richardson and James Joyce." *Journal of Modern Literature* 33, no.1 (2009): 132–53.
Gellen, Kata. "Hearing Spaces: Architecture and Acoustic Experience in Modernist German Literature." *Modernism/Modernity* 17, no. 4 (November 2010): 799–818.
———. *Kafka and Noise: The Discovery of Cinematic Sound in Literary Modernism*. Evanston, Ill.: Northwestern University Press, 2019.

Ginsburg, Michal. "Sentimentality and Survival: The Double Narrative of *The Old Curiosity Shop*." *Dickens Quarterly* 27, no. 2 (Jun. 2010): 85–101.

Gitelman, Lisa. *Always Already New: Media, History, and the Data of Culture*. Cambridge, Mass.: MIT Press, 2006.

———. *Scripts, Grooves, and Writing Machines: Representing Technology in the Edison Era*. Stanford, Calif.: Stanford University Press, 1999.

Giuliani, Élizabeth. "La réception du media." *Revue de la Bibliothèque nationale de France* 33 (2009): 9–19.

Gleeson-White, Sarah. "Auditory Exposures: Faulkner, Eisenstein, and Film Sound." *PMLA* 128, no.1 (Jan. 2013): 87–100.

Glinoer, Anthony. *La Bohème: Une figure de l'imaginaire social*. Montréal: Les Presses de l'Université de Montréal, 2018.

Godfrey, Sima. "Strangers in the Park: Manet, Baudelaire, and *La Musique aux Tuileries*." In *Baudelaire and the Poetics of Modernity*, edited by Patricia A. Ward, 45–60. Nashville: Vanderbilt University Press, 2001.

Goudeau, Emile. *Dix ans de bohème*. Paris: A la Librairie Illustré, 1888.

Gough-Cooper, Jennifer, and Jacques Caumont. *La Vie illustrée de Marcel Duchamp, avec 12 dessins d'André Raffray*. Paris: Centre National d'Art et de Culture Georges Pompidou, 1977.

Goulet, Andrea. *Legacies of the Rue Morgue: Science, Space, and Crime Fiction in France*. Philadelphia: University of Pennsylvania Press, 2015.

Greaney, Patrick. *Untimely Beggar: Poverty and Power from Baudelaire to Benjamin*. Minneapolis: University of Minnesota Press, 2007.

Griffin, Larry Don. "Walt Whitman's Voice." *Walt Whitman Quarterly Review* 9, no. 3 (Winter 1992): 125–33.

Grøtta, Marit. *Baudelaire's Media Aesthetics: The Gaze of the Flâneur and Nineteenth-Century Media*. New York: Bloomsbury Academic, 2015.

Gutton, Jean-Pierre. *Bruits et sons dans notre histoire: essai sur la réconstitution du paysage sonore*. Paris: Presses Universitaires de France, 2000.

Guy, Adam. "The Noise of Mediation: Dorothy Richardson's Sonic Modernity." *Modernism/Modernity* 27, no. 1 (Jan. 2020): 81–101.

Habermas, Jürgen. "Modernity—An Incomplete Project." In *Postmodern Culture*, edited by Hal Foster. London: Pluto Press, 1985.

Hamilton, John T. *Music, Madness, and the Unworking of Language*. New York: Columbia University Press, 2008.

Harvey, David. *Paris, Capital of Modernity*. New York: Routledge, 2005.

Harismendy-Lony, Sandrine. "Entre paraître et disparaître: Le 'Testament' de Nina de Villard." *Nineteenth-Century French Studies* 30, no. 1–2 (Fall–Winter 2001–2002): 81–91.

———. *De Nina de Villard au Cercle Zutique: violence et representation*. PhD diss., University of California, Santa Barbara, 1995.

———. "Nina de Villard, singulière Parisienne." *Nineteenth-Century French Studies* 27, no. 1–2 (Fall–Winter 1998–1999): 200–13.

Hayes, Kevin. "Visual Culture and the Word in Edgar Allan Poe's 'The Man of the Crowd.'" *Nineteenth-Century Literature* 56, no. 4 (Mar. 2002): 445–65.

Héran, Emmanuelle. "Henry Cros: le Moyen âge et la couleur." In *La Dame aux éventails: Nina de Callias, modèle de Manet*. 103–18. Paris: Réunion des musées nationaux, 2000.

Hochman, Brian. *Savage Preservation: The Ethnographic Origins of Modern Media Technology*. Minneapolis: University of Minnesota Press, 2014.

Hoffman, Tyler. *American Poetry in Performance: From Walt Whitman to Hip-Hop*. 16–55. Ann Arbor: University of Michigan Press, 2011.

———. "Walt Whitman 'Live': Performing the Public Sphere." *Walt Whitman Quarterly Review* 28 (2011): 188–208.

Hui, Alexandra. *The Psychophysical Ear: Musical Experiments, Experimental Sounds, 1840–1910*. Cambridge, Mass.: MIT Press, 2013.

Hurm, Horace. *La Passionnante Histoire du Phonographe*. Paris: Les Publications Techniques, 1943.

Ingold, Tim. "Against Soundscape." In *Autumn Leaves: Sound and the Environment in Artistic Practice*, edited by Angus Carlyle. Paris: Association Double-Entendre, 2007.

Janus, Adrienne. "Listening: Jean-Luc Nancy and the 'Anti-Ocular' Turn in Continental Philosophy and Critical Theory." *Comparative Literature* 63, no. 2 (2011): 182–202.

Johnson, James H. *Listening in Paris: A Cultural History*. Berkeley: University of California Press, 1996.

Jongh, Ariane Isler-de. "Manet, Charles Cros, et la photogravure en couleurs." *Nouvelles de l'estampe* 68 (1983).

Kahn, Douglas. *Noise, Water, Meat: A History of Sound in the Arts*. Cambridge, Mass.: MIT Press, 1999.

Kalba, Laura Anne. *Color in the Age of Impressionism: Commerce, Technology, and Art*. University Park: Penn State University Press, 2017.

———. "Hearing Voices: A Study of the Soundscape and Visual Culture of Debussy's Paris." In *Debussy's Paris: Art, Music, and Sounds of the City*. 14–31. Northampton, Mass.: Smith College Museum of Art, 2012.

Kamuf, Peggy. "Baudelaire au féminin." In *Signature Pieces: On the Institution of Authorship*. 123–44. Ithaca, N.Y.: Cornell University Press, 1988.

———. "Baudelaire's Modern Woman." *Qui Parle* 4, no. 2 (Spring 1991): 1–7.

Kane, Brian. "*Acousmate*: History and De-Visualised Sound in the Schaefferian Tradition." *Organised Sound* 17, no. 2 (2012): 179–88.

———. "*L'Objet Sonore Maintenant*: Pierre Schaeffer, Sound Objects and the Phenomenological Reduction." *Organised Sound* 12, no. 1 (2007): 15–24.

———. *Sound Unseen: Acousmatic Sound in Theory and Practice*. New York: Oxford University Press, 2014.

Kastner, Jean-Georges. *La Harpe d'Éole et la Musique Cosmique, études sur les rapports des phénomènes sonores de la nature avec la science et l'art*. Paris: G. Brandus, 1856.

———. *Les Voix de Paris, essai d'une histoire littéraire et musicale des cris populaires de la capitale, depuis la moyen-âge jusqu'à nos jours, précédé de considérations sur l'origine et le caractère du cri en général et suivi de* Les Cris de Paris, *grande symphonie humoristique vocale et instrumentale [paroles d'Édouard Thierry]*. Paris: G. Brandus, Dufour et cie, 1857.

Katsaros, Laure. *New York–Paris: Whitman, Baudelaire, and the Hybrid City*. Ann Arbor: University of Michigan Press, 2012.

Kennaway, James. *Bad Vibrations: The History of the Idea of Music as a Cause of Disease*. London: Routledge, 2016.

Kerr, Greg. "Laughing Matter: Charles Cros, from Paléophone to Monologue." *Nottingham French Studies* 59, no. 1 (Mar. 2020): 34–50.

Kieffer, Alexandra. "Bells and the Problem of Realism in Ravel's Early Piano Music." *Journal of Musicology* 34, no. 3 (Summer 2017): 432–72.

———. *Debussy's Critics: Sound, Affect, and the Experience of Modernism*. New York: Oxford University Press, 2019.

Kittler, Friedrich A. *Gramophone, Typewriter, Film*. Translated with an Introduction by Geoffrey Winthrop-Young and Michael Wutz. Stanford, Calif.: Stanford University Press, 1999.

Kursell, Julia. "Visualizing Piano Playing, 1890–1930." *Grey Room* 43 (Spring 2011): 66–87.

Kracauer, Siegfried. *Jacques Offenbach and the Paris of His Time*. New York: Zone Books, 2002.

Kreilkamp, Ivan. *Voice and the Victorian Storyteller*. Cambridge: Cambridge University Press, 2005.

Lacey, Kate. "Towards a Periodization of Listening: Radio and Modern Life." *International Journal of Cultural Studies* 3, no. 2 (Aug. 2000): 279–88.

Lacoue-Labarthe, Philippe. "L'Écho du Sujet." In *Le Sujet de la Philosophie*. Paris: Aubier: Flammarion, 1979.

———. *Musica Ficta: figures de Wagner*. Paris: Christian Bourgois, 1991.

Lajer-Burcharth, Ewa. "Modernity and the Condition of Disguise: Manet's 'Absinthe Drinker.'" *Art Journal* 45, no. 1 (Spring 1985): 18–26.

Lastra, James. *Sound Technology and the American Cinema: Perception, Representation, Modernity*. New York: Columbia University Press, 2000.

Lefebvre, Henri. *Rhythmanalysis: Space, Time, and Everyday Life*. London: Continuum International Publishing, 2004.

Lefrère, Jean-Jacques, and Michael Pakenham. *Cabaner, poète au piano*. Paris: L'Échoppe, 1994.

Levin, Joanna, and Edward Whitley, eds. *Whitman among the Bohemians*. Iowa City: University of Iowa Press, 2014.

Liénard, Pierre. "Conserver les sons." In *De Fil en Aiguille: Charles Cros et les Autres*, exh. cat., December 15, 1988–April 1, 1989, 21–26.

Littré, Emile. *Dictionnaire de français "Littré"* (1863–1877), Reverso Softissimo, 2010.

Lloyd, Rosemary. *Baudelaire's World*. Ithaca, N.Y.: Cornell University Press, 2002.

Lockerbie, I. S. "Rimbaud, Charles Cros, et le poème en prose." *Revue d'Histoire littéraire de la France*, no. 3 (Jul.–Sept. 1963): 424–40.
Lopate, Phillip, ed. *Writing New York: A Literary Anthology*. New York: The Library of America, 2008.
Loudon, James. "A Century of Progress in Acoustics." *Science* 14, no. 365 (Dec. 27, 1901): 987–95.
Mallarmé, Stéphane. *Oeuvres complètes*. 2 vols. "Pléiade" coll., edited by Bertrand Marchal. Paris: Éditions Gallimard, 1998.
Marcus, Sharon. *Apartment Stories: City and Home in Nineteenth-Century Paris and London*. Berkeley: University of California Press, 1999.
Marder, Elissa. "Baudelaire's Feminine Counter-Signature: 'Mademoiselle Bistouri'"'s Photographic Poetics." *Nineteenth-Century French Studies* 46, no. 1–2 (Fall–Winter 2017–2018): 1–25.
———. *Dead Time: Temporal Disorders in the Wake of Modernity (Baudelaire and Flaubert)*. Stanford, Calif.: Stanford University Press, 2001.
Mauté, Mathilde (Ex-Madame Paul Verlaine). *Mémoires de ma vie*. Paris: Champ Vallon Éditions, 2014.
McCloy, Shelby. *French Inventions of the Eighteenth Century*. Lexington: University Press of Kentucky, 2015.
Meltzer, Françoise. *Seeing Double: Baudelaire's Modernity*. Chicago: University of Chicago Press, 2012.
Mendès, Catulle. *La Maison de la vieille: roman contemporain*. Preface and notes by Jean-Jacques Lefrère, Michaël Pakenham, Jean-Didier Wagneur. Seyssel: Éditions Champ Vallon, 2000.
Miller, J. Hillis. *Versions of Pygmalion*. 141–78. Cambridge, Mass.: Harvard University Press, 1990.
Miller, Stewart. "Lightwaves and Telecommunication." *American Scientist* 72, no. 1 (Jan.–Feb. 1984): 66–71.
Milliot, Vincent. *Les Cris de Paris ou le Peuple Travesti: les représentations des petits métiers parisiens (XVIe–XVIIIe siècles)*. Paris: Publications de la Sorbonne, 1995.
Morris, Edmund. *Edison*. New York: Random House, 2019.
Müller-Sievers, Helmut. *The Cylinder: Kinematics of the Nineteenth Century*. Berkeley: University of California Press, 2012.
Murphy, Kieran. *Electromagnetism and the Metonymic Imagination*. University Park: Penn State University Press, 2020.
Nadar, Félix. *Charles Baudelaire, Intime, Le Poète Vierge*. Paris: A. Blaizot, Éditeur, 1911.
———. "Les Histoires du mois." *Musée français-anglais*, no. 24, Dec. 1856, 7, first column on left.
———. *Mémoires du Géant*. Paris: E. Dentu, deuxième édition, 1865.
———. *Quand j'étais photographe*. Charlieu: La Bartavelle – Éditeur, 1993.
Naeem, Asma. *Out of Earshot: Sound, Technology, and Power in American Art 1860–1900*. Berkeley: University of California Press, 2019.

Nancy, Jean-Luc. À *l'écoute*. Paris: Galilée, 2002.
———. *Listening*. Translated by Charlotte Mandell. New York: Fordham University Press, 2007.
———. *Les Muses*. Paris: Éditions Galilée, 2001.
———. "Sharing Voices." In *Transforming the Hermeneutic Context: From Nietzsche to Nancy*, edited by Gayle L. Ormiston and Alan D. Schrift. Albany: State University of New York Press, 1989.
Napolin, Julie Beth. *The Fact of Resonance: Modernist Acoustics and Narrative Form*. New York: Fordham University Press, 2020.
Nuñez, Rachel. *Between France and the World: The Gender Politics of Cosmopolitanism*. PhD diss., Stanford University, 2006.
Orgeman, Keely. "A Radiant Manifestation in Space: Wilfred, Lumia, and Light." In *Lumia: Thomas Wilfred and the Art of Light*. 21–47. New Haven, Conn.: Yale University Press, 2017.
Orledge, Robert. "After *Pelléas*: The Poe Operas (*Le Diable dans le beffroi, La Chute de la Maison Usher*)." In *Debussy and the Theatre*. 102–27. New York: Cambridge University Press, 1982.
Otis, Laura. "The Metaphoric Circuit: Organic and Technological Communication in the Nineteenth Century." *Journal of the History of Ideas* 63, no. 1 (Jan. 2002): 105–28.
———. *Networking: Communicating with Bodies and Machines in the Nineteenth Century*. Ann Arbor: University of Michigan Press, 2001.
Pahl, Dennis. "Sounding the Sublime: Poe, Burke, and the (Non)Sense of Language." *Poe Studies* 42, no. 1 (2009): 41–60.
Pakenham, Michael, et al. *La Dame aux éventails: Nina de Callias, modèle de Manet*, exh. cat. Paris: musée d'Orsay, 2000.
———. "Le 'Vaisseau-Piano' des frères Cros." *Revue d'Histoire littéraire de la France*, no. 2 (Apr.–Jun. 1964): 293–95.
Pantalony, David. *Altered Sensations: Rudolph Koenig's Acoustical Workshop in Nineteenth-Century Paris*. Dordrecht: Springer, 2009.
Pecqueux, Anthony. "Le son des choses, les bruits de la ville." *Communications* 90 (Paris: Seuil: École des Hautes Études en Sciences Sociales—Centre Edgar Morin, 2012).
Perriault, Jacques. *Mémoires de l'ombre et du son: une archéologie de l'audio-visuel*. Paris: Flammarion, 1981.
Picker, John. "Aural Anxieties and the Advent of Modernity." In *The Victorian World*, edited by Martin Hewitt, chap. 34, 603–18. London: Routledge, 2012.
———. *Victorian Soundscapes*. New York: Oxford University Press, 2003.
Poe, Edgar Allan. *Essays and Reviews*. Edited by G. R. Thompson. New York: The Library of America, 1984.
———. *Marginalia*. Charlottesville: University of Virginia Press, 1981.
———. *Poetry and Tales*. Edited by Patrick F. Quinn. New York: The Library of America, 1984.

Pound, Louise. "Whitman and the French Language." *American Speech* 1, no. 8 (May 1926): 421–30.
Prendergast, Christopher. *Paris and the Nineteenth Century*. Oxford: Blackwell, 1995.
Proust, Marcel. *Le Coté de Guermantes, À La Recherche du Temps Perdu III*. Paris: Éditions Gallimard, 1988.
———. *In Search of Lost Time, vol.3: The Guermantes Way*. Translated by C. K. Scott Moncrieff and Terence Kilmartin. New York: The Modern Library, 2003.
———. *Du côté de chez Swann, À La Recherche du Temps Perdu I*. Paris: Éditions Gallimard, 1988.
Przyblyski, Jeannene. "Revolution at a Standstill: Photography and the Paris Commune of 1871." *Yale French Studies* 101, (2001): 54–78.
Rabb, Jane, ed. *Literature and Photography: Interactions 1840–1990: A Critical Anthology*. Albuquerque: University of New Mexico Press, 1995.
Rancière, Jacques. *Le Partage du Sensible: esthétique et politique*. Paris: La Fabrique-éditions, 2000.
———. *L'inconscient esthétique*. Paris: Éditions Galilée, 2001.
Raynaud, Ernest. *La Bohème sous le second empire: Charles Cros et Nina*. Paris: L'Artisan du livre, 1930.
Rée, Jonathan. *I See a Voice: Deafness, Language, and the Senses: A Philosophical History*. New York: Holt Paperbacks, 2000.
Richter, Gerhard. *Walter Benjamin and the Corpus of Autobiography*. Detroit: Wayne State University Press, 2000.
Robida, Albert. *The Twentieth Century*. Translated by Philippe Willems. Middletown, Conn.: Wesleyan University Press, 2004.
Rosen, Jody. "Researchers Play Tune Recorded Before Edison." *New York Times*, March 27, 2008, Arts section.
Russolo, Luigi. *L'Art des bruits: manifeste futuriste 1913*. Paris: Éditions Allia, 2013.
Ryder, Robert. *The Acoustical Unconscious: From Walter Benjamin to Alexander Kluge*. Berlin: De Gruyter, 2022.
Satie, Erik. *A Mammal's Notebook: The Writings of Erik Satie*. Edited by Ornella Volta. London: Atlas Press, 2014.
———. *Mémoires d'un amnésique*, présentés et annotés par Raoul Coquereau. Toulouse: Éditions Ombres, 2010.
Saussy, Haun. *The Ethnography of Rhythm: Orality and Its Technologies*. New York: Fordham University Press, 2016.
———. "Interplanetary Literature." *Comparative Literature* 63, no. 4 (Fall 2011): 438–47.
Savery, Donna Christina. *Echoism: The Silenced Response to Narcissism*. Abingdon: Routledge, 2018.
Schafer, R. Murray. *The Soundscape: Our Sonic Environment and the Tuning of the World*. Rochester, V.T.: Destiny Books, 1993.
Schaffer, Simon. "The Leviathan of Parsonstown: Literary Technology and Scientific Representation." In *Inscribing Science: Scientific Texts and the*

Materiality of Communication, edited by Timothy Lenoir, 182–222. Stanford, Calif.: Stanford University Press, 1998.

Schivelbusch, Wolfgang. *Disenchanted Night: The Industrialization of Light in the Nineteenth Century*. Translated by Angela Davies. Berkeley: University of California Press, 1988.

Schuerewegen, Franc. *A distance de voix: essai sur les "machines à parler."* Lille, France: Presses Universitaires de Lille, 1994.

———. "Télétechné fin-de-siècle: Villiers de L'Isle-Adam et Jules Verne." Procès d'écritures Hugo-Vittez. *Romantisme: revue du dix-neuvième siècle* 69 (1990): 79–88.

Schultz, Gretchen. *The Gendered Lyric: Subjectivity and Difference in Nineteenth-Century French Poetry*. West Lafayette, Ind.: Purdue University Press, 1999.

Schultz, Gretchen, ed. *An Anthology of Nineteenth-Century Women's Poetry from France*. New York: Modern Language Association of America, 2008.

Schwartz, Vanessa. *Spectacular Realities: Early Mass Culture in* Fin-de-Siècle *Paris*. Berkeley: University of California Press, 1998.

Schwartz, Vanessa, and Jeannene Przyblyski, eds. *The Nineteenth-Century Visual Culture Reader*. New York: Routledge, 2004.

Schweighauser, Philipp. *The Noises of American Literature, 1890–1985: Toward a History of Literary Acoustics*. Gainesville: University Press of Florida, 2006.

Scott de Martinville, Édouard-Léon. "Fixation Graphique de la Voix." Paris: Impr. de J. Claye, 1857.

———. "The Phonautographic Manuscripts of Édouard-Léon Scott de Martinville." Translated and edited by Patrick Feaster. Bloomington, Ind.: FirstSounds.org, 2010.

Sebald, Bruno. "L'édition du disque." *Revue de la Bibliothèque nationale de France* 33 (2009): 31–42.

Segalen, Victor. "Voix Mortes: Musiques Maoris." In *Segalen et Debussy*. 153–187. Monaco: Éditions du Rocher, 1961.

Sené, Xavier. "L'Impression du Son," *Revue de la Bibliothèque nationale de France* 33 (2009). Naissances du disque.

Serres, Michel. *Genèse*. Paris: Grasset, 1982.

Sharpe, William. *Unreal Cities: Urban Figuration in Wordsworth, Baudelaire, Whitman, Eliot, and Williams*. Baltimore: Johns Hopkins University Press, 1990.

Shaw-Miller, Simon. "'The Only Musician with Eyes': Satie and Visual Art." In *Erik Satie: Music, Art, and Literature*, edited by Caroline Potter. London: Routledge, 2013.

Siegfried, Tom. *Strange Matters: Undiscovered Ideas at the Frontiers of Space and Time*. New York: Berkley Books, 2002.

Silverman, Kaja. *The Acoustic Mirror: The Female Voice in Psychoanalysis and Cinema*. Bloomington: Indiana University Press, 1988.

Simmel, Georg. *Simmel on Culture: Selected Writings*. Edited by David Frisby and Mike Featherstone. London: Sage Publications, 1997.

Sisiiänen, Lauri. "From the Empire of the Gaze to Noisy Bodies: Foucault, Audition, and Medical Power." In *Theory and Event*, vol. 11, no. 1. Baltimore: Johns Hopkins University Press, 2008.

Smith, Mark, ed. *Hearing History: A Reader*. Athens: University of Georgia Press, 2004.

Spann, Edward K. *The New Metropolis: New York, 1840–1857*. New York: Columbia University Press, 1981.

Stamos, David N. *Edgar Allan Poe, Eureka, and Scientific Imagination*. Albany: State University of New York Press, 2017.

Steege, Benjamin. *Helmholtz and the Modern Listener*. Cambridge: Cambridge University Press, 2012.

Sterne, Jonathan. *The Audible Past: Cultural Origins of Sound Reproduction*. Durham, N.C.: Duke University Press, 2003.

———. "Mediate Auscultation, the Stethoscope, and the 'Autopsy of the Living': Medicine's Acoustic Culture." *Journal of Medical Humanities* 22, no. 2 (2001): 115–36.

———. "The Sonic Imagination." In *The Sound Studies Reader*, edited by Jonathan Sterne, 1–17. London: Routledge, 2012.

Stewart, Susan. *Poetry and the Fate of the Senses*. Chicago: University of Chicago Press, 2002, esp. chapt. 2, "Sound," 59–105.

Szendy, Peter. *All Ears: The Aesthetics of Espionage*. Translated by Roland Végső. New York: Fordham University Press, 2016.

———. "The Archi-Road Movie." In *The Senses and Society*, vol. 8. London: Bloomsbury Publishing, 2013, 50–61.

———. "The Auditory Re-Turn (The Point of Listening)," Keynote Address, "Thinking Hearing—The Auditory Turn in the Humanities." University of Texas at Austin, October 2, 2009.

———. *Listen: A History of Our Ears*. Translated by Charlotte Mandell. New York: Fordham University Press, 2008.

———. *Of Stigmatology: Punctuation as Experience*. Translated by Jan Plug. New York: Fordham University Press, 2018.

Taminiaux, Pierre. *The Paradox of Photography*. Amsterdam: Editions Rodopi, 2009.

Taylor, Timothy, ed. *Music, Sound, and Technology in America: A Documentary History of Early Phonograph, Cinema, and Radio*. Durham, N.C.: Duke University Press, 2012.

Terao, Yoshiko. *Le fixe et le fugitif: Tiphaigne, Diderot, Mical, Castel et leurs machines audiovisuelles*. Thèse doctorale. Université Lumière Lyon 2, 2016.

Thibaud, Jean-Paul. "L'Expression Littéraire des Silences de la Ville." *La Création Sociale* no. 2 (1997): 45–70.

———. "The Sonic Composition of the City." In *The Auditory Culture Reader*, edited by Michael Bull and Les Back, 329–42. Oxford: Berg, 2004.

Thompson, Emily. "Machines, Music, and the Quest for Fidelity: Marketing the Edison Phonograph in America, 1877–1925." *The Musical Quarterly* 79, no.1 (Spring 1995): 131–71.

---. *The Soundscape of Modernity: Architectural Acoustics and the Culture of Listening in America 1900–1933.* Cambridge, Mass.: MIT Press, 2002.
Trachtenberg, Alan. "Whitman's Lesson of the City." In *Breaking Bounds: Whitman and American Cultural Studies*, edited by Betsy Erkkila and Jay Grossman, 163–73. New York: Oxford University Press, 1996.
Tresch, John. *The Romantic Machine: Utopian Science and Technology after Napoleon.* Chicago: University of Chicago Press, 2012.
---. "Technology." In *Edgar Allan Poe in Context*, edited by Kevin Hayes, 372–83. New York: Cambridge University Press, 2013.
Tyree, J. M. "Thoreau, Whitman, and the Matter of New York." *New England Review* 27, no. 1 (2006): 61–75.
Verlaine, Paul. *Œuvres en prose complètes.* Edited by Jacques Borel. Pléiade. Paris: Gallimard, 1972.
Villard, Nina de. "L'Archet." Published *en feuilleton* in *La Réforme politique et sociale*, November 25–27, 1869.
---. *Feuillets Parisiens.* Paris: Librairie Henri Messager, 1885.
---. "La Statue." Published *en feuilleton* in *La Réforme politique et sociale*, November 30–December 3, 1869.
Wade, Nicholas J., ed. *Brewster and Wheatstone on Vision.* London: Experimental Psychology Society, 1983.
Wagneur, Jean-Didier. "La Légende de Nina." In *La Dame aux éventails: Nina de Callias, modèle de Manet.* 75–82. Paris: Réunion des musées nationaux, 2000.
Weber, Samuel. *Benjamin's -abilities.* Cambridge, Mass.: Harvard University Press, 2010.
Weheliye, Alexander. *Phonographies: Grooves in Sonic Afro-Modernity.* Durham, N.C.: Duke University Press, 2005.
Weinfield, Henry. *Stéphane Mallarmé: Collected Poems.* Berkeley: University of California Press, 1994.
Weiss, Allen S. *Breathless: Sound Recording, Disembodiment, and the Transformation of Lyrical Nostalgia.* Middletown, Conn.: Wesleyan University Press, 2002.
---. "Radio Icons, Short Circuits, Deep Schisms." In *Experimental Sound and Radio.* 1–7. Cambridge Mass.: MIT Press, 2001.
Wheatstone, Charles. "Description of the Kaleidophone, or Phonic Kaleidoscope; a New Philosophical Toy, for the Illustration of Several Interesting and Amusing Acoustical and Optical Phenomena." *Quarterly Journal of Science, Literature, and Art* 23 (1827): 344–51.
Whidden, Seth. *Arthur Rimbaud.* London: Reaktion Books, 2018.
Whitaker, Robert J. "The Wheatstone Kaleidophone." *American Journal of Physics* 61 (1983): 722–28.
Whitman, Walt. *Complete Poetry and Collected Prose.* Edited by Justin Kaplan. New York: The Library of America, 1982.
---. *Leaves of Grass.* Edited by Michael Moon. New York: Norton, 2002.
---. *Specimen Days and Collect.* New York: Dover, 1995.

Whitney, Tyler. *Eardrums: Literary Modernism as Sonic Warfare.* Evanston, Ill.: Northwestern University Press, 2019.

Wilkinson, Alec. "A Voice from the Past: How a Physicist Resurrected the Earliest Recordings." *New Yorker*, May 19, 2014, 50–57.

Wilson-Bareau, Juliet, and Breon Mitchell. "Tales of a Raven: The Origins and Fate of *Le Corbeau* by Manet and Mallarmé." *Print Quarterly* 6, no. 3 (1989): 262.

Ziff, Larzer. "Whitman and the Crowd." *Critical Inquiry* 10, no. 4 (Jun. 1984): 579–91.

Index

"Al Aaraaf" (Poe), 233n54
Abbott, Helen, 248n70
aboriginal language, 141–42
Académie des Sciences, 4, 27, 52 53, 58, 220nn65,72, 221n81
Académie Française, 79
acousmaticity, 79, 80, 91, 226n24
acousmatic listening, 79–80, 225nn17–18
acousmatic sound, 78–79, 80
acoustemologies, 14
acoustical shock, 11, 108, 199
acoustic daguerreotype, 2, 14; as art, 111; Nadar and, 24, 39–40, 52, 76, 103, 104, 106–7, 109, 110, 112, 124, 200
acoustics, 46, 48, 81, 92, 210n18; music and, 171–72; panacoustic, 11, 66–73, 211n20, 223n113; technology, 38, 63, 85, 103–4, 106; urban, 11, 107, 130, 139, 143
aeolian harp, 91, 92
The Aeolian Harp and Cosmic Music (Kastner), 91
Albright, Daniel, 194
Album Zutique, 157, 181, 183, 187
"L'Alchimie moderne" (Cros, C.), 5
Alexis, Paul, 157, 179, 182–83
Algiers, 113, 113
Algonquin people, 141–42, 239n34
Allais, Alphonse, 31–32, 50, 63–64, 66–67, 248n66
All Ears (Szendy), 211n20, 223n113
alphabet, universal, 217n21
ambient sound, 125–32
"America" (Whitman), 136

Anémic Cinéma (film), 41
Anthologie de l'Humour Noir (Breton), 28
"Anywhere Out of the World" (Baudelaire), 34
Apollinaire, Guillaume, 2, 23, 27, 68, 223n115, 237n8
Arcades Project (Benjamin), 10, 98, 235n83
archaeology, media, 2
archaeophony (archaeology of sound), 1, 2
"L'Archet" ("The Bow") (Cros, C.), 59, 160, 166, 184, 244n17
"L'Archet" ("The Bow") (Villard), 160–67, 168, 172, 244n17, 245n29
Archives de la Parole, 68, 223n115, 237n8
art, 3, 23, 111, 189, 210n10; historians, 114, 220n63, 224n121, 236n89; literature and, 9, 211n21; science and, 37, 46, 61, 63, 91, 109
artistic identity, women, 167
artists, 11, 127, 169, 228n68, 245n30
"L'Art Mnémonique" (Baudelaire), 154
"art of noise," 183, 195, 196, 197
astronomy, 45, 74
Attali, Jacques, 183, 203
Au bonheur des dames (Zola), 211n22
"Au Clair de la Lune" recording, 2
The Audible Past (Sterne), 210n19, 225n18, 226n35, 227nn43,59
"audile technique," telegraph and, 86, 227n43
audiobook, 60, 62
audio newscast (*journal parlé*), 63, 66, 223nn115–16
audiovisual media, 3–5, 24, 68, 80, 171, 180–81, 198

audiovisual relations, modern, 3, 14, 202
audiovisual spectacles, in Paris, 213n35
audiovisual telecommunications, 45, 49, 68
auditory culture, 10, 11, 13, 157–58, 197, 202, 210n19
auditory hallucination, 24, 78–80, 92
auditory imagination, 11, 77, 81, 132, 196
Audouard, Olympe, 159, 169, 170
Auenbrugger, Leopold, 83, 84
Augoyard, Jean-François, 11, 21
"À une passante" (Baudelaire), 32, 121, 124, 129, 139
aurality, 122, 124, 129
auscultation, 33, 81–85, 91–92, 119, 226n32, 227n41
"Les Aveugles" (Baudelaire), 120–27, 143
Azoulay, Léon, 14

Babou, Hippolyte, 130
Bach, J. S., 184, 248nn68,70
Balzac, Honoré de, 7, 8, 21, 97, 160, 228n66
Bar aux Folies-Bergère, 41
Barret, Lindon, 225n16
Barthes, Roland, 77, 86
"Le Bateau Ivre" (Rimbaud), 35
Battu, Marie, 169
Baudelaire, Charles, 6, 50, 132, 158, 223n106, 233n59; "Les Aveugles," 120–27, 143; Bach and, 184, 248n70; city sounds and, 94–95; color photography and, 112–14; Cros, Charles, and, 29, 33, 34, 37; deafness and, 32–33, 120, 121, 124; *Les Fleurs du Mal*, 107, 114–16, 125–26, 232n44, 234n65; "une grande barbarie éclairée au gaz" and, 152–54; Haussmann and, 242n85; kaleidophonic and, 102–3, 107; listening and, 107–8, 110–11, 125; Manet and, 130–32, 235n87, 236n89; "Le Mauvais vitrier," 233n60; modernity and, 23, 107–8, 109, 124; movement and, 102, 112; Nadar and, 24, 103–4, 105, 106–7, 109–12; Paris and, 3, 121; photography and, 29, 102, 108–14, 127, 129–30, 134; Poe and, 78, 92, 96, 109, 119–20, 124, 152, 153–54, 159, 229n85, 231n16, 233n54, 242n88; rag of music and, 24, 103; sound and, 228n68; "La sourde-muette" and, 33, 121; stereoscope and, 75; "Les Veuves," 103, 125–32, 149–50; Villard and, 163–64, 167–68, 245n23; Whitman and, 122, 138, 139, 147, 148, 153, 154, 238n16, 239nn34,36, 242n87. See also specific titles
Baudelaire, l'irréductible (Compagnon), 102
"Baudelaire song project," 248n70

Baxandall, Michael, 25
"La Beauté" (Baudelaire), 184
Bell, Alexander Graham, 49, 51, 75; Cros, Charles, and, 217n21; patents, 221nn77–78; phonautograph and, 227n59; photophone and, 50, 52, 53, 71; telephone and, 49, 53, 56, 198
Bellamy, Edward, 4, 29, 110
"The Bells" (Poe), 121
Benjamin, Walter, 10, 13, 25, 80, 210n18, 235n83; "optical unconscious" and, 39, 77, 233n58; on Poe, 98, 225n22
Bennett, Léon, 47
Bentham, Jeremy, 223n113
Béranger, Jean Pierre de, 88–89, 92, 227n54
"Berenice" (Poe), 94
Bergerac, Cyrano de (1619–1655), 4, 59–60, 62, 222n91
Berliner, Emile, 27, 57, 211n21, 221nn77,85
Berlioz, Hector, 213n35
Bibliothèque nationale de France, 221n82
"The Black Cat" (Poe), 77, 83–84, 94, 142, 165
blindness, sound and, 120–24
Bobillier, Gérard, 62–63
bodies: auscultation and, 33, 81–85, 91–92, 119, 226n32, 227n41; *corps sonore*, 240n46; éclat and, 131; *Leaves of Grass* as living voice and, 242n82; listening and, 85–86; machines and, 90, 238n23; nerves, 90–92, 227n59; phonograph and disembodied voice, 136–38; social groups and, 127; sound and, 140, 146, 147; sounds of, 33, 83–85, 126, 226n35; of women and violence, 168
Boisvert, Marie, 158
Bonaparte, Napoléon, 110
Bon Marché, 222n94
books, 29, 110; audio, 60, 62; first modern illustrated, 4, 224n121
Boutin, Aimée, 24, 233n60
"The Bow" ("L'Archet") (Cros, C.), 59, 160, 166, 184, 244n17
"The Bow" ("L'Archet") (Villard), 160–67, 168, 172, 244n17, 245n29
Breton, André, 3, 28, 41, 52, 62, 75
Brewster, David (Sir), 15
"Bridges" ("*Les Ponts*") (Baudelaire), 103
British and Foreign Medical Review, 83–84
"A Broadway Pageant" (Whitman), 241n78
Brohan, Madelaine, 169
Brunot, Ferdinand, 68, 237n8
buried sound, 9, 94, 99–100, 142–43, 177, 178
buried speech, 3, 24, 137–38, 142–44
Bush, Christopher, 251n24

INDEX

Cabaner, Ernest, 156, 158, 181, 184, 187, 190, 248n68; Debussy and, 248n72; in *Madame Meuriot*, 182–83; Rimbaud and, 178, 185, 186; Satie and, 247n57; synesthesia of, 185
"Calamus" (Whitman), 242n81
Callias, Hector de, 245nn23,29
Callias, Nina de, 161
capitalist marketplace, 23, 199
Carjat, Étienne, 178
Carpentier, Jules, 181, 231n34
"The Cask of Amontillado" (Poe), 94, 177
Castel, Louis Bertrand (Father) (1688–1757), 15, 17, 23, 31, 35, 185, 213n39
Cerebral Mechanics (Cros, C.), 50
Certeux, Alphonse, 103, 230n4
Cézanne, Paul, 5, 159, 181–82, 183
Chabrier, Emmanuel, 184, 248n68
Chambers, Ross, 24, 103, 122, 147, 201, 233n60
Champfleury, Jules, 6–10, 7, 50, 137, 200, 210n11
Chaplin, Charles, 62
Le Château des Carpathes (Verne), 29, 37, 46, 47, 65, 211n22
Chat Noir (journal), 195
Chat Noir cabaret, 5, 71, 166, 178–91
Chaulnes (Duke), 27, 180–81
Chéret, Jules, 72
"La Chevelure" (Baudelaire), 120
Chion, Michel, 144–45, 225nn17–18
Chladni, Ernst, 117, 118, 213n35
chromolithography, 41, 42
La Chronique universelle (newspaper), 169, 244n18
chronophotography, 39, 41
cinema (film), 41, 43, 49, 62, 102, 180–81, 225n17; film scoring, 23, 200; as "muse of the twentieth century," 176, 246n44; photophone and, 50; wax and, 248n81
cities: acousmaticity of, 80, 91; Algiers, 113, 113; chaos sonore of, 13, 14; London, 12–13, 96–97, 98, 103, 133; muttering in streets, 98; "The Sonic Composition of the City," 210n19; sounds, 10–19, 35–36, 92–101, 121–23, 137–39, 141–43, 146–47, 212n23, 237n5; street cries, 13–14, 93, 96, 103, 233n60; urban acoustics, 11, 107, 130, 139, 143; urban noise, 11–13, 92–101, 104, 122, 147, 197, 201, 233n60. *See also* New York City; Paris
"Citizen DJ" project, 241n75
"The City Dead-House" (Whitman), 143–45
Clair, René, 200
Clarence, Geneviève, 20, 119

Clark, T. J., 235n87
Clavilux works (Wilfred), 15, 18, 19, 213n39
Coburn, Alvin, 114
Cocteau, Jean, 195, 247n58
Coeuroy, André, 20, 119
Le Coffret de santal (Cros, C.), 29, 36, 218n33
Colet, Louise, 167
Le Collier de Griffes (Cros, C.), 53
Colonial Exhibition, 14
color, 35, 185–88, 190, 213n39
color photography: Algiers, 113, 113; Baudelaire and, 112–14; Cros, Charles, and, 38, 39, 41, 54, 57, 112–14, 219n43, 231n34
color television, 232n39
Compagnie des Omnibus de Paris, 235n78
Compagnon, Antoine, 102, 112, 132–33
"Le Confiteor de l'Artiste" (Baudelaire), 228n68
Conrad, Joseph, 81, 86
Coppée, François, 182
Coquelin Cadet, Ernest, 58, 73, 221n82
Corbin, Alain, 11
"corps sonore," 240n46
"Correspondances" (Baudelaire), 167, 168
"Councillor Krespel" (Hoffmann), 161, 164, 166, 167
Crary, Jonathan, 15, 176, 210n19, 218n41
"Le Crépuscule du Soir" (Baudelaire), 121
cries: death, 177–78; street, 13–14, 93, 96, 103, 233n60
Les Cris de Londres (Certeux), 103, 230n4
Cros, Antoine, 33–35, 57, 89, 217nn24–25, 247n53
Cros, Charles (1842–1888), 75, 203; Baudelaire and, 29, 33, 34, 37; Bell and, 217n21; Bergerac and, 222n91; Cabaner and, 185; Chat Noir cabaret and, 166; color photography and, 38, 39, 41, 54, 57, 112–14, 219n43, 231n34; with convergence of technology, 61–66; Debussy and, 184; "Un drame interastral," 45–46, 48–49, 50, 52, 56, 65, 67–68; Duchamp and, 3, 28, 41, 43, 45; Edison and, 27–28, 30, 31, 45, 216n7, 220n72; "Excuse," 218n33; influence of, 3–5, 27–28; "Inscription," 28, 31, 37, 53–56, 58, 62, 65–67, 220n65; at Institut des Sourds-Muets, 31, 33, 45, 154, 221n83; legacy, 4–5, 27–30; with literature and science, 214n49; Manet and, 4, 29, 41, 42, 224n121; Nadar and, 39–40, 40, 174, 218n42, 219n43; paléophone and, 27–28, 30–33, 38, 45, 55, 57–58, 66, 247n53; paleophonic origins, 30–45; panacoustic and, 66–73; patent timing and, 56–58;

Cros, Charles *(continued)*
    patronage and, 27, 180–81, 215n2, 247n53; with phonogrammes filiformes, 59, 222n88; phonograph and, 45, 50, 57, 61, 217n25, 218n40; photophone and, 49–54; piano and, 33–35, 89; poverty and, 58; race and, 35, 218n30; with *Revue du monde nouveau*, 5; Rimbaud and, 35; scientific writings of, 5, 55, 61–62; surveillance and, 5, 23, 29, 48, 62–64, 67, 69–70; telegraph and, 218n39; trichrome photograph of Manet painting by, 29, 41, 42; vibrating diaphragm and, 211n21; Villard and, 155, 158–61, 165–66, 178–79, 187, 188, 245n24. *See also specific titles*
Cros, Henry, 34, 187
"Crossing Brooklyn Ferry" (Whitman), 122, 149–52, 154, 240nn40,47
crowds: "The Man of the Crowd," 81, 96–97, 98, 229n85; urban, 138, 139, 143–44, 147–49, 241nn62,67,69
Culler, Jonathan, 93
culture: auditory, 10, 11, 13, 157–58, 197, 202, 210n19; performance, 5, 25, 179; visual, 10, 81
Curé d'Ansacq, 79
Cutler, Edward, 98–99, 229n85

Dadaists, 25, 181, 193, 196, 249n8
Daguerre, Louis, 106, 108, 201, 247n54
daguerreotype, 14, 106; "La Légende du daguerréotype," 6–10, 7, 50, 137, 200; Poe and, 74, 76–77, 101. *See also* acoustic daguerreotype
daguerreotypie musicale, 106
La Dame aux éventails (*The Lady with the Fans*), 155, 156, 157, 170, 187, 244nn19–20
"Dead Voices" (Segalen), 14
deafness, 10, 15, 19, 35, 217n21, 243n90; Baudelaire and, 32–33, 120, 121, 124; Institut des Sourds-Muets, 31, 33, 45, 154, 221n83; sound reproducibility and, 31, 217n15
death, 8, 40, 54, 85, 165, 220n73, 238n21; "The City Dead-House," 143–45; cries, 177–78; social and artistic, 161–62; sound, voice and, 87; sound with life and, 163; violence and, 142, 168
"Death and the Shell" (Renard), 54
Debussy, Claude, 92, 100, 176, 182–84, 244n17, 247n61, 248n72
Degas, Edgar, 5, 189
De Gérando, 33
De l'Education des sourds-muets de naissance (*On the Education of the Deaf from Birth*) (De Gérando), 33

"De l'Essence du Rire" (Baudelaire), 234n62
Deleuze, Gilles, 251n22
"De l'idée moderne du progrès appliquée aux beaux-arts" (Baudelaire), 126
De Man, Paul, 234n65
"Le Démon de l'analogie" (Mallarmé), 5
Derrida, Jacques, 87, 131
Dickens, Charles, 12–13, 197
Diderot, Denis, 15
dioramas, 102, 213n35, 234n74
disability studies, 23
discs, 15, 19, 41, 43, 45, 57, 60
Dixains Réalistes (periodical), 155, 167
"Doings of Gotham" (Poe), 93, 141
Doré, Gustave, 110
"Un drame interastral" (Cros, C.), 45–46, 48–49, 50, 52, 56, 65, 67–68
dreams, 55, 89, 104, 111, 127
Dreyfous, Maurice, 157, 159, 180
Duchamp, Marcel, 3, 15, 28, 41, 43, 43–44, 45
Ducos du Hauron, Louis Arthur, 57, 113, 113–14
Du Moncel (Comte), 217n25

"ear of humanity," 85–88
echo, 82–83, 120–21, 129, 173–74. *See also* acoustics
Echo, Narcissus and, 108, 131
"L'Écho du sujet" (Lacoue-Labarthe), 120–21
éclat, éclatant and, 131
Edison, Thomas, 63, 104, 136–37, 179, 181, 214n43, 216n9; Cros, Charles, and, 27–28, 30, 31, 45, 216n7, 220n72; phonograph and, 1, 4, 27, 45, 66, 106, 110, 198, 200, 201, 217n25, 220n70
"Effarement" (Cros, C.), 223n106
electromagnetism, 90–91, 228nn63,66
electrophysiology, 90
Eliot, George, 22
Eliot, T. S., 78, 129, 142
emotions, 135, 194; electromagnetism and, 90–91; love, 45–46, 48–49, 52, 56, 68, 69, 131
Encyclopédie (Diderot), 15
"The End of Books" ("La fin des livres") (Robida and Uzanne), 29, 110
Engels, Friedrich, 97, 229n83
Engine of Modernity (Belenky), 235n78, 240n56
"The Enraged Musician" (Hogarth), 11, 12, 13
Entr'acte (short film), 180, 200
Erkkila, Betsy, 238n15, 242n81
Eureka (Poe), 5, 23, 74–77, 84
L'Ève future (Villiers de l'Isle-Adam), 27, 28–29, 62–63, 65

INDEX

"The Facts in the Case of M. Valdemar" (Poe), 77–78, 94, 165, 227n42; "ear of humanity" and, 85–88; phthisis and, 227n41
"The Fall of the House of Usher" (Poe): epigraph, 88–90; *The House of the Old Woman* and, 176–78; sounds in, 94, 99–100; wires, human nerves and, 90–92
Feld, Steven, 14
female voices, silencing of, 121, 167, 168, 170, 233n59
field of listening, 77–78, 80, 101
film. *See* cinema
"La fin des livres" ("The End of Books") (Robida and Uzanne), 29, 110
"Fixation graphique de la voix" (Scott de Martinville), 116
flame manometer, 133, 133–34, 242n86
flânerie, 13, 21, 81, 107, 235n83
Flaubert, Gustave, 53
Les Fleurs du Mal (Baudelaire), 107, 114–16, 125–26, 232n44, 234n65
Le Fleuve (Cros, C., and Manet), 224n121
Forbes, John, 83, 226n32
Forestier, Louis, 62, 222nn91,94, 223nn115–16
Foucault, Michel, 223n113
"Les Foules" (Baudelaire), 123
"found sounds," 241n75, 247n58, 249n8
"found voice," 150
Fournel, Victor, 235n83
France: legal rights for women in, 169; Poe in, 24, 158; United States and, 3, 152–53, 242n85; Whitman and, 138–39, 238n15. *See also* Paris
Frank, Adam, 87–88, 225n16, 227nn42,49
French language, 92–95, 97, 116, 119, 133, 139, 228n71, 229n76
"frozen speech," 20, 21, 97
"furniture music," 23, 198, 199–200

Gachet, Paul (Doctor), 185
gas lighting, 108, 132–35, 152, 153, 242n86
Gellen, Kata, 202
gemstones, 5
gender equality, 169, 170
Genesis (Serres), 203
Ghys, Henry, 184
Gilbert, C., 38
Giphantie (Tiphaigne de la Roche), 2, 200
Gitelman, Lisa, 4, 11, 201–2, 210n19, 250n17, 251nn24,27
"A Glimpse" (Whitman), 148
Godfrey, Sima, 130
Goncourt brothers, 5, 180, 195, 246n40
Gotham. *See* New York City

gramophone, 27, 30, 41, 43, 58, 202, 211n21, 221n77
Gramophone, Typewriter, Film (Kittler), 4, 216n7, 217n15, 220nn65,68,70
Grandfort, Marie de, 159
"une grande barbarie éclairée au gaz," Baudelaire and, 152–54
Gray, Elishah, 221n78
GRM, 183, 195
The Guermantes Way (Proust), 10, 19, 223n117
"Le Guignon" (Baudelaire), 114, 116–17, 119–20

Hanson, Miriam, 246n44
"Le Hareng Saur" (Cros, C.), 53
Harismendy-Lony, Sandrine, 157, 187
harpsichord, 9, 15, 17, 171, 172, 185
Haussmann, Georges-Eugène, 126, 132, 152, 235n78, 240n56, 242n85
Hawthorne, Nathaniel, 9
"hearings," urban vision and, 149–52
Heart of Darkness (Conrad), 81, 86
Helmholtz, Hermann von, 133, 210n10
Hérodiade (Mallarmé), 184
Hersent-Penquer, Léocadie, 167
Herz, Henri, 186
"L'Heure Froide" (Cros, C.), 35–36
Hoffman, Tyler, 136–37, 237n4
Hoffmann, E. T. A., 11, 160–61, 164–67, 172, 221n87, 245n23
Hogarth, William, 11, 12, 13
Holbrook, Curtis H., 16, 118, 133
Hoschedé, Ernest, 41, 42
The House of the Old Woman (La Maison de la vieille) (Mendès), 158, 170–76, 181, 218n30, 244n20
The House of the Seven Gables (Hawthorne), 9
Houssaye, Arsène, 104, 245n23
Hughes, David, 153
Hugo, Victor, 63–64, 139, 195

Illuminations (Rimbaud), 35
imagination, 2, 228nn63,66; auditory, 11, 77, 81, 132, 196; sound reproducibility and, 211n21, 220n73
Impressionism, 5, 29, 52, 155, 158, 184, 189
Impressions de mon Voyage au Salon de 1882 (Hoschedé), 41, 42
"Impromptu" (Villard), 189–90
industrialization, of literature, 64
"Inscription" (Cros, C.), 28, 31, 37, 53–56, 58, 62, 65–67, 149, 220n65
Institut des Sourds-Muets, 31, 33, 45, 154, 221n83
"Intonarumori," 196
Ion (Plato), 236n1

iPod, 59
Irving, Henry, 137, 138
"Israfel" (Poe), 89–90

Jaëll, Marie, 169, 186, 186–87, 248n79
James, William, 149
Janssen, Jules, 52, 75
Johnson, James, 125
"Le Journal de l'avenir" ("The Newspaper of the Future") (Cros, C.), 29, 48, 62–68, 70–71, 195
journal parlé (audio newscast), 63, 66, 223nn115–16
Joyce, James, 216n8

Kafka, Franz, 202
Kalba, Laura Anne, 114
kaleidophone, 14–15, 16, 114, 193, 194, 213n39
kaleidophonic, 9, 14, 102–3, 107, 141, 193
kaleidoscope, 9, 15, 102, 111
Kamuf, Peggy, 233n59
Kane, Brian, 79, 225nn17–18,23, 226n24
Kastner, Jean-Georges (1810–1867), 13–14, 91, 96, 106, 195, 200, 229n79
Katsaros, Laure, 95, 139, 141, 146, 229nn76,85, 239n34; on Baudelaire and Haussmann, 242n85; on Whitman and Baudelaire, 242n87; on Whitman and *Leaves of Grass*, 242n82
Kieffer, Alexandra, 182
Kittler, Friedrich A., 4, 29, 54, 216n7, 217n15, 220nn68,70; on Cros, Charles, 61–62, 65, 220n65; on Edison, 31
Koenig, Rudolph (1832–1901), 114, 133, 133, 133–34, 242n86
Kracauer, Siegfried, 132
Kreilkamp, Ivan, 81, 197
Krysinska, Marie, 166

Lacoue-Labarthe, Philippe, 120–21, 233n58
The Lady with the Fans (*La Dame aux éventails*), 155, 156, 157, 170, 187, 244nn19–20
Laennec, René, 83–84, 226nn32,35
Laforgue, Jules, 187, 242nn87–88, 248n81
Lagier, Suzanne, 169
Lamy, Pierre Franc, 155, 156, 182, 185, 187
language, 98, 122, 143; aboriginal, 141–42; French, 92–95, 97, 116, 119, 133, 139, 228n71, 229n76; sign, 31, 33, 45
laughter, 164–65, 177
Leaves of Grass (Whitman), 137–40, 148, 152, 238n21, 242n82
Leblanc, Léonide, 169
Lefrère, Jean-Jacques, 158, 184

"*La Légende du daguerréotype*" ("Legend of the Daguerreotypist") (Champfleury), 6–10, 7, 50, 137, 200
"The Leviathan of Parsonstown" (Schaffer), 224nn2,8
light: gas, 108, 132–35, 152, 153, 242n86; sound, science and, 52–53, 213n35; stars, time and, 75
"The Lighthouse" (Poe), 77, 81–83
Lissajous, Jules Antoine, 114, 116, 117, 249n4
Listen (Szendy), 210n19
listening: acoustmatic, 79–80, 225nn17–18; aurality and, 122, 124, 129; auscultative, 84; Baudelaire and, 107–8, 110–11, 125; body and, 85–86; experience, 125–26; field of, 77–78, 80, 101; "hearings" and urban vision, 149–52; in "The Lighthouse," 82; mechanical, 158, 159; modernization of, 211n22; *Modern Listener*, 210n19; performance space, 125, 180; politicized, 65–66; "Song of Myself" and, 140–41; to universe, 76; Villard with, 159–60
Listening (Nancy), 172, 240n46
Listening in Paris (Johnson), 125
Liszt, Franz, 110, 163, 245nn23–24, 248n79
literature, 6, 11, 30, 88, 241n67; art and, 9, 211n21; industrialization of, 64; science and, 23, 37, 62, 214n49, 232n50
London, 12–13, 96–97, 98, 103, 133
Longfellow, Henry Wadsworth, 115–16, 117, 232n44
"Loss of Halo" (Baudelaire), 189
Lost Children Archive (Luiselli), 14
Lottier, Louis, 113, 114
love, 45–46, 48–49, 52, 56, 68, 69, 131
Luiselli, Valeria, 14
Lumia works (Wilfred), 15, 213n39
Lumière brothers, 181, 231n34

machines, 93, 158, 159, 211n21, 238n12; bodies and, 90, 238n23; *The Romantic Machine*, 213n35; *Scripts, Grooves, and Writing Machines*, 4, 210n19
Madame Meuriot (Alexis), 157, 179, 182–83
"Mademoiselle Bistouri" (Baudelaire), 134–35
magic lantern, 102, 171, 174–76
La Maison de la vieille (*The House of the Old Woman*) (Mendès), 158, 170–76, 181, 218n30, 244n20
Mallarmé, Stéphane, 5, 61, 153, 184, 203, 211n20, 239n29, 242n87
Manet, Édouard, 5, 179, 248n79; *Bar aux Folies-Bergère*, 41; Baudelaire and, 130–32, 235n87, 236n89; Cros, Charles, and, 4, 29,

INDEX

41, 42, 224n121; *La Dame aux éventails*, 155, 156, 157, 170, 187, 244nn19–20; "Music in the Tuileries," 125, 130, 131, 132, 235n87, 236n89; *Printemps-Jeanne*, 41; trichrome photograph of painting by, 29, 41, 42
"Mannahatta" (Whitman), 141–42, 239nn34,36
"The Man of the Crowd" (Poe), 81, 96–98, 229n85
Marey, Étienne-Jules, 39
Marginalia (Poe), 227n54
Marinetti, Filippo, 195
Maupassant, Guy de, 5, 53
Mauté, Mathilde, 246n51, 249n88
"Le Mauvais vitrier" (Baudelaire), 233n60
media: archaeology, 2; art and, 189; audiovisual, 3–5, 24, 68, 80, 171, 180–81, 198; mass, 29, 63, 68, 88, 98–99, 198, 203, 227n53, 250n17; print, 66–67, 98, 110, 120, 169, 227n53; studies, 2, 198; technology and, 198
media, new, 14, 201, 237n9; premediation and, 251n24; technologies, 19, 62, 67, 199, 200, 209n5, 211n22
Meltzer, Françoise, 107–8
Mémoires du Géant (Nadar), 111
memory, sound and, 172–73
Mendès, Catulle (1841–1909), 158, 170–78, 181, 218n30, 244n20
mesmerism, 85, 88, 227n42, 238n23, 239n23
"The Metropolis and Mental Life" (Simmel), 121, 197
Meyers, Anne Akiko, 166
microphones, 15, 66, 68, 153, 193
microscope, daguerreotype and, 76–77
Middlemarch (Eliot, G.), 22
Miller, J. Hillis, 167
mirrors, 54, 75–76, 95, 116, 128, 133–34, 224n8
mnemotechnology, technology over, 220n68
modernity: Baudelaire and, 23, 107–8, 109, 124; "cult of the new" and, 229n85; *Engine of Modernity*, 235n78, 240n56; "Le Peintre de la Vie Moderne," 111; progress and, 24, 109, 126; soundscape of, 10, 202, 210n18; with time and sound reproducibility, 28; urban life and deafness, 32; visual field of, 10
modernization, of listening and sound, 211n22
Modern Listener (Steege), 210n19
Modern Times (film), 62
Morin, Gérard, 7
movement, 46, 102, 112
movie camera, 181
"The Murders in the Rue Morgue" (Poe), 80, 93, 94, 98
music: acoustics and, 171–72; aeolian harp, 91, 92; *Bad Vibrations*, 90; color and audible, 213n39; daguerreotypie musicale, 106; deafness and, 15, 31; dreams and, 55, 89; Edison and, 179, 216n9; "furniture," 23, 198, 199–200; hip hop, 241n75; human nerves and, 92; performance culture and, 25; performance space and listening, 125; player piano, 33–35, 89, 217n24; Polynesian, 14; popular "hits," 25, 183; "Proud Music of the Storm," 237n10, 238n21; rag of, 24, 103, 126, 128, 129, 132, 150; recording, 60; as "sonic materiality," 182; stenography, 35, 57; "That Music Always Round Me," 145; théatrophone and, 71, 72; Villard and, 155, 157, 159, 164–67, 169, 179, 181, 184–85, 246n51; violence in sound and, 161–62, 164, 166; of words, 239n29. *See also* opera; piano
musicians, 11, 12, 13, 195
"Musician's Day" text (Satie), 195
"Music in the Tuileries," 125, 130, 131, 132, 235n87, 236n89
musique concrète, 183, 195, 225n17
Muybridge, Eadweard, 39

Nadar, Félix (1820–1910), 2, 6, 8, 50, 178, 220n70; acoustic daguerreotype and, 24, 39–40, 52, 76, 103, 104, 106–7, 109, 110, 112, 124, 200; Baudelaire and, 24, 103–4, 105, 106–7, 109–12; Cros, Charles, and, 39–40, 40, 174, 218n42, 219n43
Nancy, Jean-Luc, 19, 129, 159, 160, 172, 236n1, 240n46
Napolin, Julie, 202
Narcissus, Echo and, 108, 131
La Nature (journal), 38, 175
nerves, wires and human, 90–92, 227n59
"The Newspaper of the Future" ("Le Journal de l'avenir") (Cros, C.), 29, 48, 62–68, 70–71, 195
New York City (Gotham), 6, 212n23, 238n12; "Crossing Brooklyn Ferry," 122, 149–52, 154, 240nn40,47; "Doings of Gotham," 93, 141; with microphones in prisons, 66, 68; omnibus in, 126, 145–49, 151, 240n57; *tintamarre* of, 92–101; urban street noise, 24, 93, 141, 147; Whitman and, 3, 139–45, 148, 154
Niépce, Nicéphore, 247n54
noise: "art of," 183, 195, 196, 197; "luminous," 11, 53, 211n20; pollution, 93, 140; Satie with, 182, 249n8; seeing, 24, 104, 116, 119, 132; traffic, 126; transatlantic, 152–54; visualization of Parisian, 114–20. *See also* urban noise

Noise (Attali), 183, 203
"Notes Nouvelles sur Edgar Poe" (Baudelaire), 32, 153

ocular harpsichord, 15, 17, 185
ocular proof, 76, 77
Offenbach, Jacques, 132
The Old Curiosity Shop (Dickens), 12–13, 197
omnibus: in New York City, 126, 145–49, 151, 240n57; in Paris, 126, 146, 235n78
On the Education of the Deaf from Birth (*De l'Education des sourds-muetsde naissance*) (De Gérando), 33
opera, 100, 169, 176, 182, 191; performance reproduced, 109, 220n70; singers and overloud orchestra, 96
"optical unconscious," 39, 77, 233n58
Otis, Laura, 22, 90
"The Oval Portrait" (Poe), 8

"Painter of Modern Life" (Baudelaire), 29, 132
The Painting of Modern Life (Clark), 235n87
paintings, sound of, 220n63
Pakenham, Michael, 158, 161, 184, 244n17
paléophone (voice of the past), 27–28, 30, 33, 55, 58, 66, 247n53; origins, 31–32, 38; sound reproduction and, 45, 57
paleophonics, origins, 30–45
panacoustic, 11, 66–73, 211n20, 223n113
panoramas, 81, 102, 113, 145, 213n35, 234n74
Parade (ballet), 180, 182, 247n58, 249n8
Paris, 1, 6, 11, 96, 139, 214n49, 222n94; "Americanization" of, 119; audiovisual spectacles in, 213n35; "Les Aveugles" and, 120–27, 143; Baudelaire and, 3, 121; Compagnie des Omnibus de Paris, 235n78; Haussmannization of, 126, 132, 152, 235n78, 240n56, 242n85; "L'Heure Froide" and, 35–36; *Listening in Paris*, 125; omnibus in, 126, 146, 235n78; Phono Museum, 218n42; "Rêve Parisien," 223n106; Salon of 1882, 41, 42; sounds, 91; soundscape, 212n23; *Le Spleen de Paris*, 35, 37, 107, 125; street cries of, 13, 14, 93; Universal Exhibition, 218n39; visualization of noise in, 114–20; *Les Voix de Paris*, 13, 195, 229n79
Paris au XXe Siècle (Verne), 62
Paris Commune, 48–49, 219n53
Parnasse Contemporain (periodical), 155
Parnassians, 155, 158, 167–68
Le Partage du Sensible (Rancière), 215n51, 243n93
Le Pâté, 183
patents, 27, 56–58, 221nn77–78

"Le Peintre de la Vie Moderne" (Baudelaire), 111
Pelléas et Mélisande (Debussy), 182
percussion auscultation, 33, 83, 84, 91–92
performance culture, 5, 25, 179
performance space, 125, 164, 179–80, 190
period ear, 25
Pernot, Hubert, 14
Perriault, Jacques, 22, 33, 40, 63, 106, 214n42, 232n47
Petite Danseuse de quatorze ans (Degas), 189
"Les Petites Vieilles" (Baudelaire), 125, 126–29, 146, 149
phenakistiscope, 15, 38–39, 41, 43, 46, 102, 112, 218n41
phonautograph: Bell and, 227n59; Scott de Martinville and, 1–2, 14, 30–31, 48, 103–4, 116–17, 117, 119, 133
phonobase.org, 221n82
phonogrammes filiformes, 59, 222n88
phonograph, 3, 210n12, 211n21, 216n8, 221n85, 237n4; *The Ancient Phonograph*, 214n42; Cros, Charles, and, 45, 50, 57, 61, 217n25, 218n40; Edison and, 1, 4, 27, 45, 66, 106, 110, 198, 200, 201, 217n25, 220n70; pinwheel, 58–61; prehistory, 20–23; sound reproducibility and, 45, 61; street cries recorded on, 13–14, 103; surveillance and, 223n11; telephone and, 29, 37, 48, 50, 65, 219n45; Verne and, 218n37; with voices disembodied, 136–38; writing and, 62–63. *See also* paléophone
phonography, 24, 30, 107, 120–21, 227n59
phonometrography, 25, 193, 249n7
Phono Museum, Paris, 218n42
phonoptomètre, 249n4
photographing sound, 6–10
photographs, 29, 41, 42, 49, 178, 187, 188
photography, 6, 8, 46, 200, 219n45; Baudelaire and, 29, 102, 108–14, 127, 129–30, 134; chronophotography, 39, 41; "optical unconscious" of, 77, 233n58. *See also* color photography
photophone, 49–54, 51, 71, 75
phreno-mesmerism, 238n23
Physiologie du Mariage (Balzac), 21
piano, 156, 172, 178, 182, 190; with fingerprint images on keys, 186, 186; player, 33–35, 89, 217n24; "Le Vaisseau-Piano," 34–35; Villard and, 155, 156, 163, 185–86, 245n24
Piatti, Ugo, 195, 196
Picker, John, 84, 210n19, 216n8, 225n16
pinwheel phonograph, 58–61
"plaque daguerrienne," 2, 104

INDEX

Plateau, Joseph, 38
Plato, 236n1
playback, 2, 32, 58, 182, 202
player piano, 33–35, 89, 217n24
"pli cachété" procedure, 221n81
podcasts, 62, 67
Poe, Edgar Allan, 3–4, 6, 8, 99, 121, 160, 184, 197, 228n63; acousmatic listening and, 79–80; acousmatic sound and, 80; acoustics and, 81; auditory hallucination and, 24, 78; Baudelaire and, 78, 92, 96, 109, 119–20, 124, 152, 153–54, 159, 229n85, 231n16, 233n54, 242n88; Béranger and, 227n54; "The Black Cat," 77, 83–84, 94, 142, 165; *British and Foreign Medical Review* and, 83–84; city sounds and, 142; daguerreotype and, 74, 76–77, 101; Debussy and, 92, 100, 176; "ear of humanity" and, 85–88; *Eureka*, 5, 23, 74–77, 84; with field of listening, 77–78; in France, 24, 158; with French language, 92–95, 228n71; immobilization and, 98; "Israfel," 89–90; "The Man of the Crowd," 81, 96–98, 229n85; mass media and, 227n53; Mendès and, 171, 176–78, microscope and, 76–77; "The Murders in the Rue Morgue," 80, 93, 94, 98; "Notes Nouvelles sur Edgar Poe," 32, 153; ocular proof and, 76, 77; with phthisis and auscultation, 227n41; with sound, 78; with sound technologies, 81–85; with "the strange and exceptional," 80, 84, 199, 225n22; telescope and, 74–77; with *tintamarre* of Gotham, 92–101; urban noise and, 11; Villard and, 164–65, 167; Whitman and, 138, 141–42, 149–50. *See also* "The Facts in the Case of M. Valdemar"; "The Fall of the House of Usher"; "The Tell-Tale Heart"; *specific titles*
poetry, 96, 104, 119
pollution, noise, 93, 140
Polynesian music, 14
"Les Ponts" ("Bridges") (Baudelaire), 103
portability, 4, 32, 58–60, 223n116
poverty, 58, 129, 234n67, 238n12
Poyet, Louis, 175
Pratella, Balilla, 195
praxinoscope, 15, 175, 175
premediation, new media and, 251n24
Prendergast, Christopher, 96, 233n60, 235n87
Prévost, Abbé, 79
Principes de mécanique cérébrale (Cros, C.), 38, 218n40, 219n54
Printemps-Jeanne, 41

print media, 66–67, 98, 110, 120, 169, 227n53
prisons, microphones in, 66, 68
"Procedure for Recording and Reproduction" (Cros, C.), 38
progress, modernity and, 24, 109, 126
Projet Bretez, 212n23
protophotographic imagination, 2
"Proud Music of the Storm" (Whitman), 237n10, 238n21
Proust, Marcel, 25, 80, 171–72, 175, 223n117, 235n76; on deafness, 10, 19; théatrophone and, 71; urban noise and, 11
Przybylski, Jeannene, 210n19
"A Psalm of Life" (Longfellow), 115–16
"ptyx" sonnet (Mallarmé), 61
"Le Public Moderne et la Photographie" (Baudelaire), 29, 108
"The Purloined Letter" (Poe), 80
Pygmalion myth, 167
Pythagoras, 79, 226n24
Pythagorean Veil, 79

Quand j'étais photographe (*When I Was a Photographer*) (Nadar), 8
Le Quart Livre (Rabelais), 20

Rabelais, François, 20–21, 78, 97, 214n42
race, 35, 218n30
Raffray, André, 41, 44
Rancière, Jacques, 22, 23, 150, 215n51, 243n93
Ravel, Maurice, 184, 247n61
"The Raven" (Poe), 78, 152
Ray, Man, 41, 194
Raynaud, Ernest, 64, 160
"Le Réalisme" (Champfleury), 6
recording, 38, 60; sound, 1–2, 14, 41; technology, 33–35, 83, 89, 159, 243n90; Whitman, 136–38
Rée, Jonathan, 225n16
reflection, resonance and, 129
La Réforme politique et sociale, 244n18, 245n27
"Le Refus" (Béranger), 88
Renard, Maurice, 54
Renoir, Pierre-Auguste, 5
reproduction, 38, 46, 109, 182, 220n70. *See also* sound reproduction
resonance, 129, 144, 160, 168, 240n46
"Rêve Parisien" (Baudelaire), 223n106
Revue du monde nouveau (periodical), 5, 248n79
Reynaud, Émile, 175, 175
Richard, Pierre, 57
Richards, I. A., 96

Rimbaud, Arthur, 30, 35, 103, 178, 181, 185–87
"The Roaring Twenties" project, 212n23
Robert le diable (Meyerbeer), 213n35
Robida, Albert (1848–1926), 29, 68–71, 69–70, 73, 110, 223n118, 224n121
The Romantic Machine (Tresch), 213n35
Rosse (Lord), 74–77, 224n2
Rotorelief no. 6—Escargot (Duchamp), 41, 43
rotoreliefs, 15, 41, 43, 43, 45
Rousseau, Jean-Jacques, 139
Russolo, Luigi, 195–97, 196, 203

Salis, Rodolphe, 63
salon, intellectual. *See* Villard, Nina de
Salon de 1846 (Baudelaire), 112, 113
Salon de 1859 (Baudelaire), 75, 108, 111
Le Salon de Nina de Villard (Lamy), 155, 156, 182, 185
Salon of 1882, Paris, 41, 42
"Salut au Monde" (Whitman), 138–39, 150
Satie, Erik, 183, 197, 203, 247nn57–58; Chat Noir and, 179–80, 181; "furniture music," 23, 198, 199–200; "Musician's Day" text, 195; with noise, 182, 249n8; phonometrography and, 25, 194, 249n7; "What I Am," 193–95, 249n1, 249nn4,7
Saussy, Haun, 198, 209n5, 210n12
Schaeffer, Pierre, 225n17
Schafer, R. Murray, 140
schizophonia, 225n18
Schultz, Gretchen, 187
Schumann, Clara, 169
Schwartz, Vanessa, 210n19, 234n74, 248n81
science, 3, 38, 119; Académie des Sciences, 4, 27, 52–53, 58, 220nn65,72, 221n81; art and, 37, 46, 61, 63, 91, 109; light, sound, and, 52–53, 213n35; literature and, 23, 37, 62, 214n49, 232n50
Science (journal), 51
science fiction, 59
scientific writings, of Cros, Charles, 5, 55, 61–62
Scott de Martinville, Édouard-Léon, 200, 232n47; phonautograph and, 1–2, 14, 30–31, 48, 103–4, 116–17, 117, 119, 133; sound and, 114, 116
Seeing Double (Meltzer), 107–8
Segalen, Victor, 14, 27
self-identity, 77, 80–82, 85, 87–88, 137
"Sept Vieillards" (Baudelaire), 229n85
Serres, Michel, 203
Shaw, George Bernard, 214n49
shock, acoustical, 11, 108, 199
"Short History of Photography" (Benjamin), 233n58

sign language, 31, 33, 45
silence, 125, 151, 213n39
silencing, of female voices, 121, 167, 168, 170, 233n59
silent films, 49
Simmel, Georg, 121, 197
Sivori, Camillo, 164
de Sivry, Charles, 179, 184, 190–91
social groups, bodies and, 127
Société Française de Photographie, 57
Society for the Encouragement of National Industry, Paris, 1
"Soir" (Cros, C.), 36–37
"Le Soleil" (Baudelaire), 94–95, 128
"Song of Myself" (Whitman), 95, 121, 136, 138, 145, 151–53, 197; buried speech and, 142–43; listening and, 140–41; resonance and, 144; urban crowd and, 147
"Song-writing" (Poe), 227n54
"sonic materiality," music as, 182
"Sonnet Astronomique" (Cros, C.), 220n65
"The Sonnet of Seven Numbers" ("Le sonnet des sept nombres)" (Cabaner), 185, 187
"Souffles de l'air" (Cabaner), 185
sound: acousmatic, 78–79, 80; ambient, 125–32; archaeophony as archaeology of, 1, 2; auditory hallucination, 24, 78–80, 92; auditory imagination, 11, 77, 81, 132, 196; Baudelaire and, 228n68; blindness and, 120–24; bodily, 33, 83–85, 126, 226n35; body and, 140, 146, 147; buried, 9, 94, 99–100, 142–43, 177, 178; of cities, 10–19, 35–36, 92–101, 121–23, 137–39, 141–43, 146–47, 212n23, 237n5; color and, 15, 35, 140–41, 186–87, 188, 190; in "The Fall of the House of Usher," 94, 99–100; found, 241n75, 247n58, 249n8; language and, 229n76; of laughter, 164–65, 177; with life and death, 163; in "The Lighthouse," 82–83; memory and, 172–73; modernization of, 211n22; of paintings, 220n63; photographing, 6–10; Poe with, 78; recording, 1–2, 14, 41; recording technology, 83, 159, 243n90; science, light and, 52–53, 213n35; Scott de Martinville and, 114, 116; silence and, 125, 151, 213n39; studies, 10, 14, 78, 198, 203, 205, 210n19, 217n15, 251n30; technologies, 81–85; timbre, 116; violence in music and, 161–62, 164, 166; voice and, 86–88, 165; wax and, 188, 190. *See also* acoustics; deafness; noise
sound reproducibility, 53, 99, 180, 197, 202; deafness and, 31, 217n15; "Un drame interastral" and, 49, 56; imagination and,

211n21, 220n73; mechanical, 3, 27, 30, 40, 58, 79, 100, 106–8, 136, 158–59, 181, 219n43; "phonograph" and, 45, 61; with photography and Impressionism, 29; portability and, 60; with time and modernity, 28
sound reproduction: Cros, Charles, and, 28, 45, 57; "cultural origins of," 83, 211n20; echo and natural, 129; paléophone and, 45, 57; phonautograph and, 30–31; pinwheel phonograph and, 58–59; as social process, 230n91
soundscapes, 140, 210n19, 216n8; of modern department store, 222n94; of modernity, 10, 202, 210n18; New York City and Paris, 212n23
The Soundscape (Schafer), 140
Specimen Days (Whitman), 145, 146, 147
"Un Spectacle Interrompu" (Mallarmé), 153, 211n20
spectacles, 90, 153, 211n20, 213n35, 228n63
"The Spectacles" (Poe), 90, 228n63
Spectacular Realities (Schwartz), 234n74
specter, 1, 6, 8, 56, 65, 196
spectre sonore (acoustic spectrum), 1, 6, 8, 116, 196
speech, 33, 87; buried, 3, 24, 137–38, 142–44; "found voice" and, 150; "frozen," 20, 21, 97
Speech and Phenomena (Derrida), 87
Le Spleen de Paris (Baudelaire), 35, 37, 107, 125
stars, with light and time, 75
state surveillance, 48, 62–63, 67
"La Statue" (Villard), 160–61, 167–69, 170, 171
steam-engine sounds, 211n22
Steege, Benjamin, 210nn10,19
stenography, musical, 35, 57
stereophony, 77–78, 86, 88, 225n12
stereoscope, 15, 75, 108, 111
Sterne, Jonathan, 11, 21, 76, 78, 210n19, 211n21, 225n18; on "audile technique" of telegraph operators, 227n43; on bodily sounds, 226n35; on phonautograph, 227n59; on sound reproduction, 230n91
stethoscope, 33, 78, 83–84, 97, 225n12
"the strange and exceptional," Poe with, 80, 84, 199, 225n22
Surrealists, 3, 10, 28, 52
surveillance, 29, 64, 69–70, 223n11; state, 48, 62–63, 67; technological, 5, 23
Symbolism, 5, 155, 168
synesthesia, 75–76, 119, 185
Szendy, Peter, 14, 66, 125, 210n19, 211n20, 223n113

"talkie" films, 43
Techniques of the Observer (Crary), 218n41
technology: acousmatic, 79, 80; acoustics, 38, 63, 85, 103–4, 106; art, science and, 3; contest and convergence of, 61–66; industry and, 140; media and, 198; new media, 19, 62, 67, 199, 200, 209n5, 211n22; over mnemotechnology, 220n68; Paris with debates on, 222n94; recording, 33–35, 83, 89, 159, 243n90; sound, 81–85; surveillance, 5, 23; telecommunications, 219n45; wires and telegraphic, 90–91
telecommunications, 45, 49, 68, 214n49, 219n45
telegraph, 211n22, 227n49; "audile technique" and, 86, 227n43; Cros, Charles, and, 218n39; electric, 49, 89–91; technology and wires, 90–91
telegraphy, 81–88, 91–92, 227nn42–43,59
telephone, 211n22; Bell and, 49, 53, 56, 198; mass information gathering and, 62, 65, 66, 67–68, 70; patent, 221n78; phonograph and, 29, 37, 48, 50, 65, 219n45; writers and, 64–65, 67
telephonoscope, 68–71, 69, 70
telescope, "Leviathan," 74–77, 224nn2,8
"The Tell-Tale Heart" (Poe), 83, 99, 114, 225n116,23; auditory hallucination in, 78; bodily sounds and, 84–85; buried sound and, 94, 142, 177; "A Psalm of Life" and, 115–16
Tennyson, Alfred (Lord), 27, 137
"That Music Always Round Me" (Whitman), 145
théatrophone, 71, 72
Thomas Edison Archives, 136
Thompson, Emily, 202, 210n18, 212n23
"Le Thyrse" (Baudelaire), 163–64, 245n23
Tilly, Émile, 38
timbre, 19, 116
time: costs and urban noise, 95–96; fugitive, 55, 56; modernity with sound reproducibility and, 28; patent timing, 56–58; stars, light and, 75
tinfoil souvenirs, 202, 251n27
tintamarre, urban noise, 92–101
Tiphaigne de la Roche, Charles-François, 2, 200
"To a Stranger" (Whitman), 139, 148
tone figures, of Chladni, 117, 118
traffic noise, 126. *See also* omnibus
transatlantic: dialogue and mass popular press, 251n30; noise, 152–54
Traubel, Horace, 136, 237n4

Treatise on Mediate Auscultation (Laennec), 83
trichrome photographs, 29, 41, 42, 187, 188
Trois Morceaux en forme de Poire, 183
Turgenev, Ivan, 5
The Twentieth Century (Robida), 68–71, 69–70, 223n118
tympanic mechanism, 211n21

Ulysses (Joyce), 216n8
Unit #50, Elliptical Prelude and Chalice: from First Table Model Clavilux (Luminar) series, 15, 18; hand-painted disc for use with, 19
United States, France and, 3, 152–53, 242n85
Universal Exhibition, Paris (1867), 218n39
universe, listening to, 76
"The Unknown Masterpiece" (Balzac), 8, 160
urban acoustics, 11, 107, 130, 139, 143
urban noise, 11, 104, 122, 197, 201, 233n60; on streets, 12–13, 24, 93–97, 126, 141, 147, 199; *tintamarre*, 92–101
Uzanne, Octave, 29, 110

"Le Vaisseau-Piano" (Cros, C.), 34–35
Valade, Léon, 183
Van Gogh, Vincent, 185
Verlaine, Paul, 4, 5, 178–79, 182, 245n24
Verne, Jules, 29, 37, 46, 47, 62, 65, 211n22, 218n37
"Les Veuves" ("Widows") (Baudelaire), 103, 125–32, 149–50
vibrating diaphragm, 211n21
video chat, 49
Vieuxtemps, Henri (1820–1881), 164, 166
Vieuxtemps Guarneri violin, 166
Villard, Nina de (1843–1884), 3, 41; on art and media, 189; Baudelaire and, 163–64, 167–68, 245n23; "The Bow," 160–67, 168, 172, 244n17, 245n29; Chat Noir and, 179; Cros, Charles, and, 155, 158–61, 165–66, 178–79, 187, 188, 245n24; *La Dame aux éventails*, 155, 156, 157, 170, 187, 244nn19–20; *The House of the Old Woman* and, 170–78; "Impromptu," 189–90; Jaëll and, 186–87; legacy, 5–6, 24–25, 155–58, 159–60, 167, 180, 183, 189; with listening, 159–60; music and, 155, 157, 159, 164–67, 169, 179, 181, 184–85, 246n51; performance culture and, 5, 25, 179; photographs of, 178; piano and, 155, 156, 163, 185–86, 245n24; Poe and, 164–65, 167; salon of, 5, 33, 36, 155, 156, 160, 164, 179–82, 184–85, 187, 190–91, 193, 199, 246n80, 249n88; "Soir" and, 36–37; "La Statue," 160–61, 167–69, 170, 171; trichrome photograph of, 187, 188; Verlaine and, 178–79; Whitman and, 248n81; women artists and support from, 169–70
Villiers de l'Isle-Adam, Auguste, 27, 28–29, 62–63, 65, 228n66, 246n42
violence, 142, 161–62, 164, 166, 168
violin, Vieuxtemps Guarneri, 166
vision: "Les Aveugles," 120–27, 143; "hearings" and urban, 149–52; ocular proof, 76, 77; seeing noise, 24, 104, 116, 119, 132
visual culture, 10, 81
visual field, 10–11, 55, 103, 183, 202
Voice Building and Tone Placing (Holbrook), 16, 113, 118
voice of the past. *See* paléophone
voices, 225n17, 236n1, 242n82; distortion, 220n72, 223n117; "found," 150; heard by gaslight, 134, 135; phonograph and disembodied, 136–38; silencing of female, 121, 167, 168, 170, 233n59; sound and, 86–88, 165
Voices of the Night (Longfellow), 116
Les Voix de Paris (Kastner), 13, 195, 229n79
Voyage dans la Lune (Bergerac), 59–60
"Voyelles" (Rimbaud), 185, 187

Wagner, Richard, 25, 110, 181, 190, 191, 244n17
Wagneur, Jean-Didier, 170, 176
Walkman, 59, 60
wax, 187–91, 248n81
Weiss, Allen, 225n16
"What I Am" (Satie), 193–95, 249nn1,4,7
Wheatstone, Charles, 14–15, 16, 75, 117, 153, 194, 213n39
When I Was a Photographer (*Quand j'étais photographe*) (Nadar), 8
Whidden, Seth, 230n2
Whistler, James McNeil, 111–12
Whitman, Walt, 4, 6, 158, 229n85, 237n10, 241n78, 242n81; Baudelaire and, 122, 138, 139, 147, 148, 153, 154, 238n16, 239nn34,36, 242n87; city sounds and, 95, 97–98, 121, 137–39, 141, 142, 146–47, 237n5; "Crossing Brooklyn Ferry," 122, 149–52, 154, 240nn40,47; France and, 138–39, 238n15; French language and, 229n76; Laforgue and, 242nn87–88; *Leaves of Grass*, 137–40, 148, 152, 238n21, 242n82; with living and buried speech, 3, 24, 137–38, 142–44; "Mannahatta," 141–42, 239nn34,36; New York City and, 3, 139–45, 148, 154; omnibus and, 145–49, 151; phonograph and,

136–37, 237n4; Poe and, 138, 141–42, 149–50; recording, 136–38; urban crowd and, 138, 139, 143–44, 147–49, 241nn62,69; urban street noise and, 24, 126, 141, 147; urban vision and "hearings," 149–52; Villard and, 248n81. *See also* "Song of Myself"; *specific titles*
"Whitman and the Homosexual Republic" (Erkkila), 242n81
"Widows" ("Les Veuves") (Baudelaire), 103, 125–32, 149–50
Wieck, Marie, 169
Wilfred, Thomas, 15, 18, 19, 213n39
wires, 90–92, 227n59
"With the Eyes Shut" (Bellamy), 29, 110
women: artistic independence, 169, 245n30; *The House of the Old Woman*, 170–78; with voices silenced, 121, 167, 168, 170, 233n59
writers, 11, 12–13, 22, 64–65, 67, 81, 214n49
writing, 4–5, 55, 61–63, 120–21, 210n19, 227n54

zoetrope, 15
Zola, Emile, 211n22
Zoom, 45
Zutistes, 5, 155, 157, 181, 183, 187

Brett Brehm is Assistant Professor of French and Francophone Studies at William & Mary.

www.ingramcontent.com/pod-product-compliance
Lightning Source LLC
Chambersburg PA
CBHW061229070526
44584CB00030B/4046